Springer Series in Design and Innovation

Volume 16

Editor-in-Chief

Francesca Tosi, University of Florence, Florence, Italy

Series Editors

Claudio Germak, Politecnico di Torino, Turin, Italy

Francesco Zurlo, Politecnico di Milano, Milan, Italy

Zhi Jinyi, Southwest Jiaotong University, Chengdu, China

Marilaine Pozzatti Amadori, Universidade Federal de Santa Maria, Santa Maria, Rio Grande do Sul, Brazil

Maurizio Caon , University of Applied Sciences and Arts, Fribourg, Switzerland

Springer Series in Design and Innovation (SSDI) publishes books on innovation and the latest developments in the fields of Product Design, Interior Design and Communication Design, with particular emphasis on technological and formal innovation, and on the application of digital technologies and new materials. The series explores all aspects of design, e.g. Human-Centered Design/User Experience, Service Design, and Design Thinking, which provide transversal and innovative approaches oriented on the involvement of people throughout the design development process. In addition, it covers emerging areas of research that may represent essential opportunities for economic and social development.

In fields ranging from the humanities to engineering and architecture, design is increasingly being recognized as a key means of bringing ideas to the market by transforming them into user-friendly and appealing products or services. Moreover, it provides a variety of methodologies, tools and techniques that can be used at different stages of the innovation process to enhance the value of new products and services.

The series' scope includes monographs, professional books, advanced textbooks, selected contributions from specialized conferences and workshops, and outstanding Ph.D. theses.

Keywords: Product and System Innovation; Product design; Interior design; Communication Design; Human-Centered Design/User Experience; Service Design; Design Thinking; Digital Innovation; Innovation of Materials.

How to submit proposals

Proposals must include: title, keywords, presentation (max 10,000 characters), table of contents, chapter abstracts, editors'/authors' CV.

In case of proceedings, chairmen/editors are requested to submit the link to conference website (incl. relevant information such as committee members, topics, key dates, keynote speakers, information about the reviewing process, etc.), and approx. number of papers.

Proposals must be sent to: series editor Prof. Francesca Tosi (francesca.tosi@unifi.it) and/or publishing editor Mr. Pierpaolo Riva (pierpaolo.riva@springer.com).

More information about this series at http://www.springer.com/series/16270

Daniel Raposo · João Neves · José Silva
Editors

Perspectives on Design II

Research, Education and Practice

 Springer

Editors
Daniel Raposo
Escola Superior de Artes Aplicadas
Instituto Politécnico de Castelo Branco
Castelo Branco, Portugal

João Neves
Escola Superior de Artes Aplicadas
Instituto Politécnico de Castelo Branco
Castelo Branco, Portugal

José Silva
Escola Superior de Artes Aplicadas
Instituto Politécnico de Castelo Branco
Castelo Branco, Portugal

ISSN 2661-8184   ISSN 2661-8192   (electronic)
Springer Series in Design and Innovation
ISBN 978-3-030-79881-9   ISBN 978-3-030-79879-6   (eBook)
https://doi.org/10.1007/978-3-030-79879-6

Preface

This book gathers a selection of chapters written by experienced authors, chosen on the basis of their relevance for the design research community out of many other contributions presented during EIMAD 2020—7th Meeting of Research in Music, Arts and Design, held on May 14–15, 2020, and published in the book Advances in Design, Music and Arts (Raposo et al., Springer, 2021, ISBN 978-3-030-55699-0).

The different chapters cover multiple areas, offering an interdisciplinary and transdisciplinary perspective on design and highlighting strategies for a better systematization of the design approach. Developed in the middle of a pandemic context, these contributions revealed new challenges and issues, associated with the unexpected situation, emphasizing the important and uninterrupted contribution of research in design. Research contributes to an ecosystem of reciprocal relations, in the cultural, social and economic dimensions of different stakeholders, and meets design practice and thinking.

The topics addressed in this book have been chosen for their particular link to contemporary concerns in terms of identity, health and well-being, social inclusion, sustainability, safety, lifestyles, economy, among others.

From diversified perspectives and themes, the authors correlate aspects of design education with research and practice in design, seeking ways to improve and contribute to the quality of life of people and the world as a whole, also contributing perspectives on the use of technology for contemporary economy and culture.

This book also highlights some important lessons learnt from experience and the resilience of those who have faced catastrophes, natural disasters and the COVID-19 pandemics.

Overall, the chapters included here are unique and have been specifically written for this book, which is organized in three main parts:

1. Design, Education and Society
2. Communication Design
3. Interior, Fashion and Product Design

The first part "Design, Education and Society" gathers some important clarifications and correlations between concepts, such as creativity, design and design thinking. It collects reflections on the foundations and relevance of the double diamond. It emphasizes strategies for design teaching, including ways to adapt educational institutions and the cities where this education takes place. This part reports on the experience of creating design courses, offers comparisons between different educational programs based on co-creation, such as one in Dublin and one in Porto, highlights the relationships between design, design education and the identity of the territory. It also presents new ideas and tools for the creation and analysis of visual thought, including new technologies and analyzing the conditions of housing and teleworking, particularly in distance design education. This part ends with the identification of some gaps and perspectives in design models.

The second part "Communication Design" studies the relationship between the teaching and practice of communication design for truly inclusive design. It discusses the role of communication design as an innovation factor, describing design as an interface in the mediation between brands and people. It reports on graphic data analysis tools for brand creation, goes through the relationship between sound and graphic narrative in videogames and ends with the study of the impact of social representations on design perceptions.

In turn, the third part of the book "Interior, Fashion and Product Design" focuses on the design of products from small to large scale, including interior spaces, and using different types of technology. It includes studies for developing contemporary jewelry and a comparative study between types of embroidery. It reports on the use of virtual reality to interpret historic interior design spaces and discusses sensorial immersion, challenge-based immersion, mental or imaginary immersion and emotional immersion. It describes how design can support business management by defining some key principles for creating dashboards, discusses the design of toys for blind or low vision children and design solutions supporting insects in their essential activity of pollination.

Castelo Branco, Portugal   Daniel Raposo
                                                                                      João Neves
                                                                                      José Silva

Contents

Communication Design

**Categorising the Sonic Experience in the Soundscapes
of Videogames**

João P. Ribeiro, Miguel Carvalhais, and Pedro Cardoso

**Social Representations of Communication Design:
Symbolic Universes**

Maria Luísa Costa, Fernanda Daniel, Inês Amaral,
and Ilda Maria Morais Massano Cardoso

Interior, Fashion and Product Design

"Playful Spaces": A Design Approach in Contemporary Jewellery

Mónica Romãozinho

Design, Education and Society

Creativity, Design and Design Thinking—A Human-Centred *ménage à trois* for Innovation

Katja Tschimmel

Abstract Although Creativity, Design and Design Thinking appear frequently in popular and business contexts, the terms are often confused. Even in the design and management communities several doubts remain about the concepts behind these terms, since they overlap, complement and sometimes contradict each other. This article seeks to throw light on the interconnected and intimate *ménage à trois*, which is the dynamic from which Innovation arises. In the analysis of the relationship between the three concepts, other terms such as Creative Thinking and Design Creativity are introduced, and the systemic perspective of Creativity and Design is discussed. The systemic approach shows that the designer/creative professional is not the only decisive element for a successful innovation. The cultural domain, the working environment and the form society judge new products must also be taken into account. At the end of the article some challenges and opportunities for Business and Design Education are identified.

Keywords Creativity · Creative thinking · Design · Design thinking · Innovation

1 Introduction

From around the turn of the century, the concepts of Creativity, Design and Design Thinking have grown in importance for the collective consciousness not only of design related fields, but also in business and management communities, and the general public.

In 2009, the European Union declared the *European Year of Creativity and Innovation*, thus highlighting the fundamental role of creative production for Europe's future. Of course, Design, itself a force for innovation, was also an

K. Tschimmel (✉)
FEP/FEUP/ID+, Porto University, Porto, Portugal
e-mail: ktschimmel@fep.up.pt

K. Tschimmel
Mindshake, Porto, Portugal

© The Author(s), under exclusive license to Springer Nature Switzerland AG 2022
D. Raposo et al. (eds.), *Perspectives on Design II*, Springer Series in Design and Innovation 16, https://doi.org/10.1007/978-3-030-79879-6_1

3

inherent part of this celebration. Thus it is not surprising that since then, more and more European cities (after Barcelona and Helsinki), became part of the *World Design Weeks*, a worldwide network for design weeks and festivals around the globe. The objective of this network of Design Weeks is the promotion of collaboration in the design field, the development of the economy of creative industries, and the support of innovation. Today we live in an alarming environment, where the spectres of nationalism, populism and protectionism loom larger than ever. Creativity, Design and Design Thinking directly counteract this trend. New thoughts and human-centred ideas only emerge when we're empathetic, open-minded, imaginative, collaborative and integrative. The *World Design Weeks* define themselves as "a force for openness", and believe in unity and inclusivity (www.worlddesignweeks.org/).

Another sign of the international recognition of the importance of Creativity, Design and Innovation is the *World Creativity and Innovation Week* (https://wciw. org/), founded in 2001, and recognised in 2017 by the United Nations, who chose the 21 of April as the official date to celebrate creativity and innovation worldwide. Thus, resolution 71/284 states that "[…] human creativity and innovation, at both the individual and group levels, have become the true wealth of nations in the twenty-first century, [...]."

Design Thinking, the third element in our conceptual 'love story', is recently also being promoted and celebrated worldwide by annual events such as the Conference of the *Global Design Thinking Alliance* (https://gdta.org/), the Dutch *Design Thinking Conference* (https://www.designthinkingconference.com/) or the Russian *Design Thinking camp* (https://en.lab-w.com/dtcamp2019). Again, the objectives of these events, besides diving deep into Design Thinking principles and methods, are contributing to solving 'wicked problems' in complex transdisciplinary fields, supporting global transformation processes and a more sustainable development, and also contributing to shape the future of education.

Although Creativity, Design and Design Thinking appear frequently in popular and business contexts, these terms are often confused. Even in the design and management communities several doubts remain about the concepts behind these terms, as they overlap, complement and sometimes contradict each other. Scientifically, these concepts have been researched since the 1950s, but with increasing intensity since the last decade of the twentieth century. This article seeks to have a look at each of these concepts to throw light on the interconnected and intimate *ménage à trois*, but also to explore their differences.

2 Creativity

In all Design literature, there seems to be no doubt, that Creativity is a fundamental element for design processes (Lawson 1990; Christiaans 1992; Goldschmidt 1999; Nelson and Stoltermann 2003). The successful designer is distinguished not only through her/his specialised knowledge, but particularly by her/his ability to think creatively. But what does that mean, thinking creatively? And are Creativity and Creative Thinking the same?

Etymologically, the term Creativity comes from the Latin word *creare*, which means "to generate" or "to produce", thus referring to a creative force that gives rise to something valuable. Creativity therefore has to do with creation and evolution, the creative person giving rise to something new and previously unknown.

In most specific literature, Creativity and Creative Thinking have been used as synonyms, creativity being defined as a cognitive capacity to develop something new. This perception is based mainly on the research from the 1950s, when J.P. Guilford developed a theory of creativity in which he described skills and attitudes that played an important role in creative thinking, introducing the concept of Divergent Thinking. Later, in the 70s, the work *Applied Imagination* (1953) became influential for the direction of creativity research. The author, Alex F. Osborn described creative thinking as problem-solving thought, having introduced techniques and principles with the help of which the creative problem-solving process can be improved. Together with Sidney Parnes, Osborn founded the *Creative Problem Solving Institute* (CPSI) in Buffalo, which is still today a leading institution in the area of creativity. Every year creativity researchers and students from all over the world meet in Buffalo for a "Creativity Training Course" (http://cpsiconference.com/). Without going deeper into creativity theories developed by a psychological approach, we can affirm that in the last century, the perception of the creativity concept gradually moved from the paradigm of the "supernaturally gifted genius" to the paradigm of the "creative person", who has the innate potential to think creatively, and who can improve creative thoughts by applying certain techniques and methods (Tschimmel 2010). Florida (2004) announced the arrival of a new creative class of people which contributes to the economic development of the future, calling the creative individual "the new mainstream". As Creativity is multidimensional and emerges in many mutually reinforcing forms, it requires a social and economic environment that can nurture its complex connections.

2.1 The Systemic Perspective of Creativity

Since the late 1980s, after centuries of humanistic observation, the phenomenon of Creativity has been increasingly investigated from the perspective of the natural sciences. A decisive contribution to the development of a new and broader understanding of Creativity was made by Systems Theory, driving a change of perception. Due to the highly dynamic complexity of Creativity, the inclusion of system-theoretical knowledge allows us to take a new view at the organisation of the cognitive system under the influence of other factors. Among the creativity researchers who are increasingly examining creativity with a systemic approach, are Amabile (1996), Guntern (1991, 1994, 1996) and Csikszentmihalyi (2004).

According to Amabile, Guntern and Csikszentmihalyi, human beings are above all creative in a "creative intersection" and not only in their cognitive capacity.

While Amabile (1996) adds into the creativity components, *domain relevant skills*, *creativity-relevant processes* and *intrinsic task motivation*, Guntern adds to personal factors the *social environment*, the *culture* in which the individual moves, elements of the *task* the creative person seeks to accomplish, and elements inherent to the *process*, understanding the creative individual as "an integral part of a field of transaction" (1991: 21).

Amongst these authors, it is Csikszentmihalyi, who elevated the Creativity concept to the systemic approach, dominant until today. According to this systemic psychologist, creativity arises from the interaction of three elements that together form a system: (1) *a culture that encompasses symbolic rules*, (2) *the individual who brings something new to a symbolic domain*, and (3) *a panel of experts who recognise and approve this innovation*. The result is a change in a symbolic domain of culture. Therefore, if there is no change in the ideas, knowledge, values, emotions or actions of people in a cultural community, in Csikszentmihalyi's perspective (2004), it is not a genuine creative accomplishment (Fig. 1).

Csikszentmihalyi understands a specialised area as a *domain*, such as Design, which could be subdivided into the areas of Product Design, Graphic Design, Service Design, etc. Each domain is anchored in a culture within which the symbolic knowledge of a certain group or even all of humanity is shared. Another component of this creativity concept is, according to Csikszentmihalyi, the *panel/society field*, which includes all the people who control access to a *domain*. In Design, the panel would consist of design professors, exhibition commissioners, collectors of 'design objects', specialised journalists and other critics, as well as employees of institutions dedicated to the domain. It is the critical part of society that decides which products will be recognised as innovative and which are worthy of commenting, preservation and remembering. The *individual* (for example the designer), the third component of the creative system, according to Csikszentmihalyi, is thus only considered creative when, based on the symbols of

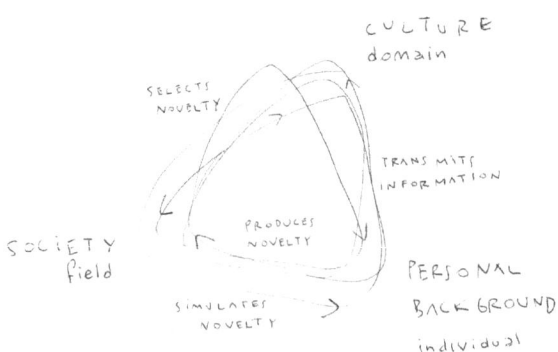

Fig. 1 The systemic perspective according Csikszentmihalyi (2004: 315) in Tschimmel (2019: 31)

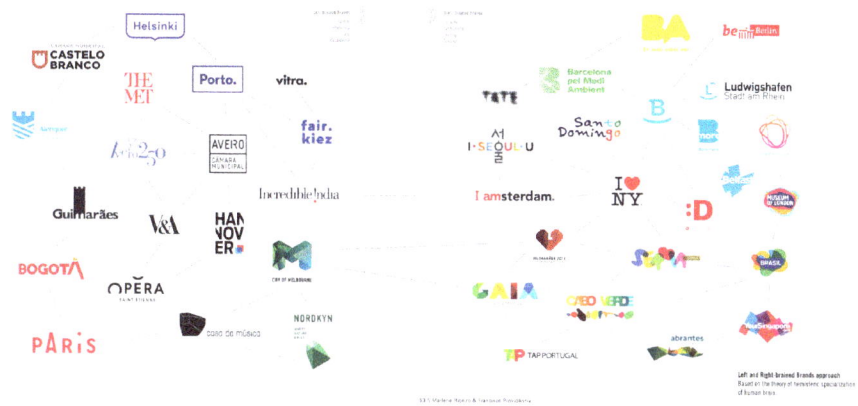

Fig. 2 "Influenza" by Marlene Ribeiro and Francisco Providência (in Tschimmel 2019: 53)

an established *domain*, the new creation is recognised by the corresponding *panel of society*, and integrated into the *culture domain*.

The study of city logotypes realised by Marlene Ribeiro and Francisco Providência (in Tschimmel 2019: 53) shows the complexity of Creativity in Graphic Design and the mutual influences. This visualisation is a brilliant example for Csikszentmihalyi's systemic approach where the designer, the cultural domain and the specialist panel/society, come together (Fig. 2).

From this systemic perspective, there are some consequences for the concept of Creativity, which are (Tschimmel 2010, 2019):

1. The characteristics of the personality and cognitive abilities are no longer decisive in determining whether a person is creative or not. What counts is the recognition of a work as a creative achievement and its integration into the domain. Since creativity results from the interaction between domain, specialists, individual and other factors not mentioned in Csikszentmihalyi's model (such as geographic or climatic factors), an individual's creative thinking can contribute to the creation of a recognised novelty, but personal creativity is not, in itself, a sufficient condition for that.

2. The systemic model explains, moreover, the frequent fluctuations in the assessment of creative results that arise over time. Think, for example, of certain painters, such as Raphael or Van Gogh or Warhol, who were alternatively considered marginal artists and established painters. They were only recognised as very creative people when a sufficiently large number of specialists became convinced that their works represented an important contribution to the field of art. And in music, in literature, and also in design, similar cases can be observed, although in the area of design, due to the functional and technological components, it is comparatively easier for a product to be recognised as innovative as soon as it appears on the market. The systemic approach clearly points to the fact that creativity and social recognition are inseparably linked.

3. Another implication of the systemic approach to creativity is that the degree of creativity in a given place and at a given historical moment does not depend only on the dimension of a capacity for individual thinking. It also depends, according to Csikszentmihalyi, to what extent the domains concerned and the corresponding panels of experts are receptive to integrating new ideas, recognising them as valuable and spreading them. In design and in areas of technological innovation, and due to economic interests, consumer needs and global competition, there has been, for some time now, an enormous receptivity to new ideas and products, a circumstance that leads to a situation in which not only is there a lot of talk about creativity, innovation and design, but also that many young designers have the opportunity to become known in the media through their projects.

Looking at the evolution of the Creativity concept, the first phase of the psychological approach to creativity brought advantages and disadvantages. On the one hand, empirical studies paved the way for a solid foundation for the phenomenon of creativity and promoted a detailed knowledge of the capacities of creative thinking. On the other hand, this investigation focused on the individual in such a way that other important factors of creative work were neglected—such as the socio-cultural context, the life circumstances, the environment, specialists in the field, etc.

Considering the systemic approach, we distinguish the concept of Creativity from the concept of Creative Thinking. While Creativity is understood to be the ability of a complex system to create something new on a symbolic level, Creative Thinking is defined as a cognitive ability to deliberately produce targeted new ideas and artefacts in a determined symbolic domain. In other words: the whole human system is creative, in that it has the capacity to produce, in a specific area, new thoughts, processes or products previously unknown. However, some people's contributions are more creative than others not only due to their cognitive abilities, but above all, due to certain systemic relationships.

2.2   Creative Thinking

Following our thoughts above, we define Creative Thinking as the cognitive capacity of an individual, or a group of individuals (collective creative thinking), to intentionally generate new ideas. For the production of new ideas, it is necessary to restructure existing elements in a domain of knowledge (as novelty never comes out of nowhere), in such a way that the new combination will be evaluated by specialists as original and useful. Once recognised, the new idea can become a driver of cultural, social, economic, etc. evolution, which is the purpose of any creative act.

Cognitive biology introduced the concept of Autopoiesis (refers to a system capable of reproducing and maintaining itself), which explains that the capacity for creative thinking is preserved and continues to develop within the cognitive system itself due to self-introduced changes (Maturana and Varela 1987). Through new connections between the elements of knowledge stored in memory and activated by perception, the human being continuously produces new mental combinations.

The more the elements that interact in the cognitive system, the more possibilities of combination that result. Systems research has shown us also that the more a creative system produces, the more changes it can make. Which means that the ability to think creatively not only preserves itself but also accelerates itself. It is common knowledge that someone who produces many new things becomes more creative with each new project. That's the reason we consider designers, artists, architects, etc. as 'creative people'. This fact allows us to claim that creative thinking can be stimulated, encouraged and improved.

Following this train of thought, the trilingual book *CriAtivaMente/The Creative Mind/CreA(c)tivaMente* (Sátiro and Tschimmel 2020) was written, in which the authors classify creative thinking into four large groups with several sub-groups: (1) Perception, (2) Interrogation, (3) Comparison, and (4) Language. Sátiro and Tschimmel developed this classification model in a dialogue format, as dialogue is the most exploratory and constructive form of co-creation. While the reader takes a mental journey through illustrated thinking exercises, she/he witnesses the dialogue about the various forms and skills of creative thinking.

The first class of creative thinking abilities, according to Sátiro and Tschimmel, is PERCEPTION. Based on the laws of *Gestalt* Theory, we individuals organise visual stimuli, so that separated elements are aggregated in the simplest way into a coherent whole that gains meaning for the perceptive and thoughtful person. In this sense, principles of rapid and habitual perception (visual, acoustic, smelling, etc.) hinder creative thinking, since the search for originality presupposes avoiding stereotypes. Thus, the ability to play with unfinished perceptions and ideas for a long time, not reaching an early conclusive rational decision (premature closure of *Gestalt*), could be considered as a specific characteristic of the most creative individuals (Guntern 1996). Beside thinking against stereotypes and norms, Perception with all Senses is part of the Perception classification group. Even though the human being predominantly perceives in a visual way, the other senses (hearing, smelling, tasting and touching, or also chronoception or thermoception) should be intentionally included, as they enrich the perceptional experience and the production of new and uncommon combinations. Considering the plasticity of our brain, it seems obvious that the stimulation of multi-sensorality enhances the capacity of creative thinking.

The second class of creative thinking abilities, according to Sátiro and Tschimmel (2020), is INTERROGATION. Questions express doubt, showing us that we are facing something problematic, which encourages our creative capacity. In organisations such as Google, for example, questions are seen as a driver of innovation. Certain questions only ask for evidence and from a given interpretation. But other kind of questions, such as provocative, procedural and imaginative questions have the power to open our minds, exploring new territories. These 3 forms of questioning reality help us to suspend the rigid judgments we normally have. Provocative questions, such as "What if it was the other way around?" or "What makes you respond the way you respond right now?", for example, defy strict rules, standards and criteria. They are questions that confront the truths and realities that we usually accept without critical reflection. Starting from an authentic doubt, provocative question generate mental flexibility, opening up a variety of possible answers and new questions. The second kind of questions Sátiro and Tschimmel (2020) explored are procedural questions, which extract, facilitate and seek the procedural aspects of creative thinking, causing a qualitative improvement in the process itself. The third kind of questions, imaginative questions, articulate visionary, dreamlike elements, not given by the perceptual consensus of others. When we ask in an imaginative way, we do not stop at dogmas, absolute certainties and stereotyped perceptions, but go through the gaps in reality and understandings about it. Imagination breaks with the ordinary course of reality, through questions such as "What would happen if …?", "Why not?" or "It's always like that? Could it be otherwise?".

According to Sátiro and Tschimmel (2020), the third group of creative thinking abilities, COMPARISON, brings together the variety of skills that are based on the relationship between similarities and differences between two or more elements. In this group we find thinking in uncommon Associations, in new Combinations and in Analogies. To reason analogously, for example, is to think of one thing as if it were another. For this reason, analogies are based on the rigorous knowledge of a certain domain or circumstance. Analogies can be found in our personal world (Personal Analogy), in the biological world (Direct Analogies), in the symbolic world (Symbolic Analogies) and in the world of fantasy (Fantasy Analogies). Analogies in a symbolic context we also call Metaphors, which express abstract ideas in a more concrete way.

The last group of creative thinking skills Sátiro and Tschimmel (2020) explored in their work is LANGUAGE, differentiating between Narrative Thinking and the Transition between Expressive Languages. Narrating is one of the ways of organising information, ordering it in a temporal and sequential way. It is also a way to transform experience into something intelligible. It is stories that give meaning to our lives and the world. In Design and Innovation, Storytelling helps to make the message more accessible, more likely to engage the audience, when presenting new products or business ideas. Language does not refer just to words, but also to visual language, sound language, the language of smells, etc. therefore translations skills are important. Knowing and stimulating other languages, in addition to oral and written, develops, at the same time, our expressive capacity and creative thinking. The translation from one expressive language to another (verbal language into visual, oral language into sign language, from rhythmic to dance, and so on) requires the reformulation of a reality and its transformation, considering the context of the subject in different perspectives.

Of course, mental life is not reducible to a list of creative thinking skills. When we create, these mental processes do not act in isolation, but are interconnected, they touch, intersect and complement each other. Designers, as creative thinkers, apply in their creative process all these thinking abilities, normally not isolated but in combined forms. Reality is always more complex than the maps that seek to explain and organise it.

3 Design

There are few areas in which there is as little consensus as in the definition of Design, thanks to its multidisciplinary and interdisciplinary character (The area of Creativity is also one, as we saw). Many authors in the design field argue that there is no universal definition of the term Design, which adequately covers all approaches and perspectives (Buchanan 2000). Frequently in design literature Simon's (1969/1996) famous phrase is quoted: "Everyone *designs* who devises courses of action aimed at changing existing situations into preferred ones". From this broad perspective, design can be understood as a constituent element of human cognition and action processes. Also Dorst (2003) understands design as a basic human activity, when he compares a designer in a metaphorical way to an explorer of unknown terrain.

By analysing definitions from historically representative design authors (from the product and graphic design fields), such as Maldonado, Archer, Margolin, Bonsiepe, Bürdek, Cross and Dorst, we can differentiate between 3 design perspectives (Tschimmel 2010):

1. Design as a project activity, with the focus on the design process.
2. Design as interface configuration. The designer processes information, focusing on the interaction between user, object and context.
3. Design as an inherent activity in evolution. The designer is just a link in the emergence and evolution of artefacts.

Each definition depends on a historical context, a cultural perspective and the professional experience from which the design activity is contemplated. In common, all these interpretations focus on the creative activity that gives rise to new material or immaterial combinations (artefacts). Perhaps we can synthesise the different perspectives in the following definition: Design—project and configuration—can be seen as an activity of a creative system, oriented towards action and inherent to the evolution of humans, to give rise to new material or immaterial products. It is important to include in this definition the creation of immaterial products, since Service Design (the design of an alive and dynamic system of user experiences) has, over the last two decades, become a more and more important design field.

3.1 Design Creativity

Design has always been closely associated with Creativity and some authors even call creativity the 'heart' of design (Baxter 2000), as new artefacts are usually expected to be original and innovative. The terminological combination 'Design + Creativity' gained visibility and meaning with the foundation of the *International Journal of Design Creativity and Innovation* in 2013. In the open article of the Editorial board of IJDCI (2013), a total of 36 researchers expressed their perspectives on Design Creativity and Innovation. Here only some perspective will be mentioned. The first opinion came from Chris McMahon, who affirmed that Creativity and Innovation are the essence of Design, creativity being intrinsic to design reasoning, both working together for an innovative outcome. Connected to design reasoning, Larry Leifer and Martin Steinert highlight the importance of Abductive Thinking in design, contrasting the normal logic of deduction and induction. Other authors, such as Martin (2009) or Dorst (2011) defend that abductive thinking is the core reasoning of design thinking, based on questions such as "What if…?" or " How many ways could we…?", questions which Sátiro and Tschimmel (2020) call Imaginative Questions.

Interesting from a systemic point of view is the opinion of John S. Gero, who defends that Design Creativity should be thought to be a social construct that involves the value of systems of many players, not only the designers. In a society where knowledge and technological advances are increasingly fragmented and challenges more complex, a systemic perspective is also needed in Design, as the designer has to work increasingly as an integrator of knowledge, and a mediator in inter- and transdisciplinary collaborative processes. This perspective fits with the new role of designers in the concept of Design Thinking.

3.2 Design Thinking

Design as a creative, complex and integrative activity is inherent in the material and symbolic evolution of societies. Thus, design thinking can be understood as a way of thinking which leads to transformation, evolution and progress, toward new and better forms of living.

If we analyse the use of the term Design Thinking, we can see that the concept has changed in the last three decades. In the 1990s 'design thinking' (dt, written in lower case) was defined by an international research group as the cognitive process of designers (Cross et al. 1992; Goldschmidt 1999), with the objective of coming closer to an understanding of the attributes that contribute to Design Creativity. Since the new millennium, the concept has been stretched. Today, Design Thinking (DT, written in upper case) is understood as a method for innovation, offering new models of processes and a set of tools which help to improve, accelerate and visualise every creative process, carried out not only by designers, but in multi- and interdisciplinary teams in any kind of organisation (Tschimmel 2012). As Design Thinking combines practical experiences with a deep base of academic research, it has a great potential for innovation processes in several domains. The new use of the term DT, specifically the combination of "thinking" and "design", offers the opportunity to apply design tools to other problem-solving-contexts not directly related with the appearance and functionality of artefacts, but with the form of businesses, services or organisational changes.

Design Thinking today is not only a cognitive process or a mindset, but has become an effective method with a toolkit for any innovation process, connecting the creative design approach to traditional business thinking, based on planning and rational problem solving. Design Thinking is promoted in the management domain as a user-centred approach to innovation, which brings creativity and human-centredness to organisations as a new way of working (Brown 2009). In the last decade, innovation literature has placed increasing importance on Design as an integral capability for organisational innovation. From innovation literature and from our own experience with companies in Portugal, we can see that organisations are trying to integrate the design approach to solve issues of organisational management, and to explore greater synergies between business strategies, product and service innovation, and complex social problems (Brown 2009; Martin 2009; Groeger et al. 2019). Design is no longer viewed as a mere creative or rational problem-solving process, but rather it is seen now as an opportunity and knowledge generating activity, which helps to deal with complex problems. According to Groeger et al. (2019), the DT concept has emerged in management debates as promising innovation to be inspired by the way designers work.

Another important factor for the spread of the new Design Thinking, was the creation of the Hasso Plattner Institute at Stanford University and later in Potsdam, Germany, better known as d.school, a teaching space where the environment is spatially prepared for the dynamics of Design Thinking. Both institutes are characterised by modular spaces, movable whiteboards, cupboards full of prototyping material, etc. Looking at these spaces and the working dynamic in the DT process, people may also define Design Thinking as a working culture, a learning process or a new innovation paradigm, and all these perspectives are also right.

Generally, and from different points of view, today DT is understood as a cross-disciplinary process of conceiving new realities, introducing designers' culture, mindset and methods into fields such as service, business, organisational, social and educational innovation. Carlgren et al. (2016) proposed a framework which classifies DT into 3 levels: (1) The DT principles, (2) DT practices (ways of working) and the DT mindset (attitudes/ways of thinking) and (3) DT techniques (methods and tools which support DT practices and the development of the DT mindset).

DT practice and research offers many descriptions of design principles, thinking modes, and creative behaviours and postures that are often subsumed under the term 'mindset'. The definition of 'mindset' varies; most authors seem to agree that, while a firm can adopt DT processes and learn new innovation practices over time, it is the DT mindset that enables innovation objectives to be achieved at a deeper and more sustainable level (Groeger et al. 2019). Design Thinking as a mindset refers to cognition and resulting behaviours that, over time, find their way into the beliefs of people, and the culture of organisations.

3.3 Design and Design Thinking

As suggested above, Design and Design Thinking are intimately connected, as the Design Thinking method and the techniques come from Design Methodology, the designers' culture and way of thinking. There is no designer who is not at the same time a design thinker.

The international *Design Thinking Research Symposium*, founded in 1992 to research design thinking as the designers' cognition, is planning its next meeting in spring 2022 (https://dtrs13.net.technion.ac.il/). Interestingly this 13th symposium aims to look at the expansion of what is understood as design (and design thinking). It is not only designers or design researchers who have been invited to present their work, but others, such as managers, marketing professionals and all sorts of experts. We can read at the website of the event: "The move from design thinking as the way in which designers think, to Design Thinking as a method embraced by the business world has brought many new actors to the table, and it is no longer clear what exactly design means and how well it is served by the expansion of its boundaries."

It will be interesting to see the answers to questions, such as "What are the new frontiers design is demarcating?" or "Can we find a new signification for the designer, which will be wider than the traditional one but narrower than 'everybody is a designer'?".

4 Conclusion—*The ménage à trois*

As a synthesis of the thoughts in this paper, we can conclude that Creativity, Creative Thinking, Design, Design Creativity and Design Thinking are intimately connected, and are the force from which Innovation arises—they are *the* innovation drivers and make change happen. If we define Innovation, according to the Oxford Dictionary, as "the action or process of making changes in something established especially by introducing new methods, ideas, or products", or according to management literature, as "the creation of a viable new offering" (Keeley et al. 2013), Design for Innovation always implies the creation of something new, and thus is always based on creative thinking or design thinking. Innovation is the driving force for the quality of life and our economy. We innovate to solve problems and to create meaningful value for ourselves, society and the planet. And that's the reason that Creativity, Design and Design Thinking are (or should be) human-centred (which these days also means planet-centred or life-centred).

Alongside Creativity, Design and Design Thinking should be understood in a systemic approach, where not only the designer and an interdisciplinary team of professionals are important for success, but also the cultural domain, the working environment, and the form we (experts and society) judge new products, and services.

4.1 Challenges for Organisations and Business Education

Considering the power, the *ménage à trois* has for innovation, we can conclude that organisations should concentrate their innovation strategies and practices on creativity and design-based methods and their mindset. To help managers develop innovation capability, many business and engineering schools have started including 'Design Thinking' or 'Creativity' in their curricula (Martin 2009; Kurokawa 2013; Matthews and Wrigley 2017). Some authors describe design thinking as a skill that every MBA student needs. However, to realise the full benefit of innovation initiatives, educational DT programmes have to do more than convey knowledge about DT and its tools. According to Kelley and Kelly (2013), they must also develop Creative Confidence. The question here is what the best way is to teach DT in Business Schools, to encourage the designerly ways of thinking and doing. What seems relevant now is how to prepare twenty-first century educators for the needs of twenty-first century business students. According to Hoidn and Kärkkäinen (2014), the question is not whether there is a 'best' teaching method, but what kind of combination of methods is the more suitable for a desired goal. The authors highlight that approaches aiming to equip business students with diverse skills for innovation cannot neglect the need to equip their teachers with a variety of effective teaching skills. Thus, a giant challenge for business education and organisational training is the professional development of lecturers and innovation trainers.

In this sense, Design Thinking as an integrative and human-centred method may be able to ensure that educational change does not just happen in every 'classroom', but everywhere in the educational system, in line with the conviction that "education is an ecosystem with many stakeholders" (OECD 2018). Looking at the landscape of business education today, in an earlier work, we considered the application of Design Thinking in the redesign of business education itself as a valid innovation methodology (Tschimmel and Santos 2018). Related to the OECD (2018) challenges, Design Thinking applied in the redesign of business education would enable it to work with others with different perspectives and find untapped human-centred opportunities, and thus contribute to change the mindset of business school educators and students. And in the end, contribute to the cultural transformation of Business Schools into Design-driven organisations.

4.2 Challenges/Opportunities for Design Education

The fact that Design shifted away from a focus on giving form and meaning to objects and visual communication to purposeful action to solve complex problems and to making design accessible now to a wider community in organisations, brings completely new challenges to Design Education.

The great advantage of the recent Design Thinking boom is that finally designers can also export knowledge developed in the discipline itself (after having imported so much knowledge from other disciplines). At last, the designer is an equal member in interdisciplinary innovation processes (instead of being called only at the end of the process), working closely with professionals in the marketing, finance, engineering, etc. departments. Not only can and should the designer be a member of innovation teams, but often he/she could take on the role of a facilitator in the generation and development of ideas, guiding 'innovation agents' or providing training on Design Thinking procedures and techniques.

Thus, the aim of teaching Design today should be to train students as creative and integrative design thinkers, who not only develop the world of artefacts but also themselves. The main objective of Design Education should be the development of a holistic thinker with intellectual and creative flexibility, creative thinking abilities, and the capacity for continuous learning and self-responsibility. Design students should become process experts with context sensitivity and a human-centred systemic view.

References

Amabile TM (1996) Creativity in context: update to the social psychology of creativity. Boulder, Westview

Baxter M (2000) Projeto de produto. Guia prático para o design de novos produtos [orig. Product design—a practical guide to systematic methods of new product development, 1995]. Editora Edgard Blücher, São Paulo

Brown T (2009) Change by design. How design thinking transforms organizations and inspires innovation. Harper Collins Publishers, New York

Buchanan R (2000) Wicked problems in design thinking. In: Margolin V, Buchanan R (eds) The idea of design. MIT Press, Cambridge, Massachusetts, pp 3–20

Carlgren L, Rauth I, Elmquist M (2016) Framing design thinking: the concept in idea and enactment. Creativity Innovation Management 25(1): 38–57

Christiaans H (1992) Creativity in design. The role of domain knowledge in designing. Lemma BV, Utrecht

Cross N, Dorst K, Roozenburg N (eds) (1992) Research in design thinking. Delft University Press

Csikszentmihalyi M (2004) Implications of a systems perspective for the study of creativity. In: Sternberg RJ (ed) Handbook of creativity. Cambridge University Press, Cambridge, pp 313–335

Dorst K (2003) Understanding design, 150 reflections on being a designer. BIS Publisher, Amsterdam

Dorst K (2011) The core of 'design thinking' and its application. Design Studies 32(6): 521–532

Editorial board of IJDCI (2013) Perspectives on design creativity and innovation research. International Journal of Design Creativity and Innovation 1(1): 1–42. https://doi.org/10.1080/21650349.2013.754657

Florida R (2004) The rise of the creative class: and how it's transforming work, leisure, community and everyday life. Basic Books, New York

Goldschmidt G (1999) Design. In: Encyclopedia of creativity, Vol. 1. Academic Press, pp 525–535

Groeger L, Schweitzer J, Sobel L, Malcolm B (2019) Design thinking mindset: developing creative confidence. In: Conference proceedings of the academy for design innovation management. London. https://doi.org/10.33114/adim.2019.09.288

Guntern G (ed) (1991) Der kreative Weg. Kreativität in Wirtschaft, Kunst und Wissenschaft. Verlag Moderne Industrie, Zürich

Guntern G (1994) Sieben Goldene Regeln der Kreativitätsförderung. Scalo, Zürich

Guntern G (ed) (1996) Intuition und Kreativität. Intuition and Creativity. Col. "Kreativität in Wirtschaft, Kunst und Wissenschaft", Internationales Zermatter Symposium. International Foundation for Creativity and Leadership e Scalo Verlag, Zürich

Hoidn S, Kärkkäinen K (2014) Promoting skills for innovation in higher education. OECD education working paper, No.100 [Online]. Available at: https://doi.org/10.1787/5k3tsj671226-en

Keeley L, Pikkel R, Quinn B, Walters H (2013) Ten types of innovation. The discipline of building breakthroughs. Wiley, New Jersey

Kelly T, Kelly D (2013) Creative confidence. Unleashing the creative potential within us all. Crown Business, New York

Kurokawa T (2013) Design thinking education at universities and graduate schools. Sci. Technol. Trends Q. Rev. 46:50–63

Lawson BR (1990) How designers think. Butterworth Architecture, London

Martin R (2009) Design of business: why design thinking is the next competitive advantage. Mcgraw-Hill Professional

Matthews J, Wrigley C (2017) Design and design thinking in business and management higher education. J. Learn Des 10(1):41–54

Maturana HR, Varela FJ (1987) Der Baum der Erkenntnis. Die biologischen Wurzeln menschlichen Erkennens. Goldmann Verlag, München

Nelson H, Stoltermann E (2003) The design way. Intentional change in an unpredictable world. Educational Technology Publications, Englewood Cliffs

OECD (2018) The future of education and skills. Education 2030. Position paper [Online]. Available at: http://www.oecd.org/education/2030/

Osborn A (1953) Applied imagination. Principles and procedures of creative problem solving. New York Charles Scribners Sons, New York

Sátiro A, Tschimmel K (2020) CriAtivaMente/The Creative Mind/CreA(c)tivaMente. Ed. Mindshake, Porto

Simon H (1996) The sciences of the artificial, 3rd edn. The MIT Press [1st. Edition 1969]

Tschimmel K (2010) Sapiens e Demens no Pensamento Criativo do Design. PhD dissertation, University of Aveiro

Tschimmel K (2012) Design thinking as an effective toolkit for innovation. In: Proceedings of the XXIII ISPIM conference: action for innovation: innovating from experience. Barcelona

Tschimmel K (Coord) (2019) The creativity virus—a book about and for creative thinking. Ed. Mindshake, Porto

Tschimmel K, Santos J (2018) Design thinking applied to the redesign of business education. In: Proceedings of the XXIX ISPIM innovation conference, the name of the game. Stockholm

The Double Diamond Model: In Pursuit of Simplicity and Flexibility

Magda Kochanowska, Weronika Rochacka Gagliardi, and with reference to Jonathan Ball

Abstract This chapter considers the foundations and relevance of the Double Diamond model fifteen years after it was first published. It draws from a lecture presented by Jonathan Ball at EIMAD in 2020. The first part of the text is devoted to the history of understanding and describing how designers work. The emphasis is on the increasing complexity of design problems, requiring designers to work with people who are unfamiliar with the design process. It goes on to describe the key phases of the Double Diamond model and comments on how they relate to universal characteristics of designers' ways of working and their thinking styles. The final section looks at different ways of working with the model, adapting it to current design challenges.

Keywords Double diamond · Design process · Design mindset

1 Design as a Process

For decades, design has been understood as an outcome of the process of designing a product, visual communication or an exhibition. This notion of a process leading to the creation of solutions that provide users with important functional, aesthetic

---

The title of this article is based on a presentation which Jonathan Ball gave in May 2020 for 7th EIMAD, Castelo Branco, Portugal.

Illustrations by David Townson, *What Could Be*.

M. Kochanowska (✉)
Academy of Fine Arts in Warsaw, Faculty of Design, Warsaw, Poland
e-mail: magda@design-provision.com

W. R. Gagliardi
SWPS University Social Sciences and Humanities, Warsaw Poznań, Poland

J. Ball
LUMA Institute, Pittsburgh, USA

19

and emotional values was a vital step in design history. Codifying the design process was crucial in making it visible and tangible.

It has been over fifteen years since the Double Diamond model was first published. From then on, the breadth of challenges taken on by designers across disciplines has been continually growing. In 2020, Jonathan Ball gave a lecture at EIMAD on the phenomenon of this diagram that shows the key phases of the design process, and commented on its current development. Ball was a member of an interdisciplinary team working on a number of projects at the Design Council that ultimately helped to shape Double Diamond in 2003–4. The Double Diamond model is brilliant in its simplicity, and has been widely used for many years, by designers and non-designers alike.

This model was not simply 'invented' by the Design Council. The notion of divergent and convergent thinking had been seen before, in the 1970s, in the work of John Chris Jones and Victor Papanek, where we find the root of the kite-shaped diagram. Ball recalls the words of Richard Eiserman, then the Design Council's Director of Design and Innovation, who initiated the project that led to the Double Diamond: 'The [Design Council] team put in the work trying to define design, process, methods, etc. What we did with the Double Diamond was codify it, rename the steps and popularise it. It was important work, but we were certainly standing on the shoulders of giants.' [quoted from: https://www.designcouncil.org.uk/news-opinion/double-diamond-universally-accepted-depiction-design-process].

2 Exploring Design Methods

Research on designers' attitudes, ways of thinking and actions dates back to the mid-twentieth century. There were many attempts to understand the approach to the problem-solving observed among design or architecture professionals. The question was, what made them distinct? Work on describing design intensified in the 1960s, when three conferences on design methods were held: in London in 1962, in Birmingham in 1965 and in Portsmouth in 1967. This was a pivotal moment in the history of design. They discovered it was possible to describe the design process and to take greater control over it (Jones 1970). The London conference (1962) marked the beginning of the British intellectual movement that laid the foundations for the Design Research Society. It was seen as an intellectual movement, because the environment in which the discussions took place was interdisciplinary, bringing together designers and scientists from various disciplines. What they had in common was their attempts to understand how design, always inextricably tied to technological development, could create a better world.

3 The Complexity of the World

In the latter half of the twentieth century, accelerating technology triggered deep changes in civilisation as a whole, and designers faced increasingly complex problems. Each new thing became part of a dynamic, interconnected system, and designers could no longer focus on the product in isolation. In approaching a design task, they were forced to recognise as wide a context as possible, to shape relations between product and the environment in which it was meant to function, and to shape the behaviour and emotions of the user (Jones 1970).

In 1962, Morris Asimow wrote that design reacts to the political, societal and cultural factors which make up the social environment. He stressed it was necessary to study this environment, as it had a significant impact on how the design came out. At the same time, designers were to recognise how the environment itself was also affected to a greater or lesser degree by the consequences of their activities (Asimow 1962). Jones, on the other hand, described four levels of design. Apart from the obvious components level (relations between the parts of a product) and the product level (as a whole, and its relations with the user and the immediate environment), he drew attention to the systems level, i.e. the relations between various products of the design (e.g. urban transport seen as a whole), and finally, the social level, understood as the relations between systems (e.g. the city as a whole). This last level made it possible to see how design artefacts affected user behaviour on a large scale, how they interacted with politics, and how they changed the image of society (Jones 1970). All these discussions expressed, among other things, the hope that there was a way to approach complexity.

4 Making the Design Process Visible

A major motivation behind investigating and describing designers' methods was the hope of creating effective ways of working with people who need to be involved in the design processes, due to the high complexity of the problems being faced. Designers needed to consider a very broad context, they had to collaborate with specialists and researchers unfamiliar with their processes. For the uninitiated, the designer's work seemed quite mysterious and rather unintuitive; some people even called designers 'black boxes'. Describing design methods and processes allowed the 'hitherto private thinking of designers' to be revealed and the process to be externalised, so that the others involved in the challenge could participate more consciously. Jones believed one of the major benefits that came from this disclosure of design way of thinking was that others, e.g. users, were able to see what was going on and assist the designer with information that was outside the designer's scope of knowledge and experience (Jones 1970).

Since the mid-twentieth century, design has undergone dynamic development. Nonetheless, these studies and descriptions of several decades ago are still relevant.

In recent decades, new areas of design have emerged, and today, they include activities that go far beyond industrial design, ones which reigned for much of the twentieth century. Most of these new areas are related to the development of digital technology and the new economic reality. We might mention UX Design, Interaction Design or Service Design, dealing with the immaterial space of human experience. The theories whose foundations were laid in the 1960s and 70s made it possible to understand a constant, universal structure of the design process, describing how designers operate, regardless of the nature of challenges and the development of civilisation.

5   Four Key Phases

The Double Diamond model outlines the four key phases of the design process: Discover, Define, Develop and Deliver. It was created through the analysis of designers' work methods, based on their practice.

The first phase, **Discover**, is about taking as broad a look as possible, conducting research. Here empathy, openness, and a variety of research tools help the designer to observe users, to discover their goals, needs and motivations. This stage should conclude with a full immersion in the context of the challenge and a good understanding of the eventual users' perspective. The lines of the diagram diverge and widen, symbolising an openness to information and inspiration.

The second phase, **Define**, is about looking at all the data you have gathered and trying to make sense of it. It is about connecting the dots, spotting patterns, hunting for insight, understanding emotions. In the second phase of the design process, discipline and order are helpful, as are tools for organising information and finding patterns in user behaviour. This is when we frame our design challenge, which often turns out different from the one we started with. With insights from the Discover and Define phases, we are able to better understand the real problems people face and frame the challenge by taking them into account, basing it no just on our assumptions. The lines of the diagram converge and meet at a key point in the process.

Then we move into **Develop** phase, which involves creativity, inventing solutions, experimenting, iterating and testing. This third phase of the design process, creativity and techniques stimulate thinking outside of the box. The team uses inspiration and their new understanding of the problem from previous phases of the project to create potential solutions that meet the users' needs. The diagram again diverges and widens, symbolising an openness to create as many potential solutions as possible.

The final phase, **Deliver**, is about working on and refining the solution. Perseverance and accuracy, along with further testing and iterations, are useful in the fourth phase of the design process. This stage concludes with a detailed description of the solution, tested by users, combined with a specific plan for its implementation. The lines of the diagram converge again and meet at a final point in the process.

6 Thinking Styles in Design

The Double Diamond diagram shows the crucial characteristics of the designer's work—a combination of thinking styles. Most theorists have agreed that design consists of a sequence of divergent and convergent thinking, analysis and synthesis.

In the first pair, designers use divergent thinking to 'expand the boundaries of the design situation to obtain a sufficiently large and fruitful search area in which the solution lies', i.e. it helps expand the understanding of the design context (Jones 1970). Convergent thinking helps them to 'eliminate doubt' and leads to the optimal version of the solution.

The second pair is analysis and synthesis. Designers use analysis to explore relationships, looking for patterns in available information, classifying objectives and finding the order and structure of a problem. Synthesis is useful in trying to move forward, to create an answer to a problem, in generating solutions (Lawson 2005). Lawson also links synthesis to evaluation, which is a critical assessment of the solutions in relation to the objectives set out in the analysis phase. Jones speaks of the three phases, divergent, transformational and convergent, where the transformational phase can be equated with Lawson's synthesis phase.

7 The Process and Its Outcome

The history of the design process emerged from industrial design, which always concludes with a physical product. The Double Diamond model shows the overall, generic structure of every design process, including both industrial design and service design teams. However, a special challenge arose when it came to such fields as service design, which often do not deliver tangible results, making them difficult to explain and their value difficult to prove. The dynamics of purchase and usage of services are unlike those of physical products. The effects of service implementation come with some delay—they can be seen in customer behaviour after several months, depending on the nature of the service. Another difficulty is measuring these effects so that the results are comparable.

The service design process does not end with the delivery of a report or service blueprint that works as a prototype. There are a many steps which still need to be taken to create what has been developed. This also highlights an important gap, which can often be seen in service design. Companies hire service designers to help them come up with innovative solutions or to improve existing ones. However, once the research has been done and analysed, the solutions developed and tested, the whole task of implementing it stays with the company. It often happens that the implementation is handed over to other teams who have not been a part of developing the solution. This poses many constraints and problems. It is still fairly rare for a team including service designers involved in the solution's development process to take part in the implementation phase. Yet in some cases, if the service design work is well distributed in the company, certain changes occur in the company's organisational culture.

8 The Double Diamond: What It Is

There are some interesting critiques of the Double Diamond model. Sometimes it is even perceived as linear, and is compared to the waterfall process. Some design agencies add diamonds before and after the Double Diamond itself to illustrate that more is happening in projects outside of the model's key four stages. All these modifications are possible because the Double Diamond model is a simple visualisation of design process, a diagram that shows a way of working. It is a point of reference and should not be seen as a detailed, step-by-step guide. The most important points of the Double Diamond process are there to illustrate how design assumptions can be challenged at the start of a project and through a series of steps, how to exercise divergent and convergent thinking, and how a challenge based on real, not imagined user needs can be framed.

9 Using the Double Diamond

Jonathan Ball recalls a workshop in Asia he ran a few years back. The participants —non-designers—were asked to question the brief and the methods they were to use, though this made them uncomfortable. They would have preferred to deliver to the brief unchallenged. How did he get them on board? He drew the Double Diamond backwards. First he made the straight line from the final point of the model—the end of the Deliver phase—to the central point situated between the two diamonds, or the moment in the process when the challenge is reframed. Then he drew the 'diamond' lines.

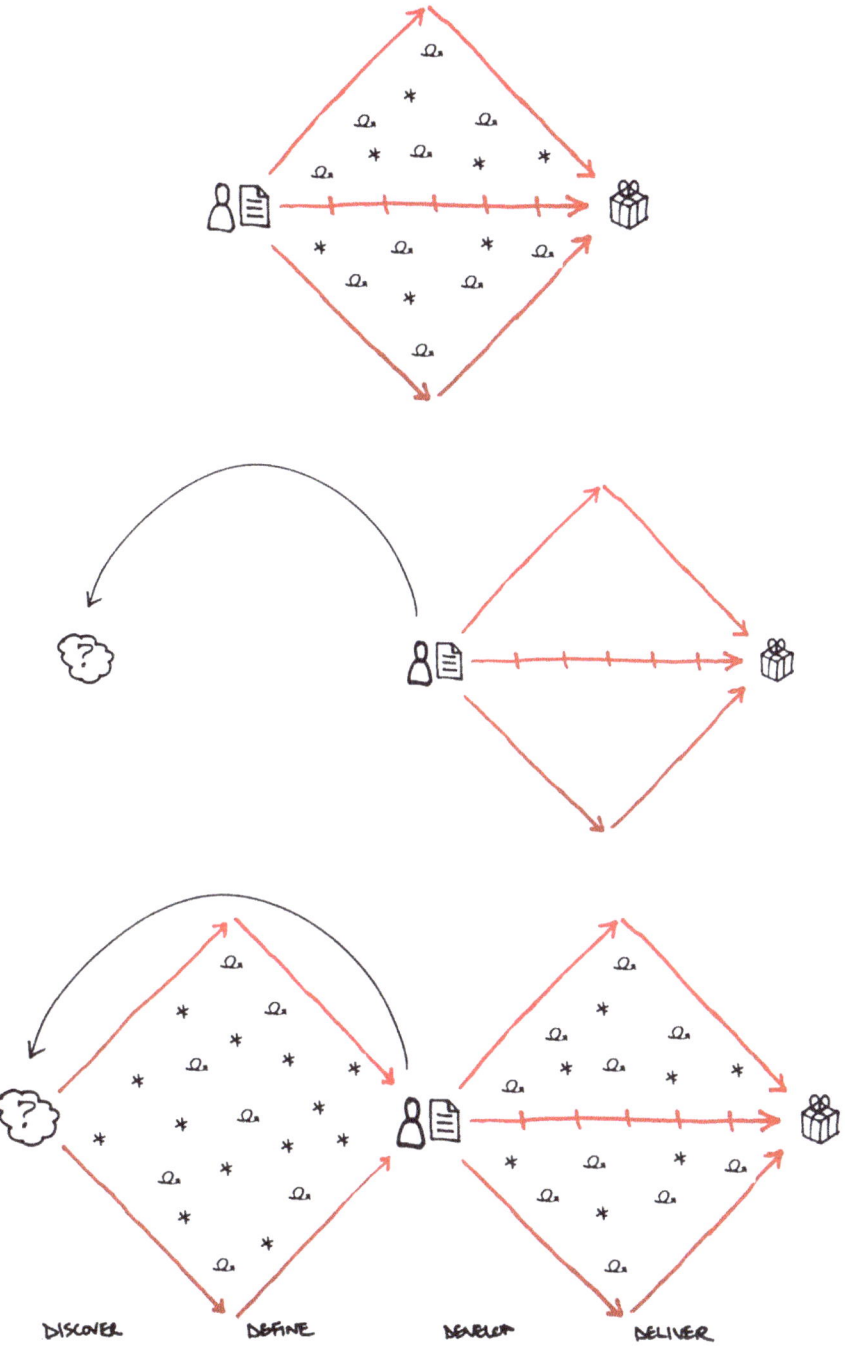

DISCOVER   DEFINE   DEVELOP   DELIVER

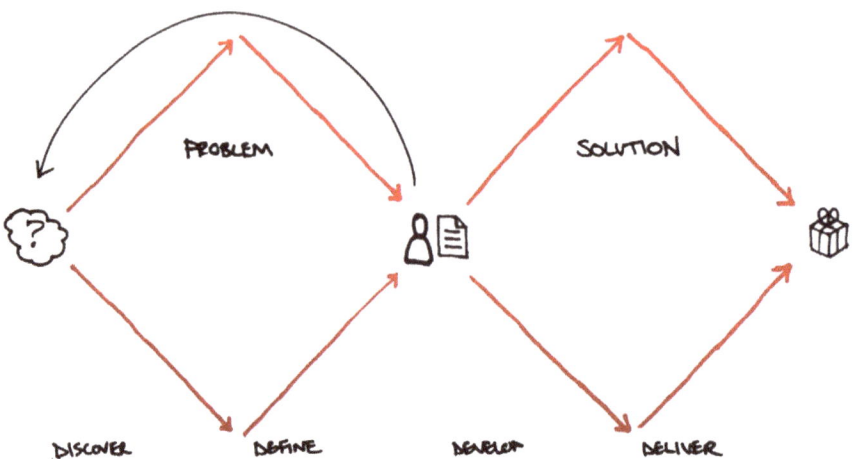

The crucial value in this visualisation is that it shows a shortcut which, once taken, leads to developing solutions that frequently fail. These failures are due to a lack of understanding the real problem. The Double Diamond encourages a design team to question the status quo, to immerse themselves in the context of the problem, and to dedicate time to gathering inspiration from the users' real lives. Instead of jumping straight to conclusions and solutions, it breaks down the standard way of dealing with challenges. Jonathan stresses that, especially for non-designers, 'the first phase of the Double Diamond is the most daunting and the most exciting, because usually it is somewhat invisible. The Double Diamond made people see and understand it'.

10   The Relevance of the Model

While discussing the relevance of the Double Diamond model in today's challenges, it should be considered that the Double Diamond is adaptable. That is why it has never gone out of date, as it is an ever-changing device. It is impossible to plan a project end-to-end, specifying every step—design challenges are not science, even though they share some principles—a question or hypothesis is followed by methods to address it. A scientific formula is limiting and, after one answer, there usually comes a new question and a new hypothesis. Designers always need to pose questions, asking themselves whether they should customise or adapt their methods and processes.

In understanding these characteristics of the design process in the Double Diamond approach, it is helpful to have a look at the theory of 'reflection in action' formulated by Donald Shön, who presented the *Reflective Practitioner* concept. Schön's theory allows us to see design in terms of 'reflective activity' and related concepts, especially 'reflective practice', 'reflection in action' and 'knowledge in action'. In 'reflection in action', doing and thinking are complementary. The doing extends thinking through experimental activities, and reflection feeds on action and its results. Each sustains and sets boundaries for the other. The Double Diamond can reflect the way of working, it can be adapted, adding extra diamonds before and after, or even inside the core model, multiplying iterations and explaining the nature of design process related to specific problem and team.

11   Double Diamond and the (Un)certainty Matrix

Another way Jonathan Ball proposes using the Double Diamond model is to look at the level of certainty in a project. This model provides a framework for assessing projects' status, especially when the certainty of an outcome is moderately or very low.

Turning to the axes: the first one, labelled '**what**', concerns the possible outcome of the design process (knowing what to design versus not knowing what to design); the second one, labelled '**how**', concerns the methods and tools that should be used (knowing how to design—not knowing how to design). Then the double diamond can visualise the complexity of the design process to be planned in a given situation. The full version of the Double Diamond reflects the most uncertain situation, when the 'what' and 'how' are not defined at the beginning of the process.

12   Can the Double Diamond Evolve?

Many different experiences tied to the creative and flexible usage of the Double Diamond diagram convinced Jonathan and his colleagues at What Could Be to go a step further and develop the Design Thinking Canvas. It starts with 'what' and 'how' questions. In their experience, these are the questions every team needs to ask itself at the beginning of a project. Others include: What is our vision? What is the impact? What challenges do we need to address? Who will be working on it? How will we communicate over the course of the project? How will we deliver the project and measure its progress?

Putting the Double Diamond model at the centre of the canvas, they formed a tool that could be a starting point for different design challenges. It looks like a visualisation of the design process and Scoping Canvas combined.

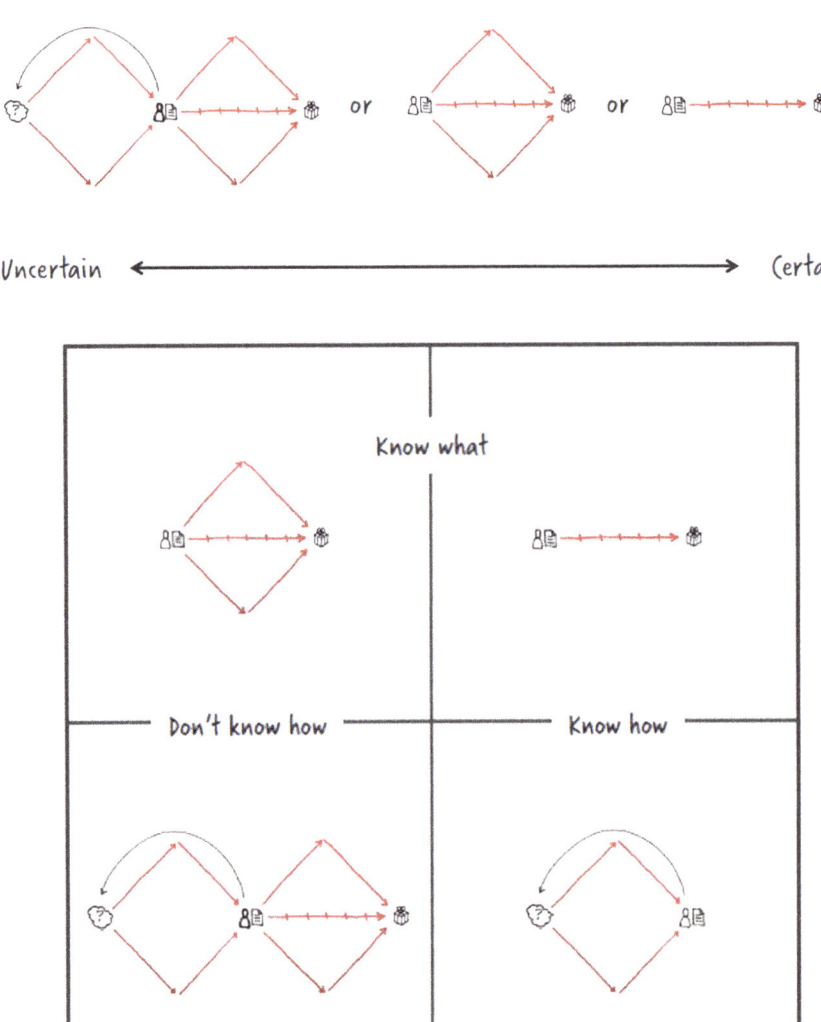

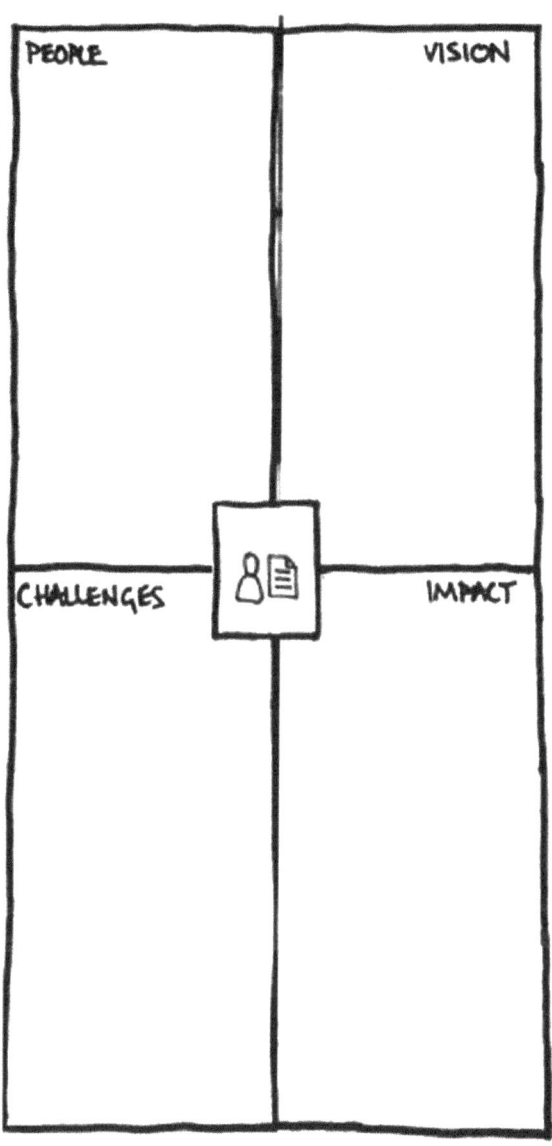

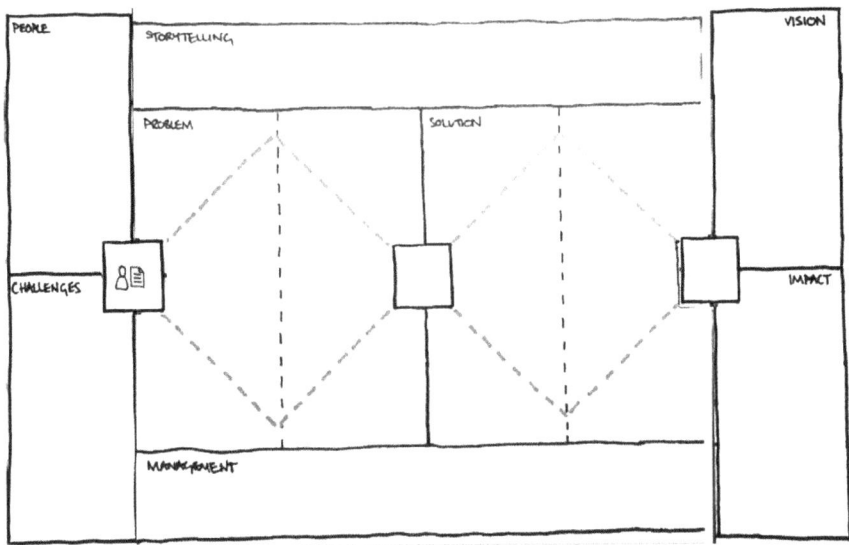

How will we deliver the project and monitor progress?

The Design Thinking Canvas is available to all via creative commons license, e.g. http://designthinkingcanvas.co.uk/. Moreover, What Could Be explains its use in a Mural webinar: https://www.mural.co/blog/what-design-thinking-could-be.

13   A Universal Model

The Double Diamond approach helps designers to collaborate in interdisciplinary teams and facilitates the introduction of new team members into a process where different ways of thinking, divergent and convergent, are alternately applied. This model helps them to participate in a process that can seem chaotic and unpredictable to non-designers. Despite the very dynamic development of design disciplines and the constant expansion of the field, and changes in social and technological contexts, the way designers work has generally stayed the same.

This article stands by the belief that the Double Diamond is a universal, flexible model that provides an explanation of the characteristic key phases of the design process. It is and was not intended to be a prescriptive approach to project planning. Design theorists and practitioners may argue it takes a linear approach; however, its narrative presentation can change the perception of the diagram. The design process itself is iterative, it is in its DNA. It is exploratory, experimental, full of surprises and various 'traps' along the way. With all these aspects in mind, the Double Diamond model is brilliant in its simplicity, helping to illustrate the principles of the process, yet leaving space to be used flexibly.

14 Conclusions

This chapter introduced an understanding of a universal structure for the design process, based on designers' way of working and thinking, irrespective of their challenges and how civilisation develops. It is especially valuable for **service design**, as it enables the work of the interdisciplinary teams fundamental to this field.

Three crucial assets of the Double Diamond diagram are discussed here:

- it makes the design process visible and enables designers to work efficiently with non-designers, who, owing to the high complexity of design problems, need to be involved
- it provides a framework for assessing the status of projects, especially where the certainty of the final outcome is moderately or very low
- it illustrates the key phases and principles of the design process, while leaving space for flexibility.

The structure of the model creates an understanding of the design process while remaining modifiable. In the hands of a creative leader, it is a tool that can be adapted to the needs of the design team and the nature of the challenge.

Bibliography

Archer BL (1965) Systematic method for designers. Council of Industrial Design
Asimow M (1962) Introduction to design. Prince-Hall Inc.
Cross N (2010) Designerly ways of knowing. Springer
Jones JC (1970) Design methods: seeds of human futures. Wiley
Lawson B (2005) How designers think: the design process demystified. Elsevier
Schön DA (1969) The reflective practitioner: how professionals think in action. Basic Books, New York [1995]
Simon HA (1969) The sciences of the artificial, 3rd edn. MIT Press [1996]

Magda Kochanowska Magda is a design expert and author of articles and other pieces for books, magazines and exhibition catalogues on issues related to design, and a curator of projects related to the promotion of design. Her background is in product and visual communications design. A co-founder of DESIGN PROVISION, she specialises in planning and implementing design processes, especially in service design. Her many years of experience and practical knowledge of various design tools and methods give her great flexibility in designing processes, products and services. Magda has run projects and training courses for such companies as: ING Bank Śląski, Santander Bank Polska, Bank Millennium, Saint-Gobain Polska, Nowy Styl Group, City of Warsaw, Nationale-Nederlandern and ING Shared Services (IBSS).

Since 2005 she has lectured at the Faculty of Design at the Academy of Fine Arts in Warsaw, where she defended her doctorate in 2010 and obtained her post-doctoral degree in 2020. She is now the Deputy Dean for Education and the Dean's Plenipotentiary for Science. Her fields are design methodologies, theory and design criticism. In 2020, she became Head of the Service Design postgraduate course and the SWPS University in Warsaw. She also teaches at the School of Ideas at the same university. She has written many texts on design and has curated design exhibitions.

Weronika Rochacka Gagliardi Weronika is a design strategist and co-founder of DESIGN PROVISION. She runs projects and training sessions in strategy building, design management, Design Thinking and service design. Thus far, she has worked with such clients as: ING Bank Śląski, ING DiBa (Germany), ING Chief Innovation Office (Holland), Santander Bank Polska, Docplanner (ZnanyLekarz.pl), Mercer Services Polska, Warsaw University and Polpharma. She gained professional experience at the British Design Council in London, where, in 2007–12, she worked as a project manager in education and support for business, the public sector and technology transfer offices.

Since 2013 she has been a lecturer, and in 2020 she became Head of the Service Design postgraduate course at the SWPS University in Poznań. She is a member of the Program Board at the School of Ideas in Warsaw (part of the SWPS University). In 2019, she joined the board of the Association of Industrial Designers (SPFP).

Jonathan Ball Jonathan started his career as a product designer in industry, experience he still relies on today as a part of a number of respected associate networks. He is a Design Associate for Design Council, a part of the team that led the creation and delivery of the Council's coaching programmes, which accelerate the commercialisation of science, speed businesses growth and transform the delivery of public services. Jonathan has worked directly with many of Design Council's clients, including manufacturing and service businesses and public bodies of all sizes. He helped shape and deliver *Innovation by Design* at the Centre for Design Innovation in Ireland and co-authored the *Business Support Canvas*; a strategic approach to the evaluation, development and delivery of publicly funded design and innovation programmes. His ongoing work includes the *Creative Decision Making Playbook* for BBC Digital, the Design Thinking Accelerator programme for V&A Dundee and the introduction of design-led strategy to many creative organisations based in north west England through The Creative Step. Jonathan is a Lead Instructor for LUMA Institute in Pittsburgh, where his work has supported LUMA's rapid growth and enables their global reach with clients that include *McDonalds, Honeywell, Autodesk, Prudential* and *DBS*, one of Asia's leading banks.

The Spirit of the Place: Challenges for the Design Education in Portugal in XXI Century

Fernando Moreira da Silva

Abstract To date, there has been little reflection on Design Education in Portugal. Especially after the revolution of 25 April 1974 and later Portugal's entry into the European Union, there was a proliferation of higher education courses in Design, in university and polytechnic education, public and private. We are aware that bridging the fields of design and education allows the construction of a social perspective, centered on the formulation of design principles and their contribution to educational practices, with a focus of design on finding solutions to problems that mediate learning, highlighting the social role of design on issues related to needs, from a sociologically localized perspective and with the development of knowledge associated with students' formation process. This leads us to a reflection on the potentialities that naturally emanate from the "spirit of the place" where a certain training in design develops, which is different from the "culture of the place", in a clear articulation with the local cultural identity. Cultural identity, besides the sense of self, provides a global significance of local knowledge and community. If we address globalization in its deeper sense, in terms of science, technology, social or even economic development, we verify that it promotes cultural identity. This work focuses on the discovery of interconnections between the teaching of Design and the educational institutions in which this education takes place, trying to value the identity of the place, its culture, in a holistic view that highlights its differences and qualities that contribute to make each institution unique and owning a specific expertise. The research was supported by a methodology of literature review crossing and interpreting fundamental authors and theories, articulated with the author's experience and direct observation. We arrived to the conclusion that each higher education school of Design in Portugal must implement a serious reflection on its role in the specific area of study and in the region, leading to value the 'spirit of the place' which is different from the 'culture of place'. To define the spirit of the place contribute and interact countless variables such as the physical place (geographic and architectural), the provided environment (interior space, rooms, laboratories, equipment), the curricular grids seen as a whole of training, the teachers who teach in the institution at a given time, the developed group synergies, the

F. Moreira da Silva (✉)
CIAUD, Lisbon School of Architecture, Universidade de Lisboa, Lisbon, Portugal

© The Author(s), under exclusive license to Springer Nature Switzerland AG 2022
D. Raposo et al. (eds.), *Perspectives on Design II*, Springer Series in Design and Innovation 16, https://doi.org/10.1007/978-3-030-79879-6_3

articulation with the environment, with the local society and their needs and desires, the contribution to the local and regional development of the institution as a whole, among others.

Keywords Design education · Identity · Culture · Local cultural identity · Spirit of the place

1 Introduction

The present work derives from a theoretical and fundamental reflection, based on studies that cross several areas of knowledge, centered on the design education and its future, taking into account the challenges facing us today and the prospects for the future. As Nigel Cross stated (2000), design as a discipline needs to develop its intellectual independence, while continuing to look for rigorous standards in other disciplines.

There is still a lot of work to develop in Portugal in order to consolidate design as an autonomous disciplinary field, with its own dynamics, processes and theoretical-practical methods, to allow a solid interdisciplinary work, but at the same time an epistemological statement of design. According to Chalmer and Fiker (1993), the development of the epistemology of this area is fundamental to consolidate scientific research in design and its product, scientific knowledge, defining what that knowledge is and what are the valid methods and processes for obtaining and justify it, since, as Cross (1982) defended in 1982, design has its own way of producing knowledge and research.

The design epistemology and the awareness of design as an autonomous discipline must lead to solid academic training and a prompt response to the challenges of the moment, aware of the diversity and specificity of the studies developed in different institutions, located in equally different regions. This study focuses on the relationship between design training and local identity, highlighting the importance of considering local cultural identity during the teaching–learning process. This leads us to a reflection on the potentialities that naturally emanate from the "spirit of the place" where a certain training in design develops, which is different from the "culture of the place", in a clear articulation with the local cultural identity.

To define the spirit of the place contribute and interact countless variables such as the physical place (geographic and architectural), the provided environment (interior space, rooms, laboratories, equipment), the curricular grids seen as a whole of training, the teachers who teach in the institution at a given time, the developed group synergies, the articulation with the environment, with the local society and their needs and desires, the contribution to the local and regional development of the institution as a whole, among others.

2 Design Education in Portugal

Especially from the 50s of the last century, design education began to develop itself, supported by several philosophical currents and with a strong support from cognitive sciences, underlining the trans, multi and interdisciplinarities which characterize the designer's practice and the researcher in design, being design training characterized by several teaching–learning theories. The positivist theories of Simon (1969) or Peirce (1975) and later Schön (1983) were instrumental in teaching design and in design project, in which stands out the pioneering role of Bauhaus, created after the first world war, in 1919, with three major periods in three different locations: Weimar, Dessau and Berlin-Steglitz. According to Maldonado (2009), this last location ends in 1933, due to Nazism.

The practice of interdisciplinarity, as a gnoseological issue, emerged in the late twentieth century, due to the need to respond to the fragmentation caused by a positivist epistemology, given that the sciences had been divided into many disciplines and interdisciplinarity allowed the reestablishment of a dialogue between them, although it did not yet rescue the unity and the totality of knowledge, a vision that was consolidated later on with cross-pollination (Instituto Paulo Freire 2020).

Interdisciplinarity involves, as a principle of its own, all areas of knowledge, including those that produce knowledge par excellence and those that apply this knowledge, and Design as a human activity that produces and applies knowledge, suffers directly the consequences of specialism. Interdisciplinarity is related to the concept of intellectual and moral autonomy, on the one hand using constructivism and on the other, serving it. As a theory of learning, constructivism understands knowledge as a result of the interaction between the subject and the environment, the role of the subject being paramount in the construction of knowledge, as well as the relationship between intellectual autonomy and interdisciplinarity is immediate. In Piaget's constructivism, the subject does not expect knowledge to be transmitted to him/her, since he/she has autonomy and constructs his/her own categories of thought, at the same time that he/she organizes his/her world and learns through his/her own actions on it (Fontoura 2011).

Multidisciplinarity implies the solution of a problem through the involvement of different disciplines, but without mutual enrichment, being the starting point for interdisciplinarity. Transdisciplinarity, in turn, promotes total integration between disciplines, eliminating the boundaries between them. Transdisciplinarity can be considered as the most profound degree of interdisciplinarity, being design interdisciplinary in nature.

The approximation of the fields of design and education allows the construction of a social perspective, centered on the formulation of design principles and their contribution to educational practices, addressing two fundamental aspects: the focus of design on finding solutions to problems that mediate learning, highlighting the social role of design on issues related to needs, from a sociologically localized perspective; and its epistemological and methodological conception, as thought, that is, knowledge associated with the formation process of individuals. All those involved in the process, students and teachers, are the originators of strategic information for the process of expanding the educational experience mediating knowledge (Coutinho and Lopes 2011).

Knowledge is no longer monodisciplinary, but interdisciplinary, and is focused on the problem, not on a specific discipline. It is produced in several areas closer to its application, having moved from academic circles to get closer to the productive business, industrial and society circles in general. It uses different means for the purposes of exchange, production and transformation into technology, being subject to different types of control, highlighting its social relevance and efficiency (Yarzábal 2002). This leads us to the "knowledge society", a society whose productive capital is the result of capturing, storing and compiling data on different aspects of life, transforming that data into understandable information for the construction of specific knowledge for a given context in which information and knowledge are essential conditions for the full exercise of citizenship in a society punctuated by technology, converging on a new workforce and capital, solving social problems with the intensive use of information and knowledge, through their accumulation, creation, reproduction and dissemination (Martins Filho et al. 2015).

In design education, it has become very important to include cognitive sciences that have a holistic approach to learning, language and memory processes. Studying the thought, the sensations, the emotions and the feelings is a structuring part of a process of conditioning mental activities for the teaching and learning processes, since in the cognitive view, an object does not assume a meaning for itself, but for the relationships established with the other objects around it (Martins Filho et al. 2015).

In the Portuguese case, the Decorative Arts School António Arroio played a pioneering role in design training in the 40s of the twentieth century, followed by IADE (Institute of Visual Arts and Design), where the first higher education design degree arises in Portugal, in 1969. Only after the 1974 revolution will higher education courses emerge in the Fine Arts schools of Lisbon and Porto (in 1975). From that moment on, many other design courses will begin to be created, producing a profound change in the teaching of this area which, as stated by Fragoso (2010), the second half of the twentieth century in Portugal is marked by important advances in design training, accompanied by theoretical and practical production. There is a progressive change in the meaning and role of the designer in society, giving him/her an own activity and field of work, increasingly inserted in society. As Frayling (1998) observed, in the field of design there has always been a difference between academia and the professional world, being, however, necessary to ensure the existence of continuous links between the two worlds, in order to consolidate knowledge, challenges, functions and points of close collaboration.

With the entry of Portugal into the European Union (EU) in 1986, there is a marked paradigmatic change in teaching, both in terms of structure and content, which culminated in the late 1990s with the adherence to the Bologna Process, allowing a marked and visible improvement in the quality and efficiency of the teaching previously practiced, boosting critical and reflective thinking. According to Dias (2018), "in the 90s, Europe undertook a challenge of modernization and globalization to standardize its higher education, through the compatibility of degrees and diplomas, in order to achieve the title of Europe of Knowledge".

The Bologna Convention, more than an obligation to adopt identical procedures across Europe, was an opportunity for transformation and enrichment, allowing for a rethinking of teaching, both in terms of academia to the exterior, and in allowing greater approximation of business tissue, industrial and society in general to academia. The Bologna process aimed to harmonize higher education across the EU, with the respective educational institutions being responsible for adapting their programs, pedagogical systems and results, to the new challenges and new demands. With regard to the design teaching, this whole process of profound change was above all an opportunity to review processes and methods, redefine goals and find a balance between traditional academy and practice in its various disciplines (Calvera 2006).

The report of the Knowledge Area Group on 'Plastic Arts and Design', developed in 2004, was an integral part of the Bologna Process Implementation plan at a national level in Portugal that aimed to create support bases in the establishment of knowledge and skills to acquire by specialty and education system, as in exemplifying nomenclatures and curricular structuring of study plans. According to Raposo and Neves (2020), the comparative analysis of the existing courses quickly made it possible to ascertain that the information did not serve the purpose, as is the case of the unequal attribution of credits to the same curricular units, even when with the same nomenclature and duration, as well as an unbalanced definition of general and specific competences, or the fitting of separate scientific sub-areas.

These researchers also pointed to the contrasting national reality strongly differentiated from some other European countries such as Spain or Germany, where the first cycle of studies in design lasts four years, and one to two years for the second cycle. With regard to the nature of design courses, they claim that this nature can relate to the schools where they are taught, and the Portuguese scenario cannot be more pluralistic and differentiated. Contrary to what happens with other areas of knowledge in Portugal, at that time there was a lack of a clear definition of the profile intended for the design and designer, both by identifying a university or polytechnic profile, as well as by the unambiguous creation of an area autonomous scientific study that would avoid a huge dispersion of the offer in the same specialties, in opposition to the spirit of Bologna.

"The imbalance of supply/demand caused, in the greater demand for higher education in the area of design, a not matured, sustained and scientifically weak training offer response" (Raposo and Neves 2020).

The teaching of design, accompanied by a decisive transformation and innovation at the technological level, further enhances the ability to solve problems and transfer knowledge, and in this way to promote research, allowing a greater visibility of the abilities and added value of the designer in society and his/her appetite at the level of leadership and to work in multidisciplinary teams, allowing to create a new vision of his/her know-how to do and know-how how to think as contribution to a more dynamic, productive and competitive business world. In other words, the human capital with training in the design area, which has a set of skills associated with entrepreneurship and innovation, with preparation in terms of transformation and problem-solving strategies combined with cognitive skills, must be considered a factor key and determinant for the success of the organization in which he/she will be inserted, given that as a creative, facing the enormous competitiveness existing in the markets, he/she can play a decisive role in the process of products and services development.

The mobility of students, teachers and researchers, which was inherent to the Bologna process, was one of the most important factors in transforming education in general and the one of design in particular, allowing for constant contamination, exchange of ideas and cultural foundations, confrontation of ways of working and investigating, transformation of mentalities, leading to transformation at the level of the social paradigm. But it also brought about a homogenization of procedures and a constant attenuation of identity differences, accentuating similarities and blurring the differences of different people and cultures, adopting similar curricular bases and procedures, ways and processes of researching and producing knowledge in everything identical. However, being inserted in an educative environment in Northern Europe or Mediterranean Europe, or even in a school in the North of Portugal or one in the center of the country, sharing with such different academic and local realities and cultures, is and must be different, having to be valued.

3 Local Cultural Identity

According to Giddens (1991), modern individuals must constantly be "self-reflective", making decisions about what they should do and who they should be. In the so-called "post-traditional" society, we are all forced to make a wide and continuous range of choices, from the most personal issues, to the deepest and broadest, with direct influence on societal procedures. The self-biographical narratives become a project that all individuals have to work on, supporting a coherence and consistency of identity. For Giddens, identity is something fluid and malleable, that the broader process of democratization allows individuals multiple possibilities to build and shape their own identities, in increasingly creative and diverse ways.

Regarding the construction of identity, Vieira (2009) refers that it consists of giving a coherent meaning to one's own existence, integrating the past and present experiences of each individual, in order to give meaning to the future. For Castells (2007) the preponderance of cultural references is central and representative in the subject's life, defining identity as the process of construction of meaning based on a cultural attribute, or on a set of interrelated cultural attributes, which prevail over other forms of meaning.

However, according to Carvalho (2014), other perspectives on identity have marked the current scenario, especially with regard to cultural identity since, as stated by Cuche (1999), the great questions about identity often refer to the culture issue.

As Pichler and Mello (2020) refer, an identity may not represent just an individual, but a group of people who live in the same place and share experiences and knowledge. These start to produce symbols and representations that unify them, turning them into an association, a neighborhood, a city, a nation, thus constituting a local identity. The place should not be interpreted as a space or piece of land where a group of people live, but also the relationships that exist between this place and the individuals who live there, their physical and material constructions developed over time and that represent their daily lives, their history and their relationships.

It should be noted that there is a very different understanding of cultural identity. Cuche (1999) distinguishes those who defend objectivist conceptions and those who follow subjectivist conceptions. Objectivists understand identity based on a number of determining criteria, considered to be 'objective', such as the common origin (heredity, genealogy), language, culture, religion, collective psychology (the 'basic personality'), the connection to a territory, among others. Within the objectivist conception (positivist), identity emerges as an essence that is not susceptible to evolve and over which neither the individual nor the group has any grasp. The subjectivist perspective (relativity) leads to the reduction of identity to a question of arbitrary individual choice, since each one is free in their identifications, emphasizing the variable character of identity, highlighting the ephemeral aspect of identity (Carvalho 2014).

The reaction of communities to the phenomenon of globalization has triggered movements of protection by local cultures and, therefore, affirmation of regional and local identities.

According to Featherstone (1996) culture is the way of life of a people through which they humanize and socialize nature. Culture is not static, growing out of reverence for selected customs and habits. It implies a value system and a network of social relationships, where human behavior and its products are central, being dependent of human beings' ability to learn and transmit knowledge to next generations.

A culture is also influenced by other cultures with which it is brought into contact. However, cultures are constructed by people, people with freedom and creativity. We are aware that creative persons contribute to introduce changes and development in a culture. People are not pieces of cultural influences: they can sift various influences and reject or integrate them (Wang 2007).

Global homogenization has a direct impact on culture, affecting directly the production and the consumers. It became normal that people use the same kind of goods everywhere. And this is affecting the way we behave, and in the present case, the way we act at the academia, the processes and models of teaching, supported by the same technologies, the same points of view, most of the times without paying attention and incorporate the important differences of local identity and culture. It is essential to focus on the mechanism of creating the notions of cultural differences or similarities.

According to Costa (2020), 'the need for the protection and preservation of Heritage (Culture) is increasingly imposed, which derives from the harmful effects that globalization has on the level of different local cultures, contributing to the indifferentiation and cultural homogenization and nullifying cultural diversity'. The local cultural heritage generates cultural diversity and guarantees sustainable development.

The concept of Cultural Identity arises from the areas of sociology and anthropology and concerns the culture in which the individual is inserted, in which traditions, beliefs, preferences, among other aspects, are shared with other members of the group. The history, the place, the race, the ethnicity and the language are, among many other factors of identity, determinant and decisive for a group to be part of a specific culture.

Cultural diversity is directly linked to the concept of identity, underlining the variety of cultures existing in a given location, which have been arising and being developed by the interaction between beings and the environment. It is also closely connected with civism, ethics and commitment to social relations, which, added to freedom of expression, citizenship, an unrestricted guarantee of human and social rights, form a set of values that connects people, groups and intellectuals, people who have in common the defense of an anthropological (re)foundation capable of altering perceptions, ways of thinking, values and establishing cooperation instead of competition and wisdom instead of logical-rational knowledge (Carvalho 1998; Campello et al. 2018).

Cultural identity, besides the sense of self, provides a global significance of local knowledge and community. If we address globalization in its deeper sense, in terms of science, technology, social or even economic development, we verify that it promotes cultural identity.

Both local culture and the environment in which the individual is established contribute to the development of their cultural identity. Since cultural identity goes hand in hand with the feeling of affection between the elements of a concrete social group and between these and their environment, local cultural identity is, therefore, the concept that best represents the idea in question.

4   The Spirit of the Place

The idea of spirit of place is directly linked with *Genius loci*, the Latin for the spirit or guardian deity of a place. For us, the spirit, even soul, of the place is defined by the several characteristics that give a place through time its uniqueness, the aspects that turn it distinctive.

The architect Norberg-Schulz (1980) proposed a phenomenological method in order to develop and explore the character of places and their meanings to the local residents, stating that place is much more than space or merely location, as there exists a 'spirit' which cannot be described by analytical and/or scientific methods. He described the 'spirit of the place' through a depiction of its physical features and an interpretation of the human experiences within that place. So, the "spirit of place" may be defined as the substance of place, the formation of the genetic order of place and its interrelations, which forms the environmental context, the origin of the place's existence, and a dialectic link in between the place and its inhabitants.

Human beings are responsible for introducing 'spirit' to place through their ways of acting, developing experiences between the place and the community, adding meaning and uniqueness.

We are increasingly subjected to the forces of globalization and homogenization. Therefore, 'authenticity' becomes an important issue for the cultural conservation, where place has a role of cultural and meaningful significance, which consists of aesthetic, historic, scientific, social and spiritual values for past, present or future generations.

The "place" can be the space of origin, the space where the individual grows, but which he/she identifies as a place of belonging, a space of belonging.

In the current scenario in which local cultures reflect signs of globalization and where identities reveal the marks of this hybridization process, the 'local' reinvents itself in new identities, making it more likely that globalization will simultaneously produce new 'global' identifications and new 'local' identifications. In this sense, the local and the global combine themselves, and create new options, establishing a relationship that is coexistent, where one strengthens the other (Carvalho 2014).

The concept of 'place' adds a social dimension to the three physical dimensions of the built environment, being a fourth dimension where space has a symbolic sense and takes on personal meaning from direct and indirect experiences, shaping our actions, thoughts and emotions. We transform space into place by adding it meaning.

According to Leite (2005), globalization, while imposing universal norms, has rediscovered knowledge and cultures that have been absent for many years from many social and educational scenarios, transporting it to the framework of organizational processes and curriculum development, a search for operating devices that take into account both the characteristics of the world in which we live and the societies that surround us, as well as local realities.

The reinvention of what exists, based on different local or global contributions, produces local cultural evolution. The balance between local culture and global culture is at the origin of design education, given the spirit of the place, guaranteeing students, but also the community in general, an education for diversity, through contact, experiences, access and respect for both singular and universal knowledge, ensuring both the knowledge of the area under study and its transfer to the local reality, thus making it stand out from the identity aspects of the local culture.

If we can respect the diversity of peoples and their cultures in this new era, it can lead to global community marked by unity in pluralism. The cultures may no longer be local in the traditional sense, but still different and plural.

Acting locally in the preservation of local cultures can contribute simultaneously to safeguard identities, reinforce memories, both individual and collective, through an involvement around common objectives and dynamics on the part of the community, thus preserving what is most differentiating and of identity each place possesses.

Given the cultural diversity that exists in Portugal, from north to south, from the coast to the interior, as well as the links that can be established locally in regional terms with society in general, it imposes an urgent reflection on the teaching of design. More than a constant struggle between schools to guarantee a good number of students annually, often with very similar educational offerings and little contextualized in the local realities and in the real needs of communities, companies and industry, it is necessary to rethink and value education in design, pointing to the specific characteristics of the 'spirit of the place' where this same teaching is practiced. Not all schools have the same capabilities, inherent to their geographical location and the space they have, the workshops and laboratories they offer, the IT and technological resources, the existing teachers, their curricula, etc. Design education should focus on the place where a school is located, on local identity and culture, on transferring knowledge to the community, on approaching the needs of the region's productive tissue, on the specific time in which it operates, on the educational strategies it uses, the creative environment generated, among many other variables. These variables are the ones that define and characterize what we defend as the 'spirit of the place', which can encourage greater bridging between design teaching schools, establishing networks and a greater spirit of sharing, pointing out and valuing differences as added value for teaching design in Portugal.

According to Aparo and Soares (2013), the design teaching method must be seen as an important contribution to the reflection on the importance of responsible teaching, in which the starting points are the result of a careful analysis and evaluation of culture of the place.

The school, as a place of teaching/learning and one of the main means of formation, is not neutral in relation to the influence of culture on the learning of its students, shaping it according to the self-experiences in a holistic way. It must be primarily an environment of true experiential learning experiences, contextualized, an environment that may lead these knowledge experiences for application and elucidation pertinent to their society, through the organization of time and collaboration and complementarity of knowledge, people, stories, information and situations. Relating education to local culture and identity, allows to build a knowledge of the world imbued with the 'spirit of the place', within a sense of belonging.

5   Conclusions

After implementing a research based on literature review focused on the design education in Portugal, the importance of local cultural identity when defining the culture of the place where the different design schools exist, we crossed this information with direct observation and the author's own experience.

In what concerns design education, we concluded that the Bologna process, aiming to harmonize higher education across the EU, with the respective educational institutions, was responsible for the adoption of new strategies by adapting their programs, pedagogical systems and results, to the new challenges and new demands. With regard to the design teaching, this whole process of profound change was above all an opportunity to review processes and methods, redefine goals and find a balance between traditional academy and practice in its various disciplines.

Contrary to what happens with other areas of knowledge in Portugal, at that time there was a lack of a clear definition of the profile intended for the design and designer, both by identifying a university or polytechnic profile, as well as by the unambiguous creation of an area autonomous scientific study that would avoid a huge dispersion of the offer in the same specialties, in opposition to the spirit of Bologna. It also brought a homogenization of procedures and a constant attenuation of identity differences, accentuating similarities and blurring the differences of different people and cultures, adopting similar curricular bases and procedures, ways and processes of researching and producing knowledge in everything identical. Global homogenization has also a direct impact on culture, affecting the way we behave, and in the present case, the way we act at the academia, the processes and models of teaching, supported by the same technologies, the same points of view, most of the times without paying attention and incorporate the important differences of local identity and culture. It is essential to focus on the mechanism of creating the notions of cultural differences or similarities.

During the study we underlined that cultural identity, besides the sense of self, provides a global significance of local knowledge and community. Even globalization in its deeper sense, in terms of science, technology, social or even economic development, promotes cultural identity. Both local culture and the environment in which the individual is established contribute to the development of his/her cultural identity. Since cultural identity goes hand in hand with the feeling of affection between the elements of a concrete social group and between these and their environment, local cultural identity is, therefore, the concept that best represents the idea in question.

If we can respect the diversity of peoples and their cultures in this new era, it can lead to global community marked by unity in pluralism. The cultures may no longer be local in the traditional sense, but still different and plural.

Given the cultural diversity that exists in Portugal, from north to south, from the coast to the interior, as well as the links that can be established locally in regional terms with society in general, it imposes an urgent reflection on design education, contextualizing it in the local realities and in the real needs of communities, companies and industry, rethinking and valuing education in design, which leads us to the concept of 'spirit of the place', relating design education to local culture and identity, building a knowledge of the world imbued with a sense of belonging, bridging the gap between academia and local society.

References

Aparo E, Soares LO (2013) Design como Veiculador da Cultura de um Lugar. In: Educação Gráfica, V.17 – N 0.02. ISSN: 2179-7374

Calvera A (2006) Treinando Pesquisadores para o Design: Algumas considerações e muitas preocupações acadêmicas. In: Design em Foco, Vol. III, número 001. Salvador, Brasil

Campello LG, Santiago MR, Andrade SL (2018) A Valorização da Identidade Cultural como desafio à concretização do direito ao Desenvolvimento. In: Revista de Direito Brasileira, vol 19, no 8, Jan/Abr 2018. São Paulo, Brasil, pp 3–19

Carvalho EA (1998) Apresentação. Ética, Solidariedade e Complexidade. Palas Athena. São Paulo, Brasil

Carvalho AFE (2014) Reafirmar a Identidade cultural local: o património cultural imaterial local como recurso. Unpublished Master dissertation. Escola Superior de Educação de Lisboa do Instituto Politécnico de Lisboa, Lisboa

Castells M (2007) O Poder da Identidade. In: A Era da Informação: Economia, Sociedade e Cultura, Vol. II. Fundação Calouste Gulbenkian, Lisboa

Chalmers AF, Fiker R (1993) O que é ciência afinal? Brasiliense, São Paulo

Costa M (2012) Design para a diversidade cultural. In: Convergências—Revista de Investigação e Ensino das Artes , VOL V (10), Retrieved from journal URL: http://convergencias.ipcb.pt. Accessed on 7 Nov 2020

Coutinho SG, Lopes MT (2011) Design para educação: uma possível contribuição para o ensino fundamental brasileiro. In: da Costa Braga M (ed) O papel social do design gráfico: história, conceitos & atuação profissional. Editora SENAC, São Paulo

Cross N (1982) Designerly ways of knowing. In: Design studies, vol 3, no 4, pp 221–227

Cuche D (1999) A Noção de Cultura nas Ciências Sociais. EDUSC, Bauru

Dias AC (2018) Transferência de Conhecimento em Design: Estratégias de Aproximação das Instituições de Ensino Superior (IES) aos Mercados e Sociedade Portuguesa, Unpublished PhD thesis in Design. Universidade de Lisboa, Lisboa

Featherstone M (1996) Localism, globalism, and cultural identity. Duke University Press, Durham, NC

Fontoura AM (2011) A interdisciplinaridade e o ensino do design. In: Projética Revista Científica de Design, V.2 l N.2 l Dezembro 2011, Universidade Estadual de Londrina, Londrina

Fragoso AM (2010) Formas e expressões da comunicação visual em Portugal: contributo para o estudo da cultura visual do século XX, através das publicações periódicas. Unpublished PhD thesis, Universidade Técnica de Lisboa, Lisboa

Frayling C (1998) Research on art and design. Research seminar on practice-based doctorates in the creative and performing arts and design. Surrey: Surrey Institute of Art and Design

Giddens A (1991) Modernity and self-identity. Polity, Cambridge

Instituto Paulo Freire (2011) Inter-transdisciplinaridade e transdiciplinadidade. In http://www.inclusao.com.br/projeto_textos_48.htm. Accessed on 11 Dec 2020

Leite C (2005) A territorialização das políticas e das práticas educativas. In: Leite C (org) Mudanças Curriculares em Portugal. Transição para o século XXI. Coleção Currículo, Políticas e Práticas. Porto Editora, Porto

Maldonado T (2009) Design industrial. Edições 70, Lisboa

Martins Filho V, Gerges NRC, Fialho FAP (2015) Design Thinking, cognição e educação no século XXI. In: Rev. Diálogo Educ., Curitiba, vol 15, no 45, maio/ago. 2015, Universidade Federal de Santa Catarina (UFSC), Florianópolis, Brasil, pp 579–596

Norberg-Schulz C (1980) Genius Loci: towards a phenomenology of architecture. Rizzoli, New York

Peirce CS (1975) Semiótica e filosofia. Cultrix, São Paulo

Pichler RF, Mello CI (2020) O Design e a Valorização da Identidade Local. In: Design & Tecnologia, 04, Pós-Graduação em Design da Universidade Federal de Rio Grande do Sul. Porto Alegre, Brasil

Raposo D, Neves J (2009) Análise da implementação do ensino de Bolonha na área do design [1]. In: Convergências—Revista de Investigação e Ensino das Artes, VOL II (4), Retrieved from journal URL: http://convergencias.ipcb.pt. Accessed on 27 Dec 2020

Schön D (1983) The reflective practitioner: how professionals think in. Basic Books, New York

Simon HA (1969) The sciences of the artificial, 1st edn. The MIT Press, Cambridge

Vieira R (2009) Identidades Pessoais. Interacções, Campos de Possibilidade e Metamorfoses Culturais. Ed. Colibri, Lisboa

Wang Y (2007) Globalization enhances cultural identity. Intercultural Commun Stud XVI 1:83–86

Yarzábal L (2002) Consenso para el cambio en la educación superior. Unesco, IESALC, Caracas

The Birth of Graphic Design in a School of Fine Arts: How the Specificity of a Learning Environment Determined a Course's Vocation

Cláudia Lima⬡, Heitor Alvelos⬡, Susana Barreto⬡,
Eliana Penedos-Santiago⬡, and Nuno Martins⬡

Abstract This study presents the context and circumstances in which the course of Design (Graphic Art) was created at the Porto School of Fine Arts in a post revolution period. This course, along with the Design courses created at the Lisbon School of Fine Arts, was the first Design course in Portuguese higher education. The study outlines the first pedagogical experiences in the field of Graphic Arts carried out in the 1960s and 1970s within the Painting course; how the course of Design was initially structured; and how its first years proved to be fundamental to its vocation. The research methodology includes document analysis and ethnography, namely life-story interviews conducted with artists and designers who played a key contextual role, both as teachers and as students. The findings show a close relationship between the Design (Graphic Art) course and both Painting and Sculpture courses, resulting from a series of factors: the first pedagogical experiences in the area of graphic arts having arisen in the context of the Painting course; the fact that when Design was created, the curriculum included several subjects in common to both to Painting and Sculpture; and the evidence that during the first decade of the Design course, the subjects were taught by professors without specialized training in the area, a majority of them having graduated in Painting or Sculpture. This close disciplinary relationship contributed to determining the specificity and vocation of the Design course, essentially oriented towards the image, visual communication, and graphic design concerns.

Keywords ESBAP · FBAUP · Communication design · Design history · Portuguese design

C. Lima (✉) · H. Alvelos · S. Barreto · E. Penedos-Santiago
ID+/Unexpected Media Lab—Faculdade de Belas Artes, Universidade do Porto,
Av. de Rodrigues de Freitas 265, 4049-021 Porto, Portugal

C. Lima
Universidade Lusófona do Porto, Rua Augusto Rosa nº 24, 4000-098 Porto, Portugal

N. Martins
Research Institute for Design, Media and Culture, School of Design, Polytechnic Institute
of Cavado and Ave, Barcelos, Portugal

© The Author(s), under exclusive license to Springer Nature Switzerland AG 2022   47
D. Raposo et al. (eds.), *Perspectives on Design II*, Springer Series in Design
and Innovation 16, https://doi.org/10.1007/978-3-030-79879-6_4

1 Introduction

The BA degree of Design was created at the Porto School of Fine Arts (ESBAP), currently the Faculty of Fine Arts of the University of Porto (FBAUP), in the school year of 1974/75. However, the first pedagogical experiments in the field of Graphic Arts at ESBAP date back to the 1960s. Initially led by Armando Alves and later by Amândio Silva and Domingos Pinho, these experiments paved the way for an approach to the teaching of Design oriented towards the field of visual communication.

This paper outlines the history and circumstances that led to the creation of the first Design course in Porto—the Design (Graphic Art) course at ESBAP—which, along with the Communication Design and Product Design courses at the Lisbon School of Fine Arts, was the first course in the field among Portuguese public higher education. The study also presents an analysis of factors that characterized the first years of the course, marked by a close relationship with the areas of Visual Arts, either through a curriculum including shared disciplines with the courses of Painting and Sculpture, as well as through the faculty, mostly graduated in Painting or Sculpture. These factors largely contributed to the definition of the specificity of the Design course, as well as a definition of an identity that, it is argued, has largely prevailed.

This study was carried out within the framework of *Wisdom Transfer: towards the scientific inscription of individual legacies in contexts of retirement from art and design higher education and research* (POCI-01-0145-FEDER-029038); the research stems from the evidence that there is insufficient inscription of individual knowledge and experience of retired professors and researchers in art and design.

2 Methodology

The research collected emic data through ethnographic methods including personal interviews with artists and teachers who led the first pedagogical experiments in the field of Graphic Arts at ESBAP: artists and teachers who contributed to the formation of the Design (Graphic Art) course, and students who attended the first years of this course. Most of the interviews were held in the context of the *Wisdom Transfer* project (Alvelos et al. 2019; Lima et al. 2020), between December 2018 and October 2020. The interviews used guidelines with open-ended questions (Quivy and Campenhoudt 2008) and were filmed, recorded, and complemented with contextual photographs, with the aim of creating a data bank for further scrutiny (Tinkler 2013). The participants were asked for permission to collect the required audio-visual material through an informed consent form (Banks and Zeitlyn 2015), provided at the beginning of each interview.

For a triangulation of information that would confirm and complement data collected in interviews, the first study plans of the course in Design (Graphic Art) and the Decree-Laws officializing the course and its structure were analyzed;

furthermore, documentation on both the History of Design and first pedagogical experiments in the context of higher education and the development of the Design (Graphic Art) course at ESBAP, were employed.

3 Findings

3.1 First Pedagogical Experiments in the Field of Design

Although Design courses in Portuguese higher education were created only after the April 25, 1974 Revolution, pedagogical experiments in this field were already a common practice at ESBAP (Lima et al. 2021a).

The first experiments were held by Armando Alves, then teacher of Decorative Painting of the Painting course at ESBAP. For Alves, who had graduated in Painting from this School and already had a considerable professional curriculum in the Graphic Arts (Lima et al. 2021a, b), "Decorative Painting" seemed out of date with contemporary artistic trends, limiting itself to the context of the Decorative Arts. Therefore, after one year lecturing on this subject, Alves proposed to Carlos Ramos, then Director of ESBAP, the introduction of the Graphic Art subject as an alternative to the Decorative Painting subject. In the absence of a theoretical framework and pedagogical experience in this area, the pedagogic approach was conceived and structured on the basis of Alves's own professional experience, as well as graphic works held by other renowned graphic artists such as Sebastião Rodrigues.

In the early years, the approach proved to be quite experimental with a strong artistic component based on crafts. For project-based work, choice magazines were used, which the students themselves brought to class. These magazines were analyzed in class, and then cut out for reuse in new graphic compositions through "cut and paste" processes. The content included clippings of letters, titles, texts, and photographs, and formed the basis of projects such as imaginary record and book covers (Lima et al. 2021b), as well as posters occasionally submitted to international competitions (Mendonça 2007).

On the classes of Decorative Painting where the contents of Graphic Arts were taught, one of the then-students, Nuno Barreto, later stated:

> We made posters, covers, a greeting card, we confronted ourselves with the dialogue of the illustration with blocks of text. Once again, what we did was on drawing paper, with gouache and paper cut-outs from magazines. There was no photography studio at the school, no silk-screen printing or lithography, that allowed us to simulate the final result of our work. As it turns out, we were still light-years away from the digital age, computers, PageMaker and PhotoShop. It was scarce, just a start without follow-up, a process of raising awareness for the students who, in their overwhelming majority, would, within a few years, be teaching Design or Visual Education in High School.[1] (Nuno Barreto, cited in Mendonça 2007, p. 62)

---

[1] All citations in this document are translated by the authors.

Also, posters and catalogues for the Extra Escolar exhibitions, annually conceived at ESBAP and subsequently exhibited in Lisbon and Coimbra, were developed within this discipline. Each student developed a proposal, and, at the end, one was selected to be reproduced (Mendonça 2007).

The outcomes of these first pedagogical experiments, visible at the two major exhibitions held at ESBAP—the Magna exhibition and the Extra Escolar exhibition —were highly appreciated and raised a growing interest in the subject of Graphic Arts on the part of the academic and student community. Soon enough, this subject began to be addressed at both levels of the discipline of Decorative Painting (taught by Armando Alves, at the first level, and by Amândio Silva, at the second level). Silva graduated in Painting at ESBAP as well and owned a company in the Graphic Arts sector—Litografia Invicta—holding considerable experience in this area.

As stated by Isabel Cabral and Rodrigo Cabral (personal communication, December 5, 2018), the approach of these two lecturers was distinct and complementary. Whereas Alves' approach was mainly characterized by the analysis of graphic works and the production of projects that often blurred the boundaries between Graphic Arts and Visual Arts, Silva's approach often included proposals for actual clients and visits to companies in the Graphic Arts sector, bringing new perspectives and knowledge to Graphic Arts and printing technologies.

When Armando Alves left ESBAP in 1973, the discipline of Decorative Painting (and its contents in the scope of Graphic Arts) was inherited by Domingos Pinho, an ESBAP Painting graduate. His connection to the Graphic Arts sector was already lasting: Pinho had been working at his father's company, Litografia Maia, since the age of 13. His knowledge in the field was acquired through practice, benefiting from contact with two of the company's employees, Joaquim Malheiro and Hernâni Tavares (Almeida 2004; Mendonça 2007).

When Pinho began lecturing the discipline of Decorative Painting in October 1973, he experimented with various techniques characterized by manuality such as drawing, cutting and collage, through exercises that combined various graphic languages and covered areas of design such as posters, comics, packaging and showroom stands. Given the absence of a defined curricular program, the nature of the taught content was closely related to the profile of the teacher at stake. This range of areas of design addressed by Pinho was the result of his own multidisciplinary professional experience: in fact, Pinho introduced concerns not only in the practical exercise of Graphic Arts, but conceptual concerns as well, thus transforming the Decorative Painting discipline into a space of experimentation of different technologies and applications. In notes provided to his students, Pinho produced a set of reflections on this very coverage of the subject:

> Decorative Painting – impossibility of a definition/why not? – interior decoration – shop windows – illustration – animation and animated film – and the scenography/Why only graphic art? (advantages of graphic arts)/and Education and visual communication/ the absence – of a syllabus – the impossibility of organizing it properly and, especially, of fulfilling it at this time of the year. (Domingos Pinho, cited in Mendonça 2007, p. 64)

These notes reflect a concern regarding the lack of a syllabus that could structure and substantiate the contents addressed. This was, in fact, a concern of Pinho who, through his years of teaching at ESBAP, endeavored to define and structure curricular contents in the field of Graphic Arts for the discipline of Decorative Painting and, later, for the course of Design (Graphic Art).

In another of Pinho's notes, an outline of a structure of contents was already evident. Under the title "Esquema condutor do programa" (Curricular blueprint), he wrote:

> Preliminary formation: Point; line; confrontation; the letter and the sign; techniques of reproduction. Specific training: illustrative graphics, graphic design exercises; typographical essays; brands and symbols; photography in the graphic arts; photographic essays?; the color; posters; packaging, exhibitions, graphic diagrams. Teamwork: creation of prints for an identity from the logo to the illuminated advertisements; relations of the graphic artist with the medium. (Domingos Pinho, cited in Mendonça 2007, p. 65)

In fact, the discipline of Decorative Painting became a space for experimentation marked by the profile of the teacher who taught it, with the practice of subjects related to the Graphic Arts as its main driver. Pinho's travels to countries such as France, Belgium, Holland, England, Denmark, Sweden or the Federal Republic of Germany, as well as the bibliography acquired in those travels (non-existent in Portugal), allowed him a deeper knowledge on international trends in art and design, knowledge that he sought to provide to his students through handwritten texts of his own.

If Armando Alves and Amândio Silva geared the discipline of Decorative Painting towards the practice of graphic exercises, Domingos Pinho instead structured and articulated its contents while aware that the domains of Graphic Arts went beyond the space of a discipline, thus beginning to envisage what could be a course in this field. A course that, according to him, should not be strictly focused on outcomes, but should include disciplines that provided a theoretical framework, namely in association with Psychology and Sociology.

3.2   The Rise of the Design (Graphic Art) Course

It was in the post-revolution period of April 1974, following several reformulations of Portuguese higher education, that the first Design courses appeared: the Communication Design course and the Product Design course at the Lisbon School of Fine Arts[2] (Fragoso 2012) and the Design (Graphic Art) course at ESBAP.[3] Various pedagogical experiments had already been tried out while aiming at the creation of these courses, as stated above, with the Design course at ESBAP being

---

[2]Approved by Decree-Law No. 38/83 of June 1, 1983.

[3]Approved by Decree-Law No. 80/83 of February 9, 1983.

structured since 1973/74; however, only in the school year of 1974/75, this was validated by the School's Scientific Board.

This post-revolutionary period was marked by moments of great instability in the country, reflected in most contexts, including the school context. At ESBAP, the meetings for decision-making followed one another, with "discussions after discussions with the students, with the teachers, with taking of stances" (Mendonça, personal communication, July 20, 2020), hindering, according to Domingos Pinho (personal communication, January 21, 2020), curricular stabilization and teaching activity itself. Everything was discussed, different school models (Mendonça 2007, p. 73) were considered, and new curricular areas and subjects that had not yet been addressed at School were proposed. This instability and precariousness in decision-making and in creating solutions resulted in a difficulty in establishing and fixing a curricular plan for the course in Design (Graphic Art) during the first years of its existence.

With the Revolution, the school year was suspended, postponing the beginning of the Design (Graphic Art) course until the following school year (1975/76). According to Mendonça (2007, p. 72), "there was great enthusiasm for the Design Course, but the circumstances only allowed the endless discussion of ideas and the will to change without enough time to reflect on the ways of changing". In this post-revolution period, curricular plans were thus outlined and soon replaced by others before even being implemented.

The political and social instability of the country and its repercussions on the School environment also postponed the beginning of the school year 1975/76 up until April 1976 (Mendonça 2007, p. 75); therefore, although the course in Design (Graphic Art) had been approved during the previous school year, in practice it only began in 1976. Foreseeing a restructuring of the existing courses at ESBAP and the curricular integration of the Design course, the document "Ante-projecto de reestruturação da ESBAP" (ESBAP's Preliminary Restructuring Project) was written by the Governing School Bodies to be presented to the Ministry of Education and Scientific Research, where it was established that the courses of Painting and Sculpture would be aggregated into a course of Visual Arts, offering the areas of Painting, Sculpture and Design (Graphic Art). This restructuring of the courses and integration in the Visual Arts reflected a close relationship (and even inter-dependency) of the recently created course in Design to the Visual Arts, which, indeed, is reflected in the document itself when it states that.

> The training of graphic artists is given as a specialized derivation of the artistic activities that are taught in this school, recognizing the creative activity of these artists as being more due to a creation of the spirit than to a matter of manual skill. (cited in Mendonça 2007, p. 76)

This document highlighted the intention to create a specialized area in design and the need to find experts for teaching in this field. The Visual Arts courses were divided into two cycles: the first, of three years, common to the areas of Painting, Sculpture and Design (Graphic Art), designated as Basic Cycle, while the second, of two years, designated as Special Cycle, offered disciplines more oriented to the specificities of each of the three areas.

Domingos Pinho, supported by Júlio Resende, then Director of ESBAP, assumed a fundamental role in this process: by structuring the curricular plan, deciding which subjects should be included in the Design (Graphic Art) course, for what purpose, defining the respective syllabuses, and largely casting specialized teachers.

In the first curricular plans developed by Pinho, only in the third year of the course a discipline devoted to the subject of design was introduced: Introduction to Graphic Design, initially assigned to Amândio Silva. It aimed at the introduction of "theoretical and practical studies of elementary problems related to Graphic Design", the reading and understanding of new visual communication media and the analysis of "relationships of dependence between design and reproduction"— that is, an understanding of the design process from the creative moment to serial reproduction. Thus, concepts on "the basic elements of graphic language (…) writing and sign" were studied as graphic elements that enhance communication (Mendonça 2007, p. 77). Other subjects devoted to design were taught in the Special Cycle, including Graphic Design I (4th year), Specialized Graphics (4th year) and Graphic Design II (5th year).

Considering that the specialization in Design only took place in the 4th year and being that the content of the first three years of the courses of Design (Graphic Art), Painting and Sculpture was shared, Pinho structured and taught the discipline of Graphic Design while aware of a need for an articulation of specific knowledge. This was needed in order "to adapt pedagogical action to the lack of basic skills and knowledge" of the students, given the scope of the first three years (Mendonça 2007, p. 77). Pinho sought to focus on aspects related to the profile and background of the students in a flexible approach that would allow them to contemplate their different areas of interest and contribute to their training. In this sense, he proposed a set of working options in the discipline's syllabus, addressing different thematic areas, namely, graphic design; cartoon and animation; illustration and comics; stands and exhibition design. As for the discipline of Specialized Graphics, it assumed a theoretical and applied character aiming at "theoretical studies on the theory of information through signs, marks, symbols and images" (Mendonça 2007, p.78).

The course also covered subjects of technological content, such as Printing Techniques, assigned to Calvet de Magalhães, aimed at the knowledge of "the range of printing techniques available on the market", understanding of the specificity, applicability and costs of each, and the knowledge of print finishing techniques (Mendonça 2007, p. 79). De Magalhães was also a teacher of Photographic Documentation which, together with Printing Techniques, were innovative disciplines at ESBAP, addressing the knowledge of technologies as photography or silk-screen printing and demonstrating their practical applicability in the context of Graphic Arts.

According to students such as Ana Campos (personal communication, June 27, 2019) or João Nunes (personal communication, February 26, 2019), de Magalhães (Director of ESBAP between 1977 and 1978), played a key role in the formatting of the course and in instituting the photography and video laboratories. Graduated in Drawing, he worked in the field of Graphic Arts since the 1940's, collaborating with companies such as Empresa do Bolhão, Litografia Vasco da Gama, La Artística and Consórcio Industrial del Miño, and authoring books such as the Manual Profissional de Artes Gráficas (Professional Handbook of Graphic Arts) or Técnicas de Impressão (Printing Techniques) (Lima et al. 2021b). His contribution was significant, in particular through the setup of video and photography laboratories, the acquisition of facilities and equipment for other laboratories, and the acquisition of bibliographic resources for the library. Even so, it was mentioned by several interviewees that bibliographic resources specialized in Design were scarce,[4] benefiting students occasionally from bibliography brought in by teachers, often acquired in travels abroad.

Given the specificity of the course disciplines, it was necessary to hire faculty members who, although not graduated in Design due to the prior absence of degrees in the field, were selected in a public tender based on their professional experience and portfolio in this area.

Dario Alves was thus hired in 1976 for the course of Design (Graphic Art), and assigned the discipline of Graphic Design (4th year). Graduated in Painting from ESBAP, since high school Dario Alves had developed graphic works for several companies including posters, stands, labels, illustration, catalogues and logos. He was member of the board of Ambar's Graphic Department from 1965 to 1966, and of Simão Guimarães' Graphic Department from 1966 to 1974 (Mendonça 2007, 75), collaborating with companies such as Estúdio Atenas or Tipografia Carvalhido.

In 1977, two other teachers graduated from ESBAP joined the faculty: João Machado, graduated in Sculpture and whose experience in design had been acquired partly through working for RTP (Portuguese State Television), where he created illustrations for Portuguese and French subjects taught at Tele-Escola (TV School) (Lima et al. 2021a, b); and Beatriz Gentil, graduated in Painting. Specialized disciplines in Design were assigned to them. And in 1978, António Quadros Ferreira (graduated in Painting at ESBAP) was hired, initially for the discipline of Introduction to Painting/Sculpture and Photographic Documentation (common to the three courses of Visual Arts) and in the following year assigned the discipline of Introduction to Visual Arts—Design.

Despite a clear intention to create a specialization in the field of design, the curriculum of the disciplines denounces the close relationship and dependence of the course of Design (Graphic Art) to the Visual Arts. In these first curricula, a more artistic perspective and the orientation of Design towards the visual realm were reflected, in part, by the proximity of the course to the area of Painting and by the predominance of faculty trained in this area, who end up filling the absence of specialized teachers in design. Changes to curriculum structure and assignment of

---

[4]According to Modesto (2016), the only publications acquired by the School library were Graphis magazines, described as "thumbnails' annuals", which, although not bad, were not compared to "a scholar's understanding of an image".

academic service during the first ten years of the course occurred almost annually. The approach to subjects tended to be flexible and could vary according to the profile of the teacher, namely their educational training and professional experience in the field of Graphic Arts.

In the school year 1977/78, the first students graduated in Design (Graphic Art). Among them, Jorge Afonso[5] stood out, becoming the first lecturer of the course with specialized training in Communication Design when hired by ESBAP in November 1978. This teacher clearly distinguished himself from the other faculties and deeply marked the academic path of those who were his students. According to Heitor Alvelos (personal communication, October 16, 2020), one of his former students,

> Jorge Afonso was of a tremendous pedagogical intensity. (...) I remember him being enthusiastic about the whole range of ideas presented in his work proposals... I remember long monologues trying to dissect the whole field of possibilities presented in each proposal.

And Providência (Silva 2016), also his former student, referred Afonso brought a different perspective from the other faculty members of the course:

> He did no illustration or painting. He did photography and typography. With Jorge Afonso I learned to give importance to letters and especially to the spaces between them. To give importance to composition and to give a lot of importance to life. (cited in Silva 2016, p. 12).

Other teachers without specialized training in Design were integrated in the faculty during the first decade of the course, most of them graduated from ESBAP in the field of Visual Arts, such as João Barata Feyo or Carlos Barreira (graduated in Sculpture), António Modesto, Jaime Azinheira, Alfredo Barros or Pedro Rocha (graduated in Painting). Seven years after Jorge Afonso was hired, new teachers with specialized training in Design were integrated into the faculty, including Francisco Providência in 1985, Eduardo Aires in 1987, Heitor Alvelos and Antero Ferreira in 1989, and Teresa Cardoso in 1990.

Although many of the faculty members of the first decade of the Design (Graphic Art) course had some experience in the field of Graphic Arts, the lack of specialized training in Design was notorious and clearly felt by the students, as reported by interviewees. As a professor, Jorge Afonso also pointed out retrospectively that, at the beginning of the course, although he shared teaching duties with "very competent teachers such as (...) João Machado, Dario Alves and, later, António Modesto, who made a remarkable contribution to the teaching of Design", their absence of training in Design conditioned his "intervention and the way in which the course evolved" (cited in Mendonça 2007, p. 185). In this context, Afonso refers to a certain "isolation" that only ended when other teachers with a

---

[5]Students who graduated this year began their higher education before the Design (Graphic Art) course commenced, having obtained equivalence to the Basic Cycle of Visual Arts and doing only the Special Cycle (2 years) in Design (Graphic Art). Jorge Afonso had the Basic Cycle in Visual Arts—Painting.

degree in Design became part of the faculty. As a consequence, his activity during the first years focused on "the assertion of the specificity of the course, valuing photography, typography, pre-press and printing techniques" (p. 185): this was ultimately his greatest contribution to the course.

Indeed, these first teachers of the Design course were in a learning process and, as stated by Quadros Ferreira (personal communication, April 12, 2019), all of them had this "collective awareness" that they were learning the Design which was emerging "within the visual arts". It was "a very contaminated design, very conditioned", from the author's view. In his approach, he sought to use a dialectic that would allow him to understand "how design could possibly stand out from the arts", leading him to reflect extensively on "what design could be". For this lecturer, the circumstances in which the Design course emerged defined a specific framework for this area within ESBAP, and an understanding of design by lecturers as "a perspective of Graphic Art", an aspect reinforced by the very name of the course— Design (Graphic Art).

Heitor Alvelos, a student of Quadros Ferreira in the 1980s, recalls that although this teacher was not trained in design, his artistic work "had a certain graphic vocation, and was very much concerned with issues of geometry, with issues of chromatic rigor". Most of the exercises he proposed to the students fitted into this framework which, for Alvelos, seemed, at the time, "to be devoted to a predominant definition of design at the time (…) very much marked by the concept of Graphic Art". It was "a very work-oriented type of training, complemented by core concepts on color theory and composition, the essentials" (personal communication, October 16, 2020).

Modesto (2016) also points out some hesitancy regarding the specificities of design. Although graduated in Painting, he attended Design disciplines, later becoming one of the teachers of this course. While a student, he recalls that there was an "awareness of extension, of applying art to everyday life", outlining the idea of the interdependence of the Design course to the Visual Arts.

João Nunes, then student, also mentions the scarcity of specialized disciplines in design, an aspect that, at the time, was unsatisfactory since he wanted to "make design and saw no sense in learning Painting and Sculpture". However, observing these learnings retrospectively and even in his daily practice, he understands how that was fundamental to his work as a designer (personal communication, February 26, 2019). This perspective is shared by Aires (2016) when he recognizes the importance of having "several teachers whose spectrum of specialized areas were very diverse", allowing him to truly understand "the integration of all Arts", rather than focusing exclusively on design and to take advantage of the wealth of multidisciplinary knowledge that the course offered him. Heitor Alvelos also considers that this multidisciplinary approach and the blurring of the Visual Arts and Design boundaries were an asset to the course, as it allowed students to have a broader understanding of different forms of visual communication, even innovative graphic languages, which could be applied to design.

Five years into the opening of the Design (Graphic Art) course, the relationship and interdependence of this course with the areas of Painting and Sculpture remained evident, both through the basic training of a large part of the faculty, and through its curricular structure, marked by several comprehensive disciplines of the three courses of Visual Arts, compared to a scarcity of specialized disciplines in Design. This perception (and concern) was expressed in a report written by one of the course teachers, Luis Demeé, where he observed the little time devoted to Graphic Arts disciplines, leading "graphic art to appear, sometimes, as an appendix to Painting/ Sculpture" (Mendonça 2007, p. 107). The specificities of the various areas of Visual Arts were also highlighted in documents by other teachers, such as Pedro Rocha and Amândio Silva, resulting in the restructuring of the curriculum in the following years —marking an increase in subjects related to the Graphic Arts and time devoted to Design subjects in the Basic Cycle. These changes revealed a clear intention to give greater prominence to the Design (Graphic Art) course through greater specialization in design-oriented disciplines. However, the predominance of contents related to visual communication and graphic design is noteworthy, with areas such as interior, product or furniture design simply not addressed.

Following the various restructurings of the course, its designation was also changed in 1981 to Communication Design (Graphic Art), but it was only in February 1983 that the courses in Design (Graphic Art) and Visual Arts (Painting and Sculpture), created in 1974/75, were formally recognized retroactively; the new course in Communication Design (Graphic Art) was simultaneously formalized (Decree-Law No. 80/83 of 9 February 1983). Despite the formal recognition, and consequent academic validation of the course, curricular changes and recurring changes in teaching assignment remained on an almost annual basis, hindering strategic and concerted coordination between curricula in the long term.

Providência (cited in Mendonça 2007) recalled that as a student he learned "more in the gardens, at the bar and canteen tables, in the library, in the local printing houses or in the neighboring cinemas, than in the classroom space itself" (p. 133). The teaching activity was fragile, with practically no "transversal curricular syllabuses or strategies" (p. 133). Nevertheless, he observed that the School experience, marked by the presence and coexistence of students in the courses of Architecture, Visual Arts (Painting and Sculpture) and Communication Design (Graphic Art), was intellectually very enlightening: "The manifestations of each group were visited and criticized by all, which greatly enriched the school experience" (p. 133).

Indeed, it was only in November 1986, when a new curriculum was approved by Decree-Law 698/86 and became effective immediately, that the course curriculum was stabilized and remained unchanged in subsequent years. The stabilization of this curriculum and the hiring of new teachers with degrees in Design that took place in the second half of this decade and decades that followed revealed a recognition of the specificities and needs of the course, gradually dissociating it from the scope of the Visual Arts. Even so, the circumstances and background surrounding the creation of the Design course, as well as a daily proximity with the activities of painting and sculpture definitely marked the patterns under which the course was developed, determining its longer term vocation towards visual communication, graphic design, and illustration.

4 Final Considerations

The present study has analyzed the circumstances that led to the creation of the Design course at ESBAP and the corresponding School context during the period surrounding the Revolution of April 25, 1974; it argues that this context had a profound impact on the academic path of the course. On the one hand, the first pedagogical experiments in the field of design appeared in the context of a discipline within the Painting course, taught by painters and focusing exclusively on the practice of Graphic Arts. On the other hand, when the Design course was structured, even though the curriculum suggested the willingness of a multidisciplinary approach with subjects such as Sociology and Psychology, in reality the disciplines remained very much associated with the Painting or Sculpture courses —both because they were shared by the three courses, and because teachers did not possess a degree in Design, but rather in Painting or Sculpture. Oddly enough, if this lack of specialization was met with some dissatisfaction on the part of students, many of these retrospectively recognize that the dynamics of this coexistence between courses turned out to be beneficial for their professional and creative skills.

The study also addressed a great level of instability of the Design course in the first ten years, a factor that weakened academic practice: during the first decade only one teacher was the holder of a Design degree; changes to the curriculum and teaching assignment took place almost annually, making strategic and concerted coordination between curricula a longer term impossibility. In fact, only when teachers trained in Design were integrated in the faculty, the specificities and needs of the course were clarified; it then became possible to format a specific curriculum, gradually dissociating Design from the Visual Arts. Even so, it is noted that the context in which the course emerged, as well as the proximity that still exists between the courses of Design, Painting and Sculpture taught at ESBAP (both in curricular content and shared infrastructures), deeply shaped the vocation of the Design course at this School, oriented towards the field of visual communication from its onset to this day.

The reciprocal dynamics between design and arts in the context of ESBAP, a result of the aforementioned fact that artists served as Design teachers, has resulted in what has been quoted in interviews as a more plastic, conceptual design approach. With the rise of industry-based private Design schools in the region of Porto (mid-1990s), and while providing for curricular content in digital technology, Design at ESBAP, now FBAUP, has consolidated a more crafts-based vocation. Silk-screen and etching workshops, ceramics and the prevalence of drawing in Design education, all have forged a Design education of a clearly distinct vocation from other technology- and industry-driven schools. To a degree, this paradigm still prevails and is treasured as a differentiating factor.

References

Aires E (2016) Retratos de gerações na primeira pessoa: Eduardo Aires/Interviewer: J. T. Santos [video]. Recuperado de https://vimeo.com/182644835

Almeida BP (2004) Domingos Pinho. ASA Editores, Porto

Alvelos H, Barreto S, Chatterjee A, Penedos-Santiago E (2019) On the brink of dissipation: the reactivation of narrative heritage and material craftsmanship through design research. In: Research & education in design: people & processes & products & philosophy: proceedings of the 1st international conference on research and education in design (REDES 2019), November 14–15, Lisbon, Portugal

Banks M, Zeitlyn D (2015) Visual methods in social research. SAGE Publications

Decree-Law no 38/83 of June 1, 1983. Recovered from https://dre.tretas.org/dre/2484459/decreto-do-governo-38-83-de-1-de-junho#anexos

Decree-Law no 80/83 of February 9, 1983. Recovered from https://dre.pt/web/guest/pesquisa/-/search/311005/details/normal?q=80%2F83+design+arte+gr%C3%A1fica

Decree-Law 698/86 of November 21, 1983. Recovered from https://dre.pt/web/guest/pesquisa/-/search/220921/details/normal?q=698%2F86+design+arte+gr%C3%A1fica

Fragoso M (2012) Design Gráfico em Portugal: formas e expressões da cultura visual do século XX. Livros Horizonte, Lisboa

Lima C, Barreto S, Alvelos H, Penedos-Santiago E, Martins N (2020) Learning ecologies: from past generations to current higher education. In 5th IAFOR international conference on education. Hawaii; The IAFOR International Conference on Education—Hawaii 2020 Official Conference Proceedings. Retrieved from http://papers.iafor.org/wp-content/uploads/conference-proceedings/IICE/IICEHawaii2020_proceedings.pdf

Lima C, Barreto S, Alvelos H, Penedos-Santiago E, Martins N (2021a) From painting to graphic arts: the unique legacy of Armando Alves. In: Martins N, Brandão D, Raposo D (eds) Perspectives on design and digital communication. Springer Series in Design and Innovation, vol 8. Springer, Cham. https://doi.org/10.1007/978-3-030-49647-0_1

Lima C, Barreto S, Alvelos H, Penedos-Santiago E, Martins N (2021b) The rise of the first design course at the School of Fine Arts of Porto. In: Raposo D, Neves J, Silva J, Correia Castilho L, Dias R (eds) Advances in design, music and arts. EIMAD 2020. Springer Series in Design and Innovation, vol 9. Springer, Cham. https://doi.org/10.1007/978-3-030-55700-3_11

Mendonça R (2007) O Cartaz e a Escola_Um Estudo Centrado nos Autores e no Curso de Design das Belas Artes do Porto (Doctoral Thesis). Faculdade de Belas Artes da Universidade do Porto

Modesto A (2016) Retratos de gerações na primeira pessoa: António Modesto/Interviewer: J. T. Santos [video]. Recuperado de https://vimeo.com/182472733

Quivy R, Campenhoudt LV (2008) Manual de Investigação em Ciências Sociais. Gradiva, Lisboa

Silva HS (2016) Da academia, Da economia, Da filosofia. In: Silva HS, Quental J, Branco V (eds) Francisco Providência. Cardume Editores, Matosinhos, pp 8–23

Tinkler P (2013) Using photographs in social and historical research. Sage Publications, Thousand Oaks

Co-creation and Co-design of Educational Programmes with Young People: A Comparative Study Between Dublin and Porto

Olga Glumac, Grace D'Arcy, and Maria Raquel Canedo de Sousa Morais

Abstract This paper analyses the youth-led and youth-centred practices of two organisations located in Dublin and Porto. The authors consider the application of educational programmes through co-creation and co-design may be relevant for informing and supporting everyday research and innovation practice and policy-making aimed at youth. The key findings of the paper stress that there is a need for: (i) building capacities in design for the intergenerational collaboration; (ii) a continuous promotion of open innovation of the study's approach to research and innovation practice and policymaking; (iii) digitalisation of education and creating new opportunities for youth-led codesign and co-creation in the school context.

Keywords Co-creation · Youth-led co-design · Wellbeing · Curriculum design

1 Introduction

This paper reflects on developing and implementing educational programmes through the use of co-creation and co-design practice with young people, within the age bracket 15–25 years old, in Dublin (Ireland) and Porto (Portugal). Educational programmes are considered as a set of learning modules prototyped and implemented with students and teachers, and other relevant stakeholders, within the formal education to build capacities in self-organisation, teamwork, co-creation/co-design and active learning. The authors believe these practices can lead to increasing the sense of self-efficacy, self-realisation and wellbeing of students.

O. Glumac (✉)
LoCY—Lab of Collaborative Youth, Porto, Portugal

G. D'Arcy
Science Gallery Dublin, Dublin, Ireland

M. R. C. de Sousa Morais
LoCY—Lab of Collaborative Youth, i2ADS—Research Institute in Art, Design and Society, Escola Artística e Profissional Árvore, Porto, Portugal

© The Author(s), under exclusive license to Springer Nature Switzerland AG 2022
D. Raposo et al. (eds.), *Perspectives on Design II*, Springer Series in Design and Innovation 16, https://doi.org/10.1007/978-3-030-79879-6_5

The topic of mental health and wellbeing as an outcome of students' participation and engagement in formal education and civic life within school settings (and beyond) has been approached differently at the national level in Ireland and Portugal. In the case of the Irish government, some responsiveness is noted through a published report on 'National Strategy on Children and Young People's Participation in Decision-Making 2015–2020' (Department of Children and Youth Affairs 2015). This strategy has proposed that children and young people should have a voice in decisions that affect their health and wellbeing, including the health and social services delivered to them. This implied using co-creation methodologies to develop support services for the mental health and well being management with young people in Ireland as the Government agreed to involve youth in policy-making. The aspect of shared and individual responsibility when it comes to physical and mental health and wellbeing was recognised by both governments at the policy level. The Portuguese government issued 'National Strategy for the Promotion of Physical Activity, Health and wellbeing 2016–2025' (Shinn et al. 2020), while the Irish government expanded a policy on 'A Healthy Ireland: A Framework for Improved Health and wellbeing 2013–2025' (Department of Health 2013). Both documents outline a vision where everyone can enjoy health and wellbeing to their full potential, hence, wellbeing is valued and supported at every level of society.

Science Gallery Dublin and Lab of Collaborative Youth are two organisations that aim to promote the added values of developing educational programmes with young people as their approaches and practices deem innovative and beneficial for the individuals and environment in which they are created. The practices show if there is a stronger inclusion and direct involvement of youth, the impact is greater on individual and collective wellbeing as shown in the examples of two educational programmes: OPEN MIND (Dublin) and Ilustracionário, à minha maneira 2.0 (Porto) (Real et al. 2019; Maylandt et al. 2020).

2   Educational Programmes Co-designed with Young People in Ireland and Portugal

2.1   Education Programming at Science Gallery Dublin

Science Gallery Dublin (SGD) at Trinity College Dublin (IE), is a public engagement space that delivers unique, transdisciplinary exhibitions, events and educational programmes with an emphasis on the intersection of art and science as a means to give power to young people. SGD was pioneered at Trinity College Dublin and its success led to the establishment of an international network of university-linked art-science cultural spaces in London, Melbourne, Bengaluru, Venice, Detroit, Rotterdam, Atlanta and Berlin. The purpose of SGD is to programme educational and exploratory experiences aimed at fostering interest-driven learning of young people. SGD has a particular target audience demographic of 15 to 25-year-olds. This group is the most vulnerable in Irish society concerning mental health. Among young people (aged 15–19), Ireland had the 7th highest rate of suicide across the 33 countries (OECD/European Union 2018). A national study profiling mental health in nearly 15,000 young people across the country found that mental health difficulties emerge in early adolescence and peak in the late teens and early 20s. The most common obstacles to wellbeing and mental health are the individual's lack of self-esteem, positive thinking and approaches to dealing with specific situations (Real et al. 2020). SGD educational programmes aspire to trigger a passion for science, technology and innovation, highlighting the rich network of interconnections between science, the arts, culture, design, business and innovation.

This paper is specifically focused on OPEN MIND, a wellbeing programme co-created within the framework of the H2020 SISCODE project. Through a series of stakeholder sessions of idea generation, idea refining and idea prototyping the group focused the challenge around 'Co-creating mental health resources with young people to use in a school setting'. The stakeholder group wanted to develop a resource that would support students' understanding of mental health and equip young people with tools to manage their wellbeing, with a focus on the importance of personal hobbies and interests. Stakeholders identified a particular year in Irish post-primary education as a major opportunity in the solution. 'Transition Year' is an optional year-long programme for Irish students moving forward from junior cycle post-primary education (usually for 12–15-year olds) to senior cycle post-primary education (usually 16–18-year-olds). The overall purpose of the Transition Year Programme is to give 15–16-year-old participants an educational experience that encourages self-directed and independent learning. A key aspect of the Transition Year Programme is that while guidelines are provided by the Government through the Department of Education and Skills, every school has the freedom to design and implement its programme.

Methodology and methods used to design programme

OPEN MIND aims to develop students' understanding of mental health and to provide them with tools to manage their wellbeing with a focus on the importance of having personal hobbies and interests. The programme consists of activities, short video content created by students, and reflection prompts. OPEN MIND was co-created through three iterations of a total of 16 hours by 9 young people, 5 mental health professionals, 2 educators, 4 parents, 5 researchers and 4 non-governmental organisation (NGO) workers who wanted to support positive mental health and wellbeing management in young people. The OPEN MIND programme was piloted in four schools nationally and validated by 71 students in a nine-week programme between September 2019 until May 2020 (see Fig. 1) (Real et al. 2020).

The co-creation was developed by an application of SISCODE co-creation journey model which distinguishes four phases such as context analysis, reframing of the problem, envisioning alternatives, and prototyping and development. This methodological approach implied consistent use of design methods, tools and techniques and development of participatory and iterative processes for sustainable engagement and

Fig. 1 Ideation generation workshop in OPEN MIND (April 2019)

youth-led innovation available in 'SISCODE Toolbox for Co-creation Journeys'. The overview of the co-creation activities is presented in Table 1.

Stakeholders' engagement

Student stakeholders who developed content for OPEN MIND first participated in a week-long education programme in SGD that was themed around youth mental health. Students were introduced to design thinking methodologies and participated in a collaborative group project. It allowed for relationship building between students and SGD and insights into areas of youth mental health that required solutions. The bottom-up engagement increased confidence of students in the space and fostered their ownership towards the project. Students were invited back to participate in multi-stakeholder events as youth representatives to ideate, refine and prototype a solution to mental health challenges in young people.

Procedures and assessment

In total, students spent 16 hours ideating, refining and prototyping the educational module, 2 hours in evaluating student and teacher feedback following the programme pilot. SGD worked with two youth representatives closely to develop the script and voice animations for the video content. SGD conducted individual reflections with students to evaluate the participatory process and collect insights. There were three educational week-long programmes for 15–17-year-olds on a theme of youth mental health. The assessment programmes were implemented through the workshops and design sprints, experiential and experimental prototyping of solutions, and reflective practice. In total, 60 students participated across three weeks and their contributions directly shaped an understanding of youth perspectives on mental health challenges.

Outcomes and added value of co-creation

OPEN MIND has encouraged young people to increase their understanding of mental health and acquire the know-how on how to address it at the individual and peer-level by developing hobbies and interests. The engagement and co-facilitation of the programme also equipped teachers with new educational plans and tools to

Table 1 Overview of co-creation activities in OPEN MIND

Session, date	Activities and design tools	Participants	Process and data documentation
Idea Generation, 12 April 2019	Getting to know each other; getting to know the project; context analysis and needs assessment; signing up for the co-ownership of the project (co-creation of the community manifesto); dividing into six groups: challenge sorting: idea generation game; group discussion, presentation of the ideas to a panel of people who have expertise in the field	9 young people, 6 mental health professionals, 2 educators, 4 parents, 6 researchers, 4 NGO workers, 8 SGD staff facilitators	Photo documentation; field notes; session plans and post-evaluation; co-facilitators' reflective discussions
Idea Refining, 26 April 2019	Idea grouping; concept evaluation; concept sketch	8 young people, 3 mental health professionals, 2 educators 4 parents, 4 researchers, 2 NGO workers, 4 SGD staff facilitators	Photo documentation; field notes; session plans and post-evaluation; co-facilitators' reflective discussions
Idea Prototyping, 28 May 2019	Solution roadmap; synthesis workshop	6 young people, 2 mental health professionals, 2 educators, 4 parents, 2 researchers and 2 NGO workers, 3 SGD staff facilitators	Photo documentation; field notes; session plans and post-evaluation; co-facilitators' reflective discussions
Prototype Feedback, 13 August 2019	Presentation of pilot roll-out and student/teacher feedback. Strategy plan workshop	6 young people, 2 mental health professionals, 2 educators, 4 parents, 2 researchers, 2 SGD staff facilitators	Photo documentation; field notes; session plans and post-evaluation; co-facilitators' reflective discussions

autonomously develop hands-on activities aiming at acquiring and/or increasing key competencies such as empathy and inclusion skills; mental health literacy; wellbeing management tools; and teamwork and co-creation skills. This implied greater involvement of youth in contributing to the development of the school environment and extracurricular programme. Each participating school has been challenged to activate the community to develop co-creation practices and a culture of resilience and student participation in decision making.

2.2   Education Programming in the Lab of Collaborative Youth

Lab of Collaborative Youth (LoCY) is an informal platform founded by two practitioners passionate about youth-led and youth-centred co-design of learning experiences and youth policies in Porto, Portugal. Since its inception in 2014, it is coordinated by professionals-volunteers of various backgrounds (design, psychology, biology, language). Insofar experience, LoCY has collaborated with three schools of basic and secondary education, two local contexts, 4 programmes and 91 students of age groups from 12 to 16 years old and 16 to 20 years old. The purpose of LoCY is to tackle the questions of self-efficacy, self-realisation and societal resilience amongst youth through intergenerational collaborative work.

The wellbeing and mental health of Portuguese youth has been affected by their socio-economic status; hence 18% of young people live in poverty (Carcillo 2016). A decrease in mental health among youth has a strong influence on early school leave and less positive expectations towards the future (Matos et al. 2016). After concluding the basic education, many youngsters tend to reach for the job market to become active workers as 18-year-olds and bring about independence and stability to their lives. This paper is specifically focused on the third programme Ilustracionário, à minha maneira 2.0, a programme co-created within the 'Learning Framework in Active Citizenship: Active Learner is an Active Citizen'(Glumac 2018). The programme addressed a challenge of active citizenship within school context and classroom; as well as testing and validating design methodologies for self-directed and peer learning. There was an attempt to include scaling of LoCY's initiative to other local schools in the third version of the Municipal Youth Plan in 2017, however, the plan was never published and the collaboration was not formalised.

Methodology and methods used to design programme

Ilustracionário. a minha maneira 2.0 was developed in a school of basic education with 11 students (5 males, 6 females) of 16 and 17 years old, 2 teachers, a psychologist, 4 volunteers of the 3 youth non-profit organisations (MEDesTU, Tudo Vai Melhorar, ConnectART), 3 LoCY members and 1 LoCY volunteer and 3 students of the master course at the Faculty of Psychology and Educational Sciences (FPCEUP). The programme lasted eight weeks and had in total of 14 sessions implemented weekly between April and June 2017 (see Fig. 2). The subjects for which it was developed were the *Oficina* and Portuguese language and literature. The *Oficina* is a subject in which youngsters of the final grade learn how to use tools for manual work. The transdisciplinary approach was applied-the form and language teacher joined all sessions and participated equitably (more as a language expert than a form teacher).

During this process, the LoCY team acted as a co-design expert and an external co-facilitator in the territorial context of the school in which it collaborated directly with the end-users and relevant local stakeholders. All actors engaged in co-owned participatory and iterative learning processes. The use of design tools and methods

Fig. 2 Prototyping stages of the visual dictionary Ilustracionário, à minha maneira 2.0

supported auditory, visual, writing and kinesthetic learning through co-design and co-production of a learning tool as a prototype. The overview of the co-design activities is presented in Table 2.

Stakeholders' engagement

The process was initiated by the LoCY team of volunteers and professionals interested in active citizenship developed and sustained through active learning and self-organisation of young people in their local school context. The educational programme development has been launched once the identified school of basic or secondary education accepted close collaboration with LoCY. In a preliminary analysis of school context, the LoCY team and school psychologist assessed and selected the most favourable class of students, subject/s, educational module and teachers according to their openness to work with an external team on curricular activities. Within the school context and during the project, young people and teachers of the same class were considered knowledge-providers and primary end-users of the educational programme while other school staff such as a psychologist, other teachers, as well as the members of the administration were considered knowledge brokers. LoCY as an external facilitator and initiator of the educational programme has managed to gather different types of relevant stakeholders who haven't worked previously with the specific local school of basic education. These were the representatives and volunteers of the local youth and art associations, master students of educational sciences, volunteers of different expertise (e.g., educational programming; performative arts), researchers and the LoCY team of facilitators.

Procedures and assessment

In total, students spent 10 hours developing a visual dictionary, and a couple of hours evaluating the participatory process, collaboration, achieved results and mastering co-design and co-production as a community of co-learners. For each phase of the process, specific design and learning tools were used as shown in Table 2. The table briefly outlines the methods and tools that supported students to think, share, create, tell stories and discuss certain aspects of the processes,

Table 2 Overview of co-design activities in Ilustracionário, à minha maneira 2.0

Session, date	Activities and design tools	Participants	Process and data documentation
WarmUp, 20 April 2017	Getting to know each other; getting to know the project; context analysis and needs assessment through youngsters' lenses as co-researchers (map of emotions, storytelling on 'what's citizenship for me?'); visual identity and name of the group	11 students, form teacher, 3 master students, 1 youth NGO representative, 1 volunteer, 1 LoCY member	Video recording; field notes; session plans and post-evaluation; co-facilitators' reflective discussions
Context analysis, 27 April 2017	Context analysis with youngsters as co-researchers (storytelling on 'what I learnt and I liked?', 'what is my role and power in the school context?', 'when do I learn better?'); teambuilding 'mission impossible'	11 students, form teacher, 3 master students, 1 youth NGO representative, 1 volunteer, 2 LoCY members	Video recording; Field notes; Session plans and post-evaluation; Co-facilitators' reflective discussions
Teambuilding, 2 May 2017	Teambuilding ('human knot'); assessment of students' and teacher's views towards the recognition of formal education and ways of learning ('agree-disagree')	11 students, form teacher, 1 volunteer, 2 LoCY members	Video recording; field notes; session plans and post-evaluation; co-facilitators' reflective discussions
Idea generation, 4 May 2017, 9 May 2017	Ideation of the meaningful concepts within themes such as art, collaboration, experience and sports; low-fi prototyping of words and their meanings; assessment of expectations and contributions and principles of co-design (flipchart with post-its to write down answers); creation of the pairs and groups	11 students, form teacher, 1 youth NGO representative, 1 volunteer, 1–2 LoCY members	Video recording; field notes; session plans and post-evaluation; co-facilitators' reflective discussions; Students taking and sending photos which may support creative processes

(continued)

Table 2 (continued)

Session, date	Activities and design tools	Participants	Process and data documentation
Idea refining, 11 May 2017, 16 May 2017	Selection of the concepts/terms for the visual dictionary; visualisation of selected terms (visual maps); introduction to illustration and techniques theory	10–11 students, form teacher, 1 volunteer, 1–2 LoCY members	Video recording; field notes; session plans and post-evaluation; co-facilitators' reflective discussions
Prototyping, 18 May 2017	'Me, as an author' (self- and peer-reflection about the others); Testing techniques for illustration	11 students, form teacher, 1 NGO representative, 1 volunteer, 1 LoCY member	Video recording; field notes; session plans and post-evaluation; co-facilitators' reflective discussions
Mid-term evaluation, 23 May 2017	Mid-term evaluation (evaluation implemented as a discussion activity through the use of physical space and positioning according to satisfaction)	11 students, form teacher, 1 NGO representative, 1 volunteer, 2 LoCY members	Video recording; field notes; session plans and post-evaluation; co-facilitators' reflective discussions
Prototyping, 25 May 2017, 30 May 2017, 1 June 2017, 5 June 2017	Prototyping illustrations in pairs/group (collage, textile, sewing); work on the cover (collage, textile, sewing); prototyping illustrations in pairs/group (collage, textile, sewing); prototyping illustrations in pairs/group (collage, textile, sewing); finalise definitions for each term; connect book pages into a final piece	9–11 students, form teacher, 1 NGO representative, 1 volunteer, 1 LoCY member	Video recording; field notes; session plans and post-evaluation; co-facilitators' reflective discussions
Final evaluation, 9 June 2017	Final evaluation (self-evaluation, peer evaluation, collective evaluation of the project); farewell party and football game	11 students, form teacher, 1 NGO representative, 1 volunteer, 1 LoCY member	Video recording; field notes; session plans and post-evaluation; co-facilitators' reflective discussions

considering their roles as peers, co-authors, co-learners and citizens. The overall assessment of the intervention was done before, during and at the end of the educational programme. The feedback from students and teachers was addressed in the consecutive sessions. The discussion and decision-making processes were stimulated through voluntary, transversal and non-frontal ways (i.e., informal and structured dialogue between everyone involved). The self-assessment and peer assessment were made individually by all students who actively participated in the programme. The evaluation process also included general discussion on the project's results, calculation of the final grade and final feedback. Furthermore, the continuous monitoring and evaluation were discussed in the meetings with the school administration, psychologists, teachers and other external stakeholders. All assessment tools were developed by the LoCY team in collaboration with teachers and other external collaborators and validated by the school community during the initiative.

Outcomes and added value of co-design

Every LoCY's programme co-designed and co-produced outputs such as: (i) new approaches and appropriation of the existing design tools for the intergenerational collaboration; (ii) building students' capacities by application of the open-ended framework with identified competencies relevant for the co-design activities, developed and validated by the primary end-users and other relevant stakeholders (Glumac and de Sousa Morais 2020); and (iii) concrete and tangible results which can serve as the learning tools and boundary objects to further sensitise, inform and promote uptake of youth-led co-design in formal education and local youth-centred policymaking. At the city level, the methodology and learning tools such as the visual dictionary on the terminology of youth participation and policies were used as proof to validate the importance of intergenerational collaboration, understanding of youth participation and use of 'language' (i.e., differences between speaking and understanding of the same subject-matter from the perspective of a youngster- and elderly-individual) (Bessant et al. 2020).

3 Comparative Analysis and Findings

3.1 Aim and Methodology for Comparative Analysis

SGD and LoCY have the same primary target audience (young people), focus on the school setting (formal education), purpose (encourage positive well being and self-efficacy, resilience, and student participation in decision making), and a similar approach to developing educational programmes (use of design methods and tools through co-creation and co-design). In this paper, the authors aim to reflect on and compare their educational programmes and explore patterns in developing capacities in intergenerational collaboration and encouraging youngsters to become active as co-authors and decision-makers of everyday educational experiences. The authors indicate the required value for developing sustainable educational programmes with youth through co-creation and co-design. In the following sub-sections, the similarities and dissimilarities in the approach and results of the two organisations are explained.

3.2 The Value of Youth-Led and Youth-Centred Educational Programmes

Considering working with young people in a school setting demands administrative approval and allocation of the activities to a specific class or classes and acceptance of those to collaborate, it is unpredictable to know what are the needs and motivational drivers before the collaboration initiates. This implies that from the very beginning the mechanisms to know about youth and their everyday experiences should vary. Some of the examples on how to do context analysis advise to include youth as co-researchers (Van Doorn et al. 2016). Both SGD and LoCY applied this approach to their context and programmes. Consequently, both cases confirm young people are not necessarily open to collaboration and/or share an enthusiasm for the suggested intervention regardless of its nature (curricular or extracurricular). Depending on their interests, young people may increase levels of empathy and participation once the intervention has captured their attention by proposing new experiences and social roles; implementing activities in a way that may highlight young people as experts; and allow them an opportunity to develop and implement initiatives they were longing for (i.e., conviviality, football match, etc.) (Glumac 2018).

The creation of a sense of ownership and responsibility among young people is not a linear process (Glumac and de Sousa Morais 2020). In the case of SGD, the taken approach was to support young people create something tangible (i.e., hobby club) which would be co-owned and co-managed by young people in synchronisation with the rest of the school community, especially the educational staff. From the teachers' perspective, this idea was not perceived as feasible on a long-term basis as students would change every year and most of the effort would be requested from teachers (Real et al. 2020). Conversely, the sense of togetherness and co-ownership has been initiated by co-creating a community manifesto with shared values and rules, to be respected by everyone involved in the programme. In the case of LoCY, the approach was to immediately sensitise students in developing learning processes and tools for their own and their peers' learning experiences. It has been initiated by developing new social roles and creating a community of co-learners and asking students to build their collective name and visual identity. Developing their visual symbol and name to describe belonging to something new was relevant and this was a prerequisite to creating new social roles and behaviours between peers but also between students and teachers and students and external co-facilitators. In both cases, having a clear and shared understanding of the envisioned milestones and tangible results was essential to sustain the motivation and empathy of students. In a practical sense, this meant utilising each session to develop concrete results which were the key milestones to reaching the final goal of the educational programme. The stimulation has been embedded by building action plans with youth, discussing methodology and methods, placing physical calendars in the classroom, rearranging the space during sessions, and using walls to visualise the progress of work by exposing the contents. The physical space was no longer an ordinary classroom but an exhibition space of students' productivity and self-organisation in collaborative work. The external co-facilitators had an important role to create power-shared relations between young and adult participants/stakeholders, as well as supporting young people to speak up in presence of adults. To sustain the motivation of all primary end-users, it was essential to keep away from false promises which do not match schools' or programme's capacity (i.e., working with equipment not available at school; working on themes such as restoration of physical spaces and assignment of new functionalities). The rewarding feeling among students who participated in the programmes has been established by knowing that they contributed to creating support tools for peers in similar situations and having developed new individual (self-empowerment) and collective skills (mutual empowerment).

3.3   The Value of Design and Design Tools for Co-creation and Co-design of Educational Programmes

In practice, SGD and LoCY apply participatory action research and promote simultaneous research and innovation practice through design methodology and design methods. SGD team has been exposed to the SISCODE's co-creation journey model, design practice and use of design tools such as idea generation, stakeholders' mapping, customer journeys, service blueprint, systems mapping, among others, that helped team members without a professional design background to learn more about service design and its application in the co-creation projects and initiatives. Besides acquiring new know-how, the team has also learnt the relevance of using design thinking to reorganise internal organisation, mindset and culture for long-term uptake of co-creation approach (Real et al. 2020). Subsequently, SGD has been involving young people already at the initial stages of initiative development such as the context analysis and reframing of the purpose/challenge for which co-creation activity has been developed (Real et al. 2020).

Conversely, the LoCY team has been already skilled in design practice for research, innovation and education, and the use and appropriation of design tools for and with young people. Consequently, the team extended its experience by involving different schools and local stakeholders, demonstrating the applicability of LoCY's methodology (Maylandt et al. 2020; Glumac and de Sousa Morais 2020). The co-design activities developed in such a framework lasted between a month to three months, depending on the modules and availability of co-facilitator-volunteers.

In addition, there are two different types of prototypes as a direct outcome of educational programmes from both organisations: (i) a non-prescriptive methodology to stage intergenerational collaboration through an application of co-design/co-creation (SGD, LoCY); (ii) co-designed and co-produced learning tools/boundary objects (LoCY). The prototype of the visual dictionary, developed in the previous LoCY's educational programme, has more success as it was validated and scaled to different schools and territorial contexts within the same cities. As for the latter, it is hard to monitor and evaluate use and effectiveness of the visual dictionary tool as the individuals have received hard copies and can use it in their individual, peer or student-teacher/student-family member learning experiences. After the conclusion of collaboration, teachers and school administration were encouraged to continue using knowledge and skills with other groups of students. SGD and LoCY have, thus, expressed interest to collaborate in future with individuals and with schools and invited them to approach organisation whenever the opportunity arises.

3.4 The Measure of Impact and Sustainability

Both organisations and educational programmes are taken into consideration for comparison utilise iteration in participatory processes during and after each session. The iteration depends on the observed and received feedback by the primary end-users (students and teachers involved), as well as the co-facilitators. The feedback was gathered through oral, written and visual means (e.g., drawing, storytelling, collage, moving within physical space, among others). The data was also gathered through photo/video recordings, notes, session plans and reflective discussion. Considering there was enough time to contemplate the process and experience achieved in each session, both organisations had an opportunity to be flexible to adapt types of activities to the encountered challenges and learning needs. The effect on individuals is immediate as it builds the capacity to address everyday experience and transform it into something more pleasurable. As for collective practice, the effect can be the same or less intense, as it depends on the existing relationships and patterns of interaction which are not necessarily easy to deconstruct. The sustainability of extended partnership may result either through the additional funding and project-based collaboration, or long-term collaboration through shared funding from the participating organisations (i.e., creation of dependency between the service provider and service user). The most visible difference between SGD and LoCY running initiatives is that SGD is linked to the university and therefore may undergo institutional bureaucracy which impacts the ability to be agile. On the other hand, the university is linked to a wider network of researchers and academics. LoCY is an informal initiative, represented by individuals and their professional affiliations has a network of local and international stakeholders, based on personal contact and relationships.

The short-term impact can be measured in the sustainability of participation and engagement of primary end-users, as well as the involvement of external co-facilitators and other private and public institutions which were interested in the process and outcomes of the programmes. Among the students, it was visible that the co-creation/co-design approaches and activities supported them in becoming more sensitive to organising collaboration and teamwork with their colleagues and teachers, as well as skills for self-organisation. Conversely, teachers who have participated directly in the development of co-creation/co-design activities have learnt that students can perform better when not competing and sharing responsibility for the common goal/result equitably. The established peer support and peer assessment was something novel in these processes and the primary end-users recognised it as relevant. The self-assessment form developed and utilised in each programme indicated to the teachers that young people with lower self-esteem but high performance were grading themselves lower than students of same or lower performance but with higher self-esteem and sense of self-efficacy. The long-term impact is hard to envision, especially among young people as these types of projects act as a catalyst which for some can be a 'mind opener' and for others just another fun-kind-of-activity. Consequently, the ones interested to extend their experiences through active engagement and participation in new initiatives have the potential to increase their capacities in understanding better their social identity and different roles in specific situations (Glumac 2018).

4 Conclusions

Mastering co-creation and co-design is time-consuming and not something easy to grasp without an experienced practitioner and co-facilitator. Regardless of who initiated the process, both approaches aim to promote sustainable bottom-up and horizontal power structures and count with equitable participation of all relevant stakeholders. There is a slight difference between co-creation and co-design, namely in how stakeholders' and designers' roles are defined—for example, in co-creation designers are experts in this topic and provide know-how, yet in co-design they encourage others to design for themselves while they co-facilitate co-design process and mitigate the existing social powers (Durall et al. 2016). A co-design practice can be a part of co-creation as relevant stakeholders can exchange their social and expert roles over time.

Through co-creation, SGD has been successful by making the final prototype/solution available for teachers on the official education portal of the Department of Education in Ireland. It aims to enable teachers to share in future the insights on the best application of the resources available. Through co-design, LoCY has been successful in scaling methodology to different schools and promoting open access to the learning tools among the teachers, NGO representatives, policymakers and other stakeholders. As an informal initiative, it is hard to work with a higher number of schools without external support. In both cases, continuous promotion of experiences and open innovation and science materials is envisioned as the participating schools became more receptive to considering students as active contributors and initiators of co-creation/co-design in a different setting for curricular and extracurricular activities.

5 Future Work

Considering some of the authors work in design education it is notable to mention that these forms of programmes should also be widely considered in design education, especially in the schools of vocational secondary education (Glumac and de Sousa Morais 2020). The authors are curious to learn if in future more collaboration can be made between art and graphic design students of secondary education and other students within the context of 'Transition Year' (Dublin) and/or traditional compulsory schooling (Porto). The authors will continue exchanging the good practices and overcoming the innovation barriers developed and encountered in different territorial contexts. Besides, SGD and LoCY believe it is beneficial to popularise the use of youth-led and youth-centred co-creation/co-design as an approach for developing/elaborating youth policies. Due to Covid-19 pandemic situation, the authors hope to stress the relevance of connections between students through digital means which can extend collaboration further than local context. There are many virtual and collaborative spaces already available, however, SGD and LoCY have keep in mind that some schools have less digital equipment and more restrictions to using digital technologies which may remain as an obstacle to a potential online co-creation and diversification of peer collaboration.

References

Bessant J, Farthing R, Watts R (2016) Co-designing a civics curriculum: young people, democratic deficit and political renewal in the EU. J Curric Stud 48(2):271–289

Carcillo S (2016) Society at a Glance 2016. A spotlight on youth: how does Portugal compare? OECD/European Union

Department of Children and Youth Affairs (2015) National strategy on children and young people's participation in decision-making, 2015–2020

Department of Health (2013) Healthy Ireland–a framework for improved health and wellbeing 2013–2025.

Durall E, Bauters M, Hietala I, Leinonen T, Kapros E (2020) Co-creation and co-design in technology-enhanced learning: Innovating science learning outside the classroom. Interact Design Architect 42:202–226

Glumac O (2018) Lab of collaborative youth: shaping a learning framework in an active citizenship. Universidade do Porto, FBAUP, Porto

Glumac O, de Sousa Morais MRC (2020) Codesigners of classroom 52: a case study for codesign in active citizenship. In: Meeting of research in music, arts and design. Springer, Cham, pp 31–49

Matos MGD, Tomé G, Gaspar T, Cicognani E, Moreno Rodríguez MDC (2016) Youth mental health in Portugal, Italy and Spain: Key challenges for improving wellbeing. Eur Health Psychol 18(3):128–133

Maylandt J, Wascher E, Kaletka C, Eckhardt J, Klimek T, Graetz C, Schulz AC, Krüger D (2020) Deliverable 2.2: case studies and biographies report. H2020 SISCODE project

OECD/European Union (2018) Health at a Glance: Europe 2018: state of health in the EU cycle. OECD Publishing, Paris/European Union, Brussels

Real M, Mantziari D, Maločić M, Stojačić I, Praça G, Bertrand G, Köppchen A, Gabriel A, Machowska M, Wlocdarczyk A, Rasmussen A, Christensen S, Merzagora M, Ghilbert A, Crispell J, D'Arcy G, Sedini C, Juarez Calvo M (2019) Deliverable 3.2: co-creation labs: solutions and policies. H2020 SISCODE project

Real M, Schmittinger F, Pistofidou A, Juarez Calvo M, Rasmussen A, Hertz Janzen M, Sedini C, Cipriani L, Gelsomini M, Maffei S, Bianchini M, Włodarczyk A, Machowska M, Gabriel A, Stojacic I, Konstantinidis E, Mantziari D, Petsani D, Bamidis P, Praça G, Marques J, Köppchen A, Bertrand G, D'Arcy G, Ghilbert A, Merzagora M (2020) Deliverable 3.4: lab's journey as case-studies. H2020 SISCODE project

Shinn C, Salgado R, Rodrigues D (2020) National programme for promotion of physical activity: the situation in Portugal. Cien Saude Colet 25:1339–1348

Van Doorn F, Stappers PJ, Gielen MA (2016) Children as co-researchers in design: enabling users to gather, share and enrich contextual data. Manuscript, Delft University of Technology, Delft

Design Teaching When It Meets Its Local Dimension

Raul Cunca and Carla Paoliello

I don't know who I am, what soul I have.
When I speak sincerely, I don't know what sincerity I speak
with. I am variously different than one I do not know if it exists
(if it is these others).
I feel beliefs that I don't have. I am enamored with desires that I
repudiate. My perpetual attention on me perpetually points me
to soul betrayals to a character that I may not have, nor does
she think I have.
I feel multiple. I am like a room with countless fantastic mirrors
that twist to false reflections a single previous reality that is not
in any and is in all.
How does the pantheist feel like a tree [?] and even the flower, I
feel like several beings. I feel that I live other people's lives, in
me, incompletely, as if my being participates in all men,
incompletely in each [?], For a sum of non-selves synthesized in
a false self.
(Pessoa 1996, p. 93).

Abstract The essay presents the paradigms of design and territory framed by identity. It discusses the potential for the development of local production. One that involves a cultural and material context and precise geography. It favors know-how of an indigenous nature that we enhance through design. That is where the object-place emerges. This product moves global without losing its natural root and its local brand. The text introduces, in the first place, the paradigms of design and identity. It presents, in a second moment, the idea of local action. In the third part, we established some territorial characteristics. Those that can manifest them self in many material solutions, valued through place knowledge. Finally, we highlighted the possible transformations in design teaching. We present The Designesart project of the Escola Superior de Artes Aplicadas de Castelo Branco. We emphasize the importance of this model as a new practice for design. We defend its reflection when it finds its local dimension.

R. Cunca · C. Paoliello (✉)
Centro de Investigação e Estudos Em Belas-Artes (CIEBA), Faculdade de Belas-Artes da Universidade de Lisboa, Lisboa, Portugal

© The Author(s), under exclusive license to Springer Nature Switzerland AG 2022
D. Raposo et al. (eds.), *Perspectives on Design II*, Springer Series in Design and Innovation 16, https://doi.org/10.1007/978-3-030-79879-6_6

Keywords Design · Design teaching · Local dimension

1 Identity and Design

Constantly reinvented, identity always reminds us of a natural identity memory. As the Polish sociologist and essayist Zygmunt Bauman observes: «the use of identity should be considered a continuous process of redefining oneself and to invent and reinvent his/her history.» (Bauman 2005, p. 13).

Affirming an identity means demarcating boundaries. It means making distinctions between individuals and between collectives. Or between what is proper and what is alien, equal and different. It is not unique but yet plural. We have several identities that are constructed and constituted by memories, experiences, environments, institutions, historical, geographical, and biological facts. All these facts enable new articulations and the establishment of new identities.

Identity is a dimension in constant mutation and transformation. Especially through the manipulation of culture, where it always finds new materials. Ideological and ritual practices also rise identity naturalness. It is this bilateral relationship between culture and environment that houses it.

Culture is the set of meanings and interconnections that can shape identities. Through symbols and representations, it identifies what is internal and unique. In-text 'The cultural turn in geography', Paul Claval establishes three concepts of culture. A first that presents it as the set of practices, knowledge, and individual values. A second is the set of principles, rules, norms, and values. The ones that determine the choices of individuals and guide their actions. And a third in which culture is the set of attitudes and customs that give the social group its unity. This one has an important role in the construction of identities.

Theoretically, we can say that we share the same values, ideas, and habits with other members of our community. If identity is the status of the individual self, it is also the result of this relationship. In its construction, the importance of others appears.

Identity is also a guarantee of cultural stability. Through the different material supports, security is transmitted. Emotional bonds are created, which, in turn, attribute greater cohesion to the cultural space.

In this conceptual dimension, the identity, besides being verified, can be reinvented. Its material set is manifested in particular typologies of a given culture. It also manifests itself in indigenous materials and production techniques. Or even in rituals that identify particular postures and users. We can drive all this source of local knowledge by design. And it can be enhanced and materialized in an artifact.

We thus defend that the territory confers identity. The territory will be that space where we live the daily life. Where we experience it and which forms our being. As exposed by the Brazilian geographer Milton Santos: «space imposes itself through the conditions it offers for production, circulation, house, communication, the exercise of politics, the exercise of beliefs, leisure, and as a condition of living well.» (Santos 2006, p. 55).

The territory is the product of social construction, place of use, cultural heritage. It reveals people's history. To perceive it is to understand these cultural, social, and historical determinations. So, we have had clues to the identities contained therein.

We relate seeing to looking and believing. Didi-Huberman explains that: « *cultus* - the Latin verb *colere* - at first designated simply the act of inhabiting a place and occupying it, cultivating it. However, it is much more than that, it is related to the place and its material, symbolic or imaginary management.» (1998, p. 155). Looking is worshiping and looking at the world is a condition, a search.

> The look is a window. Every window has two sides that communicate through it. Interior and exterior. If the landscape is a look. It is the meeting of the interior of the beholder and the exterior of what is seen as the sensorial corporeality. The landscape can be taken as the relationship between space and image. It is the meeting between them. It is the window that communicates such instances. As in René Magritte's canvas, La Condition Humaine, on which he painted an easel, with a painted canvas, in front of a window. Do you paint what you see or see what you paint? (Vieira 2006, p. 14).

Visual perception is, thus, a fundamental condition for territorial cultural existence. Yet, the visual frame of space brings only what a view includes. We understand that to perceive a place, we must have the experience of moving around it. We must smell it, hear it and feel it on the skin. In short, experiencing it in its totality of senses and stimuli. «The landscape is not a closed circle, but a displacement,» said Dardel (2011). Only then we do make and remake its meanings. And the territory will be a depository of stories, a social experience.

Proposals related to an identity merge, over time, an identity collective. Expressive values accumulate awaken appropriate solutions to new events. And material conceptions are thus a faithful depository of identity. They awaken in us the ability to imagine and envision an event from the past, the present, and even the future. All through an artifact involved in a specific context or centered on an action that originated from a geographical location.

Artifacts often materialize the values of place identity. We establish comparisons, analogies. Or we describe the path of a particular technique or way of doing. The visual repertoire is common to different identities distanced in space and time. Intervening in a territory other than yours also provides new project dynamics. This observation is only intended to emphasize the fact that the identity elements are not watertight. They are not reserved for the natural individuals of that identity. They are available to anyone who wants to meet them and work with them.

That is because identity is, in its genesis, immaterial. It takes us to a virtual space where the collective imagination of a given community lives. Where idealization and creativity can be the real axioms of their materialization. As noted by Gui Bonsiepe: «Identity does not depend so much on what each one is or has. But on what lives in the other's imagination. That is, identities belong to the *l'imaginaire*. They are artifacts of communication.» (Bonsiepe 2012, p. 71).

2 Local Design

Acting under a local identity means participating in one community. To act within local identities implies the designer's involvement in that community. Research and investigate customs, rituals, myths, materials, practices related to this territory. To handle all this knowledge in the project is to be open to new identity materializations.

We define local design as one whose set of actions and its products are demarcated by local characteristics. They are an expression of a collective, a people, or a single craftsman (Paoliello 2016, p. 261). These production objects present the peculiarities of local culture (Paoliello 2017).

We start with the tangible and intangible elements research. The ones that support project development. We use field and representation methods. Those who map architectural, pictorial, sculptural, artisanal, archaeological, gastronomic, and natural features. The values of poetry, music, customs, traditions, and cults are also sought.

We embrace the different functional, cultural, intellectual, social, technological, economic, artistic, symbolic, and environmental spheres. This allows us to choose the territory specificities. Those elements characterize historical and cultural heritage. It also reconciles different elements that take part in the local identity construction. All in the same representative support.

The designer's management of these resources consolidates the design program. They provide innovative solutions in a local context and multiple material solutions, of which we highlight: (1) the design of new objects lightens and systematizes the tasks performed; (2) artifacts present new use proposals; (3) conceptions recover a forgotten activity in the past; (4) use of ancestor's techniques and ways of making; - reinterpretations and reconfigurations of visual and material repertoires; and (5) habits, myths, and local legends are rescued.

These are some of the proposals that can result from this approach. Design can awake a local identity. It also fosters territory opportunities. We conceive cultural proximity through mediation. We allow artifacts to integrate and renew new identities.

3 Territory and Design

We have hypothesized that the landscape apprehension, as a reference, provokes identity strengthening. One which gives meaning to craft objects and the subject who does it. With this, there is recognition, respect, and appreciation of place, being, and doing.

We present the landscape as a perception, a daily way of living. It comes from memory and autochthonous material. Space never appears as neutral support in the lives of individuals. It results from human action. One that changed the natural reality and created human and humanized landscapes.

The recognition of the landscape generates the valorization of the cultural identity. It also values local self-esteem and strengthens the sense of community. It helps to build the feeling of belonging.

The *topophilia* defended by Tuan (2012) reflects this sense of territorial belonging well. It links the social to the environmental, economic, cultural, and political aspects. It is a loop of involvement that connects the person to a given part of the space. It's about affectivity. The word affection is the basis for the verb to affect. It reflects this feeling of exerting influence. The feeling of touching and of provoking a certain sensation. It is also about appropriating, fixing, taking root, and choosing what is fundamental. In the perception of each one and also in the community as a whole.

The relationship between being and space is an inseparable web of a mutual constitution (Sack 1997). The perceived interpreted and imagined territorial identity is a reflection of the sense of place. In the end, the place is being or, according to Heidegger (2001), «we are not in space: we are spatially being.» Marandola and Dal Gallo also present the being-place, whose relationship.

> (…) presupposes a mutual and simultaneous construction of both: the subject builds the place and at the same time it is built by that one. The places where the individual lived or lives are responsible for the constitution of his way of being. As well as it is guaranteeing the continuity of that being, based on experience. Through perception, sensation, cognition, representation, and imagination, the place-being is constituted. (Marandola and Dal Gallo 2010, p.411).

Cities and, in another instance, the nation, must carry the representation of each one. Men must recognize themselves in space. And in the symbolic elements that relate to territory and history.

Santos (2006) calls the process of territorial reconstruction—*reterritorialization* or the rediscovery of the relationship between place and community. This process was already explained by several other authors (Flores 2006, p. 7–8; Haesbaert 2007; Haesbaert 2001, p. 1773; Marandola and Dal Gallo 2010, p. 418; Turco 1988, p. 77). They divide it into three possibilities for action. The first one is to assign meaning or denomination and the creation and guarantee of places for cultural practices. The second moment is the control of space. We use geo symbols to understand and socio-spatially organize the territory. The third is the composition or reification time. We produce meaning and guide the creation of the territorial system. At this moment, identity is strengthened by establishing spatial links, and value is placed in the territory.

New territorialization processes promote the construction of new meanings. These lead to the appearance of other identities. Heidrich (2010, p. 6) already warned that it is possible to exist, at the same time, a national, regional, and class identity. The problem is the emergence of territories expansion. Or even the simultaneity of territorial, cultural, and economic practices. Those that provoke the appearance of dual or multiple identities. Bauman called this process of postmodern society fluidity. According to this author:

(…) Fluids, so to speak, do not fix space or arrest time. While solids, have clear spatial
dimensions, but they neutralize the impact and, therefore, diminish the significance of time.
Fluids are not very attached in any way and are constantly ready to change. (Bauman 2001,
p. 8).

The spatiotemporal rhythms have become very varied. They are the result of the
existence of dynamic and active identities. As presented by sociologist Stuart Hall:
«the subject, previously lived as having a unified and stable identity, is becoming
fragmented; composed not of a single, but several identities.» (Hall 2000, p. 12).

Even though this variety could be a problem; local products start from the
understanding that to perceive is to remember. Formal and symbolic references are
the result of memories that achieve visibility. The products establish a relationship
«between what is seen and who is seen» (Cezar 2009, p. 44), between the past and
the present. They work with memory. And transport it to the present to create
another memory. One with a strong affective link and an intense sense of belonging.

All that happens because place objects are narratives. Therefore, symbolizations
of a situation, technique, or identity, become a discourse. They become experience
events, within a network of meanings. They materialize the relationship between
man and the territory. They are also the understanding of culture interpreting these
events. From the experience itself, they are reflective products.

Everyday life contaminates the project. It values the life stories of each community; preserves local heritage, its material, and immaterial goods; understands the
characteristics of the territory or the immediate landscape; recognizes the particularities of each place.

Another dimension that artifacts get in this context is longevity. This relates to
the fact that place objects are recognized by those who interact with them. The
singularity distinguishes them from others. They make them last in time through the
values they transmit. These values can be material, environmental, social, economic, cultural, symbolic, or functional. They appeal to its preservation, reserving a
connection with the territory. The longevity of objects is a central value nowadays.
It increases the useful life and provides for their reuse. Thus, they do not subject
them to constant recycling, which raises more and more questions in environmental
terms.

The ability to preserve memories is also one of the central aspects of the objects
of local identity. Whether through the natural materials that configure them,
establishing connections to a place. Whether by the practices they support, often
referring to precise know-how.

The values of memory, tradition, and the qualities of natural materials make
these objects closer to man. These characteristics humanize us. They provide
meanings, favoring their harmonious integration in daily life.

By reaffirming local territorial identities, a possible massification generated by
globalization is combated. The relationship with the territory itself, or with the
geographic space of local production, acts as a determinant. One in the choice of
work tools and materials. What we see in this type of production is an economic
relationship based on local culture and nature.

4 Native Materials and Techniques

The local design is revealed in the act of interpreting the territory. To defend it is to discuss the value of traditions, the intimate interface with one place. And also, the symbolic relationship of the designer with the created product. The set of meanings that enable its identification is quite broad. It is the result of the interface between man and other men, and between man and the environment, apprehended in everyday life.

A fundamental value is recovered: the pleasure of doing. The action is imbued with the pleasure of handling the material. We opt for creative methods that allow corporeal proximity. The ones that approach the maker and the work. This is another dimension that local design has embedded: tacit knowledge. As stated in Saramago's book 'A caverna'

> (…) what the fingers always knew how to do best was precisely to reveal the hidden. What the brain may have perceived as infused, magical, or supernatural knowledge. Whatever they mean supernatural, magical, and infused. Where the fingers and their little brains taught it. For the brain to know what the stone was, it was necessary first that the fingers touch it. That it felt the roughness, the weight, and the density. It was necessary to get hurt in it. It was not until much later that the brain realized that from that piece of rock. One could do something that I would call a knife and something that I would call an idol. (Saramago 2000, p. XIII).

Objects that have local material characters register cultural messages. They also record sensations of the places in which they were produced. A register of a specific time–space. They are objects that keep the impressions of those who made them (Paz 1991, p. 51). They are the ones that express uniqueness and, so, authenticity.

The production of place objects materializes the symbols of a people and a place. They represent identities, stories, demands. They provide the formation of a symbolic network of meanings. A simple object manages to reflect, through the chosen materials and techniques, a cultural multiterritoriality.

5 Teaching and Design

> Enjoying and being able to handle cultural landscapes, as constantly changing, is one of the paths traced by design. This consolidates more identity to identity. Renew the landscape, transform what is useful into new and surely into beautiful. From the new rituals, new perspectives, new uses, new emotions, new feelings, new hopes arise. Unfolded in new solutions that support actions developed by local practices. These practices are changing and add new results. That starts from the observation of the local context. They merge into artifacts that reflect a new reconfiguration of actions and uses. Perspectives that address elementality, utility, and innovation. To materialize into objects capable of supporting a local ritual or practice. (Cunca in Catálogo da exposição Novos Rituais Novas Práticas Locais na Colecção Designesart, 2018).

How does identity/local design/territory reverberate in the teaching of design? How do local issues and cultural identities appear in the design curricular units?

For eleven years now, designer Raul Cunca, professor at the Faculty of Fine Arts (FBAUL) and the Escola Superior de Artes Aplicadas de Castelo Branco—ESART, among other foreign universities, has been acting as a supervisor, professor, and commissioner of the Designesart project. It is about a collection of objects that crosses traditional techniques and emerging technologies. It is about local practices that reconfigure actions and users. It is also about a school as an instrument of social and territorial construction.

There have already been three editions of this project. The first, in 2008, with the title of Designesart, had an exhibition held at the Império Galleries in Castelo Branco. The second was in 2015 entitled Designesart—Local Identity and Global Design. Exhibitions were held at the Municipal Gallery Comendador João Martins in Proença-a-Nova from October 24 to December 4, 2016, and in the old CTT building in Castelo Branco from May 7 to July 3, 2016. The third edition was in 2018, Designesart—New Rituals New Local Practices. This had exhibitions at the Centro Artístico Albicastrense in Castelo Branco from November 20 to December 31, 2018; at the Municipal Gallery Comendador João Martins in Proença-a-Nova from January 12 to March 31, 2019, and at Lagar de Varas in Vila Velha de Rodão from May 7 to September 30, 2019.

The exhibitions are important moments for recognizing the know-how of participating students and teachers. A time to view publicly the objects/prototypes made and to reflect on local cultural symbols and materials used.

These place objects can be seen in Figs. 1, 2, 3, 4, 5 and 6 (from https://www.facebook.com/projectesart/photos/). As further explained by Cunca (2018), enhance the human, popular, traditional, manufacturing, technical, technological, intuitive, and natural qualities of the Beira-Baixa region. They present identities (Cunca 2019) because they came from this project of reinvention, empowerment, discovery of a territory.

According to Margolin and Margolin (2004), social design, unlike the usual patterns of projects developed within the scope of design with an industrial and marketing focus, aims not only to please human needs. It contributes to the transformation of a community. The designer assumes the role of translator. He is a collaborator, mediator of the territory, material, indigenous technique. It is about defense and respect, valuing know-how and locality.

This practice is rooted in local traditions and ways of doing things. That is framed in the material and immaterial culture of the place. The products portray a way of being and using. They are imbued with identity meanings of the culture in which they originate.

The work is not limited only to perform, but generate a movement of identity and territory awareness in everyone involved. At this moment, the place object becomes highly differentiated. Not only it is due to its critical interpretation of reality but because it stands out as an increment. Both for its absorption by other generations as a cultural product.

Fig. 1 'Brake board' by Joana Santos

Fig. 2 'Magical boxes' by Raul Cunca

Fig. 3 'Castelo Branco's stamps' by Ana Alice Afonso

Fig. 4 'Support for drying herbs' by Joana Ramos

Fig. 5 'Spice scale' by Tiago Girão

Fig. 6 'Chili display and container' by José Simão

6 Conclusions

From these first decades of the twenty-first century, we have seen a new change in design. Based on a set of transformations, it begins to abandon, for the first time, its consolidated archetype throughout the Industrial Revolution. It implements a more flexible model where in the same space coexist techniques and technologies that bring together industrial and artisanal production practices.

The new craft is based on knowledge sharing networks. It provides its interlocutors with access to a multitude of information and the acquisition of technical skills. These structures give great flexibility to the communities of new artisans. And it explores an interesting social dimension vital to this activity. One that makes possible results that were unattainable in the recent past. Both concerning the dimension of resources, the time to reach a certain product, the final artifact quality, and its reproducibility.

Dissemination is also fundamental for the success of the entire process. The new digital manufacturing technologies promote increased quality with reduced means. It allows placing the local product on a global level. It values the region and disseminates its identity. This dissemination is facilitated nowadays through the platforms made available on the internet. As Bonsiepe states: «identity and globalization occupy a central position in the current discourse of design.» (Bonsiepe, 2012, p. 63). Everywhere became close through design.

In this new productive framework, the processes changed. Now methodologies ranging from self-production to participatory design can be applied. In this context, the design can be an important driver of local development. The different community actors are involved.

Teaching should also present this symmetrical convergence of the design strategies associated with those other different disciplines with peculiar *ethos* and logic. The intersection of design with other frontiers of knowledge is validated. These come from other ways of experimenting, thinking about everyday life, and getting to know the world. An invitation is made to immerse the academic know-how of design in the empirical know-how of local production units and vice-versa.

All because we defend the encounter of design with its local dimension.

References

Bauman Z (2005) Identidade: Entrevista a Benedetto Vecchi. Rio de Janeiro: Jorge Zahar Editor
Bonsiepe G (2012) Diseño y Crisis. Valencia, ES: Campgràfic Editors
Cezar CZC (2009) Meia paisagem e meia algumas considerações sobre o semi-visível. Dissertação (Mestrado) – Universidade Federal do Rio Grande do Sul, Instituto de Artes, Programa de Pós-Graduação em Artes Visuais. Porto Alegre: UFGRS

Claval P (2013) A virada cultural em Geografia. In: Silva, José Borzacchiello *et al.* (2013) É geografia, é Paul Claval. Maria Geralda de Almeida, Tadeu Alencar Arrais (org). Goiânia: FUNAPE

Cunca R (2018) in Catálogo da exposição "Novos Rituais Novas Práticas Locais na Colecção Designesart"

Cunca R (2019) Design, identidade e produção local. i+Diseño - Revista científico-académica internacional de Innovación, Investigación y Desarrollo en Diseño. 14, ano XI

Dardel E (2011) O Homem e a Terra: natureza da realidade geográfica. São Paulo: Perspectiva

Didi-Huberman G (1998) O que vimos, o que nos olha. SP: Editora 34

Flores M (2006) A identidade cultural do território como base de estratégias de desenvolvimento – uma visão do estado da arte. Contribuição para o Projeto Desenvolvimento Territorial Rural a partir de Serviços e Produtos com Identidade – RIMISP

Haesbaert R (2001) Da desterritorialização à multiterritorialidade. Anais do IX Encontro Nacional da ANPUR. Vol.3. Rio de Janeiro: ANPUR

Haesbaert R (2007) Território e Multiterritório: um debate. GEOgraphiaano IX, no 17

Marandola Jr E, Dal Gallo PM (2010) Ser migrante: implicações territoriais e existenciais da migração. R. Bras. Est. Pop., Rio de Janeiro 27(2):407–424. jul./dez

Hall S (2000) A Identidade Cultural na Pós modernidade. DP&A editora, Rio de Janeiro

Heidegger M (2001) Ensaios e conferências. Petrópolis: Vozes

Heidrich ÁL (2010) A abordagem territorial e a noção de representação. Anais do XVI Encontro de Geógrafos Brasileiros - Crise, práxis e autonomia: espaços de resistência e de esperanças. Espaço de Diálogos e Práticas. São Paulo: AGB

Margolin V, Margolin S (2004) Um "modelo social" de design: questões de prática e pesquisa. Revista Design em Foco, 1 (001), p.43–48. Disponível em: https://designparasustentabilidade.files.wordpress.com/2010/06/um-modelo-social-de-design.pdf

Paoliello C (2016) Relatório de Pós-doutoramento. Faculdade de Belas-Artes, Universidade de Lisboa

Paoliello C (2017) Uma "nova" metodologia para o fomento das parcerias entre designers e artesãos - uma proposta de inovação social. In: 6o Ergotrip Design, Aveiro

Paz O (1991) Convergências: ensaios sobre arte e literatura. Rocco, Rio de Janeiro

Pessoa F (1996) Páginas Íntimas e de Auto-Interpretação. (Textos estabelecidos e prefaciados por Georg Rudolf Lind e Jacinto do Prado Coelho.) Lisboa: Ática

Sack RD (1997) Homo geographicus. Johns Hopkins University Press, Baltimore

Santos M (2006) A Natureza do Espaço: Técnica e Tempo, Razão e Emoção. Editora da Universidade de São Paulo, São Paulo

Saramago J (2000) A caverna. São Paulo: Companhia das Letras

Tuan Y-F (2012) Topofilia - um estudo da percepção. Londrina: Eduel

Turco A (1988) Verso una teoria geografica della complessità. Milano: UNICOPLI

Vieira D (2006) Paisagem e Imaginário: contribuições teóricas para uma história cultural do olhar. Revista de História e Estudos Culturais, vol.3, no. 3, jul, ago, set

The Archetype of Graphic Thinking. Visual Graphic Tool that Analyses the Graphic, Creative and Project Thinking of the Product Designer

Roberta Barban Franceschi🄳

Abstract The evolution of technology towards digital and abstract possibilities combined with the evolution of culture and the intricacies of **technology** empower the designer's role in the **design process**. The virtualization of the world is a reality throughout society and a decisive factor in various sectors of design. This article introduces a tool created to analyse the **graphic thinking** involved in a project, and the participation of **new technologies** in the designer's creative process and graphic representation of his ideas. A core (the designer) that is connected to three small networks: **graphic thinking, creative thinking**, and **project thinking,** forms the archetype of graphic thinking. Outstanding designers and theoreticians in the field of project methodology, creativity and graphic representation, have been studied for the making of this tool. This **visual graphic tool** can identify the changes in the creative process and its materialization, as well as verify to what extend new technologies have paved the way not only for a change in the thinking process, but also in design.

Keywords Visual thinking · Visual graphic tool · Graphic thinking · Design process · Creative · Technology

1 Introduction

Humans has gone through various transformations in the way they work and creatives have always played a very important role in these changes. They have been constantly updating and adapting to the technologies and needs of each era.

We have seen fundamental changes in the economic, political, cultural and social areas over the last three decades. The virtualization of the world is a reality throughout society and a decisive factor in various design sectors (Cardoso 2016) and this virtualization enhances multiculturalism and globalization. Which leads us

R. Barban Franceschi (✉)
Universidad Internacional de La Rioja, UNIR, Logroño, Spain
e-mail: roberta.barban@unir.net

© The Author(s), under exclusive license to Springer Nature Switzerland AG 2022
D. Raposo et al. (eds.), *Perspectives on Design II*, Springer Series in Design and Innovation 16, https://doi.org/10.1007/978-3-030-79879-6_7

to wonder whether virtualization and new technologies have interfered in the designer's way of creating and in the graphic communication of his ideas, and to what extent have the creation process and its graphic registers changed in today's society.

The designer used to put down his ideas on paper, whereas nowadays this process can be manifested in various analogical and digital ways. What is the change that technologies have brought in the process of creating gadgets? What elements are present when a designer creates and communicates his ideas?

The evolution of technology towards digital and abstract possibilities combined with the evolution of cultural and technological complexities enhance the role of the designer in the entire design process.

For Vasconcelos et al. (2010) this context demands a high level of autonomy from the designer, in which he becomes an indispensable an essential element in every process.

The Archetype of Graphic Thinking is a visual graphic tool developed to verify this change, as well as the graphic tools involved in the ideation of the project and the factors that intervene in this ideation and creation process. This tool allows us to identify how the designer of a product communicates his ideas, and how he considers the right means to produce its shape and communication.

The methodology used in the elaboration of this tool, was the bibliographic investigation of projects by world-renowned designers, and the study of theorists in the field of project methodology, creativity and graphic representation. This research has proved that several factors coexist within the ideation process, not only concerning graphic representation, but also in relation to creative and graphic design thinking.

The visual graphic tool is an abstract graphic structure, aimed to reveal the relationships and help the understanding of coded information. It is important to highlight that diagrams, networks, charts and infographics are regular systems in visual communication and knowledge transmission (Costa 2019).

Contemporary thinking has recovered this form of expression. According to Montaner (2014), one of its features is allowing an analytical interpretation of reality, and describes it as a compliant, dynamic, ever-evolving structure, suitable for the contemporary context, since it emphasises differences. They are graphic expressions that use symbols, images and versatile elements that can be transformed (Montaner 2014).

2 Graphic Thinking Archetype

The archetype is an analysis tool created to understand how a designer's conceptual graphic process works. The concept adopted for the archetype is a network formed by a set of nodes that interact.

According to Raymond (2010), nodes are links, through which either information or knowledge flow, so the more nodes a network has, the more information and knowledge will flow through them, and the more accurate it will be. The config-uration adopted for the archetype of graphic thinking is the collaborative network, formed by small, more intimate networks connected to the core. This configuration speeds and encourages the flow of ideas.

The archetype of graphic thinking has a core (the designer) that creates and coordinates all the information. This core is connected to three small networks, graphic thinking, creative thinking, and project thinking, which have a number of distinctive features that will be explained in further detail bellow.

Core

The designer is the core of the archetype, in charge of creating the right flow of information for the conceptual process of design, in other words, he centralises the flow of information. This core sends out a signal requesting certain data and information to the networks connected to it that send back the required information. Depending on the project and the skills applied, certain areas of the archetype are activated, building each designer's own network of information and knowledge.

The designer is the key element in the whole ideation process. He uses his creative imagination and pragmatism to connect with his creative and project thinking.

The conceptual process of design is directly related to the designer, his life experience, cultural context, academic training and both graphic and project thinking. The designer is the core of the archetype, and it is up to him to establish the connections between skills and knowledge, and to start the design process using the means, skills, experiences and knowledge at his disposal (Jones 1978; Bassat 2014; Ostrower 1997) (Fig. 1).

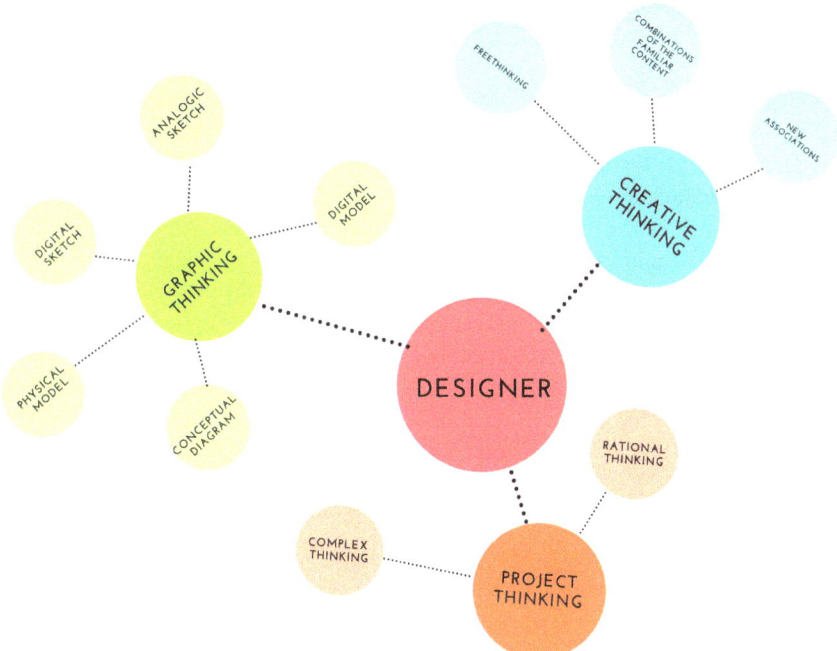

Fig. 1 Graphic thinking archetype. Author's image

3   Small Networks

They are specific fields of knowledge that make the foundation of the archetype. This core meets the specific knowledge, which is the main feature in the configuration of the archetype, and the actual responsible of it. It contains the characteristics that tell an archetype apart from another, and it is the designer's call to use one feature or another for the configuration of his own archetype.

The small networks play a fundamental role in the creation of the gadget, they work together to create the right environment for the ideas to flow. Although the type of expression and the formulation of thinking are hardly separable (Cañas et al. 2008), we will introduce the three areas of specific thinking, which are Creative Thinking, Project Thinking and Graphic Thinking.

3.1   Creative Thinking

In the researched context, these skills are related with the conception of the project, problem solving, the ideation and creation of the gadget. Creativity can be expressed as a way of projecting, freethinking, fantasy, or as the precision of invention. It covers technical, social, psychological, economic and humane aspects (Munari 1997).

Creativity can also be expressed in different ways, through combinations of the familiar content, or through the transfer of knowledge from one area to another, seemingly different (Amabile 2000), suggesting a new approach to an old context. (Bassat 2014).

Other factors that determine our creative thinking are our personal knowledge and the accumulation of references, which allow us to solve problems in an original way (Bassat 2014; Ostrower 1997).

The greater the knowledge, the more possibilities to create relationships (Munari 1997), relationships that encourage innovation (Bassat 2014). Associations are the essence of the imaginary world and they happen extremely quickly.

The route from the idea to the final product created by the designer is, according to Ryan (1997), a vital element in design, and key for the designer's creativity. He claims that the methodological process could be easy to understand and yet mysterious, since each designer has his own. A formula that is approachable and tricky at the same time. That is the essence of design, the struggle and the discovery.

Combinations and associations are fundamental elements in creativity (Ostrower 1997; Munari 1997), and they can be manifested through new associations (relationships) of familiar content, or by applying knowledge from one area to another, as well as a new approach to an old context (Bassat 2014) (Fig. 2).

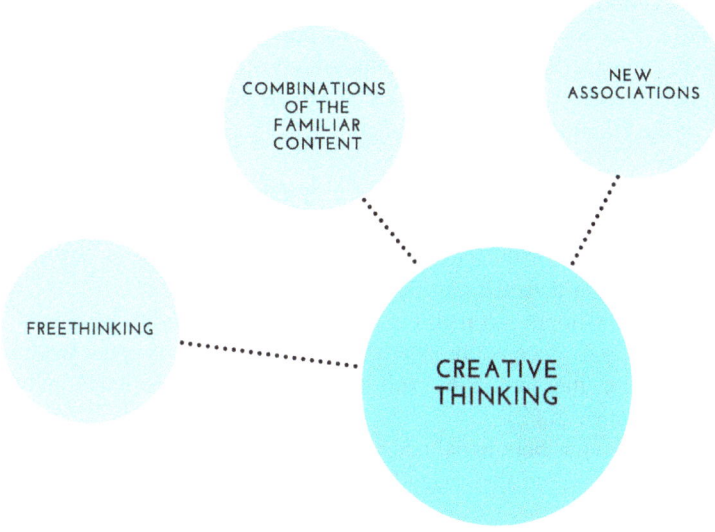

Fig. 2 Small network creative thinking. Author's image

3.2 Project Thinking

Project thinking is the core of this small network, it is the designer's ability to express, unfold and develop his ideas. Place of experiences and references, both individual and collective that shape and configure the right environment for the creation of an object.

The process of this path is irregular, it barely has fixed principles, and it is ever changing. The designer is free to split the process in several phases and sub-phases, to supply documentary evidence, decide what to photograph, how much detailed information include, and how to organize it. Documentation is an important part of the process (Dubberly 2004).

The relationship between the designer and the designed object (design process) is one of the important elements in the development of the product. Several elements participate in the creation of the designed object. The designer must follow a design process (methodology) and respect its stages to complete his work successfully.

The first design methods introduced the concept of *problem* (input) and *solution* (output) along with the development process, a vision that remains present in the design process nowadays. As well as the belief that the designer's job is to solve and get rid of problems (Dubberly 2004). A more modern approach to the subject suggests that the problem triggers innovation and experimentation, and encourages the designer to explore other ways to make a product. The architect and designer Benjamín Aranda, thinks that Design is not about solving problems but rather paving the way to new approaches.

Rational thinking is linear, it follows a sequence of steps that must be completed, and it does not allow going back to a previous point and feeding back into the process. Montaner (2002) says that rationalism timing is the linear and countable timing of production, the one of the advances in techno science. In the space and time of the relationship between function and shape, the artistic or architectural object arises.

Rational thinking seeks a language closer to industry, which will manifest itself through the abstraction of form and geometric shape. For Argan (2001), geometry is a language that transposes the individual and goes for the universal, in geometry the individual side is not detected, nor is the artist's touch.

By adopting a rational, geometric language, combined with the simple way of thinking, the designer does not broadens the possibilities. It does not work with the diverse, but with the minimum, following the most functional and rational approach. (Montaner 2002).

Complex thinking is born in an industrialized context, in a post-industrial society and a postmodern culture that magnifies dispersal and decentralization, the indeterminate, the plural, the small groups, juxtaposition and fragmented visions (Lyotard 1984). The new thinking develops a more humane and emotional language, adjusting to a world that is complex by nature.

The space–time notions are substantially modified by new (computer) technologies. Time and distance are shortened until they become immediate. The mechanisms are not linked to a specific place and move around the planet (Solá-Morales 1995).

Space and time have been two irreconcilable variables until now (Virilio 1993), and this has cleared the way to introduce new variables, associations and juxtapositions. Space–time management provided a change of perception of hyper volume, hyperspace and hypertext, also known as interfaces. In this complex context, objects are adapted for the needs of man, exploring various possibilities whether they be language wise, shape wise, materials wise, production models or graphic representations.

The computer is the interface when it comes to performing practical, organizational, cognitive and reasoning activities (Morin 1998). In project thinking, this tool has made it possible to create shapes in a virtual space, and has made the immateriality of thinking more approachable. Allowing connections and associations of ideas that would have been unreachable without the help of digital technology, be it software, hardware or the multiple professionals from various areas of knowledge.

The project carried out through digital media, aims to solve new, complex problems, or face old solutions quickly, enabling new proceeding ways, changes in the shape and the transition to new evolutionary models (Fuentes and Ureña 2011).

The digital world has brought along more freedom, promptness, and the opportunity to simulate and visualize simple and complex forms before specifying them in the matter. Allowing corrections and the exploration of several possibilities accurately and quickly.

Complex Geometry is created with the help of other tools such as computer programs. The advance in computer science, technology and materials, allows these complex forms to be created both virtually and physically. It is a revolution in the way we think and manufacture, which is encouraging new possibilities to create objects.

The combination between human mind, machine/digital mind and materials, allows us to capture the complex thinking. The old relationship between matter and form belongs to the past, since it has been outpaced by the growing discovery of new materials (Montaner 2002).

Complex geometry combined with digital manufacturing, provides endless forms and types of project thinking that share common elements creating small similar groups.

This shift towards digital joins the new industrial perception called the Third Industrial Revolution (TRI). A concept drawn up by Rifkin (2011) in the mid-90s, through which he proves the need for a new, more fair and sustainable production.

This new context of digital manufacturing brings new possibilities and ways of working. The simple thinking that defines traditional industry, that manifests through the Cartesian rational geometric form of right angles, lines and planes, differs from the complex thinking that characterizes digital manufacturing (Third Industrial Revolution) and manifests through complex geometry.

In the network of project thinking, we verify that the two available guidelines are rational thinking, defined by a linear process and an abstract geometric language that uses technology at the end of the design process. And complex thinking, defined by a non-linear process and a complex geometric language, that incorporates technology in the creation process of the object, which allows the creation of complex forms (Fig. 3).

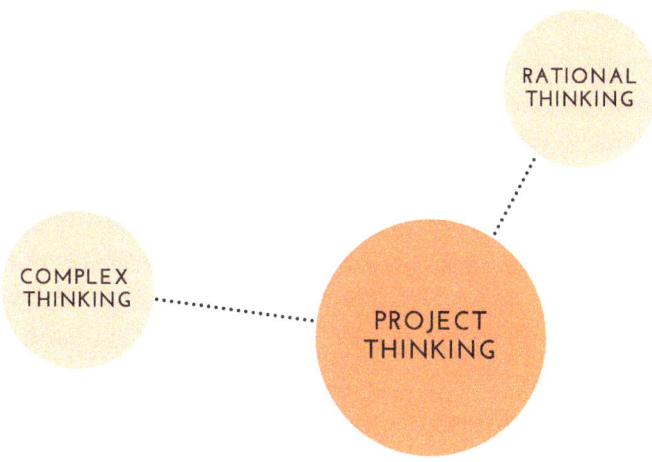

Fig. 3 Small network graphic thinking. Author's image

3.3 Graphic Thinking

Graphic thinking is formed by a variety of techniques and graphic methods, conceived to express creative thinking, where the application of one technique or another will depend on the designer's skill.

Graphic communication is a means of revealing ideas, and a tool that supports thinking (Ostrower 1997; Cañas et al. 2008). It is a subjective language, and it becomes objective through an order in the matter. This order is the reference for communication; it is the value criterion (Ostrower 1997).

Graphic thinking is the way to register experimentation and to show your visual and creative thinking. Almost every designer uses sketches, either analogic or digital, to communicate their ideas during the design process.

The three main elements of graphic thinking are research, graphic thinking as a process, which evolves as the evolution of the design process does, and flow, in which thinking and image formation are connected at all times for the communication of graphic thinking (Cañas et al. 2008).

Sketches are merely functional communications, mostly simple, cumulative and non-linear. They are actually the graphic creative thinking, and a journey of try and error, dismissing ideas and mixing proposals, that leads to new discoveries. Drawing is a tool to externalize and analyse thoughts, as well as to break down problems making them easier to understand (Pipes 2008).

Graphic communication evolves hand in hand with project thinking, and adapts to the new schools of thought and design trends. The term graphic thinking was used for the first time by Laseau (2001) to describe the thought assigned to drawing. But with the arrival of new technologies and the new creative trends, this concept could be expanded to other possibilities when it comes to expressing an idea, since currently, drawing applied to the design process is not the only way to express graphic thinking.

Research shows that nowadays designers can express themselves in different ways, on the one hand using traditional tools such as physical sketches or models, and on the other hand developing their ideas in the virtual world using digital ones, or through conceptual diagrams. These different ways of expression are part of the small network of graphic thinking. Let's see the five types.

The first one is the analogic sketch, it comprises the traditional way of sketching, putting your ideas on paper by hand. The designer uses several implements for drawing such as conventional pencils, mechanical pencils, colouring pencils, pens and fountain pens to communicate his idea. Analogical sketch is related to rational project thinking, shaping ideas in a rational, geometric way rather than complex. A very intimate communication between the designer and the conception of the object. Designers such as Alvar Aalto, Sergio Rodrigues, Joe Colombo, Lina Bo Bardi or Vermer Panton use this type of expression.

The second type of graphic thinking is the digital sketch. It uses different means than the analogic one. In this type of expression, the drawing is made on a tablet or computer, and it requires specific software. It is also connected to rational project thinking, the designer Ron Arad uses this type expression.

The third type of graphic thinking is the physical model. The designer uses real scale, three-dimensional models as a sketch of his ideas. The three-dimensional sketches are a methodology invented by Rowena Reed Kostellow (Hannah 2002) and are used at the Pratt Institute. It is a methodology widely spread in the United States and applied by several universities in Europe. Rowena named her methodology "Structures of abstract visual relationships" and divided it into three stages: three-dimensional sketches, proportional sketches and space notes. Rowena would work with abstract volumes and geometric elements through which she would lead students to develop volumetry from simple to complex compositions. Her philosophy on beauty laid on progressively polishing imperfections and finding balance.

Cabezas (2011) claims that drawing was not always the most important tool in the process of communicating ideas. Numerous architects did not use drawing to project and express their ideas. He also says that this did not happen in pre-industrial times, when creatives would make neither sketches nor drawings to communicate their ideas.

According to Parsons (2009), the essence of the three-dimensional sketch is speed, which must allow the ideas and analogic sketches to flow. Nonetheless, with a different feature, which is the aim of the three dimensional sketch to be seen and analysed to formulate a new, better version of it.

Three-dimensional sketches examine the proportions and the visual appearance, surveying the object volumetrically, and intentionally ignore other criteria such as structural strength. The model can also be closely associated with the materials instead of its shape, which allows the free exploration of its features. The choice of materials will depend on its qualities, which must be equal or similar to the ones of the final object. Designers like Konstantin Grcic, Campana Brothers, Carol Gay use this type of expression.

The fourth type of graphic thinking is the digital model. The idea is developed in a virtual way, using specific graphic tools (software). The incorporation of software as a creation tool in projects has meant a change when it comes to thinking the object. Since it replaces building lines and planes applied to perspective, by creating surfaces and geometric solids directly. These models are the three-dimensional digital sketches, created in a virtual space.

Computer modelling programs have always combined two-dimensional and three-dimensional systems, which has helped designers build more and more complex shapes (Pipes 2007), it is like returning to basic project actions like carving and sculpting solids.

The software applied to design is only useful when the designer also masters the traditional skills like analogic sketch. Programs cannot visualize on their own, therefore they need the designer to carry out the operations (Henry 2012).

Expression through a digital model allows the development of more complex shapes than in the physical model, since the digital tool allows the designer to maximize his creative potential with a wide range of shape manipulation, once they learn all the software shape-generation possibilities.

The fifth type of graphic thinking is the conceptual diagram; it is a way to create forms establishing relationships, associations or connections between things through questions and analogies. The idea (relationships, associations and connections) is represented by symbols, images or graphics that explain its reasoning. The spark that will trigger the entire process of materialization in which the relationships and associations between elements will evolve towards an object.

For Laseau (2001), these relationships, associations and connections can be established in two different ways, personal or direct, which he splits into three categories:

1. Physical: structural (structure of a tree), mechanical (like the movement of the wind through a room) or of control (like opening or closing mechanisms).
2. Organic (plants and animals).
3. Cultural (man, society or symbols).

This proves that the designer possesses a wide range of experimentation on the analogy and elaboration of diagrams (code + form) in the conceiving phase of the object.

The designer imagines, creates the idea and relationships between elements, however, he does not know the shape of the final object because the algorithm and the computer software will carry out this process. In this type of expression, we can see the influence of the software in contemporary design. The software used to take part in the final phase of the project, but now, through the insertion of the codes in the generative process, it has broaden its field of activity becoming a collaborator in the design process (Reas et al. 2010).

The great change is that the designer is still the one coming up with the idea, but after processing the data with the tools provided, the software produces a form that the designer does not control. The creator then disconnects completely from the process, and does not know the outcome. Materializing the idea is no longer the designer's task but a task for the "software", which means generating objects, which have another appearance, and whose shape does not happen in the mind.

The objects created are not rectilinear, geometric or curvilinear, they are no longer only the result of a human mind, but a hybrid between the human and the machine; they become cybernetic objects. Designers like Guto Requena, Aranda & Lasch studio, Joris Laarman, use this type of expression.

It is clear that in graphic thinking designers express their ideas in many different ways. The advancement of technology has enabled a freer thinking both in the initial phase of the project and during its development. The creative process takes places within the symbiosis between designer, idea and means of expression, whether they be analogic or digital. Looking at the five types of expression above, we can risk saying that technology has contribute a new way to conceive objects (Fig. 4).

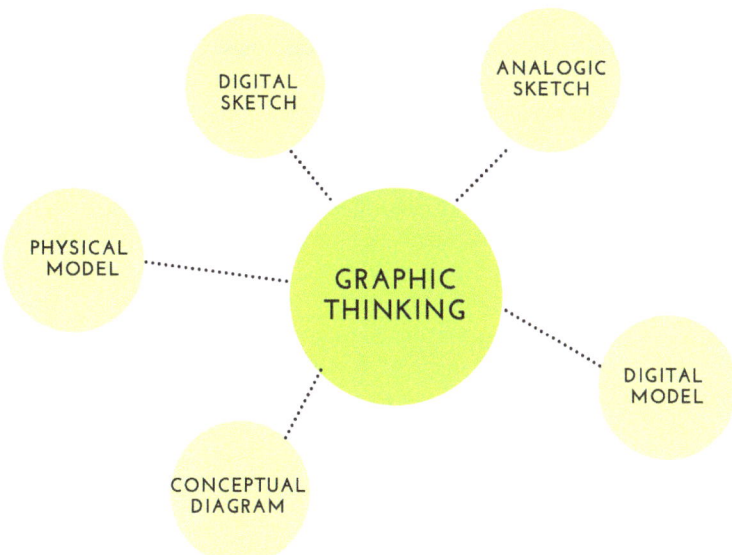

Fig. 4 Small network graphic thinking. Author's image

4 Discussion and Conclusion

The creation process and its graphic registers have changed in today's society. The technological dependency is present at all times during the creation process, and the production and reproduction of the object.

There is no question that technology changes the process of creating and materializing the shape, expanding as well the possibilities to materialize an idea into a physical figure. The arrival of the new technologies has enabled changes both in the thinking process and in the way of designing, altering the appearance of the object.

When a designer uses the conceptual diagram graphic thinking, creative thinking becomes a fundamental aspect to build associations of ideas, since it is the foundation of graphic thinking. The designer can manifest his ideas through new associations, transferring his knowledge from one field to another, approaching an old context differently and creating free associations (Bassat 2014; Munari 1997; Ostrower 1997; Amabile 2000).

The biggest change takes place in the 'conceptual diagram graphic thinking'. The evolution of technology makes it possible to start building an idea from concepts/diagrams. The initial idea travels through the synergy of the various fields of knowledge, and the technology (software) processes the information producing a shape. This process does not travel through the same path than the traditional project thinking.

The new thinking emerges as a hybrid element that flows between several areas of knowledge, combining analogic and digital elements, connecting and creating a new experimental and mutable project process.

The algorithm presents a non-quantifiable context; the designer does not possess the key parameters to carry out the design. He does not have the shape of the object in his abstract mind, or elements to help him capture the shape, which means the idea not manifested as a shape. In algorithmic design, the designer has a logical relationship with the elements, since design is a subjective process. Aesthetic matters are not at stake, the result will depend on the subjective relationships created by the designer (Reas et al. 2010).

The designer imagines, creates the idea and relationships between elements, however, he does not know the shape of the final object because the algorithm and the computer software will carry out this process. In this type of expression, we can see the influence of the software in contemporary design. The software used to take part in the final phase of the project, but now, through the insertion of the codes in the generative process, it has broaden its field of activity becoming a collaborator in the design process.

There are no fixed rules for the designer when it comes to create and communicate his ideas, neither one only interpretation of the project. It is manifested as an informal structure, and if there is indeed an order and rhythm, they are not visible, because everything depends on the starting point. According to Balmond (1999) there is not one sole interpretation of these projects: their ambiguity forces interpretation. Juxtaposition and hybrid situations are valid and not unfortunate accidents. On a small, intimate scale, local actions are supposed to expand outwards and give a sneak peek at the whole. At some point, coherence is reached, and the object is defined.

The change that technology has brought is defined by the relationship between the production of the gadgets, and new technologies for digital production serving both the industry, and small architecture, design and engineering studios. A change regarding the production of the real object that allows the designer to perform the entire process in his workplace, from the idea to the prototype.

Fuentes and Ureña (2011) point out that one of the great innovations introduced in the design process is the prototype. It enables the industry to produce the model quickly and inexpensively, just pressing a button. Aside from being visualized, the object can also be evaluated, assembled; and assembly studies can be carried out, among other applications. The union between the designer's autonomy and the digital manufacturing uses technology as an instrument of creation, not just as a graphic tool for its creators.

Complex design thinking presents a diversity of coexisting ways of thinking and making design. From a procedure based on local culture and an individual and artistic process, to a global and decontextualized one, whether it be analogical or digital.

Complex project thinking is the one that works best with technology, the computer is the interface in the execution of practical activities, and it allows the designer to create shapes in a virtual space. Bringing the immateriality of thinking closer, allowing connections and associations of ideas that would be impossible to achieve without the help of digital technology, be it software, hardware or the multiple professionals from various areas of knowledge.

The project carried out through digital means aims to either solve new, complex problems, or face old solutions more quickly, enabling new ways, changes in the form and the transition to new models that have meant a revolution (Fuentes and Ureña 2011).

We prove transformations in the way of thinking, as seen when we have approached complex project thinking. It influences the creative graphic thinking with a diversity of possibilities regarding the way in which we think the object, in the creative and conceptual phase of the design project that we have identified in the conceptual diagram graphic expressions.

In this complex context, objects adapt to the needs of man, exploring diverse possibilities whether they be languages, shape, materials, production systems or graphic representations. It made possible a change of perception towards hyper volumes, hyperspaces and hypertexts that we know as interfaces nowadays, which has paved the way for new variables, associations and juxtapositions.

References

Amabile T (2000) Harvard business review. Creatividad e Innovación. Deusto, Bilbao

Argan GC (2001) Projeto e destino. Editora Árica, São Paulo

Balmond C (1999) La nueva estructura y lo informal. Quaderns 222:38–49

Bassat L (2014) La creatividad. Penguin Handon House, Bacelona

Cabezas L (2011) Dibujo y Profesión 2. Dibujo y construcción de la realidad, arquitectura, proyecto, diseño, ingeniería, dibujo técnico. Ediciones Cátedra, Madrid

Cañas I, Bayod C, Velilla C, De San Antonio C (2008) Pensamiento crítico para el Pensamiento Gráfico. In: Anales de Ingeniería Gráfica, 19, pp 39–49

Cardoso R (2016) Design para um mundo complexo. Ubu Editora, São Paulo

Costa J (2019) Esquematismo. La eficacia de la simplicidad teoría informacional del esquema. Editorial Experimenta, Madrid

Montaner MJ (2014) Del diagrama a las experiencias, hacia una arquitectura de la acción. Editorial Gustavo Gili, Barcelona

Dubberly H (2004) How do you design? Dubberly Design Office, San Francisco

Fuentes JM, Ureña C (2011) El proyecto digital. IN Cabezas, L.: Dibujo y Profesión 2. Dibujo y construcción de la realidad, arquitectura, proyecto, diseño, ingeniería, dibujo técnico pp 309–358. Ediciones Cátedra, Madrid

Hannah GG (2002) Elements of design Rowena Reed/Anglais: Rowena Reed Kostellow and the structure of visual relationships. Princenton Architectural Press, New York

Henry K (2012) Dibujo para diseñadores de producto. De la idea al papel. Promopress. Barcelona

Laseau P (2001) Graphic thinking for architects & designers. Wiley, New York

Lyotard JF (1984) La condición postmoderna: informe sobre el saber. Ediciones Cátedra, Madrid

Montaner MJ (2002) Las formas del siglo XX. Editorial Gustavo Gili, Barcelona

Morin E (1998) El método III. El conocimiento del conocimiento. Ediciones Cátedra, Madrid

Munari B (1977) Fantasia. Edições 70, Lisboa

Ostrower F (1997) Editora Vozes, Petropolis

Parsons T (2009) Thinking: objects. Contemporary approaches to product design. Ava Academia, Lausanne

Pipes A (2008) Dibujo para diseñadores. Técnicas, bocetos de concepto, sistemas información, ilustración, medios, presentaciones, diseño por ordenador. Art Blume, Barcelona

Raymond M (2010) Tendencias: qué son, cómo identificarlas, cómo leerlas. Promopress, Barcelona

Reas R, McWilliams C, Barendse J (2010) Form+Code in design, art, architecture. Princenton Architectural Press, New York

Rifkin J (2011) La Tercera Revolución Industrial. Ediciones Paidós, Barcelona

Ryan D (1997) Enzo Mari and the process of design. Des Issues 13(3):29–36

Solá-Morales I (1995) Diferencias: topografía de la arquitectura contemporánea. Editorial Gustavo Gili, Barcelona

Vasconcelos LT et al (2010) Um modelo de classificação para metodologías de Design. In 9° Congresso Brasileiro de Pesquisa e Desenvolvimento em Design. Anhembi Morumbi Sao Paulo

Virilio P (1993) O espaço crítico e as perspectivas do tempo real. Editora 34, São Paulo (1993)

Drawing as a Strategy on Design Education

Ana Moreira da Silva

Abstract Education is more than training skills and techniques. It is an intellectual preparation for life-long learning that cultivates the abilities of the mind to encounter new situations and respond with ingenuity, imagination, and creativity.

Today's Design Education must take into account the complex nature of contemporary design, the wide range of fields in which it can operate and the new paradigm of our times.

Drawing can be an essential operational support both for teaching and professional practice. Freehand drawing is a must, not only for practicing designers but, also, for the Design students education.

Facing hand drawing as a daily mental activity for the performance of design practice could be a way for developing a drawing teaching strategy inserted in a Design Education that aims reflection and investigation in an active pedagogy process, committed to a critical posture and enhancing in each student their own creative individuality. The daily drawing practice strengthens neural networks and engages cognitive faculties at many levels. Students should sketch from the very beginning of their education and be required to use sketches to document and develop their visual ideas.

Under a qualitative research, based on literature review methodology, we intend to investigate the use of freehand drawing/sketching importance on Design Education. Through the study of several statements from various authors we verify the permanence of sketching important role. This research aims to stimulate reflection and bring new perspectives on the nowadays use of freehand drawing/sketching both in the design creative process and in Design Education.

Keywords Design education · Drawing · Sketching · Creative process

A. Moreira da Silva (✉)
CIAUD, Lisbon School of Architecture, Universidade de Lisboa, Lisboa, Portugal

D. Raposo et al. (eds.), *Perspectives on Design II*, Springer Series in Design and Innovation 16, https://doi.org/10.1007/978-3-030-79879-6_8

105

1   Introduction

This paper stems from a current post-doc research project aimed by the need of producing more knowledge and reflection on Drawing. Our post-doc main research topic is about the importance of freehand drawing as a critical instrument and as operative support within the conceptual process in design. In this project we consider the close connection between Drawing and Design. Its main objective is to investigate the importance of freehand drawing in the design process. Given that designers must conceive and develop solutions for real problems that can be of a very different nature, we intend to verify the importance of free hand drawing/sketching as an operational support for problem solving and critical analysis during the conceptual process in Design.

2   Drawing/Sketching: Definition and Function

Freehand drawing or sketching are similar denominations within the design practice.

The word Sketch, deriving from the Italian *Schizzo*, has its origin from the Latin *Schedium*, which derives from the Greek *Skhedios*, both meaning done extempore: done without preparation, improvised (Moreira da Silva 2010).

According to the Oxford English Dictionary (2020) the word Sketch means: "a rough or unfinished version of any creative work" and to the Cambridge English Dictionary: "a simple, quickly-made drawing that does not have many details".

So the word Sketch describes a quickly-made freehand drawing and its intention is to give a general overview or the guidelines of something, in relation to the intended final shape or figure, a rough drawing representing the chief features of an object or idea and often made as a project preliminary study.

Sketches are synthetic drawings, executed freehand, where the designer represents ideas that have not yet been fully defined. Sketches emerge from the need to fix those first ideas that occur in the project act and that are manifested through the first signs, coming from the thought, traced on a sheet of paper. A sketch can be like the 'thought of the hand', the hand as an extension of each thought fixed at the moment by the gesture that registers it.

A sketch assumes a peculiar and determinant character in the conceptual process, giving thought the possibility of transfiguring itself through graphics that reveal the ideas that give rise to it. It allows the anticipatory structure and the envisaged rule to be recognized (Molder and Pensamento 1995).

Sketching, not only makes the author's idea becomes visible, which until then was purely mental, but also makes possible, through graphic signs, quick and decisive ones, which help him/her to better clarify the design subject, its transformation into a project.

Sketches allow concepts and ideas to come out. If they were impossible to be formalized through words, once fixed on a sketch, become analyzable, recognizable, evaluable, modifiable, that is, became capable of being explained verbally. The main objective of this type of drawing is to fix the idea, the design global image 'in thought', which the designer gradually matures. The sketch works as a bridge between the abstract world of the imaginary and the concrete material explanation through graphic synthesis.

The act of sketching enables that reasoning and thoughts we have developed can be gradually translated and decoded throughout the drawn lines. Somehow we debate ourselves with our own ideas in this quickly-drawn lines. We scratch, we draw, we overwrite features, we configure, we represent, we visualize, giving physical form to our thoughts. There is a direct link between the thinking and the hand that performs the sketch. The hand as an extension of the brain, of the reasoning (Moreira da Silva 2017).

Our hands are like organs for thought. Sketching is a 'doing' that becomes a way of 'thinking' in which hands and thoughts are joined together.

When sketching, the designer puts into practice that critical operation capable of fixing, of suspending the flow of the idea itself in a first drawing, fast and immediate. It is through this critical process that the designer, based on successive approximations and reflections, reaches the definitive idea.

However, it is important not to confuse and clearly establish the distinction between the idea and the sketch. The idea is born out of an intellectual, mental process, not generally found when drawing; the design essentially serves to define it. The sketch is the representation of this idea.

In fact, it is through the sketch—sometimes excessive, sometimes scarce, but always essential, in its indecision, in its rethinking, in its revision—that we can penetrate the complexity of the author's 'theoretical project' to collect and retrace all the 'utopian aspects' of that delicate intellectual design process.

It is in this sense that the value of the heuristic function of the drawing is clearly revealed in the design process, momentarily conclusive as part of the research representing the genesis of ideas. It is a process comparable to the growth of the embryo that during the first phases of existence and evolution appears to be an imprecise configuration of what is predestined to become.

The path, through which sketches develop, is never straight: it is a patient and continuous redoing, it is an attempt to solidify the idea around some connections that may return to the liquid state with the introduction of an unforeseen or different interpretable data, with the glimpse of an achievement possibility, with the finding of some incongruity. Through this patient, time-consuming, tiring, manual work, the problem is explored; our knowledge, first general and schematic, then becomes the search for the final solution, in all directions; the core may exist at each point of the project, in a section, in a detail; it always becomes possible a quick total re-elaboration of the theme, while, at the same time with the knowledge, it is deepened, the definitive form becomes increasingly defined.

3   Sketching as a Project Instrument

Let us now take in consideration the value and the role that sketching occupies within the project processes and, also, on the relationship that elapses between the idea and its first representation, which is expressed, precisely, through the sketch. The role of the sketch within the design process is to allow clarifying, defining, through their own representations, our projectual ideas.

The design process requires a large production of representations of what one wants to design. Sketches are one of the most common ways to produce the images of the project proposals, which allow to create, organize and evaluate the main ideas that will rule the final project.

Embryonic ideas are quickly thrown onto the sheet of paper for primary analysis, before they disappear, relieving limited memory resources, leaving room for reflection and detailed observation of ideas, validating or discarding them, generating a constant flow of more ideas (Barreira da Costa 2019).

The world of ideas needs its external expression in order to produce their assessment, their verification, transmission, modification or elimination.

The act of projecting in Design requires multiple verifications until reaching a coherent result or a problem solving and it is through various drawings, mostly sketches, that such approaches are achieved.

Sketching allows to apprehend and express ideas that arise necessarily with great speed in the designer' mind. The designer's intuition processes, as a creator, with apparent reasoning expressed through the sketch, remain as substrates of his/her theoretical, visual and spatial referents, which allow him/her to inquire about the solution he/she will materialize through the definitive project.

Fish and Scrivener (2018) describe Sketching as the transcription of internal knowledge to visual representation, this externalization being a central part of the design process, generating knowledge and reflection like Goldschmidt (1991) and Schön state (1983).

In the early stages of the creative process, sketches are drawings that the designer essentially directs to him/herself. As instruments of this creative process, sketches are testimonies of the designer's initial attempts, of the way he clarifies his design ideas and, also helps fixing essential characteristics for his future definitive proposal. Sketching reaches its main objective when the idea is found, but it does not end at that moment, it is always present in the design process, refuting and testing hypotheses, refining the idea by organizing thoughts till the designer finds the project final solution.

4   Sketching: Designer's Monologue

In reality, sketches are perhaps the only testimony of the activity that the designer develops with him/herself. So, from a functional point of view they have an important value as a testimonies of the process and of the reflection that the designer carried out to accomplish it. These first sketches constitute what we can call 'designer's monologue'.

Neurobiology scholars clarified the ideas elaboration by recognizing that our mind uses primary data in successive and increasingly complex processes. This process of elaborating and linking ideas is organized through operations in which we assimilate data through the pre-existing mental structure in the individual who works on a particular issue. Only after this process does the initial data become significant (Zeki 1992).

The progressive knowledge of the reality takes place through the incorporation of new circuits that are activated in the brain, that is, as a theme is worked on, the mind elaborates it with higher levels of complexity. This phase is known as the association of ideas, a process that can end in the elaboration of an image much more complex than the original (Damásio 2012).

The transition from an idea to paper is one of the basic elements of the 'designer's monologue' and constitutes an important foundation to situate the relevance of the sketch as an instrument of this monologue (Lapuerta 1997).

If we accept that a design project basis is the formulation of a problem, then we can affirm that sketches are personal responses, for those who produce them, to concerns or questions that help to define and to solve the problem through successive approximations, without dependencies of rigor, scale, dimensioning or representativeness. That is, the monologue is based on a graphic instrument that allows designers to quickly define a problem, explore solutions, discard options and refine the perception of their solutions, working as problem solving strategy.

The sketch becomes the emanation of the designer's thought and the vehicle of his/her mental structures. A two-way link is established between the drawing and the mind, between thought and the action of representing it, and at the same time the character of the creative process is evidenced by allowing its self-exploration and self-evaluation. This last characteristic is important since it allows or encourages the method of qualitative approximation as it constitutes a vehicle for new modifications that optimize the original idea and open ways for obtaining new ideas.

The images are not created by sketches, these only allow them to emerge from the ideas, creating the right environment for them to be recognizable and providing a means for their expression and for their realization.

The moment when sketches are carried out is characterized by a propitiatory capacity for reflection, which allows and encourages the elaboration of new ideas.

We can conclude that it is important to recognize a creative system within the act of sketching that is part of the designer's self-investigation process about his/her work.

5   Sketching on Design Education

According to Manzini (2019), Design Education must take into account the complex nature of contemporary design, the wide range of fields in which it can operate, the multiplicity of artifacts designers can contribute to conceiving and realizing and, finally, the speed at which designers' roles and capabilities have changed in the last few years.

About today's challenges, opportunities and failures of Design Education, in 2019, Ken Friedman suggested a list of challenges for design, stating that those challenges create a new context for the design process. There are some forms of design that remain similar to what they have been for a long time but, new other forms of design emerge in response to new paradigms, new developments, new tools, new situations and new technologies (Friedman 2019).

Since everybody is typing on computers and tablets, maybe we should focus upon typing rather than writing? Questions like these make explicit not only a change in culture but also how to deal with new technologies in a rapidly changing reality. The question entails much more than typing versus handwriting. Learning how to write is learning how to organize and form thoughts and ideas on a sheet of paper, through a brain process. Handwriting connects thinking and making which is an inherent part of mankind (Sennett 2008). We can raise similar questions regarding freehand drawing within Design Education. Once, physical drawing and sketching ruled design curricula, because there was no alternative. With the several possibilities new technologies can offer in design practice, we must reconsider the several functions of Drawing within Design processes and, consequently, within Design teaching.

A sustainable definition of Drawing must go beyond the tip of the pencil and the techniques used by those who hold it, and focus on freehand drawing as an intellectually driven process of translation. A process that, in common with writing, mathematics and other forms of intellectual processing, is driven by the need to build and reconstruct multidimensional information in a readable two-dimensional format (Kantrowitz et al. 2011).

In twenty-first century, known as the digital age, with students facing constant entertainment distractions and attractions, makes it difficult for them, to assimilate information from more theoretical and abstract concepts and, therefore, their knowledge process in Design higher education. Diversified pedagogical strategies based on Drawing applied to multidisciplinary teaching in Design may offer a pedagogical experience with more meaning, facilitating the apprehension and reflection of several contents, increasing the interconnection between teacher and student, expanding the knowledge process in a more inclusive way of learning (Barreira da Costa 2019).

Buchanan (2019) considers that Education is an intellectual preparation for life-long learning that cultivates the mind capabilities to encounter new situations and respond with ingenuity, imagination, and creativity. He states that the essential elements of an educational system are, in fact, the dimensions of creativity: being *inventive* in perceiving new possibilities in the world, being open to *discovery* of new facts, being *innovative* and *imaginative* in exploring connections among diverse kinds of knowledge gained through a university education and experience in the world, and finally, be open to *intuition* in perceiving the principles, values and interdependencies in the many systems that surround. Buchanan considers that, nowadays, our culture regards innovation as the basis of creativity, and this ignores the other three dimensions of creativity: invention, discovery, and intuition.

As Design Education deals with creativity, we should take in account freehand drawing characteristics and possibilities that can lead students to explore this several creativity dimensions: discovery, intuition, invention and innovation.

It will be important to explore pedagogical strategies based on drawing that can fulfill some existing gaps in the actual Design Education, strengthening the argument that drawing can enhance critical thinking, investigating whether complemented information can generate knowledge, when accompanied by a drawn narrative. As a reinforcement of the argument, knowledge can be created. And through the process of drawing, knowledge is created sequentially, as an ephemeral iteration (Barreira da Costa 2019).

Thinking through making has largely disappeared, but design course's curricula would do well to preserve this important approach. Design thinking has demonstrated the value of a variety of thinking through making. Students should be encouraged to communicate with other design students and teachers through sketches, as a way to gain a clearer understanding of what they are designing. In design projects the first step is sketching. The point of these freehand drawings is not to represent a possible finished design but rather a starting point to bring the design student face-to-face with a range of issues and possible solutions. Through a series of specific exercises, sketching encourage expansion of the design student ideas and can inspire connections and analogies (Swanson 2020).

According to Silva et al. (2017), in a study about engaging design students reasoning through freehand drawing in classroom context, we conclude that, although drawing is being sometimes considered as an expressive tool far from the digital universe, it allows students to have a holistic perception of information, connecting associations in a timeline map, presenting the various options along the project development. In addition to its representation possibilities, sketching gives students access to a deeper learning, through the interactions and evolutions of a certain problem challenge.

Todd Kelley states that it is not enough that students know how to create design sketches, but to also know the purpose of sketching in design. First of all it is important that students understand the importance of the role that sketching plays in design, so that they naturally use this tool in the first phases to communicate their ideas to themselves and to the other students and professors, and later, to help them to try to solve the problems that arise on paper, before these problems become real in the prototyping phase (Kelley 2017).

Learning to produce accurate drawings from observation is a useful skill for design students, but more importantly, according to several authors (Kantrowitz et al. 2011; Tversky 2009; Radzikowskai et al. 2009), is the students' skills acquisition to visualize ideas, reflect on them and communicate those same ideas to others. Being these the main characteristics and advantages of sketching, it is important that students acquire them in design courses.

Sketches in design are carried out quickly, following fleeting thoughts, undergoing constant iterations and evolutions, without needing great details. They are mere initial representations, so they must be accepted as poorly defined, because the ideas themselves, at this early stage of the process, are also poorly defined. They open the way for self-criticism and reflection, for dialogue and discussion, for the debate of ideas and for the emergence of suggestions for alternatives. The very quick and rugged nature of Sketches is what makes them such a powerful design tool. As long as sketches are good enough to capture the necessary and essential elements, the drawing skill is unnecessary (Radzikowskai et al. 2009).

Sketching in design is different from sketching in the classic sense of making a work of art, artistic like drawings. Along with learning the theory and different drawing techniques, it is very important for design students to become familiar with the idea that sketching is much more than making correct drawings (Waanders et al. 2011).

In conclusion, it would suit that design drawing classes teach how to sketch in total freedom, in a rough, unfinished way, without the purposes of nice and artistic like drawings. Students must learn and practice how to use sketching for ideas exteriorization, reflection and communication in the design process and not for a graphic illustration purpose.

We must recognize in the freehand drawing a dimension, simultaneously, transversal and transdisciplinary, due to its capacity to constitute as an operational support of conception. A multidisciplinary Drawing concept in itself, allowing the qualification of environments through Drawing and, through it the human environment. Drawing teaching in a constant approach to the project methodology, fulfilling the objectives stated through well-defined phases in connection with the design process. Considering that the Drawing discipline must bridge the way for the use of drawing as an instrument for the design method throughout the Design course, based on a direct relationship with the Project and its processes.

The scientific community has shown interest in the relationship between drawing and cognition, offering arguments that drawing can enhance thinking, along with the value of drawing as visual thinking tool in design. Drawing extracts knowledge from both worlds, physical and intellectual, incorporates analysis and construction/ interpretation, can express different manifestations and multidisciplinary approaches in design, as a means, sometimes even leading the practice of design itself, uniting the analytical process and the constructivist form of design. Drawing is a way of generating knowledge. This happens through iteration during the design process. Designing reflects knowledge about what is designed, as well as the process required to achieve the final result.

In teaching practice, we should consider freehand drawing as a form of learning, as a critical conception instrument and as a means of communicating the project idea, in a posture of constant search and knowledge deepening with a constructive attitude of critical reflection. Drawing as a way to record, understand,

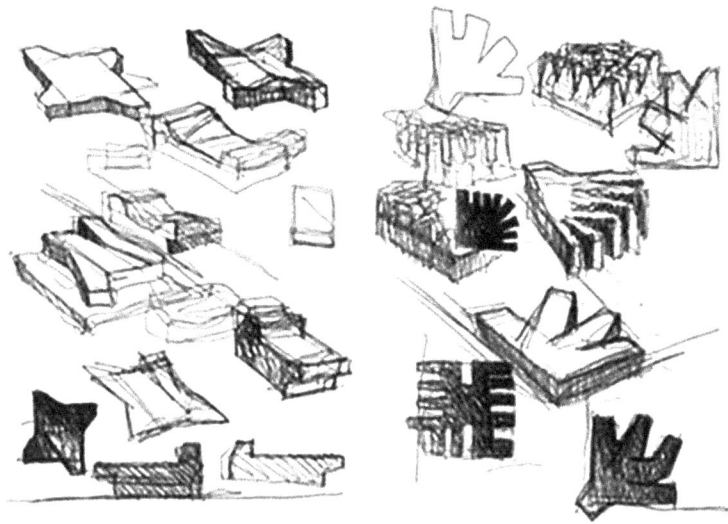

Fig. 1 Sketching allows to explore a wide variety of ideas all at once (student sketches, 2020). *Source* author

criticize and create. Considering that sketching can operate as an instrument of recognition and experimentation for the formulation and resolution of design problems (Fig. 1).

6 Conclusions

We can conclude, from several statements from various authors, as a strategy on Design Education, students should sketch from the very beginning of their education and be required to use sketches to document and develop their visual ideas.

Facing hand drawing as a daily mental activity for the performance of design practice could be a way for developing a drawing teaching strategy inserted in the reality of Design courses that aim reflection and investigation in an active pedagogy process, committed to a critical posture and enhancing in each student their own creative individuality. According to neurobiology specialists, the daily drawing practice strengthens neural networks and engages cognitive faculties at many levels, developing skills for creative solutions.

A drawing teaching strategy should be developed, inserted in nowadays design reality that aims reflection and research in an active pedagogy process, committed to a critical posture and enhancing in each student their own creative individuality.

A teaching methodology based on the concept of sketching, interconnected with the project, as an operational instrument for the conceptual process development.

Introducing a new sense of objectivity and accuracy in the Drawing course in a vision of sketching teaching, pointing to a broader freehand drawing understanding as the foundation of the design process.

Design Education should be based on an intellectual vision of Drawing as an infrastructure for the recognition of the world, promoting the development of an understanding of what we see, feel, think, idealize or want to create. Thus, developing the ability to use Drawing in the formative and operational senses. The general objectives for the discipline of Drawing based on two essential aspects: 'drawing as a way of seeing' and 'drawing as a way of thinking' to transform reality.

References

Barreira da Costa R (2019) Sketch thinking—as Ideias Não-Verbais No Território Do Design De Produto. Dissertação de Mestrado, Instituto Politécnico do Cávado e do Ave

Buchanan R (2019) In Frascara J., design education, training, and the broad picture: eight experts respond to a few questions. Retrieved from: http://www.journals.elsevier.com/she-ji-the-journal-of-design-economics-and-innovation.   https://doi.org/10.1016/j.sheji.2019.12.003, accessed on 2020.12.10

Damásio A (2012) Self comes to mind. Vintage Publishing, New York

Fish J, Scrivener S (2018) Amplifying the mind's eye: sketching and visual cognition. The MIT Press

Friedman K (2019) Design education today: challenges, opportunities, failures. In: Chatterjee Global/150th anniversary commemorative lecture, College of Design, Architecture, Art and Planning, University of Cincinnati, October 3. Retrieved from: https://www.academia.edu/40519668, accessed on 2020.12.01

Goldschmidt G (1991) The dialectics of sketching. Creat Res J 4(2):123–143. https://doi.org/10.1080/10400419109534381,accessedon2020.12.14

Kantrowitz A, Brew A, Fava M (2011) Thinking through drawing: practice into knowledge. In: Proceedings of an interdisciplinary symposium on drawing, cognition and education, N. Y. Teachers College, Columbia University (Ed.), New York

Kelley TR (2017) Design sketching: a lost skill. Technol Eng Teacher 76(8):8–12. Retrieved from https://www.search.proquest.com/docview/1913345982?ac-countid=8144%0A. http://sfx.aub.aau.dk/sfxaub?url_ver=Z39.88, accessed on 2020.12.10

Lapuerta JM (1997) El Croquis, Proyecto y Arquitectura (Scintilla Divinatis), ed. Celeste Ediciones, Madrid

Manzini E (2019) In Frascara J., Design Education, Training, and the Broad Picture: Eight Experts Respond to a Few Questions. Retrieved from: http://www.journals.elsevier.com/she-ji-the-journal-of-design-economics-and-innovation.   https://doi.org/10.1016/j.sheji.2019.12.003, accessed on 2020.12.10

Molder MFO (1995) Pensamento Morfológico de Goethe, ed. Imprensa Nacional – Casa da Moeda, Lisboa

Moreira da Silva A (2010) De Sansedoni a Vasari: um contributo para o estudo do Desenho como fundamento do processo conceptual em Arquitectura, Universidade Lusíada Editora, Lisboa

Moreira da Silva A (2017) Drawing within the design process. In Convergências - Revista de Investigação e Ensino das Artes, vol X (19). Retrieved from journal URL: http://convergencias.ipcb.pt. Accessed 2020.12.02

Oxford English Dictionary, in https://en.oxforddic-tionaries.com/ accessed on 2020.06.01

Radzikowskai M, Traynorii B, Rueckeriii S, Vaughniv N (2009) Teaching user-centered design through low-fidelity sketches. In: Proceedings of the 4th information design international conference/3rd InfoDesign Brazil/3rd Congic, Brazil

Schön DA (1983) The reflective practitioner. In The reflective practitioner. Basic Books

Sennett R (2008) The craftsman, Yale University Press

Silva J, Neves J, Raposo D (2017) Engaging students reasoning through drawing in classroom context. Reflection on an introductory module in UX design. In Convergências - Revista de Investigação e Ensino das Artes vol X (19). Retrieved from journal URL: http://convergencias. ipcb.pt, accessed on 2020.12.02

Swanson G (2020) Thinking through making. J Des Econ Innov 6(1) (Spring). Retrieved from journal URL: http://www.journals.elsevier.com/she-ji-the-journal-of-design-economics-and-innovation, accessed on 30.11.2020

Tversky B (2009) Thinking with sketches. In: Tools for innovation, pp 75–85. Oxford University Press

Waanders R, Wouter E, Maaike MN (2011) Sketching is more than making correct drawings. In: Proceedings of international conference on engineering and product design education. Faculty of Engineering Technology, University of Twente (eds) Enschede, Netherlands

Zeki S (1992) The visual image in mind and brain. In Scientific American, special edition: Mind and Brain, September. Nature Publishing Group, New York

Extending the New European Bauhaus— An Educational Initiative that is Much Needed to Transform Our Society

Jan Eckert

Abstract In 2020, the European Commission announced the launch of a New European Bauhaus aiming at collaborations between the world of art and design and the one of science and technology. The Commission deduced the need for such collaborations from the goals established in the European Green Deal and the Digital Transition. According to these goals the New European Bauhaus is meant to become a collaborative platform aiming at the redesign of our built environment and our energy clusters. Based upon a historical review and the author's observations as a design researcher and educator this text reports on the first perception of the New European Bauhaus and critically reflects the question whether referring to the original institution that had to close its doors, nearly a century ago, is still relevant. Furthermore, he sets out to understand which could be the arts and design domain's most valuable contribution to the New European Bauhaus and proposes that this contribution may lie in the art and design community's culture of creating —or in German *Entwurfskultur*—and its capacity to meet the uncertain with strategies of lifelong learning. As a conclusion, the author argues that the New European Bauhaus needs to set its aims beyond the redesign of our built environment and our energy clusters and extend to an educational initiative that transforms our society by providing the current and future generations problem-based curricula based upon lifelong and transgenerational learning.

Keywords New European Bauhaus · Lifelong learning · Problem-based learning · Entwurfskultur

J. Eckert (✉)
Faculty of Fine, Applied and Performing Arts, University of Gothenburg, Gothenburg, Sweden
e-mail: jan.eckert@gu.se

© The Author(s), under exclusive license to Springer Nature Switzerland AG 2022   117
D. Raposo et al. (eds.), *Perspectives on Design II*, Springer Series in Design and Innovation 16, https://doi.org/10.1007/978-3-030-79879-6_9

1   Introduction

In a press-statement made in September 2020, the European Commission's president Ursula Von der Leyen announced the launch of a new European Bauhaus (Von der Leyen 2020). Besides the reference to what for many people might represent our recent history's most iconic arts and crafts school her announcement stands out by shifting the attention towards the creative community in a context that usually is dominated by actors from the political sphere and the construction industry. In the light of the European Green Deal and the challenges of the Digital Transition, Von der Leyen lays out the necessity of bridging the world of science and technology with the one of arts and culture. And similar to Walter Gropius' call to unify arts and craftsmanship for the sake of good Architecture (Gropius 1919), von der Leyen sees great potential to tackle the upcoming renovation wave, together as designers, architects, artists or digital experts, scientists, entrepreneurs, students, engineers and many more (comp. Von der Leyen 2020).

Von der Leyen calls the initiative an experimentation space that is meant to provide a "forum for discussion, a lab for experimentation, an accelerator for finding solutions and a hub for global networks and experts" (ibid.). This conceptual space is planned to unfold in three phases: The first one called "design phase" is meant to explore ideas and create a movement. The second one that Von der Leyen calls "delivery phase" includes the starting point of five major European Bauhaus projects—later on in the discussion these projects are also referred to as *hubs*. And finally, a third phase aims at the dissemination of ideas, projects and outcomes as well as at opportunities to grow the Bauhaus beyond Europe's borders. In January 2021, the three phases have been complemented with the announcement of a New European Bauhaus Prize (European Commission 2021a, b) that is meant to foster competition during the first phase.

But what drives a highly influential politician to launch an initiative meant to tackle some of the most complex problems of our days by referring to an arts and crafts institution that was forced to shut down, nearly a century ago? This chapter will dive into this question by asking three follow-up questions that regard the creative community[1] itself: Firstly, if in 2021, the Bauhaus still represents a common ground to initiate collaborations between arts, design and science: how

---

[1]In this text I refer to several domains such as arts, design, music, performing arts, architecture or similar with the term *creative community*. By using this term, I mainly refer to Ursula von der Leyen's call to join people originating from the domain of design, architecture, arts or digital experts (comp. Von der Leyen, 2020) and I am perfectly aware that there are both profound differences between these disciplines and other disciplines outside the creative domain that are in their own way very creative (e.g. a molecular biologist developing a new vaccine). For the sake of a better understanding I don't intend to dive into a discussion about the differences between design and art or architecture – there are sure, many ones – but with regards to other disciplines and sectors mentioned in the call for a New European Bauhaus, these disciplines can and will be summarised in this text as *creative community* – a term that also relates to the Creative Economy including many of the mentioned disciplines.

can the creative community keep this commitment alive and avoid the New European Bauhaus being shut down as it happened both to the original Bauhaus or about 30 years later to the HfG Ulm? Secondly, what might be the creative community's most valuable contribution to a New European Bauhaus? And thirdly, which challenges come with this contribution and how might the creative community address these?

2   First Perception of the New European Bauhaus

It took some weeks for the creative community to respond to Von der Leyen's announcement—which proves that to most creatives the European Commission's call came rather as a surprise. Admittedly, it does not happen on a daily base that an archaeologist, medical doctor and highly reputable politician takes an initiative to foster the collaboration between sciences and arts—in fact, an initiative that could or should have come from the creative community, itself.

But soon, the New European Bauhaus started getting discussed and thanks to the new digital skills that the community acquired due to the pandemic, very quickly a series of online platforms popped up to do so. Amongst them a series of webinars or video call panels that all together were discussing the launch of a New European Bauhaus. Across these panels, webinars or talks two main reactions appeared to dominate the discussion.

One is the critique of a euro-centric view that is incorporated into the launch of a European-based Bauhaus—a critique that in the Dutch arts and design community even led to a petition calling for a more inclusive and less *colonising* approach of a New Bauhaus.

The second one, instead, appeared to be very supportive and trying to appreciate the European Commission's commitment to the creative community. This second response resulted in a series of statements such as the one published by the Architect's Council of Europe and other European associations (ACE et al. 2020) offering their help as networks for a holistic approach to tackle the challenges of the future built environment as stated in the New European Bauhaus' call.

Yet, another topic popped up in this first phase of discussing the New European Bauhaus. It could be described as a *race for the five hubs* that according to Ursula Von der Leyen are planned to be founded in the second phase of the New European Bauhaus' launch. Many representatives of the creative community started laying out their reasons for why their country or institution would be just a perfect match for becoming one of the five hubs. Unfortunately, this last aspect shows how much the arts and design community still depends on economic support and at the same time also reveals some of the narcissistic attitude that seems to be very common amongst some representants of the creative community—some of them hoping to step into Gropius' shoes and founding his or her own *little Bauhaus*. Needless to say, that this second aspect that has dominated quite a big part of the initial discussion, represents a rather poor reaction to what really is a great commitment to the European creative community.

All in all, it is astonishing though, how after just a few months, the New European Bauhaus triggered a rich discussion amongst people from all over Europe —even in times that are dominated by topics that could not be further away from the creative community as a main driver in tackling the challenges of our future.

3 *Ist das Bauhaus noch aktuell?* Is the Bauhaus Still Relevant?

As a design researcher and educator, I was trying to follow the creative community's first discussion about the New European Bauhaus, the best I could. Especially, because due to the large number of events taking place even at the same time (given that most of them were happening online) it was not always possible to keep track of the entire picture that was and still is evolving around the topic.

Yet, the first discussion triggered a question to me—and most likely to many others in the creative domain: is the launch of the New European Bauhaus a call from the past, or is it the most promising initiative for the creative community in a long time? Is it another try to commit to the creative realm just to realise, few years later, that some of its radical proposals are reaching out too far or the funds have been used up and it's time to cease the collaboration, again? And historically speaking I am not only referring to the shutdown of the Staatliche Bauhaus. After the original Bauhaus' shutdown other great European institutions such as the HfG Ulm in Germany or Ivrea Interaction Institute in Italy had to shut down after just being active for few years. Without mentioning many art or design schools that had to merge with other institutions to fit into the post-Bolognese system of European higher education.

And since it is not the first time in history that the creative domain receives such an attention, also the question whether referring to the Bauhaus as an appropriate model is not a new one, either. In his 1963 essay called „Ist das Bauhaus aktuell?" former HfG Ulm director, Tomás Maldonado, is asking the same question and argues:

> History repeats itself. If one were to transplant the Bauhaus of 1923, with the same people and the same ideas, to the Germany of 1963, it would undoubtedly be attacked with the same arguments that were used against the Bauhaus forty years ago and against the HfG, a few months ago. (author's translation from German,[2] (Maldonado 1963).

---

[2]Original text in German Maldonado (1963): "Die Geschichte wiederholt sich. Wenn das Bauhaus von 1923 mit denselben Persönlichkeiten und mit denselben Ideen von damals verpflanzt würde in das Deutschland von 1963, dann würde es heute sicher angegriffen werden mit denselben Argumenten, die vor 40 Jahren gegen das Bauhaus und vor wenigen Monaten gegen die HfG gebraucht wurden."

Forty-six years later, Maldonado got invited to speak at the ninetieth anniversary of the original Bauhaus' foundation and picks up the question, again: „Ist das Bauhaus noch aktuell?" Originally written in Italian and translated by Gui Bonsiepe and Constanza Pratesi into German, Maldonado decides to read his speech and being an experienced and excellent speaker, before he begins with his talk, he apologises for this fact to the audience. A few paragraphs later and for a second time in history, he concludes very quickly that:

> Personally, I am more and more convinced that the time has come to acknowledge, without nostalgia, without false remorse, the fact that the Bauhaus, as an institutional model, has ceased to be relevant, and this for the simple reason that it is no longer suited to providing adequate responses to the urgent needs of our time. (author's translation form Italian,[3] Maldonado 2009)

The fact that one of the most (if not the most) important thinkers in the design domain emphasises twice in history that the Bauhaus can no longer be considered as a role model for design and arts education might come as a very pessimistic conclusion to many inside and beyond the creative community. Even if most of us might know about Maldonado's ongoing critique on the Bauhaus and his arguments with former Bauhaus student Max Bill or his exchange of letters with Walter Gropius, his affirmation seems to wipe away all too much of the glory that many people connect to the famous institution. But besides his conclusion about the Bauhaus no longer being up to date, in his anniversary speech, Maldonado continues and provides us a key to what according to him is the Bauhaus' most important heritage:

> Nevertheless, even if we admit that the Bauhaus is no longer relevant, one question is almost obligatory: if this is really the case, as I believe it is, why does the Bauhaus still continue to be the object of widespread interest, why have we found ourselves here today, in Weimar, in the place where it all began, celebrating the 90th anniversary of its foundation? Everyone will have an own answer. Mine is very clear: what still binds me deeply to the Bauhaus today is not so much the thousands of small or large things that are usually attributed to it, but rather the great lesson that the protagonists of the Bauhaus - *the Bauhäusler* - have bequeathed to us. And that is the inalienable desire to try, with all means, to give socially and culturally innovative answers to the needs of the historical phase in which we are destined to live. (author's translation from Italian,[4] Maldonado 2009)

---

[3]Original text in Italian (Maldonado 2009): "Personalmente, sono sempre più convinto che sia arrivato il momento di riconoscere senza nostalgie, senza finti rimorsi, il fatto che il Bauhaus, come modello istituzionale, ha finito di essere attuale, e questo per il semplice motivo che non è più adatto a fornire risposte adeguate alle incalzanti esigenze del nostro tempo."

[4]Original text in Italian (Maldonado 2009, 2019): "Ciò nonostante, pur ammettendo che il Bauhaus non sia più attuale, una domanda è quasi d'obbligo: se è veramente così, come io credo, perché il Bauhaus continua a essere ancora oggetto di un interesse diffuso, perché ci siamo trovati oggi a festeggiare qui, a Weimar, nel luogo in cui tutto è cominciato, il suo 90° anniversario della fondazione? Ognuno avrà la sua risposta. La mia è molto chiara: ciò che ancora oggi mi lega profondamente al Bauhaus non sono tanto le mille piccole o grandi cose che di solito gli vengono riconosciute, ma piuttosto la grande lezione che i protagonisti del Bauhaus – i *Bauhäusler* – ci hanno lasciato in eredità. E cioè l'irrinunciabile voglia di cercare, con tutti i mezzi, di dare risposte

If we put Maldonado's thought on the Bauhaus' heritage into the context of today's call for a new European Bauhaus it becomes clear that the aspect of searching for socially and culturally innovative answers that he mentions might just stand at the core of the European Commission's invitation to the creative community joining the realms of technology, engineering and science: joining different approaches towards research and development for a more sustainable future—just as the Bauhaus managed to join artists, craftspeople and architects to focus on the art of building. From this angle the New European Bauhaus appears to be just as up to date as the original Bauhaus or other institutions have been, decades ago. But what's about the challenges or the mission that has to be faced, this time and according to the European Commission?

4   Fighting Symptoms Will Not Be Enough—Why We Need to Establish a Genuine *Entwurfskultur*

Even if in some follow-up documents that have been provided after the Ursula Von der Leyen's press announcement, the New European Bauhaus is referred to as "an environmental, economic and cultural project for Europe" (European Commission 2021a), the initial call seems to focus mainly on the upcoming renovation wave and the built environment. Which, by referring to Gropius' original Bauhaus Manifesto and its focus on the art of building (Gropius 1919) makes a lot of sense from a historical point of view. But announcing a New European Bauhaus and focusing the built environment as a key to meet the challenges of the Green Deal and the Digital Transition, for me, only represents part of the problem and could be described as symptoms of human behaviour in its natural habitat and built environment. Most of the problems caused by the act of constantly extending our artificial habitat cannot be resolved or reversed by simply retro-fitting the facades of our buildings, the redesign of our energy clusters or by fostering the use of new building materials. Even if these areas represent important starting points for the change that is so much needed, real change needs to happen somewhere else: by educating people to rethink and develop a new collective behaviour and attitude towards both our natural and artificial habitat. And I believe that compared to the launch of a series of highly-funded research initiatives meant to feed one of Europe's strongest economic sectors—the construction industry contributes about 9% of the EU's GDP (European Commission 2021b)—an educational initiative would represent a far more promising perspective of the New European Bauhaus. It could not only transform our current built environment but being part of our future society's transformation as a whole.

---

socialmente e culturalmente innovative alle esigenze della fase storica in cui ci tocca in sorte di vivere."

Recently, two colleagues of mine and I were reflecting the role of art and design schools in the context of today's VUCA world (Volatile, Uncertain, Complex, Ambigue) (Eckert et al. 2021). I our paper, we also reach back in history and try to outline whether the situation that the original Bauhaus was facing in 1919 was less uncertain than the one we are facing right now. And our conclusion was that, in fact, it is not—right in the contrary: when it comes to complexity, many of yesterday's problems got amplified by today's network society, the huge media landscape that provides access to information in real-time, an increase in mobility or global markets that got more and more interdependent. So even if in the nineteen twenties at the advent of Germany's first democratic republic or when the HfG Ulm got founded, 1953, in post-war Germany people had to tackle a certain level of complexity, one major aspect that drives today's complexity is that it extends beyond geographical or cultural borders. And perhaps that's one reason why the term *European* in the New European Bauhaus, initially has been criticised so much for a reason.

But more importantly, today's problems extend way beyond sectors or disciplinary borders. Instead of understanding the future of building or energy distribution and trying to transform our society from that perspective, today, we need to understand clusters of problems that are triggered by multiple drivers originating from a variety of starting points: human behaviour, its consequences such as the ongoing climate change, global consumption and global markets, their impact on inequality, our human society's relationship with an extending artificial and technological reality and our natural cosmos, and many more of these correlations.

While the original Bauhaus might have aimed at a transformation happening from inside out—transforming our world through good architecture, aesthetics and design—the New European Bauhaus needs to take on the question how we can collaboratively meet today's problems from a holistic point of view—from the outside of collective human behaviour towards the inside of concrete problems such as e.g., the energy consumption of our built environment. This is the reason why I see the New European Bauhaus' biggest potential and mission in its extension to an educational dimension: if we really want to keep the initiative going (and not shutting it down as soon as all awards have been assigned and the five hubs used up their funds) then the European Bauhaus really needs to extend into the transformation of our society and namely its educational system as a whole. Because due to the complexity of the problems that we are facing, today, the present and next generation will not be enough, anymore. Consequently, educating upcoming generations of change agents will be necessary to work on a long-term turnaround of the human society living in its fragile habitat. And educating future generations is a realm, where the creative domain can contribute a lot, if not the most, compared to the variety of issues tied to the call of the New European Bauhaus.

5   Transforming Our Society Through Education

In the previous section of this chapter, I laid out the reasons why I am convinced that the creative community's biggest contribution to the New European Bauhaus should not primarily and exclusively be the redesign of our built environment or the way energy is produced, distributed and used but rather the transformation of our society through education. I am well aware that reflecting upon education and the educational system as a whole would by far exceed the scope of this text. But in the following paragraphs I will try to outline what according to my experience as a design educator might be valuable perspectives that the creative community could feed into the redesign of our educational models.

I would like to start doing so by focusing the relationship between our educational system and its connection to the job world. Now, without stressing the term *employability*, too much, the transition into a professional future still represents the life phase that most likely follows up once people leave their educational pathway —and it is also the phase where people first unfold and apply their acquired knowledge and skills by facing real-world problems such as the ones mentioned in the call for the New European Bauhaus. Additionally, more and more people complement their learning biography by updating their skills and knowledge (e.g., by taking further education courses or certificates) in order to maintain their interaction with the job world. Consequently, two questions that we need to ask when talking about the future of our educational system are: How do we continue preparing people for their transition into a fast-changing job world that is exposed to a variety of dynamic and complex problems? Or from a more appropriate perspective of lifelong learning: how do we make sure people can update their knowledge and skills to stay and move on in their professional biography?

And in fact, the question about the relationship between what knowledge, skills and competencies we are able to build up in today's educational system and tomorrow's jobs is one that received more and more attention, during the past few years. Even if because of their political conviction some of my colleagues in the creative community do not like to refer to events and platforms such as the Word Economic Forum, the studies conducted by these platforms thoroughly analyse the job world on a regular base and provide an important overview over the development of work as a whole, professional fields, new disciplines or even the post-disciplinary future that we start facing, right now. When examining these studies from a design and arts point of view, two aspects appear to be very interesting. One is that the arts and design domain is very much considered when talking about the future of the job and business world. The "The Future of Jobs" (World Economic Forum 2016) report, for instance, states that "the combination of arts and science skills within businesses (is) a key feature of many parts of the Creative Industries". A fact which gets also linked to "6% higher employment growth and 8% higher sales growth" in an independent review of the creative industries in the UK by Peter Balzagette (2017).

Another finding that studies such as the "Future of Jobs Report" (World Economic Forum 2016, 2018), or the "Jobs of Tomorrow Report" (World Economic Forum 2020) continue stating is the insight that, while we might be able to track or predict occupation as a whole, we know less and less about the characteristics of future jobs or even the skillset and knowledge needed to perform in these jobs. Last year's "Jobs of Tomorrow Report" (World Economic Forum 2020) states in its first part:

> Over the next decade, a non-negligible share of newly created jobs will be in job openings for wholly new occupations, or for existing occupations undergoing significant transformations in terms of their job content and skills requirements (World Economic Forum 2020, 6).

To meet this uncertainty about the characteristics of future jobs an earlier report published by the World Economic Forum called "Towards a Reskilling Revolution: Industry-Led Action for the Future of Work" proposes "a skill-based hiring system focused on lifelong learning and flexible accreditation for navigating transitions in the labour market" (World Economic Forum 2019). It doesn't come as a surprise that such a dynamic and volatile development of the job world is putting the educational system more and more under pressure. But what could be an appropriate answer to this fast-evolving development? And asking the same question in the context of the New European Bauhaus and this text: if we agree that besides redesigning our built environment, we need to transform our society through education—what might be the creative community's contribution to the increasing uncertainty about the future of jobs and the education needed to prepare people for these jobs?

According to my experience as a design educator I mainly see two components or attitudes that we can feed into this emerging void as designers, artists, musicians, performing artists, architects or similar. One is the fact that as designers or artists we are trained to meet the unknown with critical thinking and by stating hypotheses that we are, then, able to turn into functioning prototypes of what we could call *hypothetical futures*. A very good colleague of mine, coach and service design expert, Andrew Polaine once reflected on this ability and during a panel discussion with some of my former MA students, he called it the *superpower* that designers bring into business and society: being able to deal with the uncertain and unknown with processes of design that combine methods able to deal with both hard and soft facts—something that many other sciences struggle a lot with.

In German there is a wonderful term that describes this act of projecting hypotheses in context and time and verifying them by considering soft and hard evidence—it is called *Entwurf*. And by the way, this is a term that has been also widely used by Tomás Maldonado, whom I cited, earlier in this text. There is another speech that he held at the 50th anniversary of the HfG Ulm's foundation where he explains what according to him could be a future *Entwurfskultur* that unifies people from different sectors and disciplines—people from both the world of arts and design and the one of technology and science (comp. Maldonado 2003). In other words: establishing a genuine *Entwurfskultur* and incorporating it into our educational models relates a lot to the core idea of the New European Bauhaus. And this is truly something the creative community can feed into this venture.

A second attitude that could represent a major contribution to the New European Bauhaus is the creative community's ability to adopt to constantly changing situations with strategies of (lifelong) learning. As artists, architects or designers, we are used to the fact, that mostly there isn't any *constant truth* that our work can relate to. Most of our work is characterised by changing contexts or the fact that depending on the project that we work on, we need to reach out to acquire new skills or gather information that we turn into applicable knowledge serving to conclude our project in a given context. So, what to other disciplines might come as a huge challenge due to changing metrics, emerging technologies or changing contexts, comes very natural to someone who has studied design, architecture or arts—designers, architects or artists are naturally lifelong learners!

Therefore, I see the creative community's biggest contribution to what is being discussed as the New European Bauhaus in re-thinking our educational models by integrating a genuine *Entwurfskultur* into our educational approaches and by sharing and developing strategies of lifelong learning. And by reflecting the question, whether the Bauhaus is still up to date as a model, again, the educational dimension that I tried to outline perfectly relates to Maldonado's notion on the Bauhaus' most important heritage of the creative community's "inalienable desire to try, with all means, to give socially and culturally innovative answers to the needs of the historical phase in which we are destined to live." (Maldonado 2009).

Why one the one hand this comes very natural to us as designers, architects or artists has been laid out in this section. Why it also comes with a huge challenge, on the other, will be discussed in the next one.

6   Stepping Out of Its Shoes—The Creative Community's Biggest Challenge

The big challenge, that in my eyes has been mostly ignored in the first discussion about the New European Bauhaus is the aim of "bridging the world of science and technology with the one of arts and culture" (Von der Leyen 2020). It sure represents an important perspective that in many cases and some places is being practiced, already. But if we take an honest look at the creative community and especially at arts and design schools: only few of them are really capable of forging people that are able to work across arts and design and other domains such as humanities, natural sciences or engineering by pursuing common goals and without exclusively aiming at an artistic outcome. There sure is some outstanding exceptions but few design or arts curricula include e.g., the history of technology, psychology, social sciences, ethics, ethnography, cultural studies or even computer sciences and physics to help young creatives to develop a vocabulary and skillset to collaborate with other domains by sharing common goals.

And according to my experience when studying or teaching at schools of economy or engineering, instead, it also happens the other way around: besides the wide-spread belief that teaching *design thinking* or *design sprints* to business administrators, managers or computer engineers is enough to turn them into *creatives* or even enable them to communicate with people from the arts and design community, there are few curricula that offer their learners a proper spectre of subjects that convey real knowledge and skills in the arts and design domain.

Therefore, both sides find themselves in a dilemma: it appears clearly, that today's and tomorrow's problems can only be met with a post-disciplinary, problem-based and holistic approach. Yet, we continue to learn and study in silos represented by schools, faculties, departments, disciplines or courses. Specialising in a disciplinary field is necessary when dealing with the deepness of a problem, yet most of our curricula lack to provide learning spaces that enable people to learn how to meet constantly changing contexts, cultures and issues or namely how to collaboratively engage with other experts in order to work on holistic solutions—and I don't refer to the so-called *interdisciplinary* teaching projects that, very often, just combine learners from e.g., visual communication with those from product design or building engineers that work together with architects—these are, indeed, disciplines that gather in one and the same silo, anyways.

Especially, the creative community tends to stick to an outdated and self-perceived image of the artists, architect or designer as author and individual creator of future artefacts, environments or systems. This mental image reaches back centuries in time. One of the fundamental works about the art of building, Marcus Vitruvius Pollio's „De Architectura" refers to the architect as the *head* that needs to consider knowledge from a wide spectre of disciplines (Vitruvius 1987)—an individual, who integrates a variety of knowledge in order to exceed in the art of building. But today, we have to admit that even designing a future-proof building exceeds the capacities of a single human being or even just one discipline. And yet, most of the schools of architecture that I got to know as both student or educator mainly or partially stick to the idea that the figure of the architect is the most crucial one in an architectural project (even if considering that most of the decision-making is made long before launching a building project by people involved in urban planning and urban politics). And the same applies to many schools of arts and design: the image of the designer as a "the *Gestalter* as guru and ingenious shaman, endowed with the magical gift of conjuring truths out of nothing for an astonished audience." (author's translation from German,[5] Pfeffer 2014) in many places is still the main role model or mental image that rules the curricula of the creative domain.

In a recent series of articles that have been published in two special issues on design education in SheJi Journal, amongst others, Michael W. Meyer and Donald

---

[5]Original Text in German: "Der Gestalter als Guru und genialer Schamane, der mit der magischen Gabe ausgestattet ist, aus dem Nichts Wahrheiten für ein staunendes Publikum hervorzuzaubern." (Pfeffer 2014).

Norman analyse a series of design curricula and compare them to some in the non-design domain. One of their findings is that:

> The combination of a degree in a traditional university subject— which provides a broad general education plus an in-depth education in a non-design topic—coupled with a minor in design produces a more powerful, insightful designer (...) than those who have had four years of design studies with no depth in any other discipline. (Meyer and Norman 2020)

What is expressed in these few lines, really represents one of the creative domain's major challenges: most arts and design institutions are stuck in an out-dated self-perception of *the creative* and have a very hard time to step out of this mental model and connect to curricula in other domains.

Besides the two potential contributions that I outlined in the previous section of this chapter, I think this shift in its self-perception is the main challenge that the creative community needs to face when joining the initiative of the New European Bauhaus: stepping out of the traditional mental model of the artists, architect or designer and leaving space for a new designer, architect and artist to come—one that constantly adopts to ever changing contexts, embeds into networks of collaborations, facilitates meeting the unknown or helps to establish what before has been discussed as *Entwurfskultur*.

Those readers, who know me and/or have followed some of my publications in the past years (Eckert and Mason 2010; Eckert 2018, 2020) will recognise that regarding many points that have been brought up in this text I keep repeating myself. This text, indeed, is an opinion peace that is based upon both my experience as a design researcher and educator and the thorough observation of the creative domain during the past decade of doing research in design education. But this repetition of stating that the creative realm needs to unlearn—to re-invent itself—is not based upon self-reference. It is simply the observation that amongst other disciplines we have reached the zenith of what is possibly done when staying in your own community. And besides its focus on the Green Deal and the Digital Transition the call for a New European Bauhaus is mainly about the fact that we need to accept leaving our silos and collaborate together—if we take this call seriously it might be the arts and design domain's biggest lesson learned for more than a century.

7 Concluding Thoughts

This text started off with the critical reflection of the first reactions to the European Commission's call for a New European Bauhaus. It in fact represents an own form of critique by asking the question: which could be the creative community's most suitable contribution to this venture in order to keep the European Commission's commitment alive for a longer period of time than it happened to the original Bauhaus, the HfG Ulm or other important arts and design institutions.

The text's main critique that ties up to the question whether the Bauhaus is still relevant, is the notion that simply sticking to the common image of the Bauhaus is not enough to meet today's problems, anymore. A critique that already has been thoroughly laid out by one of the most important thinkers in design, Tomás Maldonado, decades ago. According to him, the Bauhaus' real heritage that should be taken into account when referring to this historic institution is the attitude of continuously searching and researching for "socially and culturally innovative answers to the needs of the historical phase in which we are destined to live." (Maldonado 2009). An attitude that includes meeting the uncertain with the projection and evaluation of hypotheses in context and time by trying to manifest those that can be regarded as viable and valid at the present time. A process that is perfectly described by the term *Entwurfskultur* and in my opinion represents one of the major contributions of the creative community to the New European Bauhaus.

A second point that has been critically reflected in this text is the New European Bauhaus' initial focus on the built environment. It sure represents a starting point that potentially connects a large number of actors. But while mostly dealing with the symptoms of collective human behaviour it will not be enough to tackle the challenges of our times. Therefore, I tried to lay out that the real transformation should not only happen at the facades of our towns and cities but inside the core of our society: educating future generations to avoid what has been built or designed in the past. And since one generation will not be enough, we'll need to face the ever-changing context of learning with strategies of lifelong or even transgenerational learning. Which is the second area where thanks to its own capacities the creative community can feed in a great contribution.

Finally, I can only emphasise that the European Commission's initiative to launch a New European Bauhaus first and foremost is a great commitment to the arts and design domain. A commitment that needs to be handled with care, since it also holds the risk to repeat what happened before in history when great commitments to the creative domain have been withdrawn and great institutions such as the Staatliche Bauhaus or the HfG Ulm had to close their doors. Therefore, all involved actors are invited to thoroughly examine what, in-fact, could be a relevant New Bauhaus that in my option needs to extend beyond the initial idea of funding initiatives that aim at a redesign of our built environment. In my eyes the most promising extension is represented by re-thinking our European educational model —and the creative domain sure has a lot to contribute to this venture by starting to re-think arts and design education, itself. And by doing so the New European Bauhaus could not only extend its contribution beyond today's and tomorrow's generations, but it could also reacquire a humanistic view on our civilisation—a view that, nearly sixty years ago, has been pointed out by Tomás Maldonado as the *Bauhaus* that might be the most relevant, at the time and at our time, again:

> When we say that the Bauhaus is relevant again today, we are thinking of another Bauhaus. Namely, a Bauhaus that was often proclaimed but hardly ever realised; that was unable to unfold; that at the time set out, albeit without success, to uncover a humanistic view of our technical civilisation, i.e., to consider the human environment as a new „*Entwurfsfeld*". To a Bauhaus that at the time tried, albeit equally unsuccessfully, to orient Germany towards

an open and forward-looking culture. This Bauhaus, precisely this Bauhaus, is topical for us again today. (author's translation from German,[6] Maldonado 1963)

References

ACE—Architect's Council of Europe et al (2020) The New European Bauhaus. Making the renovation wave a cultural project. Retrieved December 2020 from: https://www.ace-cae.eu/fileadmin/user_upload/BH_statement_FINAL-2.pdf

Balzagette P (2017) Independent review of the creative industries. Retrieved January 2021 from: https://www.gov.uk/government/publications/independent-review-of-the-creative-industries

European Commission (2021a) Our Conversations will shape our tomorrow—The European Commission's European Bauhaus Website. Retrieved January 2021 from: https://europa.eu/new-european-bauhaus/index_en

European Commission (2021b) Internal market, industry, entrepreneurship and SMEs. Retrieved January 2021 from: https://ec.europa.eu/growth/sectors_en

Eckert J (2018) Leading the conversation—why design education should care more about leadership and stewardship in design. In: Cumulus Paris 2018—to get there: designing together, Paris, France

Eckert J (2020) Why design schools should take the lead in design education. In: Raposo D, Neves J, Silva J (eds) Perspectives on design: research and practice in communication design, fashion design, interior design, product design and intersection areas. Springer—Design and Innovation (SSDI) Epstein, D. (2019). Range—Why Generalists triumph in a specialized world, Penguin

Eckert J, Mason M (2010) From social relevances to design issues. Swiss Design Network Symposium, Basel

Eckert J, Junginger S, Noël G (2021) Rethinking & appropriating design education for a VUCA world: a conversation. CUMULUS, Rome

Gropius W (1919) Bauhaus Manifest. Retrieved, February 2020 from: http://www.dnk.de/_uploads/media/186_1919_Bauhaus.pdf

Maldonado T (1963) Ist das Bauhaus aktuell? In "ulm", 8/9, 1963, pp 5–13. Retrieved in January 2021 from: https://campus.burg-halle.de/id-neuwerk/24-short-films-about-design/wp-content/uploads/sites/31/2014/05/8-BauhausAktuell_Maldonado-1963.pdf Re-edited and complemented with its first part from Wingler (1974) From *Avanguardia e razionalità*, Einaudi, Torino 1974, pp. 156–161. Recently published in Riccini, R. (Ed.) (2019) *Bauhaus*. Feltrinelli Editore Milano.

Maldonado T (2003) «Design», Gestaltung, Entwurf – neue Inhalte. In Bonsiepe G (ed) Digitale Welt und Gestaltung. Pp 363–374. Birkhäuser, Basel

Maldonado T (2009) Ist das Bauhaus noch aktuell? Written in Italian and translated into German by Gui Bonsiepe and Costanza Pratesi. In "der bogen", Special Issue for the 90th Anniversary

---

[6]Original German text in (Maldonado 1963): Wenn wir sagen, dass das Bauhaus heute erneut aktuell ist, denken wir an ein anderes Bauhaus. Und zwar an ein Bauhaus, das oftmals proklamiert, aber kaum realisiert wurde; das sich nicht entfalten konnte; das sich seinerzeit vorgenommen hatte, wenngleich ohne Erfolg, eine humanistische Sicht auf die technische Zivilisation freizulegen, d. h. die menschliche Umwelt als ein neues „konkretes Entwurfsfeld" zu betrachten. An ein Bauhaus, das seinerzeit versuchte, wenngleich ebenso ohne Erfolg, Deutschland an einer offenen und nach vorn gerichteten Kultur zu orientieren. Dieses Bauhaus, genau dieses Bauhaus, ist heute für uns wieder aktuell.

of the Bauhaus foundation, 1, 2009, pp. 7–11. Re-edited in Italian in Riccini R (ed) (2019) Bauhaus. Feltrinelli Editore Milano

Meyer MW, Norman D (2020) changing design education for the 21st Century. She ji J Des Econ Innov 6(1): 13–49 (Spring)

Pfeffer F (2014) To Do: Die neue Rolle der Gestaltung in einer veränderten Welt: Strategien | Werkzeuge | Geschäftsmodelle. Schmidt, H, Mainz (24. April 2014). p. 20, 29

Vitruvius MP, Bücher B 1–10, Wyss B (Herausgeber), Rode A (Übersetzung) (1987) Birkhäuser Verlag; Auflage: 1. Aufl. 1987. Nachdruck (1. Januar 1987). Buch I. S. 12

Von der Leyen U (2020) Press statement by president von der Leyen on the new European Bauhaus retrieved, September 2020 from: https://www.youtube.com/watch?v=2bO8KPbzc8s &feature=emb_title

World Economic Forum (2016) The future of jobs—employment, skills and workforce strategy for the fourth industrial revolution. Retrieved January 2021 from: http://reports.weforum.org/future-of-jobs-2016/

World Economic Forum (2018) The future of jobs report. Retrieved January 2021 from: https://www.weforum.org/reports/the-future-of-jobs-report-2018

World Economic Forum (2019) Towards a reskilling revolution: industry-led action for the future of work. Retrieved January 2021 from: https://www.weforum.org/whitepapers/towards-a-reskilling-revolution-industry-led-action-for-the-future-of-work

World Economic Forum (2020) Jobs of tomorrow—mapping opportunity in the new economy. Retrieved January 2021 from: https://www.weforum.org/reports/jobs-of-tomorrow-mapping-opportunity-in-the-new-economy

Inclusive Blueprint: Designing New Blueprint Tracks to Include People with Disabilities

Diego Normandi⬤ and Cibele Taralli⬤

Abstract The Service Design is a growing professional and academic field. It is characterized by a holistic and interdisciplinary approach with focus on the processes of co-creation and co-production. It also has as one of the most emblematic tools the Service Blueprint. Nonetheless, the field still presents a gap in the proposition of tools and inclusive processes for disabled people, especially blind and deaf ones. In this paper, we propose the reflection of disabled people inclusion in the development of services, as well as we approach the Service Blueprint as an important tool, suggesting the addition of inclusive and accessible perspectives among its classic components.

Keywords Service design · Inclusion · People with disability · Disabled people · Service blueprint

1 Introduction/Contextualization

The idea of this article came out from a broader doctoral research about the inclusion of people with disabilities in cinemas. In the mentioned research, through the Service Design we sought strategies and models to enable the stimulation and use of cinema projection spaces by disabled people.

The referred research took place in Brazil, where the engagement of people with motor disability (people with para or tetraplegia, for example) is already a current practice in cinemas. On the other hand, people with sensory disability (deaf and blind ones) are still out of this kind of environment. We consider that the Brazilian

D. Normandi (✉) · C. Taralli
University of São Paulo, São Paulo, Brazil
e-mail: diegonmd@usp.br

C. Taralli
e-mail: cibelet@usp.br

© The Author(s), under exclusive license to Springer Nature Switzerland AG 2022
D. Raposo et al. (eds.), *Perspectives on Design II*, Springer Series in Design and Innovation 16, https://doi.org/10.1007/978-3-030-79879-6_10

133

legislation, due to the guidelines that regulate the civil construction in the country,[1] offer interesting conditions for the access of people with motor impairment not only in cinemas, but in other forms of entertainment (theaters, shopping centers, museums, exhibitions, etc.). In relation to people with sensory disabilities, however, even though there are feasible and accessible tools, these people are not yet included successfully.

Regarding the access to cinemas, some technologies were developed, regulated and their installation process started, to enable blind or deaf people to have access to the movies that are shown.[2] However, such devices represent only one example of access needs for the mentioned audience, which is: interaction with the accessible content[3] through devices. Other somewhat obvious needs have not been embraced by legislation that obliged accessibility in Brazilian cinemas for 2020. Among the needs neglected by both the cinema and market are the following three:

1. The access to box-office information: the movie theaters do not offer accessible systems that provide information about the movies that are playing, the prices of the tickets, the session times etc.;
2. Ticket purchase and treats: there is no definition about selling patterns that provide the best conditions for autonomy and security of the audience with sensory disabilities. In some cases, reported and noticed during our field research, for example, we attested that many places display automated teller machines without keys (touch-sensitive), which compromises the security during interaction, as, for example, a blind user is forced to inform his/her card password to pay using credit or debit.
3. Conduct and safety information: cinemas that provide videos with instructions on how to use the rooms and safety instructions do not offer information accessible to the public with sensory disabilities, nor information regarding the emergency actions focused on this kind of audience; among other barriers that cinema services in Brazil seem to neglect.

Derived from the desire to include people with different motor and sensory conditions in the cinema, we reflected that Service Design—SD could give us the conditions to design an inclusive service, as the search field assumes a holistic approach, and also embrace the problems faced from different perspectives. Nevertheless, as we will see in this paper, the SD did not present itself as an inclusive approach, whose tools for exploring problems, visualizing processes, proposing, prototyping and evaluating solutions, no matter how diverse and varied, do not take the possibility of integration of people with sensory disabilities neither in the development crew, nor as a target audience.

---

[1]Specially the NBR9050 (ABNT 2020).

[2]In Brazil, two devices were developed and approved by the regulatory agency Agência Nacional de Cinema – ANCINE for the use in cinemas. They are called: ProAccess and CineAssista.

[3]Audio description, for people with visual impairment, Brazilian Sign Language window (Brazilian Sign Language- LIBRAS) and/or descriptive subtitling for people with hearing impairment.

Thus, in this article we focused on one of the most traditional tools of Service Design, the Service Blueprint, in order to present it, discuss it, evaluate it in relation to its inclusion ability, and suggest changes in its format, so that we can promote access for people with sensory disabilities to interact satisfactorily with the resource.

2 The Service Design

The task of finding a categoric definition of Service Design seems hard at first, considering the expansion of activities in the area in recent years. In fact, it is not our objective to deal with this issue in this paper, as there are many authors who have basis for that. Nevertheless, we consider that defining terms, concepts, or at least the boundaries of the field itself is an important step. We argue that proposing definitions allows a minimal understanding of the limits between what something is and what it is not. Stickdorn et al. (2018a) has considered such debate peripheral in the field in comparison to what has been considered relevant. According to him, the most important thing is not simply translating into words what would define Service Design, but to keep in mind the results that the processes related to the SD can deliver.

In 2016, Stickdorn carried out a survey with 150 service designers, asking them to conceptualize the topic. After collecting the answers, the author sent them to the same respondents, asking them to vote for the definitions that seemed most appropriate to them. Among the most accepted responses, there is a wide variation in results, to the extent of no consensus. However, the principles that should govern Service Design are presented: (1) Human-centered; (2) Collaborative; (3) Iterative; (4) Sequential; (5) Real; and (6) Holistic.

Another author, Penin (2018) does not seek to conceptualize Service Design. Supported by the work *This is Service Design Thinking* (Stickdorn and Schneider 2011), she prefers to mention principles that surpass the concepts. Besides being "people centered", "collaborative"[4] and showing a "holistic" feature, Penin deals with the approach as "oriented by narratives" and evident through "materiality" of things that provide the service.

The principles indicated, however, can be identified in other approaches or processes in the broad branch of Design, so it seems interesting to suggest guidelines that indicate what would not be related to Service Design. In this sense, Stickdorn et al. (2018a) states that Service Design:

1. *It is not* about "decorating the cake". The Service Design does not propose cosmetic solutions; or quoting Bonsiepe (2011), the idea is not a matter of strengthening the coconut shell;

---

[4]She calls it "codesign".

2. *It is not* about "customer service". Service Design seeks to project valuable proposals, and this proposal can be understood as a kind of agreement among the actors involved, as proposed by the service-dominant logic (Lusch and Vargo 2012; Vargo and Lusch 2004a, b, 2017);
3. *It is not* about "recovery service", as it considers the service during the whole journey (before, during and after).

We add two more perspectives related to "what is not Service Design":

1. It is not an isolated activity, as it demands a wide range of transdisciplinary perceptions, which hardly ever can be carried out by a single professional or professional group of a restricted knowledge sphere.
2. According to the assumption above, it is not restricted to the designer's academic or professional training universe, as the trans and multidisciplinary characteristics of Service Design can be considered the core of any approach that involves it. Thus, a crew composed only of training designers would possibly develop less disruptive solutions than crews composed of professionals from different fields of training (Maglio and Spohrer 2008; Spohrer and Maglio 2008).

Other authors bring contributions in an attempt to translate the theme into a concept (Kimbell 2009, 2011; Kimbell and Blomberg 2011; Mager n.d.; Saco and Goncalves 2008). In this paper, however we think it is sufficient to cover Service Design based on the features that compose it, and establish the limits between what it is not.

Regarding the notions of inclusion and access to people with disabilities—when having the early contacts with the field of Service Design, and perceiving, above all, their predisposition to a holistic, co-creative and collaborative approach, we identified in the field a potential path for the development of inclusive projects. However, an immersion in the professional perspectives and Service Design research revealed a gap related to the inclusion and accessibility. The mentioned gap refers to the existence of few studies about inclusion in the field, fact also noticed in books about Service Design. The search for keywords in important reference works in SD reveals that the field has done little to promote the inclusion of people with disabilities (Fig. 1).

This assumption is also noticed when we examine tools for exploring problems, proposition, prototyping and evaluation service projects in the field. The extensive repertoire of tools is quite full of settings, but also extremely aligned with sensory interaction, which, obviously, reflects the exclusion of people with visual or hearing impairments.

One of the most emblematic design resources in SD, the Service Blueprint, is an example of a tool that presents clear barriers, as we will see later in this paper.

3   The Exclusion-Dominant Logic

Investing in practices related to Inclusive Design, Universal Design, or Accessible Design—among many others, is a necessity in any Design project. However, it should not be. Considering the fact that in an ideal society all people would have welfare, despite their motor or sensory condition. Thus, the inclusion concept would already be understood as a natural process; on the other hand, the exclusion would be something weird and unacceptable.

However, our society still accepts the exclusion, gazing it as something natural: a public square full of steps and without tactile paving does not call attention of Brazilians; whereas an available accessible parking space in a full parking lot provokes the rage in some people. Nevertheless, we think these behaviours are not caused due to bad temper, but due to the excluding mental and social model in which we are inserted. Paraphrasing Vargo, we affirm that we live the Exclusion-dominant Logic.

Thus, we need to leave behind this model. Pullin (2009) says the task of defining what is not inclusive is a role of the Design. Based on this, we consider the Design approach derived from a broader point of view, as the designer (professional with the Design background), in general, integrates a transdisciplinary production system, in which, many times, his/her work is conditioned to arbitrary decisions.

4   Design for Inclusive Services—An Overview of the Research

In the Service Design research field, Raymond Fisk (Fisk et al. 2018) studies deal with issues related to the inclusion of people with impairment. Fisk expands the notion of inclusion, as it is not restricted to the access of people with disabilities. The author also approaches the inclusion of vulnerable and/ or excluded from various interactions in society: people with low purchasing power, sexual orientation that vary from the standards established where they live/attend, as well as the migrants-especially those from ethnic minorities or excluded ethnic groups, among others.

Raymond Fisk deals with the service inclusion as a kind of "equal system capable of providing customers with fair access to a service". Thus, we can link this conception to the service-dominant logic suggested by Vargo and Lusch (Lusch and Vargo 2012; Vargo 2009; Vargo and Lusch 2004a, 2008, 2017) which presumes that in the interaction with services—during consumption and/or production—we should consider that not only the ones benefited by the service (customers) need to be served inclusively; but also, those who offer or promote the service (providers).

Based on this postulation, we add to the Fisk suggestion the need to consider service processes that promote the integration of individuals with disabilities (or other vulnerabilities) in the processes related to services. Therefore, we agree to Vargo's proposal to consider the individuals involved in the service as actors, seeking to embrace everyone as active subjects in the proposal for an inclusive service.

To promote inclusion through services, Fisk (Fisk et al. 2018) mentions four fundamental pillars: (1) enable opportunities; (2) offer choices; (3) relieve suffering; and (4) promote happiness. These are foundations already present in the daily lives of those who are not socially excluded, so we can attest that people without disabilities are individuals relatively well served by the inclusive pillars stated by Fisk.

However, we must offer compatible conditions—based on the idea of "service actors", to the person with disability, when he/she is also a service provider—a box office attendant who is blind, for example.

Hence, it is urgent to bring inclusive co-creation, co-production and co-design processes into service design discussions, that is, the ones whose project development processes are built on the principles of removing barriers (architectonic, urban, attitudinal, communicative, technological etc.).

The online file of Mark Stickdorn's book (Stickdorn et al. 2018b) can be accessed free of charge in order to show how inaccessible and exclusive the tools/ methods proposed for the development of services are.

Other platforms available online also demonstrate the lack of inclusive co-design resources (LiveWork Tools n.d.). Two of the most emblematic tools of Service Design, the Service Blueprint and the User Journey are based on visual access, that is, inaccessible to the integration of people with severe visual impairment or with cognitive impairments; therefore, it is necessary to evaluate these tools to include these actors in the improvement or proposition of new services.

5   The Service Blueprint

Perhaps the Service Blueprint is the most emblematic process of Service Design. It is difficult to imagine a service project that does not result in a Blueprint. Proposed in the early 1980s by Shostack (1982), the Service Blueprint can be considered as an adaptation of product blueprints for the service context. It is a visual, schematic representation, based on a timeline, that sets the stages of a service. The service is represented over time, through tasks that occur divided by a line of visibility in relation to who receives the service. Everything that is evident to the user is above the visibility line (called onstage); while what happens outside the customer's visibility is inserted below the line (the backstage).

The actions are segmented by the activities of customers and service providers. In addition, some evidence of the service is presented, which can be understood as everything that is tangible in the process, and also can interfere in the user's perception of value with the service. Finally, there is a line where support processes are included.

Over the years, the tool has gained space in the most diverse fields and has also received operational increases. Currently, the model proposed by Bitner et al. (2008) is one of the most cited and used reference. Figure 2 shows a configuration of the components based on the model defined by the authors.

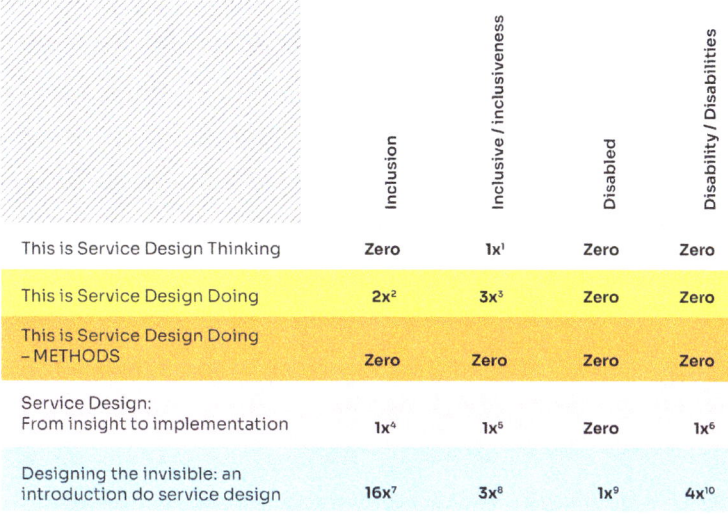

	Inclusion	Inclusive / inclusiveness	Disabled	Disability / Disabilities
This is Service Design Thinking	Zero	$1x^1$	Zero	Zero
This is Service Design Doing	$2x^2$	$3x^3$	Zero	Zero
This is Service Design Doing – METHODS	Zero	Zero	Zero	Zero
Service Design: From insight to implementation	$1x^4$	$1x^5$	Zero	$1x^6$
Designing the invisible: an introduction do service design	$16x^7$	$3x^8$	$1x^9$	$4x^{10}$

1. on page 359, quoting a book that has the word in its title

2. the expression appears twice out of the context presented in this article

3. all these words appear out of the context presented in the article

4. on page 59, out of the context presented in the article

5. on page 159, quoting Service Design as an inclusive approach

6. on page 73, as an example of empathy

7. none related to inclusion of disabled people

8. none related to inclusion of disabled people or inclusive design

9. term connected to a case study of a project involving people in vulnerable condition

10. quoting people with disability in case studies and in an interview

Fig. 1 Reference Books about Service Design, and the gap of topics related to the inclusion and accessibility

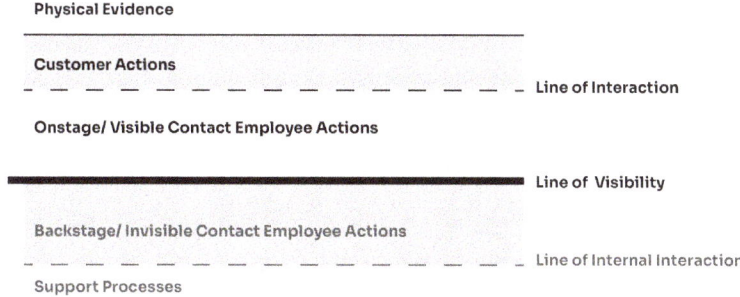

Fig. 2 Classic service blueprint

In this paper, we will not describe the process of filling in a Service Blueprint. The work of the aforementioned authors is extremely detailed and recommended for those who, perhaps, realize the need to use the tool in their projects. Likewise, the book *Mapping Experiences* (Kalbach 2016) has several examples of use, and mentions online tools for drawing Blueprints.

Here, we focus on the need to link devices to Service Blueprints to allow this type of service to be accessed, understood, and transformed by people with visual impairment. We understand that this tool is fundamental for the development of services, and, therefore, it needs to be accessible to that public.

According to Bitner, Ostrom e Morgan:

> Service blueprints allow all members of the organization to visualize an entire service and its underlying support processes, providing common ground from which critical points of customer contact, physical evidence, and other key functional and emotional experience clues can be orchestrated (Bitner et al. 2008, p. 70).

That is to say that, as this tool ignores access strategies for people with visual impairments, it also makes it impossible for this public to participate in projects that can significantly impact their lives.

In the field of Inclusive Design and Universal Design, the participation of people with disabilities in the development of inclusive and/or accessible projects is a primary need, as there is a notion that the designer without disabilities does not have the same perception of the disabled user/designer, as well as that one should not indicate the needs of the disabled user, but rather bring him/her as close to the project and use appropriate tools to explore problems, propose, prototype and evaluate solutions. Therefore, we can identify that Blueprint Service is a tool that needs accessible adjustment.

Taking into consideration the Bitner, Ostrom and Morgan's model as a reference, we suggest the integration of technologies, tools, behaviours, actions, and communication accessible in the various lines that constitute the classic Service Blueprint (see Fig. 3). We believe that the act of designing the service, taking into consideration the necessary tools to provide accessibility to disabled ones, promote inclusive services.

At this point, it is important to characterize what we classify as accessible and inclusive. We understand different perspectives in relation to inclusion, based on what we consider excluding (Fig. 4). The exclusionary perspective is the one that is usual for us on our daily practices: projects that are developed without considering the diversity of people's access conditions, for example. As this point of view does not offer accessible solutions, it excludes those who are out of the patterns considered in the development process.

There is another point of view called accessible perspective. This one is divided into two other guidelines: exclusive and inclusive. The exclusive refers to the development of solutions oriented to the access conditions of a specific target public. An elevator which has a restricted access to people in wheelchair or using crutches is an example of exclusive solution.

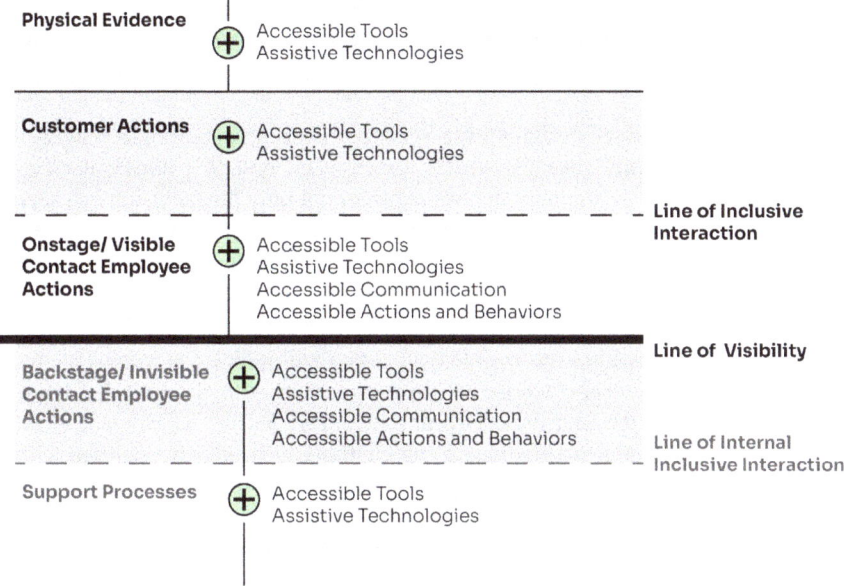

Fig. 3 Inclusive service blueprint canvas

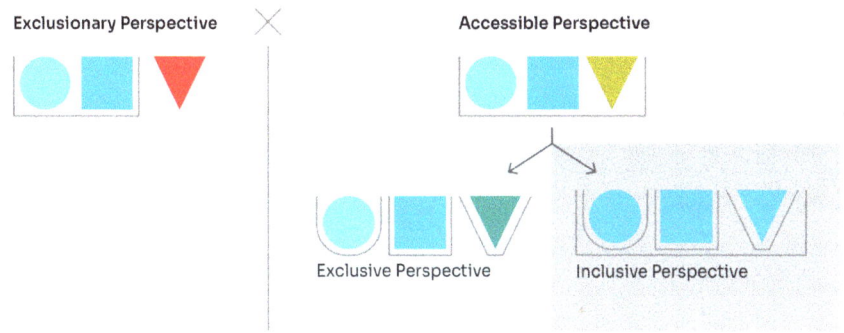

Fig. 4 Exclusionary and accessibility perspectives

Finally, we have an inclusive perspective, which aims to serve the largest number of people as possible, considering the specific needs of each group. A touchscreen smartphone with voice interaction, clicks and visual control is an inclusive example.

The inclusive model is what we try to achieve, meanwhile we consider that sometimes the exclusive format, in some cases, may be the most viable process, even though it needs improvement.

As we can see in the scheme depicted in Fig. 3, our suggestion is that when filling in the Service Blueprint, people involved in the project should ask if the desired processes are accessible to people with disabilities, in case they identify urban, architectural, attitudinal, behavioural, communicative, technological, among other barriers, is crucial to seek viable solution in order to surpass and overcome such obstacles.

During the process of designing the Service blueprint, we strongly suggest that people with disabilities take part in the process, at least to evaluate the access conditions. It is vital to highlight that we consider not only the inclusion in a service user perspective, but also in the provider point of view, as we assume the notion of an inclusive society, in which disabled people engage actively in the job market, and, therefore, they need proper tools to perform their professions. Considering this, a Blueprint oriented to accessibility and inclusion of people with disabilities should have at least two new lines (accessible tracks) that will indicate technologies, tools, behaviours, and necessary actions to support people with disabilities for every single task done by the user or service provider (Fig. 5).

Let us now imagine a situation in which the Blueprint composition process oriented to accessibility and inclusion can be conducted during its filling, or after the conventional model setting. Thus, the accessible track would work as a kind of sleigh which would ride through the service blueprint, identifying barriers and proposing inclusive solutions (Fig. 6).

Finally, we highlight the need to translate the Service Blueprints using devices and accessible technologies. We concluded that people with visual impairment are the most affected ones due to the visual feature of the tool. However, there are techniques to overcome the identified obstacle. The translation of the pictures, for example, is one of them. The creation of a system readable by screen readers

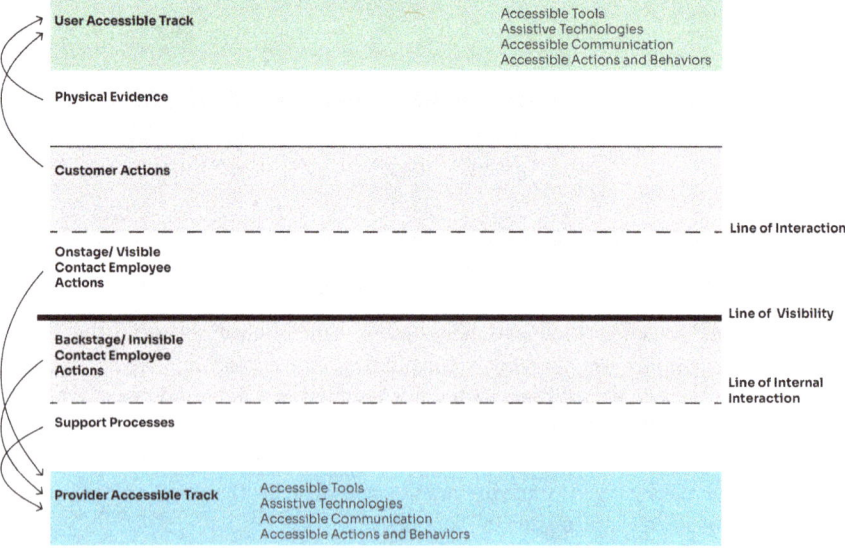

Fig. 5 Accessible tracks: for users (above) and providers (below)

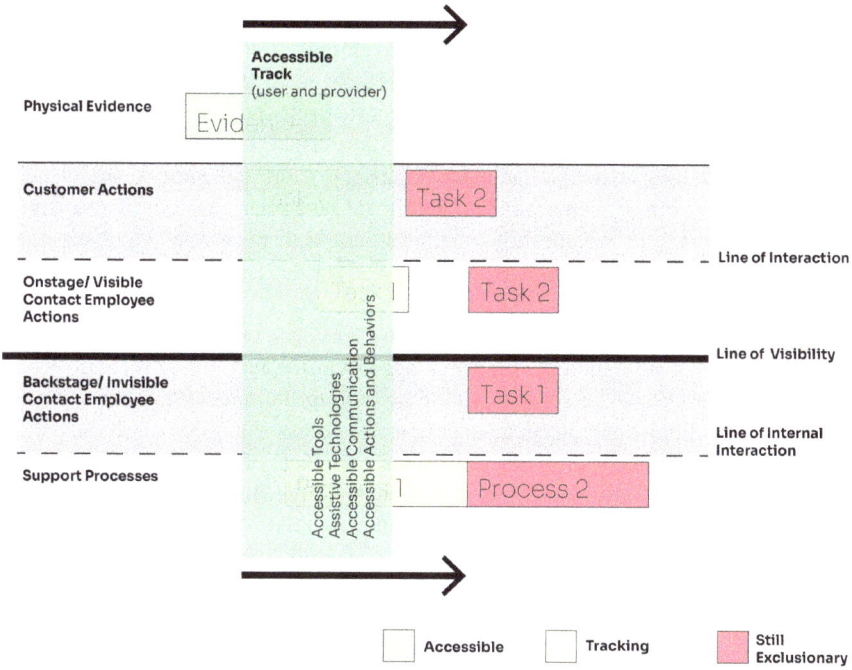

Fig. 6 Tracking taking place through a standard Blueprint

focused on the development of Service Blueprints is another possibility, which can even be enriched by the insertion of audio tracks to set the scene or even possible dialogues during the services under development. We believe that the current available technology is sufficient to include those target people in this type of project, as well as there are professionals from the Accessible Audiovisual Translation ready to enhance the tools associated to Service Design.

6 Conclusion

Is it possible to create a blueprint service that is, in fact, inclusive, according to what we considered in this paper? Or will it be necessary to create another tool which has Blueprint service similar features, but with inclusive possibilities?

One of the Blueprint Service principles is its simple creation and representation, that is, a piece of paper and a pen would be enough to design services with some complexity. Nonetheless, this method presents some excluding aspects, as it precludes the involvement of visual impaired people in the creation of proposals aligned to the tool.

On the other hand, the insertion of accessible conditions to this target audience would present challenges to the project development crews, in relation to the technologies and language techniques required, or even the interrelation between them. The picture translation techniques have a rich semantic repertoire built during many decades of scientific research in the Audiovisual Translation segment, and even though we consider that "amateur" translations are welcome in the disabled people everyday life, it seems weird to legitimate outcomes based on non-scientific processes. In this case, we question whether it would be necessary the involvement of professionals to translate the pictures in all service development crews, or at least in specific services for people with visual impairments, or in the integration of these people in the development crews.

Based on what we called the inclusive approach, the favourable scenario would be the development of the service aiming at serving the largest number of people possible, regardless their physical and sensory access conditions, whether these people are in the moment of interaction with the service, or during its development. Thus, all Blueprint should present accessible features destinated to people with disabilities. However, we face a dilemma with this kind of perspective, due to the enormous and uncountable amount of crews (small, medium, large, with low, medium or high investment budget) that can use the Service Blueprint in their professional practices. We reflect if it would be impracticable for professional interpreters to participate in all crews.

Therefore, we suggest that Blueprint Service can count on accessible resources, especially when it is designed by and for people with disabilities. Indeed, the accessible resources aligned to Service Blueprint need to be discussed in the didactic materials related to the theme. Based on this point of view, we can have, in the future, texts, authors and the proposition of new inclusive tools in the professional and academic spheres.

References

Bitner MJ, Ostrom AL, Morgan FN, Bitner MJ, Ostrom AL, Morgan FN (2008) Service blueprinting: a practical technique for service innovation, vol 50, pp 65–95

Bonsiepe G (2011) Design, Cultura e Sociedade. Blucher

Fisk RP, Dean AM, Alkire (née Nasr) L, Joubert A, Previte J, Robertson N, Rosenbaum MS (2018) Design for service inclusion: creating inclusive service systems by 2050. J Serv Manage 29(5):834–858. https://doi.org/10.1108/JOSM-05-2018-0121

Kalbach J (2016) Mapping experiences: a complete guide to creating value through journeys, blueprints & diagrams. O'Reilly Media

Kimbell L (2009) The turn to service design. Des Creativity 1–12. https://doi.org/10.5040/9781474293693.ch-009

Kimbell L (2011) Designing for service as one way of designing services

Kimbell L, Blomberg J (2011) The object of service design. Des Issues 27(3):20–34. https://doi.org/10.1162/desi_a_00088

Lusch RF, Vargo SL (2012) Service-dominant logic: premises, perspectives, possibilities. In: Service-dominant logic: premises, perspectives, possibilities, pp 1–222. https://doi.org/10.1017/CBO9781139043120

Mager B (n.d.) An emerging field

Maglio PP, Spohrer J (2008) Fundamentals of service science. J Acad Mark Sci 36(1):18–20. https://doi.org/10.1007/s11747-007-0058-9

Penin L (2018) Designing the invisible. Bloomsbury

Pullin G (2009) Design meets disability. The MIT Press

Saco RM, Goncalves AP (2008) Service design: an appraisal 68(1):10–19

Shostack GL (1982) How to design a service. Eur J Mark 16(1):49–63. https://doi.org/http://dx.doi.org/10.1108/MRR-09-2015-0216

Spohrer J, Maglio PP (2008) The emergence of service science: toward systematic service innovations to accelerate co-creation of value. Prod Oper Manag 17(3):238–246. https://doi.org/10.3401/poms.1080.0027

Stickdorn M, Lawrence A, Hormess M, Schneider J (2018b) This is service design doing—methods, vol 50(1). O'Reilly

Stickdorn M, Lawrence A, Hormess M, Schneider J (2018a) This is service design doing—applying service design thinking in the real world. In: Applying service design thinking in the real world a practitioners' handbook. O'Reilly

Vargo SL (2009) Toward a transcending conceptualization of relationship: a service-dominant logic perspective. J Bus Ind Mark 24(5/6):373–379. https://doi.org/10.1108/08858620910966255

Vargo SL, Lusch RF (2004a) The four service marketing myths: remnants of a goods-based, manufacturing model. J Serv Res 6(4):324–335. https://doi.org/10.1177/1094670503262946

Vargo SL, Lusch RF (2004b) Evolving to a new dominant logic for marketing. J Mark 68(1):1–17. https://doi.org/10.1509/jmkg.68.1.1.24036

Vargo SL, Lusch RF (2008) Service-dominant logic: continuing the evolution. J Acad Mark Sci 36(1):1–10. https://doi.org/10.1007/s11747-007-0069-6

Vargo SL, Lusch RF (2017) Service-dominant logic 2025. Int J Res Mark 34(1):46–67. https://doi.org/10.1016/j.ijresmar.2016.11.001

Design Education: The Impact of the COVID-19 Pandemic

Sara Antunes and Susana Barreto

Abstract The long evolution process that education has been through along centuries have always been affected by how society itself has evolved, which is, in turn, influenced by events like the Industrial Revolution, the appearance of Internet or a pandemic such as the COVID-19; the most significant events in the last decades were a succession of technological breakthroughs that transformed our world and our lives, the way we live, work, teach, and learn. In this study, building on existing research and review of literature to reflect on how those significant events transformed societies and economies causing subsequent adaptation in education, we have then questioned which and how lasting were the effects of the COVID-19 pandemic. Literature shows that technology advances have always triggered the need to acquire new skill sets and the pandemic has only accelerated a pathway of change that technology has started, prompting solidarity, collaboration, and new ways of working and learning. Survey results indicate the effects of the pandemic in education are long-lasting and that design education will most likely follow a blended learning model in the future.

Keywords Pandemic · Technology · Design · Education · Learning models

S. Antunes (✉)
CIAUD—Research Centre for Architecture, Urbanism and Design,
Lisbon School of Architecture, University of Lisbon, Rua Sá Nogueira,
Pólo Universitário Do Alto da Ajuda, 1349-063 Lisbon, Portugal
e-mail: sara.a.antunes@edu.ulisboa.pt

S. Barreto
ID+ Instituto de Investigação Em Design Media E Cultura, Faculty of Fine Arts,
University of Porto, Pólo de Indústrias Criativas da Universidade do Porto, Praça Coronel
Pacheco, no2 4050, Porto, Portugal
e-mail: susanaxbarreto@gmail.com

© The Author(s), under exclusive license to Springer Nature Switzerland AG 2022   147
D. Raposo et al. (eds.), *Perspectives on Design II*, Springer Series in Design
and Innovation 16, https://doi.org/10.1007/978-3-030-79879-6_11

1   Introduction

For the last few decades, the way we teach and learn has been evolving in an unprecedented way, adapting to accommodate a huge transformation in our lives and our societies, caused by a never-ending array of technological advances; education in general has been affected by technology, having gradually incorporated several available tools that did not exist before, adjusting learning models of the past to take advantage of the modern distance teaching and learning mechanisms of today.

And suddenly, as 2019 was reaching its end, the world as we knew it was attacked by an invisible enemy, one that we have not yet defeated, and has already caused such a disruption in our lives, societies, economies, and environment, that makes it hard to believe in a possible turning back, again doing whichever activity —be it working, teaching, learning, travelling or just… living, the way we were used to.

All over the world, the impact on education has been as profound as the effects felt in working environments; we moved to distance learning at a pace that was unthinkable, caused by mandatory lockdowns that have been adopted to fight the pandemic. From kindergarten to university, either in public or private institutions, we all had to quickly adapt to new ways of teaching and learning, to keep the process going while maintaining the necessary confinement measures put in place everywhere.

Design education could not avoid the path followed by all other education fields; an accelerated move to a more distance learning-based model has occurred and that might be a one-way change. The pandemic has only accelerated what technology has already started. Whether the effects of this change might bring advantages or limitations to design education, is yet to be proved.

2   Education Throughout the Centuries or the Evolution of Schooling—An Abbreviated Summary

Describing how education has evolved through times would require the recognition of a starting point and that, in turn, would require a clear definition of what is education. Defining education, when does it start, and how it has evolved throughout time, are controversial subjects that could lead us to very long discussions. Although the importance of those themes is such that has made passionate authors to write long and deep discussions about it, its profound analysis is out of the scope of this article. We will, however, in a pragmatic approach, outline basic events and ideas and advise readers on where to search further information.

The first basic notion concerns the nature of education, and how it relates to schools. Most of us would relate education to what we learn in school, but it is important to note that education is far more than that; education is the acquisition of knowledge, skills, or ideas, either by self-learning or when transferring/sharing them between each other. Wherever we are, we gather and accumulate knowledge, literally from the day we are born until we leave this world. So, let us think of education in a broader sense than by relating it to school. In fact, many authors argue that schools may not help in education at all and may get in the way of it instead. That is the case of Gary Thomas, teacher and educational psychologist, in 'Education: A Very Short Introduction'. The author quotes famous personalities such as Mark Twain, Winston Churchill, and Albert Einstein[1] to prove he is not the only one alerting to the fact that school and education are not to be understood as the same thing. The distinction between one and the other is so important for Thomas that he sometimes prefers to use the term 'schooling' rather than education, when discussing the learning activities that (should) take place in school (Thomas 2013).

We say 'should' because schools are not always as much as about education as they should be; there is now, as always have been, a lack of consensus about what should be taught at school and what methods are appropriate, this ongoing discussion also being deeply addressed by Thomas, but one we will only refer to when necessary.

Back to education as the transfer or sharing of knowledge: we have been doing this since our prehistoric ancestors, by transmitting knowledge from one generation to the next, initially by word of mouth, then using increasingly better ways of crystallizing, storing, and communicating it to others. The more knowledge we accumulate, the better we become in thinking about it and using it. As such, we may say education is a lifelong process that started since humankind appeared on Earth; the different ways we educate or get educated have evolved, and evolution also occurred in the various types of schools that we have had since then. The eldest school concept was that of ancient civilizations, such as Greeks and Romans.

Describing the long path education (here assumed as the focus activity of a school or similar institution) has been through, from an age where not all children had the right to get it until the first universities appeared in Europe and America is a task that Ellwood Cubberley has done exhaustively well; in his book 'History of Education' Ellwood indicates Greeks, Romans, Christians and later on the Germanics as the most influential peoples, among many others, in the foundations of our modern western societies. And from these four, the Hellenic people of the 5th and 4th centuries BC, especially the Greeks from Athens, as those responsible for the foundation of our education structures (Cubberley 2005).

> ...the little Greek States had developed educational systems [...] the Athenian Greeks matured and developed a literature, philosophy, and art [...] In these lines of culture the world will forever remain a debtor to this small but active and creative people (Cubberley 2005).

---

[1]Quoted by Thomas: Albert Einstein - "Education is what remains when we have forgotten everything that has been learned at school." Mark Twain – "I have never let my schooling interfere with my education." Winston Churchill – "The only time my education was interrupted was while I was at school" (Thomas 2013).

In the same way, Thomas mentions this Greek influence, outlining the similarities between their elementary schools and ephebic colleges and our elementary and secondary institutions, as well as many characteristics that our modern universities have in common with Plato's Academy and Aristotle's Lyceum (Thomas 2013).

According to both authors (Cubberley 2005; Thomas 2013), Romans, less imaginative and creative but more practical, political, and executive than the Greek, followed the Hellenic education system traditions, further developing law and order executive powers, and these two distinct but complementing cultures would have a long-lasting influence in future generations. In the Roman empire, the Christian religion got stronger and its need to pass religious values and knowledge has also played an important role in the spread of education. Furthermore, after the barbarian Northern tribes invaded Rome, almost destroying the installed progress and education values of the Roman empire, Christianism helped in recovering the Greco-Roman cultural roots.

Another influential figure was Charlemagne (aka Charles the Great), King of the Franks, who ordered all monasteries and abbeys to have their schools; and to teach a curriculum including arithmetic, astronomy, geometry, and music, created by his intellectual advisor Alcuin of York. This would become the basis for some of the first curriculums of the European universities in the 11th and 12th centuries (Thomas 2013).

Important as the role of the Church was for education, one must not forget that attending those schools was, at least initially, a privilege of nobles and ecclesiasts. In that education, as Thomas put it, learning was of a 'religious kind' and the 'province of the ecclesiastical establishment'. Only later, in the Middle Ages, other schools would appear, originated by the increase of trade and commerce, but were mainly concerned in teaching what was relevant for trading (Thomas 2013).

In the following centuries, successive scientific, industrial developments and transformations would bring schools more open to everybody; the Industrial Revolution and mass printing brought proliferation of books and cultural movements, powering the Renaissance and the interest in art, philosophy, literature, and science; the French and American revolutions brought new ideas and a modern spirit, intellectual and socio-political barriers were broken, and new values of individual freedom were installed; the Church monopoly of education gave way to State-controlled schools and all citizens got the right to public education.

Concerning the specifics of design education, the appearance of the Bauhaus school was a long lasting milestone, which still influences today's institutions.

More recent, but comparable to the invention of the press, the advent of the Internet and all Information and Communication Technologies (ICT) would bring an even wider spread of available resources that made possible the advent of other learning models, which we will approach next.

3   A Brief Review of the Main Learning Models

A possible classification of learning models is one based on the distinction of the environment where the learning process takes place, which in most cases leads to different ways of how it occurs; under an environment or context-based classification, we may then consider three main learning model types: traditional learning, distance learning and blended learning (Antunes 2021).

The traditional learning model, based on a physical classroom where the teacher lectures students mostly in a pretty much teacher-centric fashion, has been in place for centuries. This face-to-face instruction usually follows pre-defined curricula and the teacher basically manages the division of time in order to deliver pre-determined information elements that students are supposed to absorb.

To ensure that those pre-defined curricula are adhered to, a certain rhythm of lecturing must be kept, leading to student-teacher and student-student interaction being limited by the available time. As such, the tight pre-set schedules often limit an otherwise good capability of the physical environment to provide good quality collaboration experiences, by reducing opportunities for discussion and experimenting. On the contrary, as referred by Scott (2015), this traditional approach often emphasizes memorization and limits the development of students' critical thinking, initiative, and autonomy. And may also limit the development of intuitive and analytical thinking as outlined by Bruner (1978). By following a preset curriculum composed of (presumed) important subjects, the traditional model usually favours the philosophy of 'teaching facts' instead of encouraging thinking, reminding us of questions that remain to be answered since Plato and Aristotle two millennia ago, on what and how to teach, or what should be the focus of education (Thomas 2013).

However, face-to-face learning provides unique opportunities to establish social and emotional relationships, allowing for important person-to-person interaction aspects not available otherwise: "face-to-face interaction communicates a lot of facial expressions, body language, tone of voice, and eye contact. [...] the brain needs and expects these more significant channels of information" (Tayebinik and Puteh 2013). These unique characteristics of the face-to-face environment alert us to the importance of its use for learning, regardless of other options available now.

As successive technological advances appeared, a totally different learning model was made possible, one where participants are not required to be in a physical classroom: distance learning. Although other distance learning types appeared long ago and are still possible, the most common and flexible is the one based on the use of the Internet, either to look for information or to participate in online classes.

A great advantage of online learning is that it literally allows students to decide when, where and what they want to learn. They learn at their own pace, not limited by pre-set schedules, and they may choose which information they consider important, from almost unlimited resources that are available online. This is the pure e-learning environment, also called asynchronous; synchronous e-learning also is possible, but in this case some online interaction between student and teacher will occur, at agreed schedules. Some e-learning courses include both synchronous and asynchronous components (Mindflash 2020).

We consider that an ideal learning model does not really exist, as each learning context might have specific learning requirements; however, the hybrid option that includes advantages from both the traditional and online models, while also trying to avoid some limitations of both, might be a reasonable approach for most situations. Some level of social and emotional relationships is kept, as well as a desirable sense of being part of a community, while taking advantage of the facilities brought by technological innovation, such as student-centric philosophy and the possibility of choice of when, where and what to learn (Antunes 2021).

4 COVID-19—The Spread of the Chaos

On the 12th of January 2020, the Chinese Centre for Disease Control (CCDC) identified a new virus of the coronavirus family, initially called nCoV (for novel coronavirus), which led the World Health Organization (WHO) to convene an Emergency Committee meeting, on the 22nd and 23rd of the same month (International Civil Aviation Organization 2020).

Since the first cases were found in mid-December 2019 in Wuhan, in the Hubei province of the People's Republic of China (PRC), the virus rapidly spread to the neighbouring provinces and countries: on the 26th of January 2020 it had caused almost 2.800 infections and 80 deaths in 11 countries (Zhou et al. 2020); almost 43.000 infection cases and over 1.000 deaths in 25 countries on the 11th February 2020 (World Health Organization 2020b); and, as of 12 March 2020, more than 121 thousand infections and over 4.000 deaths were already confirmed, affecting 110 countries (Andersen et al. 2020).

Initially named 2019-nCoVs, the new virus would soon be renamed as SARS-CoV-2 by the Committee on Taxonomy of Viruses, due to the close relationship to the already known severe acute respiratory syndrome-related coronavirus species (Gorbalenya et al. 2020) and its related disease, the coronavirus disease named COVID-19 (Worldometer 2020). Because of the widespread of the COVID-19 outbreak, both geographically and in the number of people infected, and considering taking into account the speed of propagation of the disease, the WHO had announced it as a pandemic, on 11 March 2020 (World Health Organization 2020a).

By the 1st of August 2020, the global number of infections exceeded 17 million and more than 675.000 people had died. The pandemic almost paralyzed the world's economies, because of the forced lockdowns and border closings put in place globally, in a joint effort to limit the outbreaks.

And after an apparent calm in the summer months, we are now amid a second wave of the deadly pandemic that has already infected more than 56 million, causing the death of more than 1.3 million people (Worldometer 2020). As of 18 November 2020, several vaccines are undergoing final stages of investigation, with promising results, but availability to the public at large will not happen before the end of the year (Corum et al. 2020).

Unfortunately for all, the second wave might not be the last.

5 The Fight Back—Human Reaction to Pandemic

Solidarity is surely a characteristic of humanity. In times of difficulty, we naturally bond together, and many of these connections started to appear when a common enemy, in the face of this pandemic, threatened our lives. With actions at government level, from Non-Government Organizations or by private and even individual initiative, we have united efforts to fight the virus. Multiple initiatives have started as successive outbreaks appeared in different parts of the globe.

Groups of citizens confined at home in several countries, used the social networks to organize themselves and employed their knowledge for purposes such as providing help to the most vulnerable or creating support to frontline workers. They manufactured personal protective equipment (PPE) such as masks and visors and helped in designing ways to build or recycle ventilators. Innovation and collaboration initiatives appeared everywhere, such as the viral kindness initiative in the UK and the Tech4Covid19 technological community, initiated in Portugal and in which we had the privilege to be part of.

The sudden need for digital skills among Europeans led European Union (EU) to launch the Digital Skills and Jobs Coalition, an effort to identify and share digital skilled workers in response to a growing demand caused by the pandemic (Digital Economy and Skills 2020). Similar initiatives were taken at country level, such as the Hungarian government's appeal to unite efforts among companies and citizens in the fight against the coronavirus, through the Digital Collaboration platform (Összefogás 2020). Another example is the collaboration between the Lisbon University and industry. Together they developed an application to track people potentially useful in times of crisis, as the pandemic (Instituto Superior Técnico 2020) and produced PPE (visors) using 3D printers (Faculdade de Arquitetura de Lisboa 2020). These collaboration cases came spontaneously, as the intrinsic humans' solidarity was prompted by the global health crisis; but they showed the importance of establishing stronger links between academia, business, governments, and societies, as we mentioned earlier: "the importance and need for collaboration between academia and industries have been recognized several decades ago" (Antunes and Almendra 2020a).

6 The New Reality: Using Technology to Adapt

Well before this pandemic, mainly during the last decades, we have been watching how an unstoppable chain of technological advances kept transforming our workplaces, our schools, and our homes. Yet, a lack of digital skills adds difficulties to the lives of many, for not having adequate digital knowledge and training to cope with that transformation (Antunes and Almendra 2020b). That fact has long been assumed by the EU and in 2017 the European Commission launched its Digital Action Plan, to help preparing youngsters for a technology-driven, transformed future, where new activities and jobs will appear, while other jobs will be replaced or even disappear, stating that "Europe's digital transformation will accelerate with the rapid advance of new technologies [...] digitisation affects how people live, interact, study and work." (European Commission 2018).

This need for providing people with digital skills so they can maintain their jobs or seek for new opportunities is also recognized by Blair Sheppard, in a World Economic Forum article, also stating that one pandemic immediate economic effect is a broad effort to gain those capabilities: "Job seekers may find themselves having to compete in a digital, fast-changing digital work with which they are unfamiliar. [...] the pandemic has accelerated this need to ensure that people around the globe have the necessary technology skills and access to do their jobs." (Sheppard 2020).

By increasing the need to work remotely, which in many cases has been the only possible option, the pandemic has had this positive side: not only it has accelerated individuals and companies in self-learning digital skills and implementing remote work, but by reducing the need for commuting, it has contributed to save their own time and to reduce environment pollution.

A plan of reducing the workweek to 4 days, with longer weekends creating possible increases in productivity and stimulating domestic tourism, was advanced by New Zealand's Prime Minister Jacinda Ardern, pushing companies to try it, as reported by Miriam Berger, from the Washington Post: "I'd really encourage people to think about that, if you're an employer and in a position to do so, if that's something that would work for your workplace." (Berger 2020).

7 Education During and After the Pandemic

One week only after WHO has declared the pandemic on 11 March 2020, the estimated COVID-19 related school closures, already implemented at a national level in 107 countries, was affecting 862 million students, the equivalent to half the global student population (UNESCO 2020). By 1 April, those numbers had increased to 194 countries and 1.598.099.008 students affected (UNESCO 2020).

How did the pandemic impact education? How did it affect the different actors in the education systems?

It is true that for some education institutions around the world the impact was less noticeable, as they had been offering distance learning options for some time,[2] and, for a few, that is in fact the only option they offer; but for the majority, the impact of the pandemic was significant, at least in the short term, and there will certainly be effects in the medium and long term too. For those, the immediate reaction was to adapt and fight to maintain the right of students to continue their education, despite the disruption caused by the pandemic.

- An April 2020 UNESCO report on 'COVID-19 and Higher Education: Today and Tomorrow' describes the immediate impacts of the pandemic would include (a) for the students, being left in a completely new situation that affected their daily life, learning continuity, eventual financial problems, and limited mobility; (b) for teachers, the necessity of adapting to online teaching or otherwise risk their contracts; and (c) for non-teaching staff, a possible loss of their jobs due to the need for a reduction of costs that institutions faced. UNESCO recommended High Education Institutions to work out a plan to fight the crisis using a framework based on principles such as:
- to ensure the right to higher education for all, equal opportunities, no discrimination, leaving no student behind;
- seeing education as a continuum, from childhood to beyond higher education;
- carefully prepare the return to face-to-face learning and use that return to rethink and redesign the teaching and learning process;
- create coordination mechanisms with their governments, to better face future crises, involving students, teachers, and non-teaching staff (UNESCO 2020).

Examples of how education institutions worldwide reacted to the pandemic, including collaboration with governments and industry in the fight against the spread of the disease, and more importantly, measures taken to continue their role in society, have been continuously reported, mainly through television and Internet.

On the 15th of March, a case study presented by Wei Bao, an Associate Professor with tenure of higher education administration, of the Peking University, China, related that Chinese universities were massively closing doors and migrating to online education, following government's guidelines to fight the outbreaks while continuing their ongoing education programmes. The study indicated that other 61 countries, from Africa, Asia, Europe, Middle East, and the Americas, were closing education institutions. It also indicates "five principles of high-impact teaching practice to effectively deliver large-scale online education" (Bao 2020).

As reported by the online version of The Independent on the 5th of May, all teaching at the University of Cambridge was moved online in March 2020 and the university announced that all lectures would continue virtually, at least until summer 2021, the end of the next academic year (Independent 2020). It was the second time in its history that Cambridge University was closing, the first having

---

[2]For example, Massive Open Online Courses (MOOC) and Small Private Online Courses (SPOC) exist for some time, in several institutions.

been in 1665 because of the black plague. In the first weeks of March, the chief executive of Web Summit, Paddy Cosgrave, tweeted a story about Isaac Newton, who was a Cambridge University student at the time, confined at home due to the closure; inspired by the fall of an apple, Newton invented the laws of motion, as Goldie Blumenstyk writes in The Chronicle of Higher Education (Blumenstyk 2020).

Several Scottish universities, to include the University of Edinburgh, the University of Dundee, the Glasgow Caledonian University, Abertay University and St. Andrews were considering delays in the start of the new academic year, some of them planning to go online or using a hybrid model, according to a 20 May 2020 report from the British Broadcasting Corporation (BBC) website (BBC 2020).

Most institutions agree on the difficulties posed by a sudden change to distance learning, but also welcome the opportunities those challenges represent. The European University Association says these opportunities allow for a deeper engagement of universities, using their research and innovation capabilities to support governments in adding resilience to our societies (COVID-19 and universities 2020). We also refer the statement of the Architect Association director Gilabert, in an interview conducted by Building Design, in which several school heads gave their opinions on challenges, innovations and future, after COVID-19: "It's going to be incredibly challenging for all of us, but it's also incredibly rewarding to feel that there are a lot of things that need to be done differently (Dunton 2020).

Advice on how to teach in times of pandemic has also been widely shared, institutions and professionals trying to help those who suddenly had to move online without having previous experience, either in distance learning or in online teaching. That is the case of the American Psychological Association (APA), that after reminding us that there are millions of students who have never taken an online class, give guidance to teachers so they provide those students with a better experience, by making lessons engaging and positive, being flexible and build connections, learning from other instructors, rethink how to assess learning and picking the right technology (Abramson 2020).

"Teaching online is not rocket science but it does need a different approach from classroom teaching" says Tony Bates, who also recommends teachers to get advice from other professionals before starting online classes, to use of the right technology such as an institution-supported video-conferencing system, to get organized, and to avoid long lectures and lecture-based only classes (Bates 2020).

In turn, Wei Bao shares principles to practice high impact online education, to include what she calls 'appropriate relevance', meaning the adaptation of teaching content to the readiness and behavioural characteristics of students; 'effective delivery' implying adaptation of teaching speed; 'sufficient support', signifying after class following and supporting students; 'high-quality participation' as the measures taken to improve student's attention and participation; and 'contingency plan preparation', measures to avoid traffic overload in the online platform and also to relive student's anxiety (Bao 2020).

Finally, what does student feedback tell us so far?

An article by Yu Zhang, in the University World News, reports some concerns of the Chinese authorities about the robustness of the technology used and the potential negative impact on education, and includes results of several surveys conducted by the university of Tsinghua, trying to assess the quality of students' learning experiences. Concluding that the survey results indicate very positive experiences, the article says that "Around 40% to 55% of students feel that online teaching and traditional face-to-face teaching are equivalent in terms of general teaching quality. Around 15% to 30% of students reported that synchronous online learning is better than traditional learning. Around 30% of students thought that traditional learning outperforms live online learning." (Zhang 2020).

Students that suggested their preference in online learning based their answers in reasoning, such as better viewing information in their laptops compared to the classroom screen; feeling more relaxed; not being disturbed by colleagues; better focusing. However, some others reported difficulty in focusing. The study reports that Internet connection speed and robustness of the software used as key factors that have strong influence in learning experiences (Zhang 2020).

8   The Way Ahead and the Specifics of Design Education: Will It Ever Be the Same Again?

"Preparing designers for the 21st century involves providing them with skills to quickly adapt to a world of continuous change [...] where uncertainty is the most assured reality" (Antunes and Almendra 2020b).

In late September 2020, the European Commission president Ursula Von der Leyen unveiled that the EU plans to fund a Bauhaus-style design school, according to an article published on the architecture and design online magazine Dezeen: "We will set up a new European Bauhaus. A co-creation space where architects, artists, students, engineers, designers work together." (Block 2020).

Von der Leyen's statement proves the EU commitment in providing students with a necessary and critical set of skills, a need we have previously referred to: "… they need to acquire a diverse skill set that includes collaboration, flexibility and resilience…" (Antunes and Almendra 2020b). Whether this new school, as others in the world, will provide students with that skill set through traditional, online or hybrid learning models is yet to be seen, as scenarios like the COVID-19 pandemic, as well as others dictated by similar crisis situations, might unfortunately happen again, from time to time.

As part of a wider Ph.D. research project, we did a small-scale survey on the opinion of the design community, about possible futures of design education, specifically concerning those learning models.

The survey is still ongoing, but preliminary results were drawn from the answers received so far; those included answers from teachers (25%), researchers (28%) and professionals (46%), from 9 countries, belonging to 4 different continents. A great majority of respondents agreed on the possibility of a future pandemic or crisis in the future (94%) and on the fact that the learning environment will change because of the current pandemic (92%); most (83%) also believe that Design Education Institutions (DEI) will most likely choose a blended learning environment, although less of them (66%) consider it as the most appropriate; only 13% think the chosen model will be the traditional one, even if more (30%) consider it as the most appropriate. Surprisingly, only a minority (3%) thinks that an exclusively online learning model is the most appropriate and that DEI will opt for it in the future.

9 Conclusion

With design education in mind, we have done this study to understand the effects of the pandemic in education as a broad science, namely how we have adhered to different learning methods and which will prevail after the health crises, affecting design education in the future. We started by a reflection on the evolution of education along the centuries, and then analysed the pandemic and its immediate effects on education; and finally, we investigated which will be the remaining effects afterwards, to foresee how design education might be in the future. We concluded that the education community has learned the need to be resilient and prepared for possible future crises, and that Design Education Institutions will most likely choose a blended learning model in the future. Further investigation will eventually verify that choice and whether it will bring more advantages or more disadvantages, when compared to the Design Education of today. In any case, the pandemic has also shown that, besides the need to use technology, teachers will also increasingly rely on each other's knowledge; in summary, education will need a more multidisciplinary approach.

Acknowledgements (1) CIAUD—Research Centre for Architecture, Urbanism and Design, Lisbon School of Architecture, University of Lisbon, Portugal; (2) FCT—Foundation for Science and Technology, Portugal.

References

Abramson A (2020) Enhancing online learning: the COVID-19 pandemic has moved education online for most students. Psychologists are offering ways to maximize that shift. Monit Psychol 51(4). www.apa.org/monitor/2020/06/covid-online-learning.

Andersen G, Rambaut A, Lipkin W, Holmes E, Garry R (2020) The proximal origin of SARS-CoV-2. Nat Med 26:450–452. https://doi.org/10.1038/s41591-020-0820-9

Antunes S (2021) Education in a technology-shaped world: which learning model helps preparing for the knowledge-based societies? In: Raposo D, Neves J, Silva J, Correia L, Dias R (eds) Advances in design, music and arts: series in design and innovation (EIMAD 2020), vol 9, pp 111–125. Springer, Cham. https://doi.org/10.1007/978-3-030-55700-3_8.

Antunes S, Almendra R (2020) Collaboration: critical roles of academia-business partnerships and challenges the workforce must face. In: Rebelo, F, Soares M (eds) Advances in ergonomics in design: advances in intelligent systems and computing (AHFE 2019), vol 955, pp 370–382. Springer, Cham. https://doi.org/10.1007/978-3-030-20227-9_34

Antunes S, Almendra R (2020) Design education for the 21st century: the multiple faces of disciplinarity. Almendra R, Ferreira J (eds) Research & education in design conference - people & processes & products & philosophy (REDES 2019), pp 233–240. Taylor & Francis Group, London. https://doi.org/10.1201/9781003046103

Bao W (2020) COVID-19 and online teaching in higher education: a case study of Peking University. Wiley Periodicals LLC: Hum Behav Emerg Technol 2(2):113–115. https://doi.org/10.1002/hbe2.191

Bates T (2020) Advice to those about to teach online because of the coronavirus. www.tonybates.ca/2020/03/09

BBC (2020) Coronavirus: Some universities to delay next academic year. www.bbc.com/news/uk-scotland-scotland-politics-52738179

Berger M (2020) Will the coronavirus pandemic open the door to a four-day workweek? www.washingtonpost.com/world/2020/05/24/will-coronavirus-pandemic-open-door-four-day-workweek/

Block I (2020) This week, the EU made plans for a new Bauhaus after coronavirus. www.dezeen.com/2020/09/26/this-week-new-bauhaus-coronavirus/

Blumenstyk G (2020) Why Coronavirus looks like a 'Black Swan' moment for Higher Education. www.chronicle.com/newsletter/the-edge/

Bruner J (1978) O Processo da Educação. Edições 70, Lda

European Commission (2018) Communication from the Commission to the European Parliament, the Council, the European Economic and Social Committee and the Committee of the Regions on the Digital Education Action Plan. eur-lex.europa.eu/legal-content/EN/TXT/?uri=COM:2018:22:FIN

Corum J, Wee SL, Zimmer C (2020) Coronavirus vaccine tracker. www.nytimes.com/interactive/2020/science/coronavirus-vaccine-tracker.html

Cubberley E (2005) The history of education. www.gutenberg.org/ebooks/7521

Digital Economy and Skills (2020) The Digital Skills and Jobs Coalition compiles digital skills resources and best practices for addressing the challenges of the coronavirus crisis. ec.europa.eu/digital-single-market/en/news/digital-skills-and-jobs-coalition-compiles-digital-skills-resources-and-best-practices

Dunton J (2020) How covid-19 is changing the face of architecture schools. www.bdonline.co.uk/news/5105159.article

European University Association (2020) COVID-19 and universities, in EUA. www.eua.eu/issues/27

Faculdade de Arquitetura de Lisboa (2020) Professor Pedro Januário e Laboratório de Prototipagem Rápida produzem viseiras ergonómicas e rentáveis em impressão 3D. www.fa.ulisboa.pt/index.php/pt/portfolio-3/item/838

Gorbalenya A, Baker S, Baric R, Groot R, Drosten C, Gulyaeva A, Haagmans B, Lauber C, Leontovich A, Neuman B, Penzar D, Perlman S, Poon L, Samborskiy D, Sidorov I, Sola I, Ziebuhr J (2020) Severe acute respiratory syndrome-related coronavirus: the species and its viruses—a statement of the Coronavirus Study Group. Nat Microbiol. https://doi.org/10.1038/s41564-020-0695-z

The Independent (2020) Cambridge University to move all lectures online until 2021. www.independent.co.uk/news/education/education-news/2021-a9523236.html

Instituto Superior Técnico (2020) "Maré": Anonymous mobilization of return to normality to mitigate the covid-19 epidemic. tecnico.ulisboa.pt/en/news/mare-anonymous-mobilization-of-return-to-normality-to-mitigate-the-covid-19-epidemic/

International Civil Aviation Organization (2020) Joint Statement on COVID-19. www.icao.int/Security/COVID-19/Pages/Statements.aspx

Mindflash (2020) Asynchronous v.s. Synchronous Elearning. mindflash.com/elearning-glossary/asynchronous-synchronous

Digitális Összefogás (2020) Digital collaboration. felajanlas.digitalisjoletprogram.hu

Scott C (2015) The future of learning 3: what kind of pedagogies for the 21st century? ERF Working Papers Series, 15. UNESCO: Education and Foresight

Sheppard B (2020) A 4-step guide to thriving in the post-COVID-19 workplace. www.weforum.org/agenda/2020/05/workers-thrive-covid-19-skills/

Tayebinik M, Puteh M (2013) Blended learning or e-learning? Int Mag Adv Comput Sci Telecommun 3(1):103–110

Thomas G (2013) Education: a very short introduction. Oxford University Press

UNESCO (2020) Education: from disruption to recovery. en.unesco.org/covid19/educationresponse

World Health Organization (2020) Coronavirus disease (COVID-19) outbreak. www.euro.who.int/en/health-topics/health-emergencies/coronavirus-covid-19

World Health Organization (2020) Director-General's remarks at the media briefing on 2019-nCoV on 11 February 2020. www.who.int/dg/speeches/detail/who-director-general-s-remarks-at-the-media-briefing-on-2019-ncov-on-11-february-2020

Worldometer (2020) Coronavirus update (Live). www.worldometers.info/coronavirus

Zhang Y (2020) COVID-19 crisis is an opportunity to try out online HE. www.universityworldnews.com/post.php?story=2020031013551895

Zhou P, Yang XL, Wang XG, Hu B, Zhang L, Zhang W, Si HR, Zhu Y, Li B, Huang CL, Chen HD, Chen J, Luo Y, Guo H, Jiang RD, Liu MQ, Chen Y, Shen XR, Wang X, Zheng XS et al (2020) A pneumonia outbreak associated with a new coronavirus of probable bat origin. Nature 579:270–273. https://doi.org/10.1038/s41586-020-2012-7

Telework Episode II—New Hope for the Portuguese Academy

Cristina Caramelo Gomes

Abstract The spring of 2020 saw the spread of the virus COVID_19. The pandemic context experienced since demanded human physical distancing which results in the closure of universities and schools, ground flights, and closing spaces to stop all forms of gatherings. The forced lockdown to ensure the safety of people, and the government policies to close operations pressed and encouraged employers and employees to adopt telework notwithstanding the short time to prepare everyone for a new model of work. Before the pandemic, telework faced a slow acceptance and adoption in European countries. The pandemic was and still is a driving force for the adoption of telework, in this case considering the remote workplace employees' domestic environs. A review of literature exposes plenty of information regarding telework benefits and drawbacks, but scarce information is available about the relationship between telework and Academia. This article aims to understand the academia's experience of working from home, especially the features of home workplace and its impact on the health and wellbeing of the individuals. At the end, the main question is if academics want to stay with any form of telework. The responses obtained revealed that academics want to remain in telework several days a week and have working space conditions to do so. Literature review and online questionnaire performed the theoretical framework and contextual data to support the conclusions achieved. The answers ascertained the experience as a positive one, indicating that home workplaces have comfortable, technical and private conditions and there is a generic expectation to proceed with telework for several days a week.

Keywords Covid pandemic context · Disruptive way of living and working · Telework · Workplace environment · Academia

C. C. Gomes (✉)
Faculdade de Arquitectura, CIAUD, Universidade de Lisboa, Lisbon, Portugal
e-mail: Cris_caramelo@netcabo.pt

C. C. Gomes
Faculdade de Arquitectura e Artes, CITAD, Universidade Lusíada de Lisboa, Lisbon, Portugal

1   Introduction

The second decade of the second millennium witnessed a significant disruption in the way people, work, live and interact. Unquestionably, the world as we knew it was challenged by the spread of the Corona virus—Covid-19—and governments, supported by science, applied radical measures to save lives. The pandemic context experienced since the spring of 2020 demanded human physical distancing which results in the closure of universities, schools, ground flights, and closing spaces to impede all forms of gatherings.

The forced lockdown to ensure the safety of people, and the government policies to close operations pressed and encouraged employers and employees to adopt telework notwithstanding the short time to prepare everyone for a new model of work.

Telework can be defined as the work developed with ICT (information and communication technologies) support like smartphones, tablets, laptops, and desktop computers (and whenever possible internet) outside employer's location. Before the pandemic, telework faced a slow acceptance and adoption in European countries. The pandemic context was and still is a driving force for the adoption of telework, in this case considering the remote workplace employees' domestic environs.

Literature reveals the acceptance of telework and describe the experience during the confinement's periods and the sequent for the ones who remain in a flexible form of work as a positive experience. The review of literature show plenty of information regarding telework benefits and drawbacks, considering different geographical locations or professional backgrounds. Nevertheless, scarce information is available about the relationship between telework and Academia. Perchance, the reason for that is because academics always performed telework despite institutional recognition. This informal telework performance aims to accomplish professional achievements and deadlines, thus is always an issue of personal commitment and productivity.

To understand how Portuguese academic cluster experienced telework an online questionnaire was delivered throughout personal email and social networks. The objective was to understand the academia's experience of working from home, namely the features of home workplace and its impact on the health and wellbeing of the individuals. At the end, the main question is if academics want to proceed with any form of telework. The responses obtained revealed that academics want to remain in telework several days a week and have working space conditions to do so.

In a broader sense, the adoption of telework promotes the inclusion of minorities regardless of their nature and a new paradigm to plan the built environment where we live, work, and interact with others. Telework can define new home locations (independent of the employers' site) and contribute to the development of remote interior areas; telework can reduce the consumption of energy, time and money in commuting movements and meals away from home; telework can impact the design of home typologies and the surroundings' public spaces as well as the design of furniture, equipment and finishing to respond to teleworkers needs and expectations.

2 Telework as a Response to a Disruptive Way of Living and Working

The concept of remote work raised its importance on the late nineties. The development of the technology focused on information and communication, the portability of the physical equipment, the related reduction of costs and the spread of internet boosted the idea of producing and disseminating information from anywhere and anytime. Regardless the promises of the idea, remote work, from which we select the work from home model, has not been widely accepted. Different causes supported the opposition to the model, emerging the culture of the employers as well as employees as the most significative one. The advantages and disadvantages of the model are broadly explained by the literature and the dissemination of case studies. In accordance with the document published by European Union (2020) the diffusion of this method of work in the European countries presented a slow grow (Figs. 1 and 2).

The pandemic situation originated by the Corona virus, create a disrupted and new way of living, working, and interacting with the others also with the physical environment that is close to us, particularly home. Due to the spread of the virus and its consequent impact on human health, European countries were forced to lockdown and implement remote work from home, which we are going to mention, from now on, as telework to be in accordance with the most used nomenclature in literature review, despite its scientific or opinion nature.

In the first semester of the year 2020, with different schedules and duration, all the functions and activities possible to be performed remotely experienced

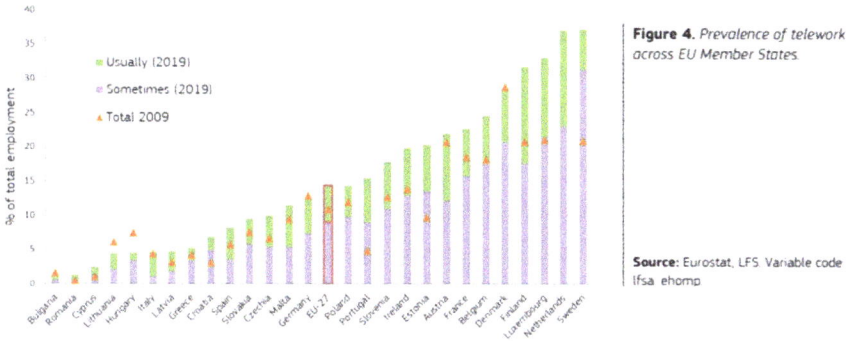

Fig. 1 Prevalence of telework across EU member states (European Union 2020)

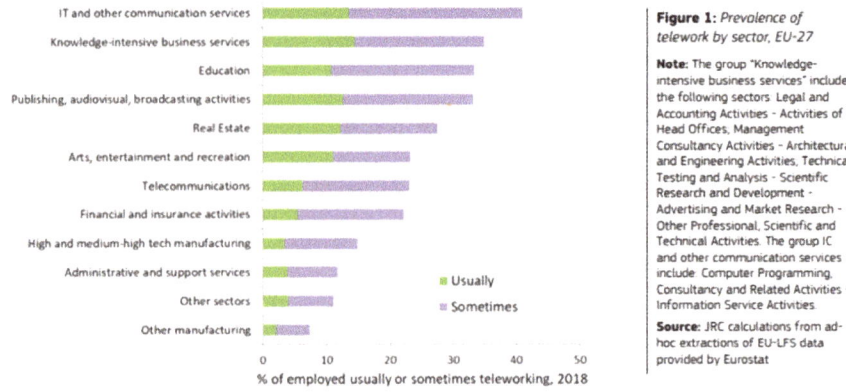

Fig. 2 Prevalence of telework by sector, EU-27 (European Union 2020)

telework. The inexistence of previous experience challenged differently functions, activities, and individuals with implication on productivity and individuals' well-being at least in the short to medium term. Although the telework reality experienced in a large geographic context and the perception of employers and employees, the future dissemination of telework will be dependent of dissimilar impacted factors such as productivity, working conditions, and the broader policies towards Europe's digital and green transitions (European Union 2020).

The pandemic context provoked the discussion around a pertinent issue and made aware the most sceptical and the most enthusiasts about its advantages and disadvantages. The evidence of this constant and lively discussion on the topic is on the number of scientific as well as opinion articles delivered and available on internet whenever the search includes telework and Covid-19. Some of them are especially focused on geographical contexts, functions, economic areas activities, productivity but not so many regarding the questions related with individuals' wellbeing, namely the impact of home office features on wellbeing and the human sense of a positive experience. As a matter of fact, the approach of these kind of issues are easier to find in opinion articles than in scientific ones.

Regardless the challenges that a mandatory adoption of telework raised, the experience of working from home was perceived as a positive one which justifies the will to preserve the possibility to work remotely, at least in a mixed model, making this way of work the normal one and not the exception as it was until the spring of 2020 (Eurofound 2020).

3   Telework and the Academia

Fleeing from the Great Plague that reached Cambridge in 1665, Newton retreated to his countryside home where he continued working for the next year and a half. During this time, he developed his theories on calculus, optics, and the law of gravitation – fundamentally changing the path of science for centuries. Newton himself described this period as the most productive time of his life. Is working from home indeed the key to efficiency for scientists also in modern times? (Aczel et al. 2020: 3)

Different models of remote work are a real option in the contemporaneous real and globalised world and a case of preference for many individuals facing the labour market, despite the nature of the work or labour contract. Notwithstanding the place location, the adoption of remote work, from home or from a co-working environment, is extensively addressed by literature tackling the issues identified as the benefits and drawbacks. Literature points out that the emergence of this model of work is the need for flexibility, from employers and employees, which can be related to the attracting and retaining talents, the reduction of facilities costs, the commuting movements, the balance between the personal and professional life, the comfort and/or accessibility of alternative work environs.

The available information regarding the benefits and drawbacks of remote work supports strategies adopted and describes case studies of dissimilar professions, most of all from the private sector. Yet, there is no representative information to document the impact of telework in the Academia (Aczel et al. 2020: 3).

The daily living of academia is characterised by a sort of activities which can be divided in collaborative ones—work developed with the colleagues or with the students, in which is included the meetings and the teaching classes—and the concentrative work, usually developed all alone which requires the tranquillity to preserve the concentration and the focus. The concentrative work that requires the attention and focus concern the reading, evaluating and correcting students' work as well as the reading, analysing, and writing activities to develop thematic skills and improve the personal contribute to research interests' areas. If there is no formal possibility to adopt telework, it is widely known that every person who works in academic environs develops at least occasionally some work from home.

Although the real possibilities to perform some sort of flexible work, repeatedly influenced by the culture of the geographical context, the university, the administrative board or the person, the opportunities offered by the improvement of ICT (Information and Communication Technologies) originated the deliverance of e-learning courses (undergraduate and postgraduate) offered throughout digital platforms that plea to the flexibility of the study according to the students' needs. As announced on these programmes of graduation, all the contacts—classes and work supervision—occur in a virtual context with synchronous and asynchronous interactions, that appeal to training according to the student's possibilities, needs and expectations. Usually, these experiences are perceived as positive ones, once increase autonomy and flexibility to manage work schedules (Shulte 2015; Dolan 2011).

During the Spring of 2020, in view of the proportion of virus' contagion, explicitly in public spaces that concentrate people such as the case of universities campuses, the universities were forced to delivered online classes and the professors and researchers were forced to work (most of all exclusively) from home. If some were familiar with the model, for the majority was a unique experience. For dissimilar reasons, such as the balance between the professional and family lives, the alternative workplace with more comfort and less interruptions, the isolation from the colleagues and some feeling of isolation, everyone experienced the benefits and the difficulties created by the context. Regardless the way each one lived and perceived the experience, literature informs that most of the people that experienced telework would like to continue with this model of work beyond the situation of Covid-19. Furthermore, the context that started in the spring of 2020 and required a disrupted attitude such as the forced implementation of telework is still an issue in the spring of 2021, once several European countries experienced different sorts of lockdown during this long year. The extensive acceptance of maintaining different forms of remote work by the Academia is in coherence with the respondents from others professional areas, functions and activities as demonstrated by Eurofound report (2020).

4 Telework and the Academia in the Portuguese Context

We started our research about telework and Lisbon Metropolitan Area during the nineties. It was long ago—during the last millennia actually, and looking back it seems, today, as it seemed then, that some sort of crazy sci-fi idea was being presented to workers, employers, companies, but especially managers that for the most part, dislike and despise telework. Before Covid-19, less than 1/3 of national companies had employees working under telework model, and the OCDE points out a percentage of 6.5% of individuals who were in remote working models (Gomes 2004; Ferrão 2020; Varzim 2020; OECD 2020) The virus took care of that…

The reasons for such a low percentage concerned the culture of the employers and employees, traditional management, and the preconceived idea that remotely the productivity decreases. The statistical data is not clear, and it is widely accepted that the numbers are higher, nevertheless they refer to informal telework, the work produced remotely but outside the formal labour contract, just a way to fulfil deadlines. The experience of last spring, where the lockdown disrupted traditional methods of work and forced telework, show the opportunity to have more flexibility and demystified the preconceived and negative ideas about less productivity and efficiency. Telework stop being a trend or modernity "nice to have" to a "requirement to have" for several employers and employees. A study developed by OECD (2020), addresses that 33.9% of the employment can be performed remotely despite some differences between the cities, namely the metropolitan ones, and the interior areas. These differences are due to the access of internet, the education level of the work force and the nature of the work of each region (Varzim 2020).

The context experienced in the spring of 2020 and which is in February 2021 (again) the reality of Portugal, as other European countries, boosted technical competencies as the use and abuse of virtual platforms such as teams, skype, zoom, etc. In general, the experience was perceived as a positive one which was demonstrated by the number of employees and employers that remain, after the lockdown, in telework. This reality can be evidenced by the study made by Walters (2020). The estimates of this study point to:

- 4% want to work exclusively on company office
- 96% want to have the flexibility to embrace remote work
- 40% work on the kitchen table or on the dinner table
- 5 in 10 reveal more autonomy
- 29% take the opportunity to sleep more hours without the requirement to commute to the office

But the efficient implementation of telework requires—as stated by João Paiva— the drop of traditional management, repeatedly supported by the lack of confidence in employees and the persistence on management practices oriented to instrumental monitoring if not even policing. It is required to delegate, trust, and evaluate, demanding for responsibility and measure productivity. The crisis' experience exposed the consistency of productivity levels in remote work context and in many cases its expansion (Paiva 2020).

Paiva's statements are consistent with Robert Walters' report which declares that 44% of professionals expand their productivity and the causes that contribute for this achievement were:

- More flexibility on time schedules
- More autonomy
- Working in a more comfortable and relaxed environment
- Higher capacity of concentration and less distractions
- Less meetings

The drawbacks presented by the same report were:

- The inexistence of a proper office at home
- Isolation from the colleagues
- More meetings or check-ups to understand the development of particular activities
- Distractions caused by domestic environment

More important, 96% of professionals manifested the intention to maintain telework after the pandemic context (Walter 2020).

The information delivered on the previous paragraphs is not a diagnosis of a professional area, still, it is also representative of the academia work environment.

In the academic environment daily routines there is a considerable volume of work that is or can be done remotely. However, the work developed remotely is like a phantom activity because despite its existence it is not institutionally recognised. Regardless some labour contractual differences between public and private institutions, both sectors are characterised by basing on an instrumental monitoring practice and not on productivity.

The reason why academics prefer to work remotely, even just for some sorts of activities or periods of time, relates with the physical and technical conditions of the institutions. Some institutions do not have enough physical space to provide personal working spaces for collaborators; others provide the required space but rarely offers generous dimensions, comfort, or a peaceful environment; ergonomic considerations towards the teaching rooms and (possible) personal working space are repeatedly inexistant. The bureaucratic work goes along with the use of paper physical support hindering the options enabled by technology. ICT equipment is scarce and frequently out of date.

The available statistical data does not refer the academia collaborators (which include not only professors but also administrative employees) in particular, but maybe they were part of the sample that allowed the reports of INE (2020), OECD (2020) and Walters (2020). Walters' report goes further and show information related with the place from which people work: 40% are working from home on the kitchen or dinner table, 57% have an office and 4% from an exterior area. The overlapping of numbers is due to the possibility to work from different areas depending on preference or availability of the space. However, the working space is not described beyond its location in the functional area of domestic environment.

As a brief end note, from the information presented on the previous pages it is evident that remote work is a working model that will remain beyond the present context. Broadly speaking, most people who have experienced working from home during confinement want to preserve the opportunity to develop their activities in a remote work environment.

The academia cluster is not an exception. The mandatory experience of teaching and working remotely using the potential offered by ICT highlighted the advantages and challenges of working from home on a level of personal experience. Professors and researchers as well as institutions, in a broadly sense, define the experience as a positive one, and the desire of supporting flexible forms of work; others describe the experience as an unbalanced challenge.

The gap founded on literature review regarding working from home and academia, raise the purpose of electing this group as the target of this study. The aim is not to establish the group productivity, once professors and researchers always performed, although in an informal way, remote work, but to understand if working from home is a pattern to preserve, how to characterise the domestic workspace, and how this space contributes for human wellbeing. Moreover, the main drawbacks evidenced by literature related with working from home are part of the confinement context and consequently all the family members are at home performing any kind of tele-activity.

The results of the study must be an awareness for our work environments as well as a reminder to architects and designers once we do strongly believe that the general acceptance of working from home, by choice or lack of it, impact considerably housing location and typology, furniture, and finishing (Gomes and Aouad 1999).

5 Telework Workplace and the Academia—A Study of Portuguese Reality

The main purpose of this study was to understand academia's experience of working from home, namely the features of home workplace and its impact on the health and wellbeing of the individuals. For achieve our goal, an online questionnaire was delivered through personal emails and social networks. The personal and social relationships between collaborators were decisive for a diversified sample from different universities from coastal and interior areas of the country. At the end it was possible to receive 182 responses. The quantity and the provenience support the sample validity.

The questionnaire was available from the 27 of January up to the 15 of February. The choice of the launch date and response collection period was for the reason that during that period it was defined another period of mandatory confinement due to the numbers of infected and deaths by Corona virus. Facing another cycle of mandatory telework, the individuals are more attentive to the home workplace requirements towards personal safety, comfort and wellbeing.

The questionnaire had 182 responses from public Academic institutions (45%) and private ones (34%). Some respondents declined to inform their generic affiliation, for reasons best known to themselves…, or not. From the sample 95.6% teleworked during the second semester of 2019/2020 academic year. Women were more responsive to the questionnaire with 62.6% of responses against 37.4% of men. Most of the respondents are between the 36 and the 67 years old. Half of the respondents, 55% have more people working from home and 47% have people on e-learning programs in their households.

The functional domestic area most used for work was the home office followed by the living and dining rooms. The dominance of a personal office is certainly related with the provenience of the responses: responses came from academic institutions across the country, both bigger metropolitan areas and smaller cities. If in the metropolitan areas the homes are mainly apartments, homes outside the main cities present more generous dimensions which allow more space to dedicate to a personal office. Others organise the layout of the living and dinner rooms to have a dedicated space to work. Although inside a traditional functional area, is perceived as an autonomous area to work. Furthermore, the age range that most respondents fall into, indicates that most do not have children to care for or have already left home, resulting in more space available (Fig. 3).

In teleworking from home, where do you develop your professional activity?

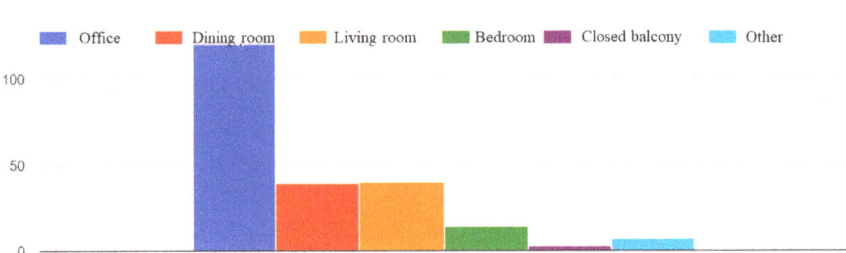

Fig. 3 Home workplace location

What are the reasons (more or less positive) that you associate with user wellbeing at the home working place

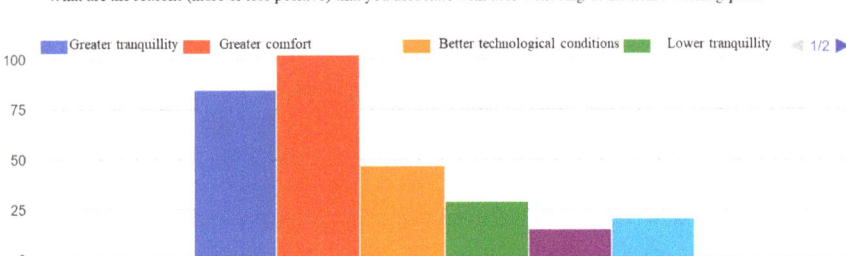

Fig. 4 The reasons more and less positives associated with user wellbeing at the home working place

The predominance of working from an office at home, supports the privacy that 82% of responses indicated. Most of the answers state that the working space was not shared or at the most is shared with one person. The same situation occurs with the use of the computer.

The answers revealed the conditions related with the sense of wellbeing of the working place, evidencing the greater tranquillity and comfort, and better technical performances (Fig. 4).

Regarding the ergonomic conditions of the working space, 52.7% have a table dedicated to work, 57% have an ergonomic chair, 18% have footrest, 83% use a laptop and 22% a desktop, 60% use the mouse but only 8.8% have an ergonomic mouse. For 41% of the respondents the superior limit of the screen is at the eyes level, 13.7% above the eyes level and 33% below.

The access to internet was split with 67.6% with fixed broadband internet and 36.8% with mobile broadband internet.

The responses indicate that 98.4% of the working spaces have a window and 86.7% a comfortable temperature. The used artificial light is characterised by the direct, indirect and task light in a descendent sequence.

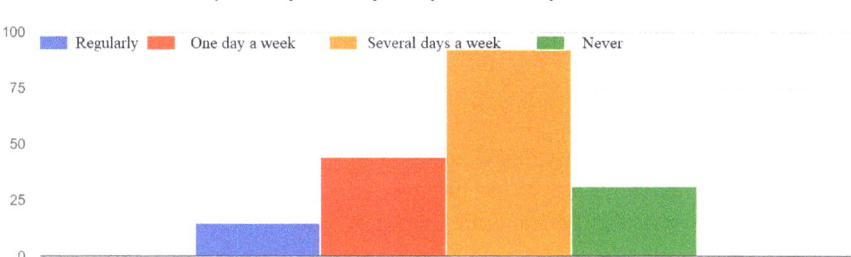

Fig. 5 Would you like to preserve the possibility to work remotely?

It was also questioned the main symptoms at the end of the working day. In a descendent order were mentioned the tiredness of immobility, cervical pain, back pain, low back pain and dry eyes.

Certainly, these symptoms were related with the continuous time online, between teaching classes, meetings, and general work on the computer; the cervical and back pain must be related with the unbalance between the seat plane and the working plane which promotes bad postures, the height of superior limit of the computer screen and the lack of footrest.

Asked about the experience of telework, most of the answers revealed the most positive factors as the less time spent in commuting, less money spent with fuel and food, the alternative work environment comfort, time management, privacy. Some negative factors were shown such as ICT addiction, increase of sedentary routines and difficulty to disconnect from work.

When asked if they would like to maintain any form of working from home the majority answered that they would like to have several days working from home followed by the answers that preferred one day a week in telework. Some people also expressed the desire of not working from home (Fig. 5).

The answers also revealed that the respondents would like to invest on their home working space environ, in a descending order, on the chair, on technology, on the layout of the place and some reveal the intention to change the workspace to another functional area of the house.

6 Discussion

The way to work and interact with students and colleagues changed profoundly last year. Covid-19 and IT disrupted the boundaries of physical space and time. Physical location and established time schedules were challenged by the when, where, and how are mostly subject of our adjustments.

The pandemic exposed a neglected reality which is all the work always performed by professors and researchers off campus. Although the reality experienced by every professor or researcher, this work was not considered as a time spent at work or an element included in remuneration. The work performed remotely aimed, generally, to fulfil individual professional goals and deadlines. The availability of Academia to achieve professional goals is the primary indicator that the performance and productivity during this time of sequential confinements (spring of 2020 to spring 2021) and the adoption of telework will contribute to improve productivity and if not, the reason is based on aspects of the context such as the balance between professional and personal life particularly for those with child or elderly care.

Regardless the available information on the different approaches to the subject of telework and employers and employees' experiences of telework, the information that relates telework and the Academia is scarce, although the identification of this cluster as a target one to adopt telework. This gap encouraged the author to develop a study to support this article.

The main objective of this study—supported by literature review and by a questionnaire to comprehend the Portuguese context of Academia and telework experience—is to find out if it is possible for Academia to work remotely; to understand if the experience was perceived as a positive or negative one; identify the benefits and drawbacks of this experience and consequently the intention to proceed or not with some sort of remote work; perceive if the Academia cluster have the right conditions to work from home and figure out how the workplace environment impacted the health and wellbeing of the user.

The responses gathered allow us to announce the most significant achievements: Academia perceived the telework experience as a positive one and wish to preserve the possibility to perform telework several days a week. The benefits identified by the respondents were the savings in commuting, fuel, transports and food, and an alternative work environ with better condition and comfort. As drawbacks, the physical isolation, addition to technology and difficulty quitting work were the identified ones.

The information related with the workplace aspects, revealed that an office is the functional area more used to work. The responses showed the predominant use of laptop; mouse (not an ergonomic one); an ergonomic chair and a table to support the work gadgets; the relation between the computer screen and the eyes level showed the sharing of responses between the superior limit of the screen at the eyes level and the limit of the screen below the eyes level. Just a few responses demonstrate the use of an ergonomic mouse and a footrest. The work environments have a window which allows natural light and contact with exterior, and when artificial light is required the direct light is the most significant choice.

These workplace' attributes support the symptoms felt by respondents at the end of a working day, such as the tiredness from immobility, cervical and back pains and dried eyes.

The answers identified a good network connection, with predominance of fixed broadband internet. The sharing of working space, the sharing of the personal computer and privacy were not an issue once most of the answers declared the exclusive use of space and equipment and the possible virtual background of virtual meetings' platforms to protect the home setting.

The intention to invest on workplace environ is not enthusiastic, however, there are significant answers that show the purpose of investing in a chair and technology.

The study has several limitations. The range of time in which the survey took place, the unfamiliarity of respondents with some technical expressions, and the need to introduce more questions to a more accurate understanding about workplace layout and attributes. Nevertheless, the results achieved are irrefutable by the number of responses obtained and by the diversified nature of academic institutions —public and private ones placed in different locations of the country—where the respondents were based.

With this piece of research, we just tackled the topic, but we do understand that the subject of telework, regardless the professional target associated boost a resource of research areas of interest, particularly in the architectural and design domains.

Acknowledgements We acknowledge the inspiration of the Star Wars saga for this title. When we first started, last millennia, talking and researching about Telework we felt like Leia or Luke, but definitely some sort of Skywalker. Let us hope the next episode won't be the "Empire Strikes Back". We will keep you posted.

References

Aczel B, Kovacs M, van der Lippe T, Szaszi B (2020) Researchers working from home: benefits and challenges (Online). Available at: https://osf.io/preprints/metaarxiv/52ezd/

Dolan VLB (2011) The isolation of online adjunct faculty and its impact on their performance. Int Rev Res Open Distrib Learn 12(2):62–77

Eurofound (2020) Living, working and COVID-19. COVID-19 series, Publications Office of the European Union, Luxembourg

European Union (2020) Telework in the EU before and after the COVID-19: where we were, where we head to (Online). Available at: https://ec.europa.eu/jrc/sites/jrcsh/files/jrc120945_policy_brief_-_covid_and_telework_final.pdf

Ferrão F (2020) Teletrabalho sim. Mas não a 100%. Jornal Expresso (Online). Available at: https://expresso.pt/economia/2020-07-03-Teletrabalho-sim.-Mas-nao-a-100

Gomes CC (2004) A conceptual model to introduce telework in Lisbon. Universidade Lusíada Editora, Lisboa

Gomes CC, Aouad G (1999) Telework, housing and urban planning. In: Telework 99—Aahrus, 22–24 September, Aahrus. European Commission, pp 139–155

INE (2020) COVID-19: acompanhamento do impacto da pandemia nas empresas (Online). Available at: https://www.ine.pt/xportal/xmain?xpid=INE&xpgid=ine_destaques&DESTAQUESdest_boui=431950311&DESTAQUESmodo=2&xlang=pt

OECD (2020) Productivity gains from teleworking in the post COVID-19 era: how can public policies make it happen? (Online). Available at: https://www.oecd.org/coronavirus/policy-responses/productivity-gains-from-teleworking-in-the-post-covid-19-era-a5d52e99/

Paiva J (2020) Teletrabalho em pós-pandemia: uma verdadeira oportunidade para o b-work (Online). Available at: https://www.publico.pt/2020/04/28/opiniao/noticia/teletrabalho-pospandemia-verdadeira-oportunidade-bwork-1914066

Schulte M (2015) Distance faculty experiences: a personal perspective of benefits and detriments of telecommuting. J Contin High Educ 63(1):63–66

Varzim T (2020) OCDE diz que um terço dos portugueses pode trabalhar a partir de casa (Online). Available at: https://eco.sapo.pt/2020/11/28/ocde-diz-que-um-terco-dos-portugueses-pode-trabalhar-a-partir-de-casa/

Walters R (2020) 44% dos profissionais em Portugal consideram que a sua produtividade aumentou com o teletrabalho (Online). Available at: https://www.robertwalters.pt/hiring/hiring-advice/produtividade-portugueses-aumenta-com-teletrabalho.html

Design Requirements for Sustainability and Disaster Resilience in Flood Situations

Lara Leite Barbosa⑩

Abstract Resilience and sustainability are topics that are intrinsically interconnected. This paper selected among the 17 Sustainable Development Goals (SDGs), those who seek resilience. The term appears in the 1st (No poverty), 11th (Sustainable cities and communities), 13th (Climate action) and 14th (Life below water) goals. Thus, the paper describes examples of projects that promoted resilience and sustainability focusing on flood situations with emphasis on the selected goals. From this analysis, required conditions are extracted that can deliver significant benefits if they are multiplied by disaster risk reduction practitioners. Aims to build project requirements from design to sustainability with those who carry out projects that address the problems of rain-related disasters.

Keywords Design for sustainability · Disaster risk reduction · Floods · Resilience · Sustainable development goals

1 Reversing an Apocalyptic Scenario

Apocalyptic scenarios of submerged cities, ruins after the devastation of earthquakes, mass refugees seeking shelters and many other chaotic situations are current realities and have been repeated with increasing frequency. These are not prophecies or futuristic predictions of a civilization that ends, but of the imminence of disasters in our contemporary risk society. The article seeks to contribute with considerations for the development of solutions and changes that can reverse this picture.

The first part presents the fundamental concepts and terms, addressing the issue of disaster risk management in a broader perspective, with some particularities of hydrological aspects.

L. L. Barbosa (✉)
Architecture and Urbanism School, University of São Paulo (FAU- USP),
São Paulo 05508-080, Brazil
e-mail: barbosall@usp.br

The second part highlights among the SDG those referring to the theme of resilience and presents projects that illustrate the possibilities of simultaneously addressing resilience and sustainability for flood situations.

As a conclusion, it presents design requirements that can be adopted by architects, designers and project developers who can contribute to achieve changes in this chaotic scenario.

2 Disaster Resilience

After a disaster, the structures that sustain the functioning of a city are shaken, which requires urgent measures to avoid escalating problems. According to the magnitude of the event, the provision of telecommunications and electricity as well as water supply may be interrupted; the means of transport and access by bridges, roads and airports to be blocked and the availability of rationed fuel. The absence of essential public services spells out the urgency of re-establishing order after chaos when emergency responses are put into practice. If the system is able to return to the state it was in before the disaster again, after a concussion occurs, it can be said to be resilient.

Widely discussed in the context of disaster risk management, the concept of resilience comes with the consequences in crisis cases, indicating responsibilities and directing the paths to be adopted. Resilience was the focus of the United Nations International Strategy for Disaster Reduction (UNISDR) global campaign to increase awareness and commitment to sustainable development practices, reducing vulnerabilities and providing citizens with well-being and security (UNISDR United Nations Office for Disaster Risk Reduction 2012).

Originally, resilience is a physical property of elasticity related to the adaptability of something that has suffered some kind of shock. This approach can be literally applied to material behavior, but if applied to the context variables after disaster, the interpretation gains figurative character (Macaskill and Guthrie 2014). A crucial point of the figurative interpretation is not only to return to being as it was before, but to overcome the initial state, to gain benefits, to become better than before.

The word "crisis" in Mandarin is composed of two characters: danger combined with chance or opportunity. Through a crisis, it is possible to rescue deep problems and reformulate a new structure. This concept raises a new look at the transformations arising from institutions that collaborate with the rehabilitation and reconstruction of cities after being affected by natural disasters.

Due to the flexibility of meanings it may possess, a resilient design should consider the term's interdisciplinary approach, as Macaskill suggests. It also includes ecological, environmental, institutional, infrastructural, organizational, economic, social, community, family and individual systems, all acting simultaneously and at different levels of resilience, the results of this interaction are complex and dynamic (Macaskill and Guthrie 2014).

Aguirre realizes that resilience is not just the ability to react, but what really drives improvements is their ability to anticipate crises and drive change through planning and recovery (Aguirre 2006).

Macaskill (2014) proposes a framework to assist the interdisciplinary approach of the term with the following subdivision of resilience:

1. Application
1.1 Object:
1.1.1 Physical property;
1.1.2 System property;
1.1.3 Governance/process.
1.2 Perspective:
1.2.1 Structural;
1.2.2 Organizational/Institutional;
1.2.3 Socio-political.
2. Context
2.1 Societal:
2.1.1 Developed; 2.1.2 Developing.
2.2 Chronological:
2.2.1 Pre-disaster; 2.2.2 Post-disaster.
2.3 Scale:
2.3.1 Local/Community; 2.3.2 City/Regional.

The objective of the framework is to highlight the similarities and differences that the interpretations of resilience allow according to the categories listed. This tool can help develop proposals or even support comparative analysis.

3   Risk and Disaster Lifecycle

Richard The concept of risk is paramount for understanding disasters and demystifying the concept that the physical phenomenon (hazard or threat, explained below) is solely responsible for the damage caused by so-called "natural disasters". Ulrich Beck, a sociologist who coined the term "risk society", explains that this perspective of certainty, security and control over the natural world is the result of a predominantly technocratic interventionist stance (Beck 1992). Consequently, man is organized to solve the problems created by himself, since it is our own society that produces the risk conditions that result in disasters.

The well-known speech of the inventor of the magnitude scale of earthquakes, Charles Francis Richter "Earthquakes do not kill people, buildings of the" rescues that truth. This phrase warns about the responsibilities of architects and engineers and shows the other side of the closeness of their creations to the people that can bring disastrous consequences.

The approach to risk as a result of factors other than technical and physical is expressed by the formula, with some variations: Risk = Hazard × Vulnerability × Exposure. It means that the risk is directly proportional to the Hazard, the physical phenomenon (that can be caused by climate change); increased by vulnerability (a human factor, the result of social and economic processes); potentiated or controlled by the exposure (structural mechanisms that can regulate the previous ones). What this "disaster risk formula" demonstrates is that risk stems not only from physical factors, but from the vulnerability that concerns social processes that develop in prone areas, characterized by their fragility, susceptibility or lack of resilience of the population to threats of different types.

For Disaster Risk Management, three periods are established: normal, disaster risk reduction with mitigation and prevention activities, prior to the disaster; the period of emergency response, with the portion of humanitarian assistance immediately after the disaster, and the recovery period that may include the preparation linking the two types of effort for rehabilitation and reconstruction (Baas et al. 2008). The disaster approach presented in this paper is in line with the disaster lifecycle, simplified to the moments before, during and after disasters.

3.1   Before

Before the disaster, mitigation and prevention activities are measures that reduce the risk of disaster. The World Bank manual recommends that all mitigation options, even those that are politically difficult, should be considered. "The principal mitigation measures are: locational mitigation, in which damage or loss is reduced by avoiding the physical impacts of an event; "structural mitigation, in which damage is resisted through bracing of buildings or construction of a levee; operational mitigation, in which damage or loss is minimized by interventions such as emergency planning, tsunami warning, or other temporary measures; and risk sharing, in which the cost of the damage is shared" (Jha et al. 2010).

Faced with the reality of risk, it is not possible to build something fragile. The threat, that is, the physical event such as flood, may not be accurately predictable, but the intervention arising from it must be anti-fragile, according to Nassim Nicholas Taleb's concept (Taleb 2017). He reports the investment in protection measures that consider the occurrence of the disaster, in the impossibility of containing its consequences, reducing the dependence of the forecasts.

International efforts are focused on disaster prevention, mitigation and reduction in general, as the harm associated with the consequences is exorbitant. Depleted cities require the rebuilding of their public buildings, the restoration of urban infrastructure and can be virtually redefined when the previous model had structural problems.

3.2 During

The most important response organizations and major institutions of security and people protection originated after major events that caused many deaths.

Conditioned to occur after a shocking event, such initiatives are built after some kind of disaster and are based on previous experiences. The efficiency of immediate relief is related to the planning and preparation of the infrastructure that will receive the facilities and the temporary shelter itself even before the disaster occurs (Zhen et al. 2015).

The response phase receives a lot of attention from the media, which will report restoring essential services and often dramatizing relief to those affected and also requesting assistance to victims. To restore reputation and preserve the organization's continued success even after the crisis, the Red Cross and other non-profit organizations understand that communicating with their audiences is critical. Advertising should also be listened with caution, as there are political interests in conveying the message "everything is under control" when in reality nothing is.

In this sense, the performance of architects or designers needs to consider the availability of resources with simplicity and try to solve existing problems, instead of bringing greater difficulties with complex propositions, which instill new factors for the population to deal with.

How to rescue order after chaos? If everything went out of control, would an apparently random organization have already taken over a kind of self-structuring?

3.3 After

Reconstruction begins on the day of the disaster. This is one of the statements in the disaster reconstruction handbook prepared by the World Bank's Bank for Reconstruction and Development, a team entitled "Safer Homes, Stronger Communities." The publication alerts project managers and policymakers alike to a series of decisions that must be made urgently, but which have long-term impacts, changing the lives of people affected by the disaster in the coming years (Jha et al. 2010).

The slogan "Build Back Better" is the fourth priority of the Sendai Framework for Disaster Risk Reduction (2015–2030). It was popularized after the Indian Ocean Tsunami in 2004, indicating that this moment should be perceived as an opportunity for introduce resilience, and become better than it was before the disaster. However, the shortcomings of reconstruction projects are very recurrent, reaching as high as 50% in Africa by the year 2000 by the World Bank. These cover issues of backlog, resources, community involvement, poorly funded reconstruction, preliminary assessment, lack of coordination, corruption and policies to rebuild better and safer, quality of works, land issues, cost overruns and a shortage of technical personnel (Ismail et al. 2014).

The reconstruction process, which in the disaster timeline occurs after the response phase, can extend for 2 years or more. Field experiments help collect information for transitional shelter scheduling and the initiation of reconstruction and repair programs in the urban context, which is crucial to ensure a sustainable recovery (D'Urzo et al. 2012).

4 Design Requirements for Sustainability in Flood Situations

According to new global SDG, proclaimed by the Heads of State and Government and High Representatives, meeting at United Nations Headquarters in New York from 25 to 27 September 2015, the term resilience has been quoted a few times. When mentioned in the new Agenda, resilience is about communities that host refugees and in another section, it presents the promotion of sustainable tourism and resilience to disaster risk reduction. Among the seventeen SDGs, resilience appears in the text quoted in goals 1, 11, 13 and 14. Goal 1 is about building resilience of the poor and those in vulnerable situations by reducing exposure and vulnerability to extreme events. Goal 11 addresses the adoption and implementation of integrated policies and inclusion plans, with resource efficiency, mitigation and adaptation to climate change and disaster resilience by cities and human settlements. Goal 13 indicates the strengthening of resilience and adaptability to climate-related risks and natural disasters in all countries. Goal 14 addresses the resilience of marine and coastal ecosystems and take measures to restore them in order to reach healthy and productive oceans.

Sustainability design requirements related to goals 1, 11, 13 and 14 are presented, containing the theme of resilience, from the description of some cases that may be appropriate to flood situations. Although an initiative proposed by the project will trigger benefits for more than one goal simultaneously, the following description will focus on the aspect indicated by the selected goal.

4.1 Goal 1. "End Poverty in all its Forms Everywhere" (UN United Nations 2019)

The first objective is quite ambitious as it intends that exposure to disasters, whether economic, social or climate related to poor and vulnerable people, should be reduced by 2030.

The example project that represents this goal is an irrigation innovation awarded by the World Bank and the UN for the eradication of poverty and adaptation to climate change called Bhungroo, which means straw or hollow tube in Gujarati (see Fig. 1). This is an efficient and effective water system as it filters and pipes a

The Bhungroo

The technology is open source so that it is scalable in other places. Bhungroo does have a non-negotiable principle, however—that the technology should be used by poor people only.

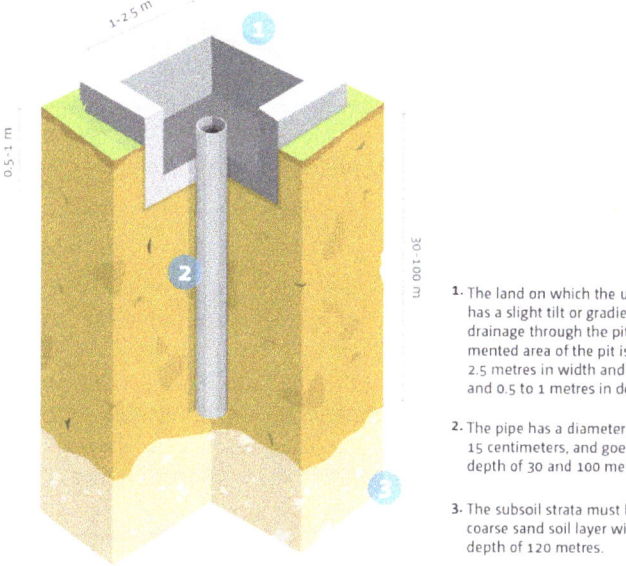

1. The land on which the unit is made has a slight tilt or gradient to ensure drainage through the pit. The cemented area of the pit is usually 1 to 2.5 metres in width and breadth, and 0.5 to 1 metres in depth.

2. The pipe has a diameter of 10 to 15 centimeters, and goes to a depth of 30 and 100 metres.

3. The subsoil strata must have a coarse sand soil layer within a depth of 120 metres.

For more information, visit Momentum4Change.org

Fig. 1 Drawing that synthesizes Bhungroo technology by Naireeta Services (2018)

floodwater into an underground well. Thus, when the flood occurs, it drains the waters to the ground and when the drought occurs, it supplies this water stocked for agriculture.

Technology, not patented to reduce cost and expand access, is implemented primarily by empowered women who benefit from this source of income. Potentializes the effects, since irrigation is unrestricted at zero cost and reduces the time of cultivation.

4.2 Goal 11. "Make Cities and Human Settlements Inclusive, Safe, Resilient and Sustainable" (UN United Nations 2019)

The eleventh objective is based on the Sendai Framework, in which both cities and human settlements need to be scaled up to put in place concepts of inclusion,

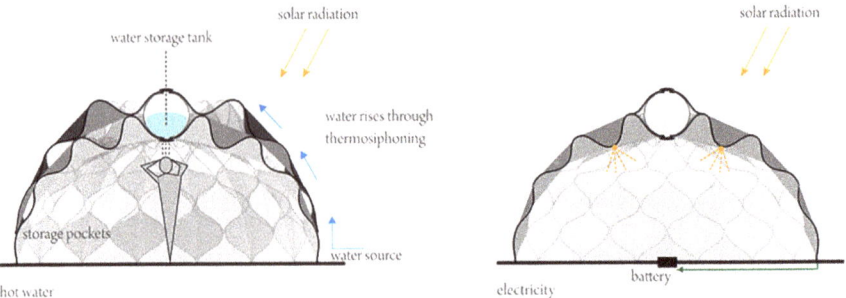

Fig. 2 Scheme for the use of solar radiation and water storage in weaving a home by Abeer Seikaly (2019)

resource efficiency, climate change mitigation and adaptation and disaster resilience at all levels by 2020.

In Jordan, Abeer Seikaly elaborated the project of a shelter that seeks to gather the properties of the structure and the textile covering with possibilities of formal variations and dimensions (see Fig. 2). Based on the concept of weaving a house, it proposes a design that allows compaction for transportation and adaptability to different climates. To do this, it proposes to take advantage of rainwater, ventilation flows, energy and solar radiation. "Weaving a home" received the Lexus Design Award in 2013.

4.3   Goal 13. "Take Urgent Action to Combat Climate Change and its Impacts" (UN United Nations 2019)

Thirteenth objective broadly aims to increase resilience and adaptability to climate and natural disaster risks.

If it is necessary to adapt to the inevitable climate changes, mainly to the fact that many cities will be affected by the rise of the level of the oceans, the projects that consider the interaction with the water are very important.

The Makoko Floating School is a collaborative knowledge platform for aquatic communities such as Makoko in Lagos in Nigeria proposed by the NLÉ architects office (see Fig. 3). As a floating architecture, it is a response to the continuity of classes in periods where populations are stranded due to flooding of rivers or even temporary flood situations. Produced with pre-fabrication and quick assembly, this structure was exhibited as Atlas of WATERFRONT at the 15th International Architecture Exhibition—La Biennale di Venezia in 2016.

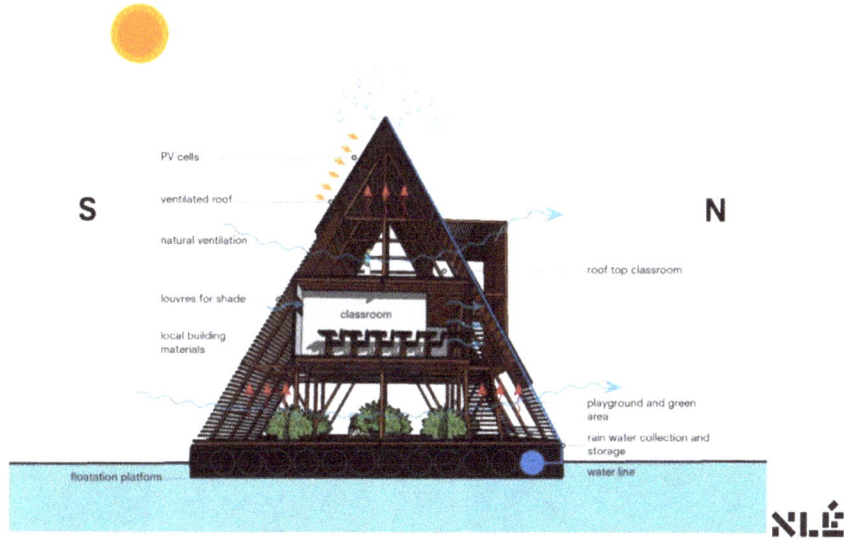

S

N

PV cells

ventilated roof

natural ventilation

louvres for shade

classroom

local building
materials

floatation platform

roof top classroom

playground and green
area

rain water collection and
storage

water line

Fig. 3 Section in perspective of Makoko Floating School by NLÉ Architects (2019)

4.4 Goal 14. *"Conserve and Sustainably Use the Oceans, Seas and Marine Resources for Sustainable Development" (UN United Nations 2019)*

The fourteenth objective proposes addressing marine and coastal ecosystems, reducing harmful impacts and seeking resilience in order to achieve healthy and productive oceans by 2020.

It is important to remember that diagnosing the causes of flooding resumes urban problems caused mainly by consequences of acts of disrespect to nature, such as polluting rivers and dumping garbage causing clogging. When flooding occurs in cities, it generally worsens when drainage systems are deficient with excessively paved streets and sidewalks, reducing the infiltration surface. Other factors that interfere are when there are heavy rainfall with insufficient rainwater network and when there is overflow of normal gutter from rivers, seas, lakes and reservoirs, which generates the accumulation of water in the streets and in the perimeters urban areas (SEDEC Secretaria Nacional de Defesa Civil 2019).

The recycled park is a proposal that meets the resilience of marine ecosystems and brings benefits to coastal cities (see Fig. 4). It is based on an international approach on marine litter with four key elements: litter trap, circular products, education and cleanups. Recycled Island Foundation in collaboration with the City of Rotterdam has developed a floating park made from building blocks with recycled plastics of household products made with HDPE (High Density Polyethylene), where vegetation grows in an area of 140 m^2. Through the park,

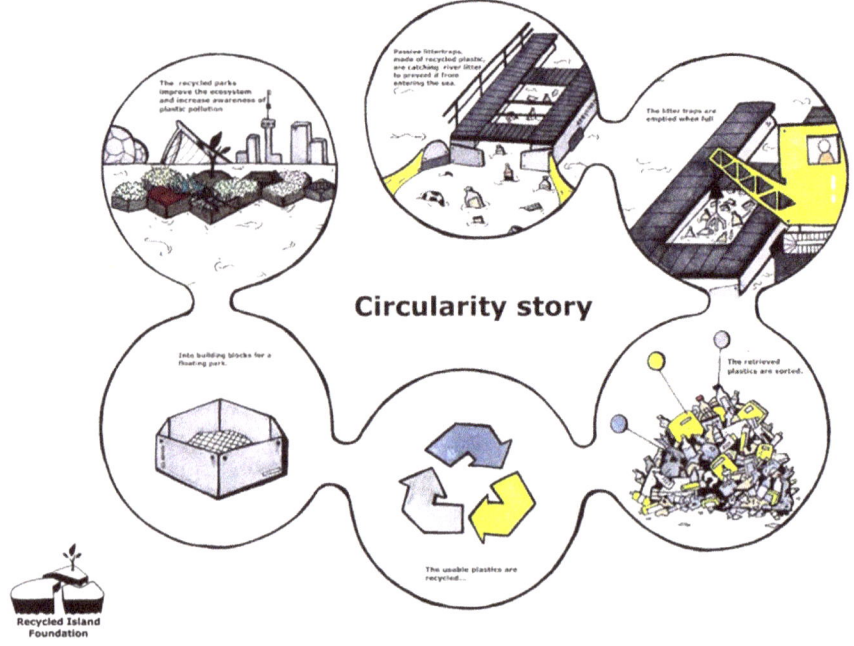

Fig. 4 Recycled Park concept by The Recycled Island Foundation (2019)

consisting of 28 hexagonal blocks of 5 m^2 each, runs a small channel about a half meter deep where birds, fish and microorganisms find food, fertile ground and shelter. There is also an educational aspect in the proposal, for awareness of the damage caused by plastic pollution and the potential for recycling plastic waste.

5 Conclusion

By 2020 and 2030, many advances will be possible if we reconcile resilience and sustainability as key principles in decision-making. The seventeen SDGs with 169 associated goals through 2030, which are integrated and indivisible, seek global development and "win–win" cooperation.

The projects that illustrate this article present requirements that, if multiplied by more initiatives, could provide benefits at broader scales. We can list some requirements such as:

– For protection measures: consider planning, preparing and pre-assembly, so that the implementation or installation of the required infrastructures is quick and efficient.

- For mitigation and prevention: explore in all projects the potential to expand awareness about environmental problems and measures that mitigate the evil effects.
- For response actions: enjoy the natural resources and passive processes to promote both ventilation and heating; for the capture and treatment of water, as well as for the immediate solution of resources for survival.
- For security and protection: propose a technology that gives people a tool that can stimulate new ways of thinking, aiming at empowerment that will promote people's autonomy.
- For reconstruction and recovery: apply eco-efficiency strategies that can combine the available energies: solar, photovoltaic, solar thermal, wind, hydropower, geothermal to sustain the consumption required for its operation.
- For rebuild and repair: adopt the cyclical approach that helps to create a circular economy on the management of raw materials used, manufacturing processes, distribution, use and disposal of waste.

In order to develop solutions capable of reversing the apocalyptic scenario we are working on, all professionals involved in Disaster Risk Reduction need to reduce vulnerabilities (reducing occupancy of risk areas, increasing knowledge about prevention, relief and recovery measures, etc.) that comes being aggravated by the man himself. Applying the concepts of resilience and sustainability helps achieve results that make the quality of life of people affected better than it was before the disaster.

Acknowledgements This study was financed in part by the Coordenação de Aperfeiçoamento de Pessoal de Nível Superior—Brazil (CAPES)—Finance Code 001.

References

Aguirre BE (2006) On the concept of resilience. University of Delaware, Disaster Research Center

Baas S, Ramasamy S, Depryck JD, Battista F (2008) Disaster risk management systems analysis. A guide book. Food & Agriculture Organization, Rome

Beck U (1992) Risk society: towards a new modernity. SAGE Publications, Los Angeles, London

D'Urzo S, Young M, Shneider C (2012) Sustainable reconstruction in urban areas. A handbook. Swiss Resource Centre and Consultancies for Development Foundation (SKAT), International Federation of Red Cross and Red Crescent Societies (IFRC), 2012. Available: https://www. humanitarianlibrary.org/sites/default/files/2018/11/Urban%20reconstruction%20Handbook%20IFRC-SKAT.pdf. Accessed 2 Dec 2018

Ismail D et al (2014) Project management success for post-disaster reconstruction projects: international NGOs perspectives. Proc Econ Financ 18:120–127

Jha A, Barenstein KJD, Phelps PM, Pittet D, Sena S (2010) Safer homes, stronger communities: a handbook for reconstructing after natural disasters. World Bank, Washington, p 348

Macaskill K, Guthrie P (2014) Multiple interpretations of resilience in disaster risk management. Proc Econ Financ 18:667–674

Naireeta Services (2018) Bhungroo. Available: https://www.naireetaservices.com/wp-content/uploads/2017/05/Innovation-as-technology-1-1024x1024.png. Accessed 27 Sept 2018

NLÉ Architects (2019) Makoko floating school. Available: http://www.nleworks.com/case/makoko-floating-school/. Accessed 6 June 2019

Recycled Island Foundation (2019) Recycled park. Available: https://www.recycledisland.com. Accessed 6 June 2019

SEDEC Secretaria Nacional de Defesa Civil (2019) Como se proteger das enchentes. Coordenadoria Estadual de Defesa Civil, São Paulo. Available: http://www.campinas.sp.gov.br/governo/secretaria-de-governo/defesa-civil/volante_enchente.pdf. Accessed 3 June 2019

Seikaly A (2019) Weaving a home. Available: http://www.abeerseikaly.com/weavinghome.php. Accessed 6 June 2019

Taleb NN (2017) Antifrágil. Coisas que se beneficiam com o caos. Best Business, Rio de janeiro

UN United Nations (2019) Transforming our world: the 2030 agenda for sustainable development. Available: https://sustainabledevelopment.un.org/content/documents/21252030%20Agenda%20for%20Sustainable%20Development%20web.pdf. Accessed 6 June 2019

UNISDR United Nations Office for Disaster Risk Reduction (2012) Como Construir Cidades Mais Resilientes- Um Guia para Gestores Públicos Locais (translation of: How to make cities more resilient—a handbook for mayors and local government leaders). Escritório das Nações Unidas para a Redução do Risco de Desastres, Genebra, Suíça

Zhen L, Wang K, Liu H (2015) Disaster relief facility network design in metropolises. IEEE Trans Syst Man Cybern Syst 45(5):751–761

Reflections on the Design Ecosystem Model

Rui Monteiro, Bruno Giesteira, Anne Boddington, and Cristina Farinha

Abstract This paper aims to undertake a closer examination of the design ecosystem model, considering it has recently emerged to justify and support the implementation of design policies within the systems failure theory. It does so by identifying and analyzing diverse perspectives and some of the gaps in the literature, and to propose adaptations in the model by looking at design capabilities as its substance, and as well to identify avenues for further research.

Keywords Design · Design ecosystem · Design policies

1 Premise and Approach

The use of systemic approaches in policymaking, also known as systems failure theory or systems theory in policies, has been around for several decades (Stewart and Ayres 2001). In turn the design ecosystem as a model, an application of the systems theory to policymaking in the design sector, has been slowly emerging for the past five to ten years. It is therefore an approach still taking its first steps, building-up and catching-up on an extensive pool of knowledge and literature.

From a public policy perspective, the usefulness of this approach is based on the motivation that policies are put forward to essentially rectify an identified problem —or system failure—in order to achieve, over time, a state where that problem ceases to exist (Woolthuis et al. 2005).

The 'design ecosystem' approach picks up on this rationale and was created as a support to the development of effective design policies. Given the role of design in fostering creativity and innovation (Medyna et al. 2013), a design ecosystem

R. Monteiro (✉) · B. Giesteira
Faculty of Fine Arts, University of Porto, Porto, Portugal

A. Boddington
Kingston University College of Art and Design, Kingston upon Thames, UK

C. Farinha
Institute of Sociology, University of Porto, Porto, Portugal

approach would therefore appear to be well-positioned to unearth and identify existing problems and to act in the light of expanding the use of design, in and for society. In effect, the design ecosystem model has been essentially theorized and proposed using the innovation system model as a blueprint (Monteiro et al. 2021). But it is also true that while design studies usually take innovation as a result, innovation studies most often overlook and neglect the role of design (Mortati 2013).

In this line of thought, and taking into account the recent nature of the design ecosystem model, its expected role in design policy-making and how it has arisen confined within a design-to-innovation perspective, we argue on the importance of looking at and assembling different viewpoints which combined can offer an enlarged understanding of the model.

Considering the extensivity of systems theory, we also found it beneficial to feed this discussion by first doing a brief recap of the systems theory principles. This is useful to ensure a debate within the parameters of a systemic approach.

Accordingly, and picking up from Whicher's design ecosystem model (2017) as a base and trigger arising from an innovation framework, we propose to examine a set of literature references that are useful from a systems perspective to coherently identify and analyse insights. As a result, we propose three branches that offer complementary views: (1) a design and innovation perspective, as the context where the 'design ecosystem' term has been coined, (2) a cultural and creative ecosystem perspective where design is considered as an integral part, and (3) looking at the design ecosystem from within, as a way to detect its internal mechanics.

In the final section of this paper, we propose a set of adaptations to the model that aim to fill in some of the identified gaps, while keeping it framed within the systems failure theory. In turn, this provides new future lines of inquiry.

2 Systems Principles and Application in Policies

The advantage and underpinning principle of the systems failure theory is based on the ability to bring to the table an holistic and integrated matrix of variables that together aim to depict 'reality' to the best possible extent (Bertalanffy 1969). It then attempts to provide a coherent and understandable model from which to plan and to act if a system failure is identified that appears to be preventing or slowing down the attainment of a desired state.

More recently, the term 'ecosystem' has become more commonly used, not because it proposes fundamental change of methods or goals of the systems approach, but rather because it recognizes systems as more responsive, flexible and 'organic' instead of more rigid or pre-determined structures (Mercan and Göktas 2011).

As such, considering how the design ecosystem is delineated from a systems perspective, this section intends to ground the discussion on what are the system's fundamentals and its implications, firstly by looking at the key components as they stand independently of where they are to be applied and secondly on the relation between systems and policy-making.

2.1 The Key Components

One of the most important scholars on the subject defines a system as an arrangement of elements which are interconnected in ways which accomplish a certain goal, whatever that goal may be (Meadows 2009). This implies that to define a system the following should be established: elements, interconnections/rules and purpose/function (of the system). Meadows also derives a set of principles:

- elements change have the least impact on a system;
- changing the interconnections or rules can lead to great alterations in the system; and
- changing goals can also have drastic effects.

This implies that the system boundaries need to be clearly defined, and that a certain linkage between elements must exist responding to the same set of rules, otherwise it is not a system or might not belong to the same system. Moreover, the direction or function of a system needs to be deduced based on evidence, instead of being stated what is believed or wished to be.

Systems also require a nonlinear mindset, which is the result of the existing interconnections, feedback loops, causality or how they continuously change over time. The 'ecosystem' term is then a way to recognize and reflect this nonlinear philosophy more accurately.

In this regard, it is necessary to understand what the steps are to model a system, as these are the ones leading to its dynamic understanding. Oruç (2010) picks up on previous scholarly references and structures the systems modelling process according to five iterative stages: (1) Problem articulation (boundary selection), (2) Dynamic hypothesis, (3) Formulation, (4) Testing, and (5) Policy Formulation and Evaluation.

According to this arrangement, this paper is located at stage 1. Indeed, the hypothesis raised and how it proposes as important to scrutinize diverse perspectives to substantiate the design ecosystem model, subscribes as plausible that a proper boundary selection has not yet been undertaken.

2.2 Systems and Policy Making

Prior to the use of systemic approaches in policies, the market failure perspective was the norm, by opposing and attempting to balance offer and demand, but as knowledge, science and technology were quickly evolving, it was also becoming clear that all sorts of blind spots were not sufficiently considered by the market point of view (Bleda and Rio 2013). The systems school of thought has then been successful in making the case for its value as a helpful, convenient, flexible and practical tool. Policy makers have then picked up on this approach as to better understand and act on identified system failures.

The scope of systemic approaches also goes well beyond policies. In fact, systemic approaches have their principles rooted in the biology and environmental fields and have been applied in areas as diverse as chemistry or information technologies (Badziili et al. 2019).

But as pointed out by Walker and van Daalen (2013), policy models, as opposed to scientific and engineering system models, are faced with the increased challenge of a limited availability of empirical data to develop and validate a system model. A consideration which is particularly true given the large pool of information it needs to capture. Consequently, as also argued by Walker, policy models usually tend towards applicability and purpose, instead of accuracy. It is then expected this shall be helpful to include a larger number of variables considered important, even if they lack precision, as to compare and test different policy options. However, such trade-offs must be carefully considered, otherwise the relevant system failures might not be properly identified in subsequent stages of the modelling process. In turn, the policy options to be developed and considered might be ill-adjusted.

Policy makers therefore use systemic approaches to understand and shape what defines a given system, namely its elements, rules, and direction.

3 The Design Ecosystem

Considering the systems theory framework put forward in the previous section, we now intend to look at diverse perspectives that can feed an enlarged view of the design ecosystem. It thus follows that this discussion aims to roll out relevant insights that are beneficial to articulate the 'design ecosystem problem' in the sense of helping to establish its boundaries. It also follows that the design ecosystem failures will not be addressed in this section nor in this paper, as this would be a subsequent step, as pointed out in the methodology used to define and understand a system. Three main points of view are considered: the design and innovation perspective, the cultural and creative perspective and insights which can elicit on the internals of the design ecosystem.

3.1 Departing Point: The Design and Innovation Perspective

The 'design ecosystem' as a model has arisen within an innovation perspective, that is, it was portrayed within the rationale of the innovation system framework, which in turn is used to support innovation policies. This paper is based on this approach, more precisely, it departs from Whichers' design ecosystem model and from there identifies and examines other approaches that were considered helpful to complement the design and innovation perspective.

In this regard, pioneering work by Whicher (2017) was crucial for using a structured process to map and understand the design ecosystem. This was based in a previously theorised design ecosystem model, framed according to the innovation system model. Through a set of interviews and workshops bringing together both policy makers and design professionals, a model of a design ecosystem was fine-tuned aiming to inform policy makers. This resulted in a nine-component ecosystem, grouped in three major roles: demand (users, support and promotion), supply (research, education and designer) and supply & demand (actors, policy and government, and funding). The terminology used also reveals and indicates a certain positioning and role in the wide ecosystem for each element. It does so by using an articulation from systemic approaches, as it differentiates the elements as different players and a language from the market perspective, by grouping them in terms of supply and demand.

This process was considered beneficial as it was able to demonstrate the ample presence of design across different fields to policy makers and to convey the possibilities design can offer to innovation as a user-centred approach.

Other representations have preceded the "Whicher" model, and have influenced its construct. In effect, these previous approaches have also categorised a variety of components. They are also an evidence of the model evolution until its current form, from "design infrastructures", to "national design systems" and now to "design ecosystems". Subsequent work has also provided further clarification on how design policies overlap with innovation policies, and how this can be problematic for understanding where one ends and another one starts (Mortati and Maffei 2018). A multitude of root causes were identified: the variety and often not explicit policy lines and actions supporting design, the diverse understandings of what design is, or even the definition of a design policy were some of the explanations provided. It also pointed out how Whichers' model might be located or interpreted in a position either tending towards design professionals as its focus and beneficiaries or for the wider benefit of society. This thus raised questions on its rationale and approaches, namely on what the expectations for design and design policies were. As pointed out by Mortati, other scholars clarified that even if design policies target design professionals, the bottom line would still be to serve society's interests at large. But further clarifications were still considered helpful.

It was within this context that Mortati proposed a design policy ecosystem model, addressing identified gaps, and aiming to benefit policy makers for better substantiating design policies. This approach was based on a previous existing structure from an innovation perspective. Instead of looking at the innovation system structure, this baseline picks up on innovation policy goals and divides them in three groups: demand-side of innovation, supply-side of innovation in terms of human enhancement and supply-side of innovation in terms of technical enhancement. Mortati then establishes a comparative categorization for design policies: framework development, human development, and asset development, respectively, based on an extensive mapping and analysis of design policy lines and actions found in Europe. From a macro perspective, this grouping process has the same terminology as Whicher's model, by taking a supply and offer framework. On a finer look, the difference lies on how each group from Mortati's model is then focused on specific types of policy actions, instead of roles and organisations as seen before for Whicher's model. At the end of the day, this process therefore seems to show how design is difficult to locate within the wider innovation policy and system framework, as it seems to bring the design and innovation perspectives closer.

Around the same period as the previous references, another approach looked at the Oslo Manual to establish comparisons and ground design policies (Gonzalez et al. 2018). As the innovation reference handbook, the Oslo Manual is used around the world by policy makers, as it provides a baseline on what constitutes innovation, having as its background the innovation system. This research first analysed and categorized design policies in six European countries and applied a SWOT analysis to each category. This was followed by a proposal which establishes a relationship between these categories and the ones from the Oslo Manual. This thus showed to be a practical tool for portraying an alignment between design policy strategies and design ecosystem agents with the diverse agents of the innovation system. But while an alignment is proposed, it does not however provide clues on the sort of alignment it is in play, namely where each piece exactly fits from a systems perspective. That is, it seems difficult to scrutinize where exactly design is located from a systems perspective.

3.2   The Cultural and Creative Perspective

The existence of a design ecosystem, at least in the sense of locating and debating design through a systemic perspective, is not limited to the design-driven innovation rationale. We can also find diverse references to the positioning of design from a "cultural and creative industries" perspective.

Despite some existing criticism of this approach, as it bundles a diversity of disciplines in one single sector, it has been successful as a framework of analysis and policy making. One of the references for defining the cultural and creative industries was proposed back in the late nineties (DCMS 2001), where design has since been an integral part and presence in this proposition. This has been mostly a static model, where the different disciplines that compose this sector are essentially stated as they are. From then on, several models to describe how the cultural and creative industries functions across the economic and social landscape and within the sector itself have been developed.

One of the most known proposals is the Concentric Circles Model (Thorsby 2008) which aggregates four distinct layers depending on their cultural content and value attributed directly to the creative arts. The core inner circle includes disciplines such as literature, music, performing arts and visual arts, followed by another layer which includes, for example, film or museums, succeeded by the layer which includes publishing and print media, sound recording or video and computer games, and finally, on the outer circle, it is where we find the location for design.

The concentric model is by itself static, but the dynamics of the cultural and creative ecosystem are nevertheless recognized and highlighted also by Thorsby (2010) by referring to the existence of several inputs and feedback loops which sustain a creative ecosystem, instead of a set of linear, non-complex, interconnections. A description which is in harmony with systemic approaches. It is interesting to note how all four layers have connections among themselves and how design is therefore linked to the cultural and creative industries, but also hints on its privileged position to bridge with other fields. Indeed, the location of design in the outer layer suggests how it is positioned within the edges of the cultural and creative ecosystem and therefore with blurrier boundaries with other systems.

And while this model is an analysis within the confinement of the cultural and creative industries, other scholars have also been precursors in proposing how this sector is articulated with other fields. Most especially, what value has this sector been offering within the larger economic and social panorama.

The Creative Class Model (Florida 2002) is a widely known example of representing the cultural and creative industries as embedded in the wider economic and social fabric. It states that its functioning, as a system within systems and along other systems, is considered a critical factor for development. Florida's work has therefore been an important contribution to help change the impression of the cultural and creative sector as a siloed field.

To better understand how the cultural and creative industries are installed within society at large, several other works have also been developed, such as the Cultural and creative spillovers in Europe report (2015). This study mapped and categorized evidence supporting the wider impact of this sector at large and found three main visible areas where this takes place: knowledge, industry, and network spillovers. But it also states that strong and across the board evidence is limited due to a lack of adequate available evaluation methods while also pointing out to the existence of negative spillovers that should be considered. From a systems perspective, the presence of positive and negative spillovers is however beneficial as it provides clues on the existing interactions. The reported types of negative spillovers found in a few situations, such as negative impacts on wages and housing speculation, are also useful illustrations of interactions with other systems.

It might seem that untangling the cultural and creative ecosystem is not particularly useful for the context of this paper. But ultimately, one needs to consider that design is indeed included in most if not all definitions of the cultural and creative industries. Most importantly, there are a variety of examples of public policies that target the cultural and creative industries, and consequently, design.

Therefore, the relevance of this point of view is that it seems to model an ecosystem which departs from an independent direct or explicit relationship to innovation, as it rather proposes to uncover where that connections exist, but only after the ecosystem is defined. It looks at this ecosystem as it sits and on what has been offering in terms of its added value, instead of pushing towards a certain predetermined "innovation direction".

3.3 Uncovering the Design Ecosystem Internal Functioning

Up until this moment, this paper has been mostly discussing the location of design from two different ecosystem perspectives regarding their overall frame of reference. But as already pointed out, systems are not merely defined by their boundaries, but also by how they function. The perspectives from within are therefore crucial to put forward, as they can provide clarity on the system internals. But while there is an extensive debate on design methods or approaches and even on the meaning of design, there seems to be limited available literature that is useful from a systems perspective. Such a statement might look like a paradox, however a system analysis also requires an understanding of the micro scale and what sort of interactions take place. It is this sort of scrutiny that has not yet been fully undertaken. Nevertheless, we attempt here to produce an analysis based on a selection of references that still reveal interesting systemic views.

As a starting point, the design sector has produced an analysis within the European context based on a slightly modified version of Whicher's ecosystem model (BEDA and PDR 2018), focusing on a strength and weakness investigation. This analysis is advantageous as it provides a look at the internal machinery of the design ecosystem through a macro perspective.

Still, what can be distilled from a systems perspective is limited. But there are interesting observations that we can take from BEDA's report, namely some impressions which are useful from a systems 'internal perspective'. For example, the variety of disciplines within design (even if they seem isolated from each other), a good and diverse offer of design education, or the lack of any official stamp on the designer as a profession. Additionally, and while there is a widespread popularity of design, there seems to exist a limited exchange with other sectors, with the public, and with enterprises and politicians, when it comes to awareness raising, cooperation and research-to-market knowledge transfer. Such limitations are presented as opposed to a higher number of existing connections among designers. In a sense, these are or might be interpreted as an initial recognition of possible system failures within the design ecosystem. Another interesting aspect is that such analysis does not seem to investigate or understand the direction of the system, rather one can try to extrapolate what is wished or expected it to be. In this regard, what can be derived or even speculated is an underlying and desired goal to strengthen the innovation possibilities within the wider innovation ecosystem and social and economic landscape, as it departs from the potential of design for innovation.

And while focusing on the design ecosystem functioning, this analysis entails what is only an indirect understanding of what are its boundaries and, in this perspective, does not provide clarity on what exactly is within and outside the ecosystem.

In 2001, the Danish Design Centre developed the Design Ladder, a tool divided in four sequential levels, to map the use of design within an organisation. The premise was simple: the more embedded design becomes, the higher its positive impacts; a link which was proven true, most especially when it comes to gross revenue growth. In turn, this also served as a base to establish a correlation between investment in design and economic growth, which was decisive to make the case for design policies. From a systems perspective, this approach tells that increased interactions, within the context of embedding design, result in clear positive impacts. In effect, as the ladder is divided into four stages, starting in the no design level, followed by design as providing form, then design when used as a process and finally when design is used as strategy. This brings to light that the more ingrained and solid are design interactions within an organisation, the more effective and visible the design ecosystem seems to become. What remains unclear is exactly what sort of interactions are this and who is operating them, regarding to what kind of skills or activities are taking place.

On this last point, Conley (2010) thoughts on what may be the design core competences provide further clarity. Perhaps one of the central arguments put forward lies on the need to separate the design expertise from what are widely used keywords, such as creativity, strategy, and innovation, which are considered transversal with other disciplines. This differentiation can reveal an important systemic mind-set: informing an ecosystem model based on a more precise knowledge of the underlying mechanisms. Such micro perspective entails, according to Conley, seven core competencies which define the catalogue of what are exclusive design activities and knowledge. They are: (1) capability to understand and frame a design problem, (2) capability for adequate abstract reasoning, (3) capability for modelling and visualizing even with limited data, (4) capability to develop and assess diverse scenarios as possible solutions, (5) capability to create value along the process of arranging the different available components for a possible solution, (6) capability to create relations between the solution components, the solution and the background where it sits and, (7) the capability to transform ideas into form and communicating their value. According to Conley, these competencies are at the core of design.

Subsequent work has picked up on this reasoning and developed it further. The recent work by Morelli on service design capabilities (2021) is representative of such undertakings. By chiseling and shaping several key related concepts, it proposes an updated understanding of what service design is and the required skills to successfully use them. The relevance of this work for a system analysis within design is that it also captures and provides clarity on the expansion of design into new territories. Moreover, it raises the same type of questions put forward by Conley. In effect, Morelli's proposal picks up on Conley's approach and defines a set of eight competences, also referred as skills, or talents, or abilities, or capabilities, this last term being preferred given its largest significance. It has thus also been able to delineate a set of design capabilities as unique to this discipline. But it also adds and states that such core capabilities are not permanently enclosed within design professionals, in the perspective that designers can also foster design capabilities that are underlying in other contexts.

Such propositions, while not visible at first sight, can therefore be useful to understand the inner working of the design ecosystem. They seem to tell us that beneath a 'design ecosystem' a set of core capabilities are at its root and there is still a complex and wide debate taking place.

4   Circumscribing the Design Ecosystem

The variety of points of view and understandings as to where design stands in an ecosystem seems to be, as seen in the previous discussion, and among many other factors, the reflection of a long and complex debate with multiple origins, including the definition of design, its methods, its relation to innovation and practice, its position as seen by the cultural and creative industries, or the expansion of design into new areas. A debate which is not under detailed discussion here. But it is this same diversity that should be used, in our perspective, as a guide for understanding the design ecosystem.

This section therefore aims to intersect what are the key takeaways when looking at different perspectives, by re-centering them in the systems rationale and principles. The goal is to provide a coherent perspective on how to frame a design ecosystem.

4.1   Underlying Issues

Looking at the above discussion on the different 'design ecosystem' perspectives, several contrasting and complementary views have been scrutinized, adhering as best as possible, to an analysis from a systems perspective. Table 1 summarizes the key points, by placing on the left column what are the key takeaways from the discussion in the immediate previous Sect. 3 and on the right column the related observations taken from a systems point of view, based on Sect. 2 of this paper. That is, the right column intends to frame the discussion within the parameters of a systemic perspective, which will be helpful to propose adaptations to the model.

When looking at such considerations, it becomes clear how there is still a large knowledge gap to be produced to substantiate the 'design ecosystem' model from a systems perspective. The following section intends to work on the existing available information to propose adaptations to the design ecosystem model, while leaving to the conclusions section a set of observations and gaps that can be useful to further explore in the future.

Table 1 Intersection analysis between takeaways from design ecosystem perspectives (Sect. 3 of this paper) and systemic guidelines (Sect. 2 of this paper)

Takeaways from diverse perspectives on the design ecosystem	Systemic considerations on the takeaways
Differentiating the design ecosystem from the innovation ecosystem seems problematic	Systemic analysis requires clear boundaries between systems
There is an unawareness regarding the direction of the design ecosystem	A system direction needs to be deduced from evidence and is difficult to capture for large systems
There is an expectation and desired goal for the design ecosystem to foster innovation	This reflects what is the wished direction of a system and therefore the expected role of policies
Design ecosystem perspectives from innovation and cultural and creative viewpoints have not yet been sufficiently bridged	This shall help clarify the design ecosystem boundaries and internal mechanics
There is a recognition and evidence on the interactions and impact in other sectors	The articulation with other systems is key not only to define each one boundary but also to understand the direction its taking
There is evidence that increased "design interactions" have positive effects	Such interactions and impact can be useful in deducing the direction and functions
There is a limited understanding on the sort of interactions taking place	A clear discernment of existing interactions is key for understanding the system
There has been an effort in articulating and clarifying design core capabilities	These endeavors allow to better understand what sort of interactions and functions are specifically employed by design
There seems to be limited, systematic and evidence-based knowledge on the sort of system failures within a design ecosystem	Such knowledge is fundamental as to know where to act from a systems (and policies) point of view
The design ecosystem seems diverse in terms of its disciplines, its territories of action or its interactions within and with other systems	This points towards an organic and dynamic and complex nature

4.2   Can We yet State that a Design Ecosystem is Clearly Established?

Going back to the initial hypothesis on the importance of scrutinizing different viewpoints on the design ecosystem model, we have found several pointers which indicate the design ecosystem frontiers are still blurry. From a systems perspective, and even a policy-making perspective, this can be problematic. Most especially, as those frontiers are the ones that will help define which data is to be collected, which is key to identify the system interactions, rules, and possible system failures.

As such, it seems plausible that the boundaries of the design ecosystem model require further adaptations so that they are as clear as possible, even if within a certain rigor for relevance tradeoff, as pointed out by Walker. We will therefore discuss the design ecosystem by following the key components and guidelines of systems theory as to build adaptations that sit within systemic parameters.

Subsequently, we first need to look at the elements of the system which we propose as the professionals making use of a set of design capabilities, such as the competences identified by Conley and Morelli. Indeed, this critical mass is what substantiates this debate, and the core design capabilities therefore seem to be the glue of a design ecosystem. And if the system elements are clear, so are its boundaries. Moreover, circumscribing an ecosystem also requires that it be distinctive from other systems, even if it is located within or connected to other systems. That is also why we argue that it does not seem plausible that a design ecosystem has its perimeter entirely within the innovation ecosystem. And this is because defining the design ecosystem with the same kind of elements and even terminology of the innovation system makes it challenging to define its boundaries. In this perspective, referring to the professionals who use design capabilities seems to provide clearer frontiers, especially as opposed to those who do not use such capabilities. Moreover, the cultural and creative perspective is a reminder of how design seems to permeate across different contexts, independently of its role (or no role) in innovation.

Secondly, it is also important to look at the existing interactions within elements, as systems theory states that one of the prerequisites for classifying a system is when elements interact among themselves. Indeed, there are examples that proof such interactions as the case pointed out by the design ladder, most especially as the further we climb up the ladder the more interactions among professionals using design capabilities take place. Moreover, there is also a perspective on limited connections with other sectors, as opposed to existing a higher level of relationships within the professionals using design capabilities, as noted in BEDA's analysis. And additionally, Morelli also points out how design capabilities can be fostered in other contexts. This thus raises the question on how design capabilities are applied, transferred, permeate, and evolve within the design ecosystem and other systems, and on how such interactions take place. This seems to further subscribe how design capabilities play a crucial role in defining the design ecosystem boundaries and function.

The third and last point is about the design ecosystem direction. This is perhaps the most complex and difficult point to scrutinize, as it would require an extensive evidence-base study. Simultaneously, at this stage, that is also an advantage as a direction already implies that a system exists and/or is clearly defined.

As to summarize this discussion and translating this framework into an adapted version of the ecosystem boundaries and identity the following is therefore proposed:

- the elements are set in all active professionals, working in any kind of context, as long as they are employing design capabilities;
- the rules of the ecosystem refer to the way the interactions among these elements and with other systems are established, which seem centred on design capabilities; and
- the direction of the entire ecosystem is the sum of the directions of each element, as at this stage is difficult to provide further clarity on this point.

What we are then proposing is to reduce the scope and reposition current understandings of the design ecosystem, towards its critical mass: professionals using the set of design capabilities. By organising the design ecosystem in this perspective, it seems more in tune with systems principles as it delineates more clearly its elements and how they interact with each other and with other systems.

However, it is also clear that further information and data must be collected and analysed to fine tune this proposition. Prospects to be carried out are then proposed in the upcoming section.

5   Conclusions and Way Forward

In this paper we have dissected different perspectives concerning the design ecosystem approach. From these, it is clear on the existing diversity of proposals, which are not yet sufficiently covered in a coherent and holistic perspective. As such, we have argued that such a variety of views is also a reflected on the complexity and difficulty in understanding and delineating a design ecosystem. Which was why it was considered useful to apply what are settled notions and principles from systems theory to support an adaptation of the design ecosystem model.

By re-framing the design ecosystem towards the professionals using the set of design core capabilities as its elements and the ones leading on the existing interactions, this has also led to raising further questions that are important to reflect. The relevance of these issues also lies at the core of the systems theory approach and how the current stage of problem articulation and boundary selection indicates how moving forward to subsequent stages might yet be too soon. Moreover, settling the main unsolved issues for bounding the design ecosystem model will be crucial for helping to detect what are the design ecosystem specific failures and exactly how a policy should then act.

A set of issues and questions that follow from the previous discussion and proposal and which therefore remain open are raised in Table 2.

Other issues can certainly be derived for future research; these ones seem to relate more closely with the systemic approach for policy-making.

Table 2 Considerations for future research

Issues	Considerations for future research
Ecosystem failures	As systems failures are at the core of how a policy is developed, it becomes clear on the need to further study this aspect for the design ecosystem. There are already several clues and research undertaken in this regard, but such work has not yet been conducted through a systemic approach
Direction of the ecosystem	While the direction of the design ecosystem has not been here under detailed scrutiny, given how difficult it is to have a clear picture, it is worth raising this discussion. The concept of "direction" in this case can have a multiplicity of meanings and, most especially, ways of determining such direction. Whatever the evidence, this issue is a clear sign on the importance of defining ways to evaluate this dimension
Target of policies	Within the approach we propose, while design policies exist because professionals are the ones substantiating the ecosystem, this does not necessarily imply that a design policy should focus alone on such professionals. In fact, a design policy should focus on what are the identified failures
Limits of action	By centering the ecosystem in professionals using the set of design capabilities, this also means there is a maximum radius of action that such an ecosystem and eventual respective policy can have. In turn, this raises the question on the need to further study core design capabilities to articulate them as clearly and distinctly as possible
Confluence with other policies	The existence of different perspectives on where design sits in terms of ecosystems comes along with different policies sitting in different policy areas. Innovation and cultural and creative policies were the examples provided. Special consideration is then required when building-up design policies as a closer look is vital as to prevent negative reinforcements with other policies

Acknowledgements R. Monteiro—This paper was developed within the context of the author Rui Monteiro FCT Research Scholarship (FCT - Fundação para a Ciência e Tecnologia e Fundo Social Europeu), PD/BD/150494/2019.

References

Badziili N, Richards D, Cruickshank L (2019) Disruptive innovation ecosystems: reconceptualising innovationecosystems. Academy for Design Innovation Management Conference, London, UK

BEDA & PDR (2018) Design action plan for Europe 2.0? Workshop Transcript, Thes-saloniki, 07.06.18. Retrieved from https://www.interregeurope.eu/fileadmin/user_upload/tx_tevprojects/library/file_1533120355.pdf. Accessed on 28 Jan 2019

Bertalanff LV (1969) General system theory: foundations, developments, applications. George Braziller, New York

Bleda M, del Rio P (2013) The market failure and the systemic failure rationales in technological innovation systems. Res Policy 42(5):1039–1052. https://doi.org/10.1016/j.respol.2013.02.008

Conley C (2010) Leveraging design's core competencies. Des Manag Rev 15(3):45–51. https://doi.org/10.1111/j.1948-7169.2004.tb00171.x

DCMS (2001) Creative industries mapping document 1998, 1st edn. Department of Culture, Media and Sport, London, UK

Florida R (2002) The rise of the creative class. And how it's transforming work, leisure and everyday life. Basic Books

Gonzalez C, Lecuona M, Hernandez M (2018) Concordancia de las políticas de diseño con el marco de medición de la innovación del Manual de Oslo. Revista 180:62. https://doi.org/10.32995/rev180.Num-41.(2018).art-359

Meadows DH (2009) Thinking in systems: a primer. Earthscan , London, Sterling

Medyna G, Coatanéa E, Christophe F, Bakhouya M, Choulier D, Forest J (2013) Creativity from design and innovation perspectives. In: Carayannis EG (eds) Encyclopedia of creativity, invention, innovation and entrepreneurship. Springer, New York. https://doi.org/10.1007/978-1-4614-3858-8_32

Mercan B, Göktas D (2011) Components of innovation ecosystems: a cross-country study. Int Res J Financ Econ 76. EuroJournals Publishing

Morelli N, de Götzen A, Simeone L (2021) Introduction. In: Service design capabilities. Springer series in design and innovation, vol 10. Springer, Cham. https://doi.org/10.1007/978-3-030-56282-3_1

Mortati M (2013) Systemic aspects of innovation and design. https://doi.org/10.1007/978-3-319-03242-9

Monteiro R, Giesteira B, Boddington A, Farinha C (2021) Current issues in design policies: balancing tensions. In: Raposo D, Neves J, Silva J, Correia Castilho L, Dias R (eds) Advances in design, music and arts. EIMAD 2020. Springer series in design and innovation, vol 9. Springer, Cham. https://doi.org/10.1007/978-3-030-55700-3_39

Mortati M, Maffei S (2018) Researching design policy ecosystems in Europe. She Ji: J Des Econ Innov 4(3):209–228. ISSN 2405–8726. https://doi.org/10.1016/j.sheji.2018.04.002

Oruç S (2010) Modeling dynamic systems of creative industries: the case of film industries. Master thesis, The Middle East Technical University

Stewart J, Ayres R (2001) Systems theory and policy practice: an exploration. Policy Sci 34(1):79–94. Retrieved 6 Dec 2020, from http://www.jstor.org/stable/4532523

TFCC Tom Fleming Creative Consultancy (2015) Cultural and creative spillovers in Europe: report on a preliminary evidence review

Throsby D (2008) The concentric circles model of the cultural industries. Cultural Trends 17 (3):147–164

Throsby D (2010) The economics of cultural policy. Cambridge University Press, Cambridge, UK

Walker WE, van Daalen CE (2013) System models for policy analysis. In: Thissen W, Walker W (eds) Public policy analysis. International series in operations research & management science, vol 179. Springer, Boston, MA. https://doi.org/10.1007/978-1-4614-4602-6_7

Whicher A (2017) Design ecosystems and innovation policy in Europe. Strateg De-sign Res J 10 (2). https://doi.org/10.4013/sdrj.2017.102.04

Woolthuis R, Lankhuizen M, Gilsingc V (2005) Technovation 25(6):609–619. https://doi.org/10.1016/j.technovation.2003.11.002

Communication Design

The Empty Tide

Mafalda Sofia Almeida

Abstract Contemporary society it is marked by the strong transformations that has been felt, recently, in all social, educational, cultural and political levels. It seems that we are facing a society that drastically empties itself of its values and ways of acting, trying to reconfigure itself at every step, a redoubled effort required of all of us, in order to respond to the demands and challenges that we face every day. This empty tide, full of uncertainties where we are called to make deeper reflections on the way we have been proceeding along our academic and professional path, can also become a turning point in the history of mankind. We now have, more than ever, the possibility of renewing ourselves and being able to open new pathways by adopting more conscious and constructive attitudes, inside and outside the academic environment. We have the possibility to train young people who are more aware and more attentive to society and their fellows. The text presented, intends to bring a reflection on how to make a difference, in communication design, promoting and sensitizing students, to issues related to social inclusion and to the realization of projects in which they contemplate, accessibility and inclusion. Transformative Education; Raising Awareness for the Inclusion Thematic; Communication for all; Accessible and Inclusive Communication are some of the topics that we will cover in this section.

Keywords Transformative education · Awareness for inclusion · Accessible and inclusive communication · Communication for all

1 Introduction

Currently, the strong transformations that we have been felt, within society at all is levels, social, educational, cultural and political, show us how worrying is the direction we are taking and the urgency of a more sustainable change.

M. S. Almeida (✉)
Universidade da Beira Interior, Rua Marquês d'Ávila e Bolama, 6201-001 Covilhã, Portugal
e-mail: mafalda.almeida@ubi.pt

© The Author(s), under exclusive license to Springer Nature Switzerland AG 2022 205
D. Raposo et al. (eds.), *Perspectives on Design II*, Springer Series in Design
and Innovation 16, https://doi.org/10.1007/978-3-030-79879-6_15

This tide, which has promoted the loss of many loved ones, due to the COVID-19 pandemic, forces us and confronts us with what we are and what we really want. We are obliged to reflect about the course we have taken and what values are really important and which we want to defend. When we arrived here, and as teachers, we realized that the challenges that we often pose to our students are superfluous and without added value. This sad reality, which many will probably want to hide, must not impede progress and the urgent changes that are being felt.

In a moment, as delicate as the one we are experiencing, in which all Humanity suffers, on the most varied levels, whose uncertainties of the future are enormous, we have the possibility to put into practice more innovative techniques, methods and teaching–learning processes. We have in front of us a golden opportunity. Because new paths can be traced, teaching can be made more dynamic, flexible and easily adapted to circumstances and means, extracting from them the guidelines and challenges necessary for the formation of young people and new generations. We can take advantage of the tide to challenge and promote in each student the ability to transform obstacles into challenges, an important factor for motivational development in the search, exploration and experimentation for more innovative and inclusive solutions.

It is known that education can be transformative, as it can produce new ways of seeing and thinking in each of the beings. Sensitizing and disseminating reflections, knowledge and practices on the importance of real and contemporary themes on life in society and about social inclusion, is, in our view, the duty of any teacher, who is interested in promoting a more just, more tolerant society and more inclusive. We believe that raising awareness of the themes of accessibility and inclusion, in the field of communication design, with future designers, opens the way for new reflections and approaches in the development of products and services, with added value, which may come to generate strong social changes.

Communication is an extremely important and powerful medium, because it is through it that we make ourselves understood, we understand the others and everything that happens around us. It is, therefore, fundamental to create mechanisms that allow us to have a communication that does not discriminate, that includes, that democratizes and that guarantees the participation of all citizens, both of them, women and men. We are surrounded by communication problems and according to Werneck (2020), the biggest question is: who is really interested in practicing accessible communication? Making communication more democratic and more inclusive? Regarding this aspect, we think that communication designers have a decisive role in planning, awareness and execution of all types of projects and products of this nature.

2 Transformative Education

It is known that education can be transformative, a capable means by which each individual can operate his own transformation and renewal. When well-dosed and worked, education has the necessary powers to change social positions and behaviours, an extremely important factor at a time when the quality in education is sought so much, but as Freire and Shor (2006) said, a new "quality" is needed, which welcomes everyone. For UNESCO (2001, p. 1) educational quality is a "Dynamic concept that must be permanently adapted to a world that is experiencing profound social and economic changes. It is very important to stimulate the ability to forecast and anticipation. The old quality criteria are no longer enough. Despite differences in context, there are many common elements in the search for quality education that empowers everyone, women and men, to fully participate in community life and to be citizens of the world". Education is undergoing very significant changes and disruptions, in an increasingly digitalized era, with increasingly sophisticated resources and with increasingly sustainable premises, is an important time to be able to make changes and give a new meaning to education. This means looking for a more flexible education that encourages respect for everything and everyone, implying diversity, acceptance, cooperation, mutual help and that rejects any type or form of discrimination, oppression or domination. It was important to create more malleable forms of teaching, to give space for students to pursue their own interests and choose the path that was most convenient for them. Promoting in this way, a culture of innovation and experimentation to a more sustainable and inclusive development.

All the experiences we are exposed to, regardless of the environment in which they happen, are processes that provide us with some type of learning. Like Berg (2012), we believe that everything happens in our life with a greater purpose. We believe that the greater the obstacle, the greater its potential for reward and the greater the difficulty, the greater will be our learning.

It is important to move towards teaching renewed with new approaches encouraging students to think beyond the obvious, to use their creativity to the fullest, to experiment with new ways and means of proceeding, analyzing and correlating information, to accept error as an integral part of the process and to work with action research methodologies, in which fieldwork is a decisive stage of knowledge acquisition.

To Lino (2020), the school must guarantee equal opportunities, stimulate curiosity and creativity and encourage talents and skills. It is par excellence the place where each citizen develops critical thinking and sense, and citizens are the basis of a society, plenty of reasons for schools not to fail. Câmara (2010), alerts us to the fact that our curriculum, in the twenty-first century, they remain completely misfit, because they do not form people to be more human, more supportive, more competitive, more innovative, who take risks, who have confidence (…). According to him, one of the biggest challenges, in this age of global knowledge, is to create a new generation of explorers to act at different levels of our society. For Kawasaki (1990), in the book "The Macintosh Way", Apple's human resources manual, it can be seen that the skills they were looking for in their workers had little to do with the school curriculum. When analysing the characteristics, they were looking for, we found that these are much more linked to the individual's training and emotional intelligence, because they were looking for people, with passion, energy, self-confidence, people capable of dealing with stress and ambiguity, to work in groups, people capable of leading and able to achieve.

Well then, it is necessary to educate beings capable of analyzing, creating, developing, criticizing and innovating. It is necessary students/designers who have postures of self-reflection, reflection, analysis and criticism about the challenges that are thrown at them and that they face every day, to take them to the conscious deepening of decision making.

3   The Designer as Educator and as Sensitizer

According to Gadotti (2013), we live in a constantly connected and moving society, a space of numerous opportunities for acquiring knowledge, a society of "global learning" in which brings consequences for the school, for teachers and for teaching. According to him, "it is essential to learn to think autonomously, to know how to communicate, to know how to research, to know how to do, to have logical reasoning, to know how to organize one's work, to have discipline, to be subject to the construction of knowledge, to be open to new learning, to know the sources of information, to know how to articulate knowledge with practice and with other knowledge" (Gadotti 2013, p. 7). Within this perspective, the teacher becomes a mediator of information and learning, leaving the classic format of lecturer to become an organizer of knowledge, he becomes a constant learner, a collaborator and co-operator, a constructor of meaning, an information manager that helps to connect and relate information, which indicates a possible path.

In recent times, it has been felt that there is a great deal of installed inertia, since a great majority of students seem not to have the glow of other times, they seem to walk in school with little motivation. However, when challenged their posture changes radically, gain strength and advance at full speed. When stimulated, we believe it is important to give the message, that they should not be content with doing for doing, they should do the best they can or know, because indifference has never helped anyone to renew themselves let alone succeed. And if they have something to do, they should do it with pride. And if they want a good result, they must set the goal beyond the excellent.

Câmara (2010), at the conference "which curriculum for the twenty-first century", he exposes a particularity, which he finds interesting, and that the main world schools, whether at secondary or higher level are concerned and that Portuguese schools do not give any importance - the hidden curriculum. The one that is not written anywhere and that is so lacking in the formation of our young students.

According to Robinson (2006), it is necessary an education that encourages students to think, and for that, it is necessary to encourage them to be adventurous and not to be afraid of failing, it is important to create environments in which it is okay to be wrong.

For Gadotti (2013, p. 11), "the quality of teaching depends a lot on the quality of the teacher". That is why it is so important for the teacher, in addition to his professionalism, to be an educator, who stimulates, guides and makes students aware of real problems. The teacher must have passion and be happy to teach and learn, be ethical and set an example, be empathetic and humble, know how to listen and try to understand their students, be willing to work in a team, not make value judgments, be supportive and, and, above all, to know how to promote spaces for learning, reflection and criticism, respecting and shaping the attitudes and language of their students, so that they become future citizens and professionals, more aware that they express themselves and communicate more effectively and efficiently.

We are convinced that there are two fundamental axes in the training and learning of a communication designer: the curricular knowledge, but also training for citizenship. Because a good awareness and orientation made from school over the years can come to make all the difference in the future choices and professional conduct of the students.

4   Raising Awareness for the Inclusion Thematic

In education we should look for inclusive and sustainable values for the development and progress of our own society, based on fundamentals such as: acceptance, respect and sharing of knowledge and ideas, cooperation between all elements, experimentation, discovery and innovation. We need to value individuals and their needs and not constantly promote simply commercial values. Since the 1970s, from the nineteenth century, authors and activists such as Victor Papanek and Ezio Manzini have called for a design approach based on a more responsible and sustainable posture, looking to projects for social, moral and ecological value at the expense of a design purely mercantile and disposable.

If we believe that young people have all the potential to be able to be drivers of change, we know that awareness-raising must start right from the start, both at home and in schools. We can read on the website of Associação Salvador, in the section what we do that "The awareness of this early instils an attitude of respect towards difference" (AS 2008). It is very important to talk and raise awareness among children and young people about respect for others, disability, equal opportunities and the importance of inclusion.

If we want to create an inclusive communication culture, we must, first together with our students, future communication designers, analyse and understand the reality that exists and how objects or services are being created and if they are or not inclusive.

This preliminary phase may open the door to discussions on exclusion, integration and inclusion. We believe that in this way young designers can be more attentive and more critical in relation to the products/services that surround them, also becoming aware of their future projects.

According to the Guide to Good Accessibility Practices, of the General Directorate of Cultural Heritage and Tourism of Portugal, a communication to be relevant, must appeal to the various senses, so that each individual can enjoy reading and interpretation in the way that suits him best (Mineiro Clara et al. 2017). This encouragement in the use of multisensory[1] and multimodal[2] communication, is the closest awareness of respect for human beings, which regardless of their physical or cognitive condition, offers them multiple forms of experience and learning.

We believe that one of the biggest challenges today is to bring delicate themes into the classroom, valuing and promoting with students the development of projects, with added value, those that contemplate, in addition to the rest, concerns and inclusive solutions. This attempt to call for the construction of communication products and/or services, taking into account the different senses, of the human being, promotes the possibility of ensuring a more meaningful and valid learning and experience for all.

5   Communication4all

An empty tide is conducive to the implementation and development of important requirements, such as accessibility and inclusion, in a selfish, selective and increasingly deprived society with social values. Aspects that in the background because in the eyes of many, they are not relevant, since they do not add commercial value.

It is common for a constitution to exist that preaches a more fraternal, more pluralistic society, without discrimination and prejudice while at the same time experiencing the exact opposite. And this happens, because we do not have an education aimed at creating a more awake and inclusive society, we do not promote a culture of acceptance and appreciation of diversity and pluralism. This dehumanization and self-centeredness lead each of us to discriminate and exclude in a natural way, without realizing the gravity of the situation (Werneck 2020).

---

[1]Multisensory communication is a communication that involves two or more senses simultaneously.

[2]Multimodal communication is a communication where several communicative modalities coexist (speech, gestures, text, images, description …). Multimodal text is one whose meaning is realized by more than one modality, that is, a code: Linguistic or non-linguistic (images, color, sound …). Each modality has its potential for representation and communication, produced culturally (Kress and Van Leeuwen 1996).

Communication is an extremely important and powerful medium because it is through it that we made understand us, we understand each other and all that is happening around us. It is, therefore, fundamental to create mechanisms that allow us to have a communication that does not discriminate, that includes that democratizes and that guarantees the participation of all citizens, men and women.

We don't realize it, but there is a lot of discrimination throughout the communication process. According to Werneck (2020), all people have the same human value, regardless of their physical, psychological or cognitive condition, no matter if the person is blind, deaf or dumb, no matter how the human body manifests itself on planet earth. The fact is that nothing changes human value[3] of any person, because this value is immutable. According to the same author, for there to be an inclusive and accessible communication, which is the basis of communication for all, every society must be convinced that all people have the same human value and, therefore, everyone must have the same opportunity to communication, this being the basis of barrier-free communication.

We are surrounded by communication problems, and our performance is as serious as our lack of commitment to the barriers that we create and that exist in communication. If we reflect and analyse, we realize that there are many people, who for various reasons, are discriminated against and fail to exercise their right to access information and, even more serious, to be able to communicate. It is wrong that a given social group can only communicate, thanks to the generosity of some who promote projects and develop some resources so that these people can also participate, although, in a limited way, of what should be an essential good for them and a legal right.

For example, a book, in addition to being printed, should include several other forms and formats for presenting its contents, so that everyone could access it. We speak of the possibility of sound description, not only of the text, but also of images and other graphics elements, of the possibility of creating a format using the language of "libras[4]" and subtitles, and so on. Here it is also necessary to create means and ways to understand what people, especially those who have some type of disability, can also tell and transmit us. We are ignorant, in relation to some fields of social evolution, because we have no interest and do not want to know about the values and knowledge that these people can give us.

For Werneck (2020), the biggest question is who is really interested in practicing accessible communication? Making communication more democratic and more inclusive? With regard to this aspect, we think that communication designers have a decisive role in the planning, awareness and execution of all types of projects and products of this nature.

---

[3]According to the author, the human value is different from social value. The human value is transversal to all human beings, because we are born, live and die all in the same way. The social value is different, because it refers to the person's form, status and behavior. These can be corrupt, heterosexual, homosexual, pedophile, rich, poor, formed, without studies …

[4]Libras is the term used to designate sign language.

6 Accessible and Inclusive Communication

Today the concept associated with accessibility is vast and with many facets, it is a term that applies to all projects, strategies, activities and means developed, to minimize physical, intellectual and social barriers, allowing access to the largest possible number of people to goods and services. Ensuring accessibility is a fundamental condition to ensure the quality of life of any person, being even a necessary element, so that the rights and duties of citizenship, conferred to any member of a democratic society can be exercised (INR 2020).

When a communication designer participates in the development of any product or service, he must always keep in mind, important issues such as accessibility and inclusion, because as Clarkson et al. (2017), refers, each decision made of the design, they have the potential to include or exclude people.

For the National Institute for Rehabilitation, universal or inclusive design aims to simplify everyone's life, regardless of age, status, creed or ability, making products, structures, communication/information and the built environment usable, at low cost or without cost extra, so that all citizens, and not only those with special needs, even if temporarily can fully integrate into an inclusive society (INR 2020).

Therefore, a pedagogical practice that seeks to develop communication projects with concerns of accessibility and social inclusion, will have to undergo some modifications in the educational procedure, as it must meet real and not fictitious or utopian work proposals.

In view of the diversity, we believe that communication projects that aim to reach people with different needs, should contemplate, at least, two principles:

- Flexibility, where it is expected that each human being may need different forms and/or means of communication to understand information. And that not everyone acquires information at the same pace and time.
- Cooperative and participatory work where is expected, in the projects, the participate of the target groups. Is therefore, accommodation is important, where a period of time is established so that students can be integrated into environments, conducive and indicated, so they can observe and better understand the needs and challenges that the target audience are facing, seeking and exploring together, with them, more correct solutions.

For Manzini (2008) it is just as important to develop the capacity for recognizing the value of social innovation projects as it is to foster with designers the ability to design solutions that can be reproduced or adapted in different contexts. According to him, "are cases of social innovation, basic innovations (…), which indicate how, sometimes, diffuse design skills are capable of creating ways of being and doing at the same time creative and collaborative…".

7   Creativity and Social Innovation

Throughout the twentieth century, we have seen the phenomenon and the concept associated with creativity growing and passing from a mere individual capacity, to processes capable of generating wealth and bringing collective benefits.

Following hand in hand with creativity, also innovation, has become a key element in the transformation of various sectors and modes of life and the importance of which, today, is not contested (Giglio et al. 2009).

For Alencar (1997), creativity is intimate with the thought process and is easily associated with imagination, invention, intuition, inspiration and originality. He also mentions that creativity carries with it something magical and mysterious, since creative ideas usually appear unexpectedly and not when we want to.

However, for Kao (1997), creative people are those who more quickly assimilate conflicts, needs and problems that need to be solved, they are also those who more easily find the hidden connections that can be related and explored in order to obtain something innovative. Bruno-Faria et al. (2008), refer that an individual is creative when he meets the following characteristics: Has initiative; he likes what he does, he is not afraid of taking risks, he is not afraid of making mistakes, he has confidence in himself and he has flexible thinking. Added to all these characteristics, those that we also consider to be important, in the profile of a creative person: he must be humble and receptive, be attentive, assertive, explorer, curious, questioning and honest.

The concept of creativity can also extend to the phenomenon of generating new ideas, processes and services that can contribute in some way to social good. Within this context, creativity and innovation do not seek originality but different solutions for real and concrete problems.

Innovation has always accompanied humanity throughout its evolutionary history a fundamental factor and driver of civilizational and social progress. Any empty tide is fertile ground for innovation, as it creates the necessary conditions, to drop paradigms that no longer serve to respond to the needs that emerge. Only an innovative path will be able to add knowledge, technological capacity and experience to seek and develop new approaches and new ways for communication and information transmission.

Although creativity and innovation are interconnected and related, they are distinct processes. The first comes from an internal process of processing and linking ideas. The second concerns to the practical and objective application and operationalization of the idea.

For Alencar (1997), innovation is the way to introduce, adopt and implement new ideas (goods or services), in response to a problem, transforming the new idea into something concrete. However, and according to Antónia (2007), for innovation to happen, changes must happen, soon right from academic training, because if organizations are transformed, training must also be transformed in order to keep up with the changes that take place. Here it is not just about recycling materials, but rather incorporating new practices. To innovate, we must overcome "the "culture of poverty", in which the scarcity of resources annuls all risky projects, as also the conservatism, which penalizes heterodoxy and asphyxiates innovation. It is important to accept that not all projects will be successful, but nevertheless be willing to take the risk of experimenting" (UNESCO 2006).

The teaching understanding and formative interdisciplinarity can allow the future designer to acquire skills to aggregate and process instructions of all kinds, placing him in privileged conditions, as he will be able to present concrete solutions to various problems.

Every student should be challenged to promote their ability to turn obstacles into challenges, an important factor for motivational development in the search for innovative and inclusive solutions.

The student of communication design must seek to position himself as a responsible professional capable of contributing to the development of communication projects, capable of being interpreted and reaching as many people as possible. It is obvious that a designer cannot change the world but he can help and contribute to the design and construction of a better, fairer, more informed, more tolerant, more inclusive and sustainable society.

8 Conclusion

An accessible and inclusive communication is one that allows any citizen to have access to information and knowledge without any barriers. To make communication more accessible, it is important to know how to adapt the means and the information, so that all people, including those with intellectual disabilities, can understand the content. We believe that promoting reflections, concerns and moments of sharing and raising awareness on sensitive issues, among young people, such as social exclusion/inclusion, can promote in them a construction of a new conscience.

Taking as a starting point that creativity and social innovation can be used in all areas of our life and that are based on the search for new solutions or reformulation of the design of objects or services. An innovative social challenge is one that seeks processes, means and forms, to solve the different problems and challenges, which go far beyond what is common. However, encouraging the use of creative capacities and innovation, oriented to the theme of inclusion, as a concept of the activities to be developed, in the classroom space, will depend a lot on the dynamics that are created between teachers and students. According to Robinson (2006), we are trained in a fast-food educational system, in which everything follows rules, is standardized and closely linked to the industrial era. It is important to change this educational system to one that is more malleable and organic so that it stops being so linear and becomes more dynamic in order to adapt to different circumstances. Education should instruct us for to in the future have a profession but also to be a good citizen. It is necessary to create good conditions for our young people to see school as a space for learning, investigation, reflection and appreciation, where they feel stimulated to explore and learn, where they are not afraid to fail, to speak, to ask, a space of acceptance open to discussion and progress. As we have already mentioned, we need students/designers who have positions of self-reflection, reflection, analysis and criticism about the challenges they are faced with and which they face, to lead them to the conscious deepening of decision making.

In a world that was created for everyone where we all have the same human condition, the existence of discrimination in access to communication does not make any sense. We are convinced, as well as Werneck (2020), that the exercise for the realization of objects that allow an inclusive communication is the way to build a more sustainable society, that is, a society that welcomes the contribution of all people without exception. It is for this reason that the student of communication design must seek to position himself as a responsible professional, capable of contributing to the development of communication projects, with added value, those that include in addition to the rest, concerns and inclusive solutions. Because we recognize that this attempt to call for the construction of communication products and/or services taking into account the different senses of the human being, can promote the possibility of ensuring a more meaningful and valid learning and experience for all.

We are in an important period that allows us to make significant changes for the whole of society. It is time to take new paths, to be courageous to innovate and to be persistent for not give up on the first obstacles and to believe that it is possible, because only then will we become pioneers. It is up to us to accept the new challenges that lie ahead and take advantage of this empty tide to create the necessary conditions so that the tide, again filling up, fills up in a consistent and renewed way in order to sustain the new generations.

Bibliography

Alencar ELS (1997) The management of creativity. Makron Books, São Paulo

Antónia N (2007) The role of the archive professional in the development and innovation processes. In: Proceedings of the National congress of librarians, archivists and documentalists, no. 9,Portugal

Associação Salvador (2008) Awareness in schools. https://www.associacaosalvador.com/o-que-fazemos/sensibilizacao-em-escolas/140/. Accessed 20 Oct 2020

Berg Y (2012) The power of Kabbalah. 13 Principles for overcoming challenges and achieving fullness. Pergaminho

Bruno-Faria MF, Veiga HMS, Macedo LF (2008) Creativity in organizations: analysis of national scientific production in journals and books on administration and psychology. Psychol Mag. Work, Florianópolis, vol 8(1), Jun. Retrieved from http://pepsic.bvsalud.org/scielo.php?script=sci_arttext&pid=S1984-66572008000100009&lng=pt&nrm=iso

Câmara A (2010, June 7) DESAFIOS COLOCADOS À ESCOLA PORTUGUESA[Intervenção]. QUE CURRÍCULO PARA O SÉCULO XXI? (Colóquios e Conferências Parlamentares), Lisboa, Portugal

Clarkson J et al (2017) Inclusion design toolkit. University of Cambridge, Cambridge. http://www.inclusivedesigntoolkit.com/whatis/whatis.html . Accessed 21 Oct 2020

Freire P, Shor I (2006) Fear and daring: the teacher's daily life, 11th edn. Peace and Earth, Rio de Janeiro

Gadotti M (2013) Quality in education: a new approach. In: Basic education congress: quality in learning. Municipal Education Network from Florianópolis. Retrieved from http://www.pmf.sc.gov.br/arquivos/arquivos/pdf/14_02_2013_16.22.16.85d3681692786726aa2c7daa4389040f.pdf

Giglio Z, Wechsler SM, Bragotto D (orgs.) (2009) From creativity to innovation, 1st edn. Papirus, São Paulo

INR (2020) National Institute for Rehabilitation. Accessibility. Retrieved from https://www.inr.pt/acessibilidades

Kao JJ (1997) The art and discipline of creativity in the company. Campus, Rio de Janeiro

Kawasaki G (1990) The Macintosh way (1st ed.). Longman

Kress G, van Leeuwen T (1996) Reading images: the grammar of visual design. Routledge, London & New York

Lino C (2020) 15 | 25 What the school does for students? Evening Newscast. SIC News. 24 Nov 20, 22h03. Retrieved from https://sicnoticias.pt/programas/1525/2020-11-24-1525.-O-que-e-que-a-escola-faz-pelos-alunos-

Manzini E (2008) Design for social innovation and sustainability: creative communities, collaborative organizations and new project networks (trans: coordination Cipolla C, team Spampinato E, Silva AL). E-papers, Rio de Janeiro, 2008 (notebooks of the high studies group, vol 1)

Mineiro C, Garcia A, Neves J (2017) Guia de Boas Práticas de Acessibilidade Comunicação Inclusiva em Monumentos, Palácios e Museus (1st ed., Vol. 1) [E-book]. Turismo de Portugal, I. P. Direção Geral do Património Cultural. Retrieved from http://business.turismodeportugal.pt/SiteCollectionDocuments/all-for-all/guia-boas-praticas-acessibilidade-monumentos-museus-jun-2017.pdf

Robinson (2006) Do schools kill creativity? [Video]. TED. (Portugueses trans: Caseiro N, reviewed by Lopes S). Retrieved from https://www.ted.com/talks/sir_ken_robinson_do_schools_kill_creativity?language=pt

UNESCO (2001) The countries of Latin America and the Caribbean adopt the Cochabamba declaration on education. In: Anais da Office of Public Information for Latin America and the Caribbean. Retrieved from http://www.iesalc.org

UNESCO (2006) United Nations decade of education for sustainable development (2005–2014). Contributions to its dynamism in Portugal. UNESCO, Lisboa. Retrieved from https://www.dge.mec.pt/sites/default/files/ECidadania/Areas_Tematicas/contibutos_dnuds.pdf

Werneck C (2020) All communication must be accessible and inclusive [Video]. TEDxPUCMinas, 19 Oct 2020. Retrieved from URL: https://www.youtube.com/watch?v=GTfcWtFo8J4

Communication Design Playing a Role in Social Innovation

Ana Melo and Marco Neves

Abstract Design for social innovation aims at solving community problems by recombining available resources, creating new social relationships, and strengthening stakeholder networks. Social innovation presents itself as one of the most promising proposals for responding to systemic problems that manifest themselves both at a global and local level, and the use of design methodologies, tools, and skills enables social innovation to become more resilient and sustainable. Communication design is a particularly relevant area in this context, as it meets the needs for visibility, visual materialization, creation of future scenarios, dissemination, and replication. Through an in-depth case study of three social innovation initiatives, we collected evidence regarding different roles that design is called upon, although they are not exclusive to communication design. Some of the main roles relate to triggering the initiatives themselves as well as the social debate that sustains them, facilitating processes of ideation and co-creation, mediating actors and prototyping products, services or events.

Keywords Communication design · Design for social innovation · Case study · Social innovation

1 Introduction

This article presents preliminary results of a multiple case study carried out on three social innovation initiatives, with the central objective of observing and describing communication design role throughout the process as well as the opportunities to

A. Melo (✉) · M. Neves
Faculdade de Arquitetura, Centro de Investigação em Arquitetura, Urbanismo e Design, Universidade de Lisboa, Rua Sá Nogueira, Polo Universitário, Alto da Ajuda, 1349-055 Lisboa, Portugal
e-mail: amelo2@edu.ulisboa.pt

M. Neves
e-mail: mneves@fa.ulisboa.pt

expand its performance. This case study is part of an ongoing doctoral research about design for social innovation and the role communication design plays in this context. The doctoral research intends to address several aspects of how communication design takes part in social innovation projects. Namely to characterize what this intervention is, how it proceeds (project methodology, methods, resources, tools, dynamics established with other disciplines and intervening actors, as well as with other design areas), when it occurs (at what stages of the social innovation processes) and why (the relevance of communication design in social innovation initiatives and what characterizes its specific intervention in comparison to other areas).

Design for social innovation (Thackara 2005; Manzini 2015; Amatullo et al. 2016) appears in the contemporary context as a practice-based design response and as a research field interested in addressing open, dynamic, interconnected, and complex problems (Murray et al. 2010; Ceschin 2014; Nicholls et al. 2015) that confront social, economic and natural systems. In face of profound disruptions at multiple levels that jeopardize planet's sustainability, social cohesion, and democracy resilience, there is a demand for new ways of action that take on an ecosystem approach (Scharmer and Kaufer 2013). On the other hand, the transformative capability of engaged citizens and communities, to form coalitions between personal, public, and private domains has never been higher (Manzini 2019). Constant connectivity, as provided by information and communication technologies that configure the fourth industrial revolution (Schwab 2015), is one of the main factors that enable new networks of interest and action (Manzini 2019) both at global and local levels.

It is in this context that design expands its more traditional intervention (Sanders and Stappers 2008), shifting from producing physical artifacts to more immaterial outcomes such as interaction, services, experiences, or systems (Davis 2008; Grefé 2011; Norman 2018). Design for social innovation thus relates to emerging areas that have as their main objective "design for" a purpose (Sanders and Stappers 2008; Manzini 2011; Meroni and Sangiorgi 2011), moving away from material, controlled, and finished products that characterized most of design activity in the twentieth century (Buchanan 2001). Design skills, tools, and methods are applied to social innovation processes (Mulgan 2014) and placed at the service of projects initiated by citizens and communities to facilitate, mediate, co-design, and enhance initiatives. These may be rooted in a specific time and space but can be disseminated and replicated in other situations, giving rise to possibilities of systemic transformation (Manzini 2015).

Communication design is an area capable of adding value to social innovation processes due to its specific contributions (Melo and Neves 2020), in close collaboration with interaction design, strategic design, system design, or service design. By reframing issues or problems (Dorst 2012), circulating new meanings and new narratives of the future (Ehn et al. 2014; Manzini 2015; Emilson 2015), establishing an infrastructure (Hillgren et al. 2011), and design coalitions (Jégou and Manzini 2008), communication design can expand social innovation possibilities and actions.

2 A Multiple Case Study Method

We considered a multiple case study method to be the most appropriate since our main goal was to attain a deep understanding of how communication designers took part in three social innovation initiatives. We combined the methodological steps described by Yin (2018) with the Social Innovation Biographies (SIBs) methodology (Kleverbeck and Terstriep 2017) bearing in mind that the study would focus on social innovation initiatives.

A case study method is particularly suitable when the object of study is contemporary (as opposed to historical) and when there is no control by the researcher over behavioral events (Yin 2018). It allows direct contact with the phenomenon and its context, allowing to describe, understand, and explain it in detail (Tellis 1997). Regarding the situated, contextual (Dorst 2010), and unrepeatable nature of a design process, the case study method becomes even more relevant.

We used multiple sources of information, allowing in-depth data collection and analysis. Through a descriptive approach, we correlated observed phenomena with constructs collected during the literature review.

SIBs intend to address flaws in social innovation case studies that mainly focus on describing implementation and dissemination. This methodology ensures the collection of information and analysis regarding three different levels: individual, structural, and conceptual. The goal is to capture data from "development paths, knowledge trajectories and stakeholder interactions at the micro-level" (Kleverbeck and Terstriep 2017, p. 3). It combines evidence from interviews with key stakeholders and other actors with an analysis of the network woven by the initiative.

Our multiple case study was developed in three phases. In the first phase, we carried out the planning and definition of the case study protocol and selected the cases. In the second phase, we guaranteed triangulation (Yin 2018) by collecting evidence from multiple sources such as semi-structured interviews, structured online questionnaires, desk research, and documentation analysis. In the third phase, we coded collected data in tables and diagrams, allowing for the systematization of information and for analyzing each particular case.

2.1 First Phase—Planning the Action

In the planning phase, we developed a protocol for a multiple case study, pointed out as essential by Yin (2018). This document contains the study's objectives, research questions and propositions, criteria for selecting cases, and procedures regarding evidence collection. The protocol serves as a guide for data collection and analysis, ensuring a consistent and standardized line of action (Yin 2018) in multiple cases, and thus contributing to obtain comparable data between them. It also served as a sort of road map, allowing to clarify and facilitate the research process.

The objectives of the study were to describe three processes of social innovation, mapping stages and milestones, interventions of communication design and resulting tasks and outputs, main actors in the process (individuals, institutions, communities), and network of relationships between them. Parallel to mapping the initiatives, it was also an objective of the study to describe the presence of categories and concepts present in the literature about design for social innovation.

Regarding the selection of cases, one of the main criteria was that each initiative had to fit in a certain description of social innovation, one that combines existing resources (social, economical, productive, i.e.) to solve a community problem, to achieve shareable and sustainable benefits, and to create, recreate or strengthen social relations in the process (Murray et al. 2010; Manzini 2015). Another selection criterion was the existence of communication designers' intervention in the initiatives.

Due to the need to elaborate an in-depth study that allows comparative analysis of results, another criterion was the possibility of collecting data in adequate quantity and depth (Yin 2018) and access key actors in the process (Kleverbeck and Terstriep 2017). The selected initiatives must also be related in some way to problems of human desertification of inland territories or have place-making (Manzini 2015) purposes.

The three selected initiatives were: Loulé Design Lab (LDL), Laboratório Cívico Santiago (Santiago Civic Laboratory/LCS), and Loulé Sou Eu! (I am Loulé/LSE).

2.2   Second Phase—Data Collection Proceedings

Data collection derived from multiple sources of evidence that could provide rich, detailed, and in-depth information. We applied the principle of triangulation so that the findings converged from two or more sources of evidence, thus contributing to construct validity (Yin 2018).

Preliminary desk research was carried out for each case, analyzing official communication material such as websites, social networks, and press clippings.

Afterward, we conducted semi-structured interviews with a key stakeholder (Kleverbeck and Terstriep 2017) to obtain detailed information from someone deeply involved in the initiative. Interviews focused on initiative objectives, structure, activities, the role played by the interviewee, and on the contributions of design and communication design to the process.

Later we sent a structured questionnaire via e-mail and Google Forms to interviewees. It aimed at delving into some specific themes related to the role of design, which required some reflection on the part of respondents. We also analyzed documents provided by interviewees about the initiatives and a field diary was used to collect the researcher's observations and reflections throughout the research process.

In the Loulé Design Lab case, we also had the opportunity to visit the facilities and to undertake direct observation of the project's ecosystem: co-working space for resident designers, workshops, store, and coordination team offices.

2.3   Third Phase—Coding and Analysis

To systematize collected qualitative data, as well as to establish the connection between the occurrence of certain phenomena and their description in the literature, we developed some tools to facilitate comparative analysis of the information: tables and diagrams.

Tables function to code data in a way that makes it easier to detect relevant patterns, serving as a basis for the analysis. The analysis process in the case studies should also, as far as possible, be anticipated and, in some way, planned when elaborating the study protocol (Yin 2018). In this regard, the use of word tables was productive since it ensured all relevant information was being collected, in addition to clarifying which data to collect.

Diagrams allow, clearly and immediately, to obtain a visualization of the operating structure of the initiative and the various phases of the process. They are especially useful in fulfilling functions of recording, understanding, and communicating information (Bertin 1983), generating a systemic view, and leading to the generation of knowledge and insights (Roxburgh 2014; Frascara 2015; Figueiras 2016).

We developed a table of concepts that characterize or are associated with design processes for social innovation (Hillgren et al. 2011; Meroni et al. 2013; Manzini 2014, 2015; Amatullo et al. 2016), recording which of them are identifiable in each case through the collected evidence (Table 1). We also developed an ID table of the initiatives, with relevant data to characterize each one (Kleverbeck and Terstriep 2017); diagrams of the network of stakeholders identified in data collection; diagrams representing the various stages of the process with the recording of moments of communication design intervention and a table of visual artifacts produced by communication design.

We used all these tools for analysis, that unfolded through a cyclical strategy described by Yin (2018): consider evidence collected, draw preliminary conclusions, and re-examine data, to ensure the findings are supported by evidence and observing the principle of linking evidence.

2.4   Study Limitations

Main limitations are related to time constraints for collecting information, as well as the availability of interviewees to allow for an extended interview time, which sometimes needed continuation to deepen some of the topics.

Another limitation stems from the difficulty of obtaining explicit information about the designers' work process, which is sometimes in the domain of tacit knowledge (Schön 1983). Also, when non-designer participants were implementing design strategies, they may not have the vocabulary to explicit their activity in terms of design processes, methods, or tools.

Table 1 Observable DSI concepts in the three cases

Design for social innovation/concepts	LDL	LCS	LSE
Participant interaction			
Design network	✓	✓	✓
Expert design	✓	✓	✓
Diffuse design (non-experts)	✓	✓	✓
Strategies for building consensus/common goals	✓	✓	✓
Creation of new social relations	✓	✓	✓
Design intervention			
Purpose (problem-solving/sensemaking)	Both	Both	Both
Placemaking strategies	✓	✓	✓
Tooling up	✓	✓	–
Framework project (strategy)	✓	✓	✓
Design initiatives	✓	✓	✓
Infrastructuring	✓	✓	✓
Defining an exit strategy	–	–	✓
Results			
Dissemination	✓	✓	✓
Replication	–	–	✓

The existence of two cases from the city of Loulé in the multiple case study is due to the unexpected opportunity to have access to in-depth information about LSE when we were conducting semi-structured interviews in LDL. It was an unforeseen opportunity, but the initiative proved to fit all the selection criteria explained above.

2.5 Case 1—Loulé Design Lab

Loulé Design Lab is an initiative integrated with Loulé Criativo, a project promoted by the Municipality of Loulé, in Algarve, a region in the south of Portugal that has tourism as its main economic activity. Loulé is a small town of about 25,000 inhabitants located a few kilometers from the seashore but still affected by the problems resulting from the concentration of critical thinking (namely in the creative field) in Lisbon and Porto areas, the largest cities in the country.

LDL was created in 2017 to function as an incubator for design projects that incorporate endogenous resources of the region, preserving and expanding the municipality's cultural identity. These resources include a large body of ancient artisanal knowledge that still exists in the community but is increasingly at risk of being lost, due to the aging of the population and by a scarcity of younger people interested in continuing traditional crafts. The synergy model between promoters and the local community bases itself on facilitating opportunities for co-creation

Fig. 1 LDL—visual identity, workshops, and exhibitions. Published with permission from LDL

between resident designers and local artisans. LDL works through a dynamic of long-term residences and the support of a dedicated logistics and human resources structure, with an industrial designer as coordinator and curator and a communication designer in the core team (Fig. 1).

2.6 Case II—Laboratório Cívico de Santiago

Laboratório Cívico de Santiago took place in Aveiro, a city in Portugal's central coast, to implement a civic laboratory methodology (Freire 2017; García 2018) in the Santiago neighborhood, an area with a past of social and economic problems. LCS was promoted by a group of researchers and people connected to the University of Aveiro, some of whom were designers.

The idea was to launch this project as an experience to revitalize social relations in the community, facilitating citizens' initiatives that could contribute to this goal. The public process began with a public call for ideas to improve the neighborhood. Afterward, the promoting team selected ten proposals and organized groups of volunteers from the community for project implementation. A set of prototyping sessions followed with the participation of the involved community and promoting team, which ensured mediation. As a result, there was a photojournalism exhibition, recipe sharing sessions from African cuisine, and painting of public spaces with children from local schools, among others. Projects were developed within a limited timeframe and shared with the Aveiro community in general through a final event (Fig. 2).

Fig. 2 LCS—call for ideas, co-creation workshops, website, and final event. Published with permission from LCS

2.7 Case III—Loulé Sou Eu!

Loulé Sou Eu! was generated in the context of a master's final project by a communication designer at the University of Algarve in Faro. The project reactivated a traditional shopping street in downtown Loulé, in decline due to the increasingly widespread shopping centers. Traditional stores, owned by small local merchants, showed difficulties with the increasing absence of passers-by and consequent lack of customers. Main downtown street, Rua de Portugal, was selected to implement this project.

The promoting designer created a communication plan to showcase each store, involving shopkeepers in an initial action of community creation and engagement with the project. As a follow-up, the promotor and the community of shopkeepers created an event to attract visitors, including street entertainment, decoration of shops and public space, and various other sharing activities between merchants and visitors. The event had great public acceptance and was replicated various times over the course of several months. This project originated an invitation by the Municipality of Loulé for the promoter designer to join a team from this public body to revitalize the downtown area and traditional commerce (Fig. 3).

3 Preliminary Results

Preliminary results of the multiple case study refer to three aspects: presence of concepts or structuring themes relating to communication design intervention in social innovation projects; the roles communication design plays, closely related to the needs of initiatives; lastly, the milestones of communication design intervention regarding one model describing the DSI process (Meroni et al. 2013).

Fig. 3 LSE—event, posters, visual identity, and postcards. Published with permission from LSE

3.1 Concepts

Table 1 lists main concepts that come into play in design for social innovation activities collected from the literature review, describing which were observable in each case.

Social innovation initiatives allow reframing problematic situations to generate new meanings (Dorst 2012; Zurlo and Cautela 2014; Emilson 2015; Manzini 2015). In doing so, they are capable of circulating new narratives socially and thus facilitate deeper change processes. Sense-making ability was observed in the three cases and equated in terms of importance to problem-solving by the various interviewees. This kind of action was carried out by the participating designers, but also by other team members.

All the cases showed the existence and importance of a place-making strategy (Pierce et al. 2011; Manzini 2015), i.e. the production of new meanings that transform a specific space or geographic location into a place. This process of creation implies various communities that relate to it and intentionally produce it. We collected compelling evidence in the three cases of the promoters' intervention as mediators and enablers of establishing and strengthening active communities linked by a shared sense of place.

In the three cases, we were also able to verify the existence of a strategic plan for the development of the initiative. That is, the elaboration of a design program, or framework project (Manzini 2014, 2015), which defines a strategic orientation that can frame and guide the remaining steps. All initiatives, through their promoters but not always through designers, previously defined a macro and medium or long term vision that brought together, coordinated and directed the meaning of a series of specific design initiatives.

The concept of infrastructure (Hillgren et al. 2011) fits in with the need for social innovation initiatives to establish a support system that helps them to be more resilient and flexible. This allows them to sustain themselves over time and support the nature of temporary and sometimes superficial involvement of some participants (Manzini 2019). Design can play a crucial role in creating, managing, and maintaining a network of relationships between actors and in enhancing synergies between them (Hillgren et al. 2011). These are key steps for the creation of infrastructure, which can also be composed of physical spaces, digital platforms, communication, and design services, or logistical services (Manzini 2015). It became clear in the three cases under analysis that various actions were taken to build elements that work as infrastructure. LDL is the most expressive of the three, with physical structures, institutional partnerships, and a permanent support team.

3.2   Roles

In the LDL and LSE cases, designers took part from the beginning of initiatives, acting as promoters, facilitators, mediators, and triggers of social conversations. They also fostered synergies among stakeholders that gave rise to new social relationships as well as the circulation of resources and knowledge in the network of each initiative. In the LCS case, these roles were performed mostly by specialists from other areas.

However, despite these roles do not need to be performed exclusively by designers, they exhibit the use of design strategies (Lawson 1997; Swann 2002; Dubberly 2005; Almendra 2010). These design strategies include mapping and systematizing information about available resources; strategic planning; project management; use of prototyping tools and materialization of ideas; tooling up, that is providing ways for community members to equip themselves to move forward with projects autonomously; story listening and storytelling as a way of attending the motivations, needs and wants of the community and the participants; co-creation.

It is noteworthy that in the three initiatives, these roles were never done in a closed, pre-determined, specific, or isolated manner. On the contrary, this type of activity can be characterized as flexible, open, fluid, and always evolving (in the sense that needs and formats of action are frequently updated and adjusted). Also, these interventions take place in a community context and imply sharing knowledge, solutions, and insights between participants, experts, and non-experts.

Mediation is very present in the three cases since it is necessary to establish bridges of dialogue between stakeholders, trying to determine a common language among participants with different backgrounds, managing consensus, resolving conflicts, and actively contributing to creating new social relationships.

At LDL it is essential to mediate the relationship between designers and artisans. It is evident the extreme care on part of promoters to foster an egalitarian relationship between the two, concerning authorship and protagonism, and based on proximity and partnership. The need for translation between a more technical language, specific to designers, and the artisan's more traditional approach is also a point worth noting.

At LCS the process was executed through workshops with groups of volunteer citizens who co-designed solutions for the neighborhood. So, it was essential for promoters to make sure that projects pushed through beyond some critical moments, resolving deadlocks and fostering synergies between teams.

In the case of LSE, mediation was crucial at the start of the initiative. There was a previous communication campaign addressed to shopkeepers of Rua de Portugal, generating awareness, goodwill, and gathering efforts around the project's objectives. Furthermore, the project was implemented through teamwork between shop owners to carry out shop decoration and street animation.

The facilitation role is also highlighted in the LDL and LCS cases since in both there were participants who proposed to develop specific projects: ideas for the Santiago neighborhood in the LCS case and products or services that build upon the local resources of Loulé in the LDL case. A constant effort by the promoting team was necessary for providing technical and logistical support, highlighting and encouraging possible partnerships with other community members, and maintaining a constant, motivating, and productive work rhythm.

In all cases, communication design participated as creative producer of design devices (Manzini 2015), developing a visual identity, communication of initiatives, digital communication, and promoting of events. These are tasks that require more specialized skills in communication design since they presuppose the use of specific techniques, tools, methods, as well as graphic and image editing software.

3.3 Process

All the initiatives observed were of medium to long duration, with LCS being active for four months (but with many more months of prior preparation of the promoter team), LSE with a length of more than one year, and LDL with more than three years of existence. Data collected on all three processes show the need for involvement of promoting teams in a deep and committed way, as well as the existence of infrastructure that allows initiatives to sustain throughout its duration. It is also clear that there is a substantial difference in these processes when compared to more traditional modes of design, characterized by occasional interventions responding to a specific briefing and limited to a defined timeframe.

To conclude how the design process for social innovation unfolds we developed a diagram based on the model by Meroni, Fassi, and Simeone (2013) in which we mapped the evidence collected in all three cases (Fig. 4).

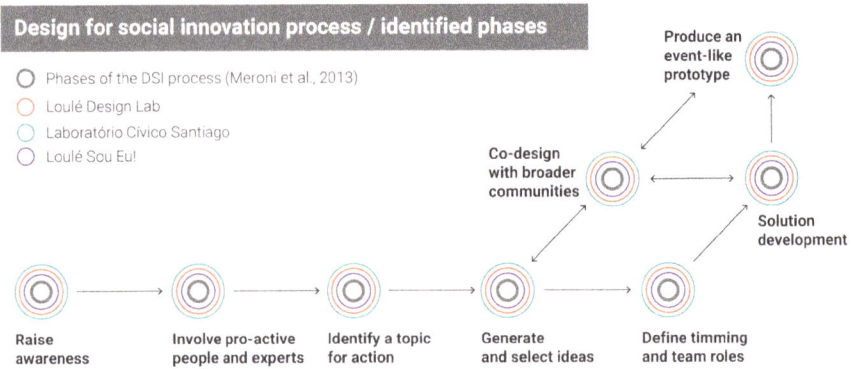

Fig. 4 DSI process adapted from Meroni et al. (2013), with identified phases in each case

4 Discussion

Table 2 shows the study's propositions, based on our literature review, with an indication of their verification in each of the three cases.

4.1 *Recommendations for Further Research*

Concerning the multiple case study, it will be necessary to do a complete comparative analysis, as well as to produce final conclusions and the case study report. Another recommended step will be to share the report with interviewees for review, as a validation procedure (Yin 2018).

Table 2 Confirmation of study propositions on each case

Multiple case study propositions	LDL	LCS	LSE
Design process methodology, characterized by cycles of goal setting, creation of possible solutions, and implementation tests (Lawson 1997; Design Council 2005; Brown 2009; Almendra 2010) is used in social innovation processes, even when stakeholders who implement it are not design experts	✓	✓	✓
Various tools of the design process (Laurel 2003; Stickdorn et al. 2018) are used, contributing to initiatives to reach their goals	✓	✓	✓
Communication design acts in multiple phases, moments, and tasks of a design for social innovation process	✓	✓	✓
Communication design generates specific outputs and results that are relevant for social innovation initiatives to achieve their goals	✓	✓	✓
Social innovation processes benefit from multiple areas of design, like strategic design, design for services, interaction design, or project management	✓	✓	✓

To broaden the research about the role of communication design in social innovation processes, it is recommended that more cases can be studied. Also, the use of design ethnography and design probes could prove beneficial since the application of these methods will allow the in-depth and context-specific collection of data, from differentiated nature of those already collected. Keeping up with initiatives as they unfold, thus originating specific moments of immersion (Martin and Hanington 2012) from the beginning to the end of the process, would bring benefits in terms of knowledge about effective participation of designers and other stakeholders in less explicit tasks, such as strategic development or others where outcomes are immaterial.

Participant observation aims to obtain information and generate interpretations about behaviors, activities, cultural and social meanings (Atkinson and Hammersley 1994). Applied through design ethnography, it will be especially useful to collect data on the context of design interventions, the dynamics between stakeholders, and to make explicit tacit knowledge in a real work context. It allows questioning people while observing them and ask for explanations about their actions and motivations at specific moments of social innovation initiatives.

Probes, called cultural probes (Gaver et al. 1999) or design probes (Mattelmäki 2006), are physical or digital tools used to collect evidence in a way very close to the research phenomenon. These instruments allow an intentionally informal, flexible, and open collection of inputs, trying to instigate user participation and provoke the sharing of information about aspects of their inner life such as reflections, emotions, or motivations (Martin and Hanington 2012). Another advantage of the method is to reduce the incidence of bias due to the absence of the researcher at the time of data collection, which facilitates the authentic expression of opinions and reflections by the subject (Stickdorn et al. 2018). Deployment of probes can thus allow the collection of information of subjective nature, difficult to obtain by other methods, and possibly generate valuable insights about the role of designers in the DSI process.

5   Conclusions

Although it is necessary to deepen research through comparative analysis of the cases that make up the study, it is possible to observe that design processes for social innovation present challenges that extrapolate the more common model of design intervention. These difficulties are related to working in direct collaboration with communities, co-designing with non-experts, and sharing the conducting of the design process with specialists from other areas. The need for medium and long-term involvement in projects is also problematic, since initiatives may be driven by voluntary personal involvement, making it hard for designers to manage other professional activities.

Our multiple case study allowed us to identify the need to produce communication artifacts to communicate internally, trigger community contributions, attract participants, create a visual identity, generate documentation, and allow presentation of results. These are situations in which communication design contribution becomes more material, depending on expert capability to generate communication artifacts and systems.

But social innovation initiatives require other roles from designers, like fostering close personal relationships and trust, managing conflicts and consensus, and establishing a design network that helps sustain the initiative over time. Although some of the identified roles are not exclusive to design and can be played by other participants, they make use of methods, tools, and skills that are specific to design. When deployed by designers that are trained and experienced in using these tools, their results can be amplified.

In this sense, regarding communication design, results point to some specific skills like enabling communities of interest and action, tooling up, facilitation, and mediation that must be present to add more value to the processes of social innovation.

Acknowledgements This work is funded by Programa de Bolsas de Doutoramento through Universidade de Lisboa and Faculdade de Arquitetura da Universidade de Lisboa.

References

Amatullo M, Boyer B, Shea A (eds) (2016) Leap dialogues: career pathways in design for social innovation. Designmatters at Art Center College of Design, Pasadena

Almendra R (2010) Decision making in the conceptual phase of design processes. [Unpublished doctoral dissertation] Faculdade de Arquitetura, Universidade Técnica de Lisboa

Atkinson P, Hammersley M (1994) Ethnography and participant observation: handbook of qualitative research 1:248–261

Bertin J (1983) Semiology of graphics. University of Wisconsin Press, Wisconsin

Brown T (2009) Change by design: how design thinking transforms organizations and inspires innovation. Harper, New York

Buchanan R (2001) Design research and the new learning. Des Issues 17(4):3–23

Ceschin F (2014) Sustainable product-service systems: between strategic design and transition studies. PoliMI Springer Briefs

Davis M (2008) Toto, I've got a feeling we're not in Kansas anymore. Interactions 15(5):28–34. https://doi.org/10.1145/1390085.1390091

Design Council (2005) A study of the design process. Eleven lessons: managing design in eleven global brands

Dorst K (2010) The nature of design thinking. In Design thinking research symposium. DAB Documents

Dorst K (2012) Frame innovation: create new thinking by design. MIT Press, Cambridge, MA

Dubberly H (2005) How do you design? Dubberly design office. Available from: http://www.dubberly.com/articles/how-do-you-design.html . Last accessed 23 Jan 2020

Ehn P, Nilsson EM, Topgaard R (2014) Introduction. In: Ehn P, Nilsson EM, Topgaard R (eds) Making futures: marginal notes on innovation, design, and democracy. The MIT Press, Cambridge

Emilson A (2015) Design in the space between stories: design for social innovation and sustainability: from responding to societal challenges to preparing for societal collapse. Mälmo University, Mälmo

Figueiras A (2016) How to tell stories using visualization: strategies towards narrative visualization [Unpublished doctoral dissertation]. Faculdade de Ciências Sociais e Humanas, Universidade Nova de Lisboa

Frascara J (2015) What is information design? In: Frascara J (ed) Information design as principled action: making information accessible, relevant, understandable and usable. Common Ground Publishing

Freire J (2017) La emergencia de los laboratorios ciudadanos. Retrieved 2 Dec 2020, from https://juanfreire.com/la-emergencia-de-los-laboratorios-ciudadanos/

García M (2018) Los laboratorios ciudadanos en los sistemas de experimentación e innovación. Abrir instituiciones desde dentro. Hacking inside Black Book, pp 105–112

Gaver B, Dunne T, Pacenti E (1999) Design: cultural probes. Interactions 6(1):21–29. https://doi.org/10.1145/291224.291235

Grefé R (2011) Experience design is the only design. Des Manage Rev 22(4):26–30. https://doi.org/10.1111/j.1948-7169.2011.00153.x

Hillgren P, Seravalli A, Emilson A (2011) Prototyping and infrastructuring in design for social innovation. CoDesign 7(3–4):169–183

Jégou F, Manzini E (eds) (2008) Collaborative services. Social innovation and design for sustainability. Polidesign, Milan

Kleverbeck M, Terstriep J (2017) Analysing the social innovation process: the methodology of social innovation biographies. European Public & Social Innovation Review, 2(2):15–29

Laurel B (ed) (2003) Design research: methods and perspectives. The MIT Press, Cambridge

Lawson B (1997) How designers think: the design process demystified. Architectural Press

Manzini E (2011) Introduction. In Meroni A, Sangiorgi D (eds) Design for services. Gower, Farnham

Manzini E (2014) Making things happen: social innovation and design. Des Issues 30(1):57–66

Manzini E (2015) Design, when everybody design: an introduction to design for social innovation. MIT Press, Cambridge, MA

Manzini E (2019) Politics of the everyday. Bloomsbury

Martin B, Hanington B (2012) Universal methods of design: 100 ways to research complex problems, develop innovative ideas, and design effective solutions. Rockport Publishers

Mattelmäki T (2006) Design probes. Aalto University

Melo A, Neves M (2020) Communication design within social innovation. In: Raposo D, Neves J, Silva J (eds) Advances in design, music and arts: 7th meeting of research in music, arts and design, EIMAD 2020, 14–15 May 2020. Springer, Berlin

Meroni A, Sangiorgi D (2011) Design for services. Gower, Farnham

Meroni A, Fassi D, Simeone G (2013) Design for social innovation as a form of designing activism: an action format. In: Social frontiers: the next edge of social innovation research. Nesta

Mulgan G (2014) Design in public and social innovation: what works and what could work better. Nesta

Murray R, Caulier-Grice J, Mulgan G (2010) The open book of social innovation. Nesta

Nicholls A, Simon J, Gabriel M (eds) (2015) New frontiers in social innovation research. Palgrave Macmillan, London

Norman D (2018) Why design education must change. Retrieved 30 Nov 2020, from https://jnd.org/why_design_education_must_change/

Pierce J, Martin DG, Murphy JT (2011) Relational place-making: the networked politics of place. Trans Inst Br Geogr 36:54–70

Roxburgh M (2014) Depiction as theory and writing by practice: the design process of a written thesis. In: Rodgers P, Yee J (eds) The Routledge companion to design research. Routledge, London, pp 346–363

Sanders EB-N, Stappers PJ (2008) Co-creation and the new landscapes of design. CoDesign, 4 (1):5–18

Scharmer CO, Kaufer K (2013) Leading from the emerging future: from ego-system to eco-system economies. Berrett-Koehler Publishers Inc., San Francisco

Schön D (1983) The reflective practitioner: how professionals think in action. Basic Books, New York

Schwab K (2015) The fourth industrial revolution: what it means and how to respond. Foreign Affairs

Stickdorn M, Hormess M, Lawrence A, Schneider J (eds) (2018) This is service design doing. O'Reilly

Swann C (2002) Action research and the practice of design. Design issues, 18(1):49–61

Tellis W (1997) Application of a case study methodology. The qualitative report, 3(3):1–9

Thackara J (2005) In the bubble: designing in a complex world. The MIT Press, Cambridge, MA

Yin R (2018) Case study research: design and methods. Sage Publications, Thousand Oaks, US

Zurlo F, Cautela C (2014) Design strategies in different narrative frames. Des Issues 30(1):19–35

Communication Design as an Educational Tool for a More Sustainable and Social Development of the Future

Caio Vitoriano Carvalho⬤

Abstract This article explores the important relationship between design, information and education for a more sustainable social conscience, through a brief bibliographic exploration and critique of the contemporary world's strategic-political scenario. It also discusses the relevance of interdisciplinarity associated to design and other disciplines in the construction of a communication committed to inform, alleviating possible interferences in the understanding of the message. As the problems of the world, in relation to sustainable issues, become more and more complex, design is an instrument that incorporates collaborative and participative methodologies in search of solutions in the most varied social areas. Thus, in this context and sense, the article brings two 'cases' exemplifying the good use of communication design (purpose and sustainable purpose) as a resource to guide a proposal of an informational message more inviting and thought to the intended audience. The text provokes the reader with some questions and ends with a reflection on our contemporary scenario, in an attempt to build a coherent contribution in the body of knowledge in this area.

Keywords Communication design · Sustainability · Education

1 Introduction

One of the ways in which we can reach a more sustainable social conscience is through information. Starting from this premise to develop projects in communication design, both for digital and non-digital media, in order to educate and that are thought naturally with the aplomb of mitigating the 'noise' (some interference in the message that compromises its full understanding). However, there is not always a professional with sensitivity or interdisciplinary training to see such adverse and complex scenarios, in addition to an understanding of the receiver (public) of information.

C. V. Carvalho (✉)
Universidade de Aveiro (UA), Aveiro, Portugal

In this way, Morin (2002) qualifies that the human being at one time is physical, biological, psychic, cultural, social, historical. But "this complex unity of man's nature is disintegrated in education through the disciplines, instituted in the nineteenth century with the formation of modern universities" as Mousinho (2018) states. Thus, in the early 1970s, interdisciplinarity emerged as the prospect of breaking through limits predisposed to the division of disciplines and advocated diversifying the levels of knowledge integration.

Interdisciplinarity presents itself as a renewal of the way of thinking, or self-pagination, and according to Piaget (1973) proposes the possibility of mutual exchange and reciprocal integration among various sciences. Or even more, through Japiassú's (1997) affirmation in concluding that "interdisciplinarity is characterized by the intensity of exchanges among specialists and the degree of integration of a research project. Thus defragmenting the expert view and, as Fazenda apud Mousinho (2018) says, "preventing the establishment of the supremacy of a particular science to the detriment of other equally important contributions". In other words, a professional who must seek interdisciplinary training and, in this way, understand how to adapt information without harming the content, optimizing language and learning, observing the needs of the target audience. And undoubtedly it is no use "counting on the most expensive and innovative technological resources if there is no knowledge to make good use of these tools", as Pinto (2020) concludes.

Thus, from the point of view of professional training, we can state that an intercession between communication design, other areas of knowledge in partnership with teaching added to the technological contribution resulted in the educational designer. This is a professional, among other collaborators, who contributes to the improvement of the quality of education by facilitating the learning process by uniting teaching institutions with technology, adapting information to the online, in-person and semi-in-person context. Substantially according to Pinto (2020) "the educational designer is the professional responsible for the improvement of learning processes. He needs to be collaborative, multidisciplinary and able to plan, coordinate and evaluate educational processes with the use of new technologies".

That said, in a scenario that is not everyone's reality, a hybrid teaching context is reached, which is a concept that combines face-to-face and distance learning methodologies with the objective of optimizing and improving the learning process. This strategy is increasingly common, considering that digital devices are part of everyday life for a portion of the population and the Internet is an environment for information research. When thinking along this path, if educational institutions invested more in people with this interdisciplinary background we would have, in thesis, more people with integrative reasoning applying design.

By assuming this inclusive characteristic, design must be structured in the interaction between the user (public) and the product (message) to facilitate effective actions in adapting Bonsiepe's speech (1997). In line with this statement, I can state that the reasoning of the designer and cognitive scientist Donald Norman and the educator and articulator of Brazilian pedagogical thought Paulo Freire complement each other and are equivalent.

Norman (2004) is recognized for his studies in which he qualifies that the design (as a project) should be user centered. His study cutout is the interaction environment mediated by digital screens, in which he comes to conclusions that design must focus on the human and that its interfaces must be intuitive interfering 'positively' with the user's experience and choice. In a teaching context, Paulo Freire also focuses on the human and in his researches considered learning within a social and political context, without underestimating the practices of popular culture and the periphery. Freire (Alves 2017) "proposes a work that does not move the apprentice, but rather moves the content and object of learning and makes the object and content work and adapt to the apprentice's learning and not the other way around". Thackara (2005) reinforces from the point of view of design that most solutions must involve integration between designers, localities and citizens in close understanding of local reality contemplating citizens and their habits in search of solutions.

It is clear that the framework proposed by the article is not one of teaching–learning in a school or academic environment, but how communication design associated with this educational perception in its practice can positively influence a socially sustainable attitude. Martins and Couto (2015) lists some points of design-based learning in which one of them says that "the importance of learning issues related to the environment and the built environment, connecting the teaching of design with education for conscious consumption" is fundamental. At the core is the desire to learn with the will to teach through communication. Explaining better concepts of the sustainable lexicon that are literally launched to the public as an advertising slogan, knowing why to buy better and what beneficial consequences this brings. To rationalize to the general public what is "green economy" and what sustainability is more than recycling and that expands on concepts such as fighting extreme poverty, improving health and gender equality. These are some of the obligations that sustainable communication design must propose.

1.1 Internet and Sustainability: Construction of a Future Thinking and Means Marketing Actions

In a world where the climate crisis is always on the agenda, the concept of sustainability appears as a miraculous and saving imperative. Companies and governments feel an ethical obligation to move towards more ecologically responsible thinking, which used to be a distant concern, now becomes something emergency.

In the umbrella of what is considered sustainable, a series of measures are being sought to repair the "damage" of uninterrupted decades of a robust economic system with profound consequences today. Like the European Ecological Pact (Comissão Europeia 2019) which details actions necessary for the transition of the economic bloc to a clean economy by 2050, but experts say (Clima Info 2020) that the total figure of 30% for climate action is insufficient.

Attentive, according to Orange (2016), a penetration through the state is the example of the Swedish government, in partnership with the Social Democratic Party and the Green Party, which introduces fiscal incentives for the repair of durable objects (bicycles, washing machines) in order to delay disposal together with other measures to reduce carbon emissions. In the same country, however, through private initiative, Ikea (furniture and utensils net) proposes that its clients return with the used and sometimes damaged products to restore them, and thus prolong the life cycle. Carvalho (2020) defines this movement as "a contemporary proposal to adjust to a commercial scenario in which customers are increasingly informed, and sometimes engaged in attitudes to minimize the impacts of their consumption. However, this is a reality in Sweden, not a global reflex, and it is clear that a public–private partnership is important.

For another bias and according to Fiore (2020) the UK intends to regulate large technology companies like Facebook and Google by presenting a statutory code of conduct that aims to give more options to users and outsourcing companies more autonomy. This proposal interferes mainly in the online advertising issues suggested by such platforms making the market more competitive and giving more freedom to users. In other words, Fiori (2020) adds "this could allow any internet user in the UK to choose not to be exposed to any advertising based on their online behaviour, something unthinkable on the internet today". And consequently, it interferes with consumer habits, which reflects in the possible decrease in environmental impact.

However, in Portugal, according to the National Institute of Statistics (2019), in 2019, 80.9% of households participate in social networks and of these 78% have access to broadband. Among the residents aged 16–74 who use the Internet most are students of higher education and high school, and among other surveys it is important to note that in this same survey it is seen that 38.7% reported having conducted e-commerce (an increase of 2% compared to 2018). Now in 2020, according to the same Institute (Instituto Nacional de Estatísticas de Portugal 2020) there was an increase of 3.6% in relation to 2019 to access the Internet through home connection via broadband, which notes that "Internet and e-commerce users have increased significantly and more than doubled the percentage of users for educational reasons". However, it is important because of the COVID-19 factor and the teleworking conditions for the increase of internet data consumption.

The Internet is an extremely strong means of access to information and consumption of products and services. Virtual events also help to discuss and disseminate new practices in education and foster an innovative mindset thinking in a twenty-first century context. Like the Virtual Educa Lisboa (2020) international education and technology event that took place in an online format, under the theme "Transforming educational policies in Europe", it discusses topics such as "Public education: the engine of change in Portugal", "Europe adapted to the digital age", "Projects for the transformation of education", "Scenarios for the future of education" among others in tables with names of politics and international education.

Portugal expands the consumption of internet data and also invests in events that foster social responsibility. But does the penetration of these messages really reach those who are interested or only specialists and researchers?

From a practical perspective, like the micro plastic pollution affecting small soil organisms reported by The Guardian (Watts 2020) which is specific information but of interest to many people. Because such action may affect the life and economy of many people, however it is restricted to a segment interested or researching the subject. It is true that the pollution of the oceans by plastic is gradually being alerted by the press, documentaries and attitudes of private initiative, but there is no succinct and clear explanation for the layman. Are the communities dependent on fishing being educated about this via some mechanism of public order? I question it.

Another point of attention is pointed out by author Kendra Pierre-Louis (2012) when she says "by positioning environmental sustainability as a market choice, similar to choosing a milk whipped or not, we downgrade the urgency of our current ecological situation. Manzini (2004) ponders when considering that "the success of sustainable solutions and the fact that they are adopted globally by society depends on a change in our idea of well-being and the way we act to achieve it. Our posture as a society can change and can be guided by serious information with politically credible intentions and not guided by brands, because many concepts and words from the sustainability lexicon, or even the processes, are announced in a simple and shallow way.

Like the iconic tennis brand Converse which "launched Renew to find solutions for post-consumer and post-industrial waste using recycled fabrics and recycled cotton canvas blends" (La Publicidad 2020). Following the trend, the Brazilian popular footwear and sandals brand Rider (Alves 2020) in recent initiative to reduce environmental impact launches a line of four shoes based on 4Rs—Reduce, Reuse, Recycle and Recreate. As he notes "the idea is to show that it is possible to do something new through sustainable design". They announce that all the products are vegan and produced with recycled material from the residues of the own plant, also reducing water consumption and with a packaging proposal on recycled paper with spelling made with ink of less environmental impact. In fact the real innovation point, in relation to Rider's action (and for being in Brazil), is that the sandals, after being used a lot, can be discarded on selective collection points.

However, the plastic recycling previously seen as a virtue is increasingly weakened as a solution to the waste crisis, because with the devaluation of oil and gas the cost of manufacturing new plastic, which is already low, becomes lower. This is plastic for consumption that has become economically unviable to recycle. More rigorous measures voted by the European Union (Rankin 2019) such as the prohibition of single use plastic until 2021 are more assertive directions.

The initiatives are sustainable in nature, but they put on the market another similar product of high value. In other words, it is not totally sustainable. They could change all the lines for the sustainable contribution since they perceive real indications of reduction of environmental impact. They also bring terms in English or call themselves vegan, but they do not explain such concepts. Are they really concerned about forming a solid base of educated and interested public or just follow the commercial flow?

The perception is that there is always the need of provoking the consumption through the perception of the new product, a point of view coming from the market, of the offer expansion. In other words, one more option to consume and not an alternative in definitive. They use design and publicity to make communication and to transmit their intentions of sustainable marketing, but it is only marketing. They don't stop to make an exclusive campaign or informative material with the specific reason to educate, to create a mentality, to foment a movement.

2   Methodology

This article is based on bibliographic review, recent literature, journalistic articles and academic articles. In this way a theoretical context for its argumentative development is structured, which through two 'cases' (one in Portugal and one in Brazil) exemplifies the importance between design, information and education for a more sustainable social conscience.

Thus, through these 'cases' that have different approaches and target audiences it is possible to create a comparative intersection to show that the communication design designed for social and sustainable education can have positive effects.

3   Cases

Here we go to two interesting examples about the adequacy of the communication design in proposal for an effective action in what sensitizes sustainability, one in Portugal and another in Brazil. Places completely different in their intentions and public, however it is important to highlight that both, even minimally, there are resolutions involving public policies and state as supporter or financier.

Both strategies are happy because they think about the message and how it will reach the audience. Either through integrated communication involving printed and virtual media or through a booklet (kind of folder), one must know to whom the message is intended and in this way think about the format and language most appropriate for the success of the action. Both examples are concerned with informing.

One detail that should be highlighted is that the first 'case' trails through a strictly textual solution (typographic) and the second seeks the illustration in its entirety. By seeking a positive end result, in an intuitive or pragmatic way with the help of field research, project developers put into practice methodologies based on Norman (2004) or Thackara (2005) by being concerned with the functionality and scenario that the message fits.

3.1 UAUbike (Uaubike.Web.Ua.Pt) | 2020

At the University of Aveiro (Portural) it promotes an initiative that consists in distributing bicycles (mechanical and electrical) to members of the academic community, stimulating the behavior of leaving the car at home when travelling to the university campus. The demand was greater than the number of bicycles available according to Público (Lusa 2020) and through a press release it states that "the 239 contemplated with bicycles committed to do about 16 thousand kilometers per week, leaving the car at home when traveling to the University". The university also offers a point for the maintenance of the bicycles in case of any breakdown, the service is available to members of the academic community and outside (in occasional situations).

The justification is a cause proposal for cleaner air and consequently provide fewer cars in circulation, besides stimulating a healthy habit in a flat topography city that facilitates the practice of cycling. According to reports, the action is in line with the European Union's commitment to the UN's global goals for it to become a carbon neutral continent by 2050, also foreseen in the European Ecological Pact (Comissão Europeia 2019).

The initiative is communicated through informative signs and posters in the university space, in addition to its own website and dissemination through the electronic address of the University of Aveiro with the help of social networks. The website is bilingual (Portuguese and English) and in its entirety informative, with simple black texts and explanations about basic color backgrounds. This way, added to a responsive site architecture, i.e., adaptable to mobile devices without hindering the understanding of information, the information circulates easily in online and offline media (Fig. 1).

There is also a unity in discourse in which visual programming (colors, typography) and textual load are contemplated, thus facilitating the identification and recognition by those who are impacted by outdoor ads, websites and social networks. From the point of view of graphic design is a campaign not very rich visually, extremely minimalist in relation to the elements that compose the graphic pieces because it does not use photographs and illustrations only composed by text. It is a visual path that risks little in seduction and focuses strictly on the text message. Creatively weak, but extremely efficient.

It is important to put in the lens of analysis that the context of a university environment is theoretically formed people with education, access to information and technology, besides minimally with interest in subjects of sustainable vocation. Added to this is the familiarity with the language of social networks and the desire to have a means of transporting clean energy. This scenario also contributes to the success of the action associated with all communication designed to engage this type of audience.

Fig. 1 Color study and typography. *Source* uaubike.web.ua.pt

3.2 Government of the State of Rio Grande do Norte (Brazil) | 2017

Completely different from the university environment of the previous example, the Government of the State of Rio Grande do Norte (in northeastern Brazil) through the BR 8276 Loan Agreement with the World Bank formatted the Integrated Sustainable Development Project (RN Sustentável 2020). The objective is to reverse the scenario of low socioeconomic dynamism, supporting actions to modernize the management of the public sector in order to improve the quality of life of the population of Rio Grande do Norte.

Among the strategies is the Sustainable RN Project that seeks to train the beneficiaries, partners, managers and technicians involved in the Project through training and qualification to ensure the improvement of various services in the implementation and sustainability of state investments.

That said, the idea of the booklet "Um Dia" (One Day) with support from UFGE (The Umbrella Facility for Gender Equality) for residents of rural areas, places usually with scarce resources, with limited access and work routine where women are usually overloaded with agricultural work and domestic obligations. The

Fig. 2 "Um Dia" (One Day)
cover. *Source* rnsustentavel.
rn.gov.br

booklet is thus intended as a tool for discussing gender relations in family farming, with a view to transforming ways of living together and overcoming inequalities (Fig. 2).

The material is printed and has the appearance of a colorful and very lively comic book designed to attract attention. There is practically no written text, the whole story is narrated without balloons or dialog boxes and through two readings (front and back) you can follow the routine of a family that works with agriculture associated with other daily activities. On the one hand you can flip through the equitable routine between husband and wife, and on the other hand the routine with the functions overwhelming the woman. The final concept is to pass on a positive message of division of labour and at the same time small pieces of advice on how to make family farming more sustainable.

It is important to say that the designers who conceived the visual project went to the field, and in research they understood that most of the people that the booklet is intended are illiterate or have difficulty in reading. Thus, the solution of being something didactic of unsophisticated graphic-visual language, of not having written text and choosing the almost majority use of eye-catching and vibrant designs was assertive and generated results.

Knowing who the information is meant for is fundamental and understanding what kind and how this message should be conveyed as well, the genius of this material is precisely in the process of understanding the surrounding system and presenting an appropriate solution.

4 Concluding Remarks

Let us realize that here we are discussing perceptions and movements of a dynamic daily life, however the process of learning and practice is proportionally slow. For, before pro-sustainability actions or movements it would be important to explain what sustainability is and all the concepts that permeate its context. What we see, in great majority, is the superficiality of information in the attempt to educate people and the impression that is transmitted is that the sustainable movement is something elitist.

Communication design, when well-articulated in consonance with technology and education associated with the sensitivity of an interdisciplinary professional, can lead to more efficient results. In the two cases we discussed we see the concern in this sense, when thinking about the referential cultures, political, economic, sociological scenarios and the employability of the message in the media with the role of educating and opening a platform for dialogue, in search of more awareness.

The important thing is to realize that in a global context the disparities are great, from educated people with access to technology to people with minimal resources. Thus, when we talk about educating or passing on some informational content that requires some effort from someone, as an obligation or duty, this type of information can most likely generate disinterest. In general, people don't want to feel obliged to do anything, they do it for pleasure or for something in return. In the case of a sustainable consciousness this 'something in return' doesn't come immediately, because today's actions reverberate, but the results appear over time.

It is more immediate and preferable to buy a 'green product' and feel the debt paid in relation to the sin of irresponsibility of the ecological non-consciousness. Buying won't make the world more sustainable, now it may change its attitude.

Therefore, in the midst of the challenges of complexity in a world of immediate problems, information is needed and through the inclusive design of interdisciplinary posture the message can come to convince whom it is meant for. Education is discipline and at the same time posture, and a posture of sustainable consciousness needs to be transmitted with coherence. Inform to form and from this transform.

References

Alves M (2017) Teorias Pedagógicas e Design: considerações sobre o método de Paulo Freire como guia para a construção de animações gráficas educacionais. In: XIII EDUCERE e IV Seminário Internacional de Representações Sociais, Subjetividade e Educação – SIRSSE e o VI Seminário Internacional sobre Profissionalização Docente (SIPD/CÁTEDRA UNESCO), promovendo discussões em torno do tema "Formação de professores: contextos, sentidos e práticas", pp 9351–9364. ISSN 2176–1396

Alves S (2020) Rider lança sua primeira coleção sustentável. https://www.b9.com.br/134440/rider-lanca-sua-primeira-colecao-sustentavel/. Last accessed 5 Nov 2020

Bonsiepe G (1997) Design do material ao digital. FIESC/IEL, Florianópolis

Carvalho C (2020) Point of view on dialectics in the commercial scenario of the circular economy. In: Raposo D, Neves J, Silva J, Correia Castilho L, Dias R (eds) 7° EIMAD—Encontro de Investigação em Música, Artes e Design de Springer series in design and innovation, pp 589–599. ISBN 978–3–030–55699–0

Clima Info (2020) EU: pacote de recuperação econômica corta recursos para ação climática. https://tinyurl.com/yyxbx9t6. Last accessed 22 July 2020

Comissão Europeia (2019) Pacto Europeu. https://tinyurl.com/vgcx36q

Fiori M (2020) Reino Unido quer regulamentar gigantes tecnológicas e propagandas online. https://tinyurl.com/yxcpn2n3. Last accessed 27 Nov 2020

Instituto Nacional de Estatísticas de Portugal (2019) Sociedade da Informação e do Conhecimento - Inquérito à Utilização de Tecnologias da Informação e da Comunicação nas Famílias: 80% dos utilizadores de internet participam em redes sociais. Instituto Nacional de Estatísticas de Portugal, Portugal

Instituto Nacional de Estatísticas de Portugal (2020) Sociedade da Informação e do Conhecimento - Inquérito à Utilização de Tecnologias da Informação e da Comunicação nas Famílias: Aumentaram significativamente os utilizadores de internet e de comércio eletrónico. Mais que duplicou a percentagem dos utilizadores por motivos educativos. Instituto Nacional de Estatísticas de Portugal, Portugal

Japiassú H (1997) Interdisciplinaridade e patologia do saber. Imago, Rio de Janeiro

La Publicidad (2020) Converse Crea Una Nueva Colección Con Telas Recicladas y Mezclas de lonas de Algodón Reciclado. https://tinyurl.com/yxqwqxfl. Last accessed 14 May 2020

Lusa (2020) Universidade de Aveiro distribui bicicletas "para que os carros fiquem em casa". Público, https://tinyurl.com/y387exyn. Last accessed 03 Nov 2020

Manzini E (2004) El Diseño como Herramienta para la Sostenibilidad Medioambiental y Social. In: Macdonald S (org.) Temas de Deseño En La Europa Hoy. BEDA, Barcelona

Martins B, Couto R (2015) Design-based learning: a pedagogy that strengthens the paradigms of contemporary education. In: Spinillo CG, Fadel LM, Souto VT, Silva TBP, Camara RJ (eds) Proceedings [Oral] of the 7th information design international conference, CIDI 2015 [Blucher design proceedings, no 2, vol 2, pp 424–438]. ISSN 2318–6968, ISBN: 978–85–8039–122–0, https://doi.org/10.5151/designpro-CIDI2015-cidi_217. Blucher, São Paulo

Morin E (2002) Cabeça bem-feita: repensar a reforma, reformar o pensamento. Bertrand Brasil, Rio de Janeiro

Mousinho S (2018) A interdisciplinaridade ao alcance de todos. https://tinyurl.com/y4txn9vo. Last accessed 24 Nov 2020

Norman D (2004) Emotional design: why we love (or hate) everyday things. Basic Books, New York

Orange R (2016) Waste not want not: Sweden to give tax breaks for repairs. The Guardian. https://bit.ly/3278DNa. Last accessed 19 June 2019

Piaget J (1973) Problemas gerais da investigação interdisciplinar e mecanismos comuns. Bertrand, Lisboa

Pierre-Louis K (2012) Green washed: why we can't buy our way to a green planet. Ig Publishing, New York

Pinto D (2020) Descubra agora o papel e a importância do designer educacional. https://tinyurl.com/y4h7no2b. Last accessed 24 Nov 2020

Rankin J (2019) European parliament votes to Ban Sigle-use plastics. The Guardian. https://tinyurl.com/yyqtyrbz. Last accessed 20 May 2020

RN Sustentável. https://rnsustentavel.rn.gov.br. Last accessed 02 Nov 2020

Thackara J (2005) In the bubble: designing in a complex world. MIT, Cambridge

Virtual Educa, https://virtualeduca.org/foroglobal/live. Last accessed 24 Nov 2020

Watts J (2020) Microplastic pollution devastating soil species, study finds. The Guardian. https://tinyurl.com/y34uxech. Last accessed 20 Sept 2020

The Brand as Mediation Through Design

Marlene Ribeiro and **Francisco Providência**

Abstract Portugal is receiving international recognition for its competence centres in various activity sectors, mostly located in the North of the country (wines, textiles, footwear, wooden furniture, technology). This region still enjoys a creative frenzy that is an innovation enhancer. Despite that, the perceived strength of Brand Origin for Portuguese Made products is lower than Swiss Made or German Made products. Optimistically, we can see this as space and opportunity for growth of the Brand Portugal, but which presents itself as a demanding challenge for the territories through their local agents. Considering this ecosystem, we affirm the indispensable contribution of Design in the economic valorization of the industrial product and the sustainable growth of cities, regions, and nations. Thus, we bring to this reflection a review that articulates the theoretical statements of Design as Cultural Mediator and Brand Design, looking for the stabilization of concepts associated with them, and we left as a contribution, the possibility of The Brand as Mediation through Design.

Keywords Design as cultural mediator · Brand design · Country of origin · Brand origin · Made in

1 Introduction

In a market thought applied to places (Puig 2009), the cities that gain the global world's competitiveness and benefit from attention and wealth develop anticipation strategies. They do not react, but they propose. In this sense, symbolically characterizing a territory through Brand Design, attributing qualities beyond its origin, confirms the intrinsic value of Design as an agent of change and a source of creative

M. Ribeiro (✉) · F. Providência
University of Aveiro, Aveiro, Portugal
e-mail: marlenefribeiro@ua.pt

M. Ribeiro · F. Providência
ID+ Research Institute for Design, Media and Culture, Aveiro, Portugal

transformation (project) (Castillo 2018). It also reflects the critical role of Design (reflection), fundamental to creating an environmentally sustainable, economically viable, socially equitable, and culturally diverse world (Montréal World Design Summit 2017). Brand Design also values the collaborative, holistic, and integrated work of scientific, economic, and political agents to promote Design as a standard benefit. This value is also the value of persuasion of those who have chosen or will choose the territory to invest, visit or live.

The collection of the theoretical basis that supports this contribution is structured based on the two themes immediately announced in its title: "The Brand as Mediation through Design". Thus, we highlight the Design as Cultural Mediator and the Brand Design, preceded and proceeded by Introduction and Conclusion. To fulfil the objective of stabilizing concepts related to the themes under reflection, we started the approach to point 2. Design as Cultural Mediator with the presentation based on the concepts *Medium, Interface, Mediator*, a strategy also followed in the first part of point 3. Brand Design, where we articulate the Power of the Country of Origin, from the concepts of *Cluster, Made in, Country of Origin, Brand Origin*. Taking a collector approach in the first part of these two points, we refer to each point's second part as a prospective stance. In point 2. we continue the discussion of Design as a Mediator, trying to anticipate the future of the Design research, undertaken by the research group MADE.PT—Critical Design Lab for Growth and Prosperity, that welcomes both authors of this reflection. In the second part of point 3., we reinforce the imperative of a collaborative strategy to create and manage Place Brands.

2 Design as Cultural Mediator

2.1 Medium, Interface, Mediator

In the 60s and 70s of the twentieth century, the theorization of Design practice, through creating Design methodology, supported Design as a distinct process activity, enhanced its autonomy as a discipline, and inaugurated Design Research as a mediator.

Archer (1979, p. 18) refers to the Design activity as "is not only a distinct process, comparable with but different from scientific and scholarly processes but also operates through a *medium*, called modeling, that is comparable with but different from language and notation".

Remembering Design as a means of critical reflection on culture, through objects, Naylor and Ball propose, based on the functionalist heritage of Louis Sullivan *Form follows Function*, its most generous openness, and updating, declined in *Form follows Ideas*. This publication is a demonstration "that design itself can be a critical *medium* for cultural reflection without recourse to interpretation by the design critic who writes about the artifact" (Naylor and Ball 2005, p. 6).

Bonsiepe (1999), heir to the German industrial functionalism of Design (trained at School of Ulm), presents, after his experience as a designer in a software development company (user-centered perspective), his new approach to Design as *Interface*. "I developed a reinterpretation of design as the domain of the *interface* where the interaction between users and tools is structured" (Fathers 2003, p. 51). *Interface* with social, technological, commercial, but above all, cultural *mediation*.

Design as a "cultural *mediation* activity (through artifacts, devices, and services) between the past and the future, between companies and people, between people, or even between objects" is the ontological proposal for framework the discipline, which Providência (2012) defends. Under this reflection, we develop the proposal to promote *Brand Design as a Territorial Mediator* between scientific (Universities), economic (Industries), and political (Municipalities) agents.

We also resorted to the *Design Dictionary* (Board of International Research in Design BIRD 2008), where we searched for the terms that we highlighted from the review of authors communicated here and, *medium* records numerous occurrences (with use in different contexts as a means of communication, means of production, means of reflection, means of visualization, means of perception, technique, method) among which we cite that which refers to Design as cross-cultural "from this perspective, Design constitutes a flexible universal language and a powerful *medium* of cultural exchange that is rapidly being appropriated for business, politics, and other purposes" (Board of International Research in Design BIRD 2008, p. 99). The term *interface* is the one that is most often repeated (usually in the context of Interaction Design, Web Design, and Engineering, applied as *User Interface—UI* or *Interface Design*, but also referring to an interface between the theory and practice of Design or as a cognitive and emotional interface) and, referring to the relationship between human and artifacts. We highlight, "a common definition of design is the organization of the *interface* between humans and the "made world", that is, the interaction between people and our artifact" (Board of International Research in Design BIRD 2008, p. 27). Finally, Design as a *mediator* originates in this dictionary two entries, is exposed as a *mediator* between areas of knowledge "urban design is the *mediator* between urban planning and architecture" (Board of International Research in Design BIRD 2008, p. 423) and underlines the role of the designer in this *mediation* "designers play a decisive role in this process as expert mediators among the participating disciplines" (Board of International Research in Design BIRD 2008, p. 446).

2.2 Design Mediator of Future

Based on the reflection of Tim Benton, who, referring to the novelty of Modernism, tells us "Architecture and Design should be socially emancipatory, not just responding to the exiting needs of society, but contributing to revolution or change" (Benton 2006, p. 154) we see Design not only by solving common problems but by creating new problems and understood as the need to communicate utopia. Thus interpreted, we think schools are the epicenter of the questioning, reflection, and experimentation (and also of error) of Design, as an essential contribution to design our collective future.

The University of Aveiro (Portugal), and more broadly the Higher Education Institutions, have as their central mission Teaching, Research, and Cooperation with Society (knowledge mediation). Intending to observe, discuss, and thinking about school, teaching, and research in Design in the national ecosystem context, *REDE —Meeting of Design Schools* had its first edition in 2017 at the University of Aveiro. An approach of broad-spectrum served as the first diagnosis of a community's concerns and issues characterized by a great diversity of geographical contexts and the heterogeneity of the respective social and economic environments (Borges et al. 2018). Thus, this *REDE* presents itself as a space for sharing and designing the future of Design Schools in Portugal.

Also focusing on the responsibility of the approximately 35 Design Schools in Portugal for mediation through Design, the *Schools* project of the *Porto Design Biennal*, demonstrating the national culture of Design (Design of the future), contributes, through work and talent (knowledge and creativity) of students, lecturers and schools themselves, for the economic, social and cultural development of the country, Europe and the world.

> Schools are, perhaps, the biggest and most fruitful critical resource for research and development in Design, reconciling it with the reality of each territory and culture. Therefore, it has been mainly in the schools and by the schools that has passed the production of knowledge in Design (Providência 2019b).

As an internal observation of the research produced at the University of Aveiro, through the ID+ Research Institute for Design, Media and Culture, more specifically by the research group MADE.PT Critical Design Lab for Growth and Prosperity, which welcomes the authors of this article, we invited its director Francisco Providência, to position the contribution of the researchers he leads, assessing the impact of the portfolio of shared competencies for a Society, Economy and Policy based on knowledge in Design. From the answer to the question—*Design Research by the MADE.PT group—mediate what future?*—we emphasize:

The MADE.PT group brings together research in Design that starts from the observation of national productive practice, for the design of its futures, focusing its scientific activity on the project, that is, on the Design carried out, in doing Design and in the inherent innovation.

In anticipation and convergence with the scientific and economic ideals of the European development framework, the MADE.PT group primary objective is contributing to development through the strategic affirmation of Design with the Economy and Society, so that new opportunities can be generated in the market and, consequently, more wealth that, in addition to the national economic sovereignty of an EU member state, can be translated into more prosperity and social well-being.

The high concentration of industrial companies in the Aveiro region and, more broadly, in the Northern Region of Portugal constitutes an important circumstance and opportunity for applied Design Research. If the contributions of science have been centered on technological knowledge transfer and adaptation to the markets, they should, in the future, focus on the qualification of the designed product. In this context, new industrialization that integrates Design Management will reflect social and environmental knowledge in a more responsible, more sustainable, and socially more inclusive economy, thus assuming itself as European ecology, this time understood as a large, complex, and diverse ecosystem, culturally mediated by Design, which will take the place of its creative booster (Providência 2019a, pp. 8–23).

To fulfil the mediation of the future that Design Research demands, the MADE. PT group proposes to conceive, install, and promote an operational instrument to support the management of Northern Portugal's industrial fabric, aimed at guiding the creative management of the Design as creation of artifacts, services, and cultural mediation devices, under the condition of innovation. Establish a Creative Innovation Lab is the answer project, idealized as a space for producing content (generic and specific) to be made available to industries. It wants to constitute itself as a production machine (and consequently a social and future modeler for producing new consumption arguments) and not just for monitoring ideas.

3   Brand Design

3.1   The Power of Brand Origin

Assuming Design as a cultural mediator aligned with the objectives of valuing the industrial product, Brand Design has a fundamental role and contribute to the economic sovereignty of regions and countries.

Under the premise that the *Brand Origin* is an essential factor in evaluating products by its consumers (Johnson et al. 2016), we reflect, at this point, on the origin associated with the offer of products and services under the brand. For this, we verify the impact on consumer choice and the added value that territories can bring to brands, and reciprocally, the benefits of this economic valorization of products and services for territories (Suter et al. 2020).

Increasingly enlightened, consumers have gradually demanded greater transparency in the identification of the product supply chain. This theme was analyzed in *Forbes magazine* (Webb 2015), "consumers do look at the *Country of Origin* labels and are curious to learn more about the supply chain. This is a novel development for manufacturers", thus exposing the *Brand Origin* as a challenge for companies and territories.

In a literature review article specifically on *Country of Origin*, Dinnie (2004) found a first reference on the subject. In his 1965 study, Schooler observes that there is an effect of the *Country of Origin*, a theme explored through the *Made in* concept. Several authors have explored the *Country of Origin's* impact on consumers' purchase intention (Johnson et al. 2016; Sharma and Kaur 2020) and are associated with different consumption behaviors.

One factor analyzed concerning the *Country of Origin's* impact is growing importance, attributed by consumers, to the demonstrations of corporate social responsibility, which leads to consumption trends using domestic markets. The Greek study by Pouliopoulos et al. (2017) demonstrates, through statistical evidence, loyalty, willingness to pay more and purchasing behavior that favors local production over foreign companies.[1]

In another dimension of the willingness to pay more, there are consumers of luxury goods. Here, too, the *Country of Origin* is considered, but its emotional appeal has a more significant influence. So, *Brand Love* has a more direct relationship with *Perceived Strength of Brand Origin* than *Country of Origin* (Siew et al. 2018). However, these two possibilities compliment us for a fundamental question. The relocation of industrial production, mainly to the East, created entropy to the system of associating a product with an origin. It is recurrent evidence, in large organizations, that their production is dispersed in several countries. Considering, in addition to the final assembly facilities, the suppliers, we find an extensive list of origins that we can associate with Apple products (Apple Inc., 2019). Therefore, if on the one hand, "some consumers may perceive a Louis Vuitton handbag or an Apple iPhone as being "very French" or "very American", whereas other consumers may feel these brands are not so French or American, after all" (Siew et al. 2018). In this context, the power of *Made in* seems to lose strength, a trend already analyzed by Olins (2005), placing the challenge on the brands' communication strategy, thus allowing them to distance themselves from the territorial origin of the brands, where counterfeiting and the image of the low quality of industrial production, reported in the West.

Even among the brands that deliberately use the national flag in communicating their visual identity, we can observe some contradictions. The graphic brand *Havaianas*,[2] whose visual communication is part of the Brazilian flag, communicates verbally using another territory's name (Hawaii). In addition to the Norwegian flag, the *Neutrogena*[3] brand uses the signature "Norwegian Formula", despite being marketed by an American company. Some of the Swiss brands of most significant international value, namely in the segment of watches (luxury and high consumption), chocolates and cheeses, besides integrating the national flag in their visual communication, often reinforce with the verbal element *Swiss Made* and are

---

[1]In the case of a 2017 study, we must consider that the recent memory of Greek consumers prior to the austerity packages and successive financial bailouts contributed to adhesion or collective awareness of the imperative of their contribution, through the consumption of the national product level, to encourage the economic recovery of your country.

[2]*Havaianas* is a brand of the Brazilian company *Alpargatas* (Havaianas 2021).

[3]*Neotrogena* is a brand of the American company *Johnson & Johnson* (Neotrogena 2021).

an example of the recognition of the *Power of the Country Brand*,[4] as a way of establishing a quality standard for products. Thus, this sharing of roles between countries and companies that Olins (1999) has considered for more than 20 years that *Trading Identities* is a mutual benefit. In the same vein, but focusing on brands, Anholt (2011) recognizes the decisive role of places and products using the brand to reduce inequalities and contribute to the development of the poorest countries, having presented the *Brand New Justice* concept.

In Portugal, many companies have, in recent years, integrated national references into their *Brand Communication* after years of the national and international devaluation of their products. There is also a deficit in the market positioning through its brand, thus subordinating the national industry to the competition of supply at a lower price, a space led by countries geographically located in Asia, and condemning the economy to impoverishment. This context that we observe in the territory of Paredes (Northern Portugal), where a large concentration of wooden furniture industries went into decline and, intending to reverse this reality, the municipality launched the *Art on Chairs* project converging through mediation and Design management, efforts by scientific, economic and political agents to reposition the Paredes brand and the industries located here (Ribeiro and Providência 2014). What happened in the first edition of the project in this territory was the demonstration of the economic valorization of the industrial product through Design, an example similar to the *cluster* of furniture industries in Milan (Northern Italy), where the Designer António Citterio (1950) played an essential role in promoting, mainly in the 1990s (Lencastre and Pedro 2007).

The concept of the *cluster*, widely disseminated by Porter (1990) as a driver of innovation in the industry, is seen by the author as an essential competitive advantage since national prosperity is not inherent but the result of strategic action.

Competitive advantage is created and sustained through a highly localized process. (...) There are striking differences in the competitiveness patterns in every country; no nation can or will be competitive in every or even most industries. Ultimately, nations succeed in particular industries because their home environment is the most forward-looking, dynamic, and challenging (Porter 1990, p. 73).

In the sector of cultural and creative industries (understood as a *cluster*), which Florida (2014 [2002 1st ed.]) observed as an economic driver of the territories, the benefits of bringing culture to the economy are recognized, since professionals of this sector have a more significant economic contribution (Design Council 2018) for basing their activity on entrepreneurship and innovation, thus attracting new services, investment and activities to the place where they settle. A geographic concentration of these companies is frequent, often rehabilitating abandoned industrial spaces, which also promotes the urban requalification of the city, as

---

[4]Switzerland ranks third in the *Country Index 2019* (Future Brand 2019, pp. 72–81).

observed in Lisbon (LX Factory[5]), Madrid (Matadero Madrid[6]), or Eindhoven (Sectie-C District[7]).

In Portugal, it has been mainly the Northern region, heavily industrialized, to stand out in this sector, thus contributing and benefiting from *Brand Origin's* power for the international recognition of the North as a creative region of Portugal (Fundação Serralves 2013).

Finally, the important contribution of the organization of mega-events (cultural, technological, sports, political, religious, or others), which has not been dissected here, deserves our mention since it acts as a catalyst for the *Brand Image* of the territories of the host countries and cities. In addition to the local dynamism, the multicultural concentration of people with geographically dispersed origins directly impacts the local/national economy before, during, and after the event's time. The national and international media coverage associated with these events places the territory in the collective memory of a broad audience, anticipating the experience of the place and making it desirable as a future destination, in a *Competitive Advantage* that goes beyond the temporal frontier of the event and the geographical frontier, since it also mobilizes to neighboring territories.

The concepts *Cluster, Made in, Country of Origin*, and *Brand Origin* that we have mentioned here do not seem to leave any doubt about the need for a collaborative strategy to boost industries and territories economically.

3.2 Place Brand, Collaborative Strategy

It is in a highly competitive environment that territories compete for investment, tourism, and talent. The adoption of brands by cities, regions, and nations (for greater and more immediate differentiation than the heraldic system of insignia in the form of a coat of arms did not satisfy) brought them the novelty of the need to see the world as a global market, and of positioning themselves through the adoption of strategic management of the brand, a resource that products and services have used for the longest time.

Anholt (2005, p. 247) from Porter (1990) describes this paradigm stating that there is no other way for a country to prosper but considering itself a competitor in the single market. In a globalized world, all nations need to compete for the world's attention and wealth. Azevedo et al. (2011, p. 34) consider territorial competitiveness as the capacity of a given territorial community to ensure its sustained development's economic conditions. Kotler et al. (1993) referred in the 1990s to the *Competitiveness of Places* as a new challenge. These references, some of which have been around for two decades, demonstrate that the growth, prosperity, and

---

[5]See more at https://lxfactory.com (Retrieved February 6, 2021).

[6]See more at https://www.mataderomadrid.org (Retrieved February 6, 2021).

[7]See more at https://www.sectie-c.com/site/ (Retrieved February 6, 2021).

sustainable development of the territories is not a recent concern, but is as we know in the political agendas (Ribeiro and Providência 2019).

Today we see Design expresses itself strategically and instrumentally from the management sciences, technology, and aesthetics, but the greatest ambition of Design efficiency in the *Design of Place Brands* is the mediation of a tripartite relationship, articulating the production of university innovation, the economic and productive fabric and the power of local administration, thus imposing a collaborative dynamic between scientific, economic and political agents. Management and marketing refer to agents of the territory as *stakeholders*, giving them a central role in *Place Brands*.

In addition to evaluating and adopting the strategic actions of the territory's agents (which achieve holistic coherence through the management of Design), it is necessary to involve the public immediately after hearing them. Thus, questioning a group of residents, it was possible to determine in Porto (Casais and Monteiro 2019) and Barcelona (Compte-Pujol et al. 2018), which reflect widespread recognition of values that the two brands intend to transmit, verifying, however, that residents recognize that they are brands aimed at a tourist attraction, rather than to reinforce the citizens' connection to the territory.

Resuming the competitiveness of the market to which brands are subject, Keller (2002) warns of the imperative of leveraging brands, proposing, in line with the collaborative dynamic of mutual benefit that we tried to demonstrate in the previous point, the need to link the brand to different entities, people, places, things, other brands. According to the author, this leverage favors *Brand Knowledge*, that is, the brand's meaning stored in the consumer's memory. Thus understood, the concept of *Brand Knowledge* is similar to that of *Brand Image*. However, it seems to us to refer to a more enlightened dimension on the consumer, which in the case of *Place Brands* is also a more reflected consumption because it is about his choosing a place to invest, visit or live.

4 Conclusion

To comply with the mediation of the future that research in Design demands, in the MADE.PT —Critical Design Lab for Growth and Prosperity, part of the ID + Research Institute for Design, Media and Culture at the University of Aveiro—Portugal, we believe to be the result of the convergence of investment efforts of the different agents operating in the territory through their brands, the guarantee of the economic sovereignty of the industries, the region, and the country.

This convergence may be the reason for the growth of the *Portuguese Country Brand*, with more significant evidence in the tourism sector, but with some consolidation in trade (exports) and business (foreign investment). We can confirm this growth through different rankings such as Bloom Consulting (2020a, b, 2017), Future Brand (2019) or Brand Finance (2020).

References

Anholt S (2005) Branding de locais e de países. In: Newspaper TE (ed) O mundo das marcas. Actual Editora, Lisboa

Anholt S (2011) Brand new justice: how branding places and products can help the developing world. Routledge, New York

Apple Inc (2019) Apple supplier responsibility 2019. Retrieved 3 Feb 2021, Supplier List website: https://www.apple.com/supplier-responsibility/pdf/Apple-Supplier-List.pdf

Archer B (1979) Whatever became of design methodology? Des Stud 1(1):17–20

Azevedo A, Magalhães D, Pereira J (2011) City marketing—myplace in XXI (2nd edn). Vida Económica, Porto

Benton T (2006) Building utopia. In: Wilk C (ed) Modernism: designing a new world 1914–1939. V&A Publications, London

Bloom Consulting (2017) Digital Country Index'17. Retrieved from https://www.digitalcountryindex.com/digital-country-index-executive-summary.pdf?601c007202029

Bloom Consulting (2020a) Country brand ranking 2019/2020 trade edition. Retrieved from https://www.bloom-consulting.com/en/pdf/rankings/Bloom_Consulting_Country_Brand_Ranking_Trade.pdf

Bloom Consulting (2020b) Country brand ranking 2019/2020 turism edition. Retrieved from https://www.bloom-consulting.com/en/pdf/rankings/Bloom_Consulting_Country_Brand_Ranking_Tourism.pdf

Board of International Research in Design BIRD (2008) Design Dictionary: perspectives on Design Terminology.In: Erlhoff M, Marshall T (eds) Birkhäuser Verlag AG

Bonsiepe G (1999) Interface—an approach to design. Jan van Eyck Akademie, Maastricht

Borges A, Silva AC, Modesto A, Cunca R, Costa R, Branco V (2018) REDE #01: Reunião de Escolas de Design. Retrieved from http://hdl.handle.net/10773/24199

Branco V, Providência F (2017) Design as cultural mediation between matter and what matters design as cultural mediation between matter and what matters. Design J 1–9. https://doi.org/10.1080/14606925.2018.1396025

Brand Finance (2020) Brand finance nation brands 2020. Retrieved from https://brandirectory.com/download-report/brand-finance-nation-brands-2020-preview.pdf

Casais B, Monteiro P (2019) Residents' involvement in city brand co-creation and their perceptions of city brand identity: a case study in Porto. Place Brand Public Dipl 15(4):229–237. https://doi.org/10.1057/s41254-019-00132-8

Castillo G (2018) El diseño ha muerto, viva el diseño: Los nuevos desafíos que están transformando al diseño y la manera en que impacta a nuestra sociedad. Procorp, Universidad Andrés Bello and Campus Creativo Universidad Andrés Bello, Santiago, Chile

Compte-Pujol M, de San Eugenio-Vela J, Frigola-Reig J (2018) Key elements in defining Barcelona's place values: the contribution of residents' perceptions from an internal place branding perspective. Place Brand Public Dipl 14(4):245–259. https://doi.org/10.1057/s41254-017-0081-7

Design Council (2018) The design economy 2018—the state of design in the UK. In: The design economy 2018. Retrieved from https://www.designcouncil.org.uk/sites/default/files/asset/document/Design_Economy_2018_exec_summary.pdf

Dinnie K (2004) Country-of-origin 1965–2004: a literature review. J Customers Behav 3(2). https://doi.org/10.1362/1475392041829537

Fathers J (2003) Peripheral vision: an interview with Gui Bonsiepe charting a lifetime of commitment to design empowerment. Des Issues 19(4):44–56. https://doi.org/10.1162/074793603322545055

Florida R (2014) The rise of the creative class, revisited. Basic Books, Philadelphia, PA

Fundação Serralves (2013) Estudo Macroeconómico para o Desenvolvimento de um Cluster de Indústrias Criativas na Região do Norte, Porto

Future Brand (2019) Future country brand index 2019. Retrieved from https://www.futurebrand.com/uploads/FCI/FutureBrand-Country-Index-2019.pdf

Havaianas (2021) Havaianas—history. Retrieved 4 Feb 2021, from https://www.havaianas-store.com/en/history

Johnson ZS, Tian Y, Lee S (2016) Country-of-origin fit: when does a discrepancy between brand origin and country of manufacture reduce consumers' product evaluations. J Brand Manag 23 (4):403–418. https://doi.org/10.1057/bm.2016.13

Keller KL (2002) Brand synthesis: THE multidimensionality of brand knowledge. J Consum Res 29(4):595–600. https://doi.org/10.1086/346254

Kotler P, Haider D, Rein I (1993) Marketing places: attracting investment, industry, and tourism to cities, states, and nations. The Free Press, New York

Lencastre P de, and Pedro M (2007) Quatro Designers, Quatro casos: Caso Antonio Citterio - Cluster de Milão (Itália). In: Lencastre P de (ed) O livro da marca, pp 373–385. Publicações Dom Quixote, Lisboa

Montréal World Design Summit (2017) Montréal design declaration. Retrieved from http://www.montrealdesigndeclaration.org/

Naylor M, Ball R (2005) Forms follow Idea: an introduction to design poetics. Black Dog Publishing, London

Neotrogena (2021) Neotrogena—Origem do Creme Neotrogena. Retrieved 4 Feb 2020, from https://www.neutrogena.pt/origen-creme-neutrogena

Olins W (1999) Trading identities: why countries and companies are taking on each others roles. The Foreing Policy Center, London

Olins W (2005) Made in… o que significa e o que vale. In: A Marca, pp 140–157. Editorial Verbo, Lisboa

Porter ME (1990) The competitive advantage of nations. Harvard business review, (March–April). Retrieved from https://hbr.org/1990/03/the-competitive-advantage-of-nations

Pouliopoulos L, Pouliopoulos T, Triantafillidou A (2017) The effects of country-of-origin on consumers' CSR perceptions, behavioral intentions, and loyalty. In: Tsounis N, Vlachvei A (eds) Adv Appl Econ Res. Springer Proc Bus Econ 303–316. https://doi.org/10.1007/978-3-319-48454-9_22

Providência F (2012) Poeta ou aquele que faz: a poética como inovação em Design. Universidade de Aveiro. Retrieved from http://hdl.handle.net/10773/9218

Providência F (2019a) MADE.PT Design Crítico para o desenvolvimento e prosperidade. UA Editora—Universidade de Aveiro, Aveiro

Providência F (2019b) Y_Desenhar Portugal. Porto Design Biennal 2019, Porto

Puig T (2009) Marca cuidad: cómo rediseñarla para asegurar un futuro espléndido para todos. Paidós, Barcelona

Ribeiro M, Providência F (2014) Gestão vertical do Design no território: o caso Paredes. 3ª. Conferência Internacional Em Design e Artes Gráficas—Do-It-Yourself. Instituto Superior de Educação e Ciências, Instituto Politécnico de Tomar, Lisboa

Ribeiro M, Providência F (2019) Políticas baseadas no Design para a Inovação Sustentável do Território. In: Providência F, Quental J, Ramos I, Cardoso JM, Afreixo L, NevesL, … Rodrigues YW (eds) UD18 7° Encontro de Doutoramentos em Design, pp 329–335. UA Editora—Universidade de Aveiro, Aveiro

Sharma A, Kaur N (2020) The effect of country of origin on purchase intention. Int J Creative Res Thoughts (IJCRT) 8(7):104–109

Siew SW, Minor MS, Felix R (2018) The influence of perceived strength of brand origin on willingness to pay more for luxury goods. J Brand Manag 25(6):591–605. https://doi.org/10.1057/s41262-018-0114-4

Suter MB, Borini FM, Coelho DB, Junior MM de O, Machado MCC (2020) Leveraging the country-of-origin image by managing it at different levels. Place Branding Public Diplomacy 16(3):224–237. https://doi.org/10.1057/s41254-019-00149-z

Webb J (2015) Consumers demand more visibility into the supply chain. Forbes. Retrieved from https://www.forbes.com/sites/jwebb/2015/10/26/consumers-demand-more-visibility-into-the-supply-chain/?sh=67e0ae6b5b70

Mapping of Graphic-Semantic Representations in Design Teaching

Cátia Rijo

Abstract This article proposes a reflection on the visual thinking tools used in graphic design teaching as an active methodology that help the synthesis process of the expressive code and support graphic expression and semantics in design practice. It´s intended to analyze more specifically the use of mood boards as an imagery tool in the creation of a brand mark and its relationship with expressive codes. In order to build a relevant and meaningful brand mark, it is important to be aware of the semantic elements used. Tools like mood boards help students with the aesthetic-symbolic references of the form and make the semantic concepts more perceptible. At the end we analyze mood boards and their relationship with semantics in the creation of brand marks.

Keywords Design teaching · Mood board · Brand Mark · Semantic · Graphic-semantic Expression Map

1 Introduction

It's intended to analyse the methodological tool used in design teaching that helps the delimitation of graphic-semantic elements in the creation of brand marks.

Expressive ability is essential to the skillset of a designer, since the evolution of the project depends on its ability to externalize, record and communicate ideas. The development of a design project implies the experience of observation, analysis, and synthesis cycles. For this to happen, tools are needed that support perception, demonstration and the sharing of results. Working with aesthetic-formal codes is one of the central challenges of the design activity in its various fields of activity.

In the context of graphic design teaching, expressive capacity is worked as a way of managing project knowledge, as well as emphasizing the importance of creating a visual support for the semantic meaning of the created artifacts. Considering these

C. Rijo (✉)
Higher Education School of Lisbon Polytechnic, Campus de Benfica do IPL, 1549-003 Lisbon, Portugal

© The Author(s), under exclusive license to Springer Nature Switzerland AG 2022
D. Raposo et al. (eds.), *Perspectives on Design II*, Springer Series in Design and Innovation 16, https://doi.org/10.1007/978-3-030-79879-6_19

aspects, we intend to analyze the methodological tools that allow the mapping of graphic expression and that synthesize the aesthetic-symbolic concepts in graphic design teaching, and their importance in brand mark creation, as well as validating whether the immersive learning context can be a facilitating space for learning, creative thinking and for the generation of new ideas.

2 Active Methodologies and Graphic Design Teaching

In graphic design teaching, the intention is to recreate the experience of a designer in a real work context for the students. Through the use of active methodologies, the student is the main agent of their learning. This method encourages criticism and reflection, which, although accompanied by the teacher, the student is the center of this process, making it possible to guide learning in a more participatory way. The active methodology improves the student's individual autonomy developing it, in this way, they can understand aspects in their various areas of knowledge. This methodology requires an active role from the student, to make them autonomous, responsible and able to update their potential. The active methodology involves research, analysis, reflection, and the development of ideas individually or in pairs.

In this context, strategies are planned to facilitate the transformation of context variables into delimiters for the materialization of a solution that establishes an effective dialogue, where each project involves investigating contexts, identifying problems, formulating objectives, synthesizing concepts, experimenting with proposals, and communicating solutions.

Design, being an interdisciplinary and coordinating activity, requires the student to develop the ability to relate variables in order to find the best solution for the integration of the project's bounding?? ABUNDANT?? factors. However, project knowledge is consolidated through a reasoning structure marked by cycles of advances, setbacks and displacements of thought (Lawson, 2011). Through recurring cycles of analysis, synthesis and evaluation, aided by specific methods, the act of developing the project matures and converges towards the clarification of the project concept.

In the design project, each action is complemented by a combination of processes of thought to decide what procedures should be adopted. The process involves the interaction of information, the synthesis of concepts and the transformation of these concepts into meaningful knowledge to produce a coherent answer.

In the educational field, it is essential to create an environment conducive to active participation by students in the strategies they use to articulate this path. The teaching / learning context is also a space to reflect on design practice, where students should be encouraged to decide on the methodological strategies they will use. Ausubel (2003) proposes that, in addition to the content indicated by the teacher, the student's prior knowledge is valued during the learning process.

According to the author, this helps to build mental structures and schemes and to provide effective learning.

3 Methods and Techniques Applied to the Project

There are several learning methods in the scope of active methodologies, among them there is a collaborative learning model. This model consists of collaborative learning in which one of the main goals is to encourage teamwork. In its original definition, collaborative learning is a situation where two or more people learn or try to learn something together (Dillenbourg 1999). Through this method, students work as a team, sharing experiences and applying their knowledge directly, on the project. This model presupposes the involvement of all participants in all phases of the project and is intrinsically linked to cooperative learning since students should work in a group with several tasks.

Another method widely used in design teaching is learning based on the investigation of case studies, which is characterized by the research process in the development of a particular person, group, or situation over a period of time. This method is characterized by establishing questions, problems and hypotheses to arrive at the best solution for the problem or exploratory research, which is characterized by the initial investigation to clarify the exact nature of the problem to be solved. This methodology in teaching design is often used in the early stages of the design process in order to gain knowledge of the problem in question. In the creation phase this method helps the foundation and applicability of the proposed solution.

The Project Based learning (PLB) method is a very focused approach to design teaching, where students are involved in research, since the objective is for students to seek solutions to problems, questioning, debating ideas, collecting, and analyzing data, communicating information, their ideas and creating artifacts (Blumenfeld et al 1991).

As its name implies, it concerns learning based on problems applied to the act of designing. It is a type of active learning methodology widely practiced in the teaching of graphic design, since it allows the student to acquire skills, such as critical thinking, creativity, communication, and problem solving, characteristics essential to the function of a designer. This methodology assumes that students acquire knowledge from a concrete problem, in favor of an abstract concept, allowing them to learn to think and express their learning through the execution of a project. Project-based learning refers to the process, in which the objective is to arrive at a viable final product, based on research and on a problem, stimulating critical thinking and the respective skills of each student, leading the student to collaborate and share experiences with other students.

These methods are just a few used in design teaching, however there are many others, and it is important to keep in mind that new or readapted methods of others are always emerging, because of the experience of teachers in the area.

If the methods consist of the research and collection process that guides towards the intended objective, the techniques are the resources used to implement the method.

In graphic design teaching, there are several techniques that support the implementation of the active methodology, techniques that also help the designer in the exercise of his profession. According to Lupton (2011), in the initial phase of project design development there are several methods and techniques that help problem definition and stimulate creativity at the time of project creation: brainstorming, concept maps, interviews, focus groups, mood boards, graphic diaries, among others.

Specifically, in a graphic brand creation project, the use of mind maps, mood boards[1] and concept boards, is very common as tools that help students with project definition, stimulating their creativity at the same time.

4 The Importance of Visual Thinking Tools in the Design Process

As previously mentioned, in the development of a design project, there are several processes or steps in the act of creation and there are several techniques used during the process in graphic design teaching.

All design projects begin with the brief delimitation of the problem and, after that, the process passes through several stages until the project is completed. However, the order in which the different stages are performed isn't watertight, according to Lawson (2011), the process is marked by a cycle of advances, setbacks, and changes in thinking.

Many authors define the different phases of design in the development of a design project, but in all of them there are three main phases: analysis, synthesis and evaluation.

According to Jones (1992), there is a predominant thought in each of the phases and classifies the stages of the project into: divergence (includes actions to expand the points of view about the problem, originates questions giving different perspectives on the same issue); transformation (giving space to the structural exploration of the problem and the creation of creative concepts to establish connections in the search for a solution) and convergence (actions are channeled towards the definition of a solution, reducing uncertainties through evaluation strategies).

Cross-cutting to all development processes of a design project is the need to conduct research and assess the concept of the project, because the project definitions are taken based on the knowledge of the project itself.

---

[1]This is a tool with different interpretations, in this context we find this tool as a semantic panel similar to some authors (Baxter 2011; Cassidy 2011; De Wet 2016; Endrissat et al. 2016; Garner and Mcdonagh 2001; Lucero 2012).

In a simplistic way, we can define research as a way to seek answers to the questions raised. Preliminary research can be called exploratory research, tas this type of research helps to better understand the context to be worked on in the project. After this investigation, it is essential to carry out the analysis and synthesis of the collected data into a visual support, to measure patterns that help the understanding of the whole.

After investigating the issue in question, the concept of the project should be verified, a concept that will support the choices made in the different stages of the process. A concept is the idea behind the design, it is the main idea of the project, what is intended to be conveyed. To define the concept, it is important to know what you want to communicate, what the diagnosed need is and what the final objective of the project is.

In design teaching, in the early stages of project development—research, problem definition and concept definition—students obtain a lot of visual information through images. For this reason, visual thinking is an essential tool, as it helps to clarify ideas, the visualization of images that represent concepts helps in the interpretation of the problem and triggers associations of ideas. In this way, the images are treated as information and innovative ideas are created. In this context, the most frequently adopted tools that explore visual thinking in the context of graphic design teaching and that help students in visualizing and communicating the concept, are concept boards, inspiration panels and mood boards (Fig. 1).

According to Lupton (2011) in the first phases of the project-research and creation of ideas—it is common to use concept boards and mood boards as forms of organization and analysis of visual thinking.

Design is a creative activity and inspiration is an essential factor Designers look for inspiration from various types of sources, which may be intentional (sought by themselves) or unintentional. For Lupton (2011) the design process includes aspirations for art, science and culture. Ambrose and Harris (2010) state that designers cross reference from different elements of contemporary life, along with references from the past, returning to the traditions of art and history of design and looking at them as visual stimuli. This inspiration is fundamental in any creative activity. According to the authors, there are many creatives who register the inspiration process through a book of ideas - collection of clippings, photographs, doodles, color palettes, typographic examples, among others.

In this way, the use of tools such as a mood board, concept board and inspiration panel (among others), operate as agents of creation and mediation in the scope of creating a project, since they use visual resources as a form of project design.

5   Mood Board: An Imagery Tool

Slade-Brooking (2016) defines a semantic panel as a visual collage that projects a particular emotion or theme through the selection of various visual elements. Considered as a qualitative tool of visual inspiration (Cassidy 2011; Garner and

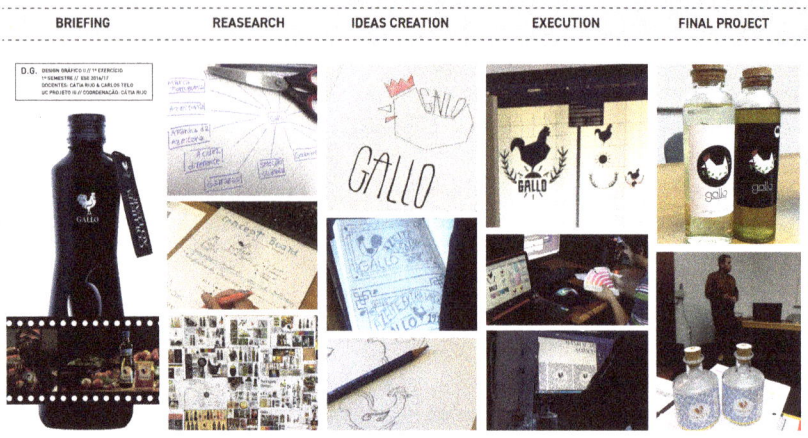

Fig. 1 Example of project design phases are visible in the use of mind map, concept board and mood board in the research. Photos of the author and work of students from graphic design classes at Escola Superior de Educação, Politécnico de Lisboa

Mcdonagh 2002), in the scope of design and when applied during the development process of a project, it serves as a source of sensory reference, especially visual, that uses aesthetic and symbolic elements to define the shape of a product (Löbach 2001). For this reason, it is a visual analysis technique that helps to define the aesthetic sense or style of a project and is often used in the conceptual phase of the design process since it is at this stage that the designer must be able to summarize the symbolism of the project in an image.

For Bürdek (2015), the visualization of images helps in the process of interpreting the meaning of words, for this reason the use of mood boards in the project scope presents itself as an agent of creation and mediation, making the collected data more synesthetic.

This technique offers a visual way capable of stimulating and inspiring the process of project development, "which must be considered because they are more logical and empathic to the design context than the traditional approach centered on verbal code" (Denton and Mcdonagh 2002, p. 63).

The creation of mood boards, according to Gusmão (2012), should be guided in stages to ensure the effectiveness of the technique. Jacques and Santos (2009) enumerate five distinct phases: 1st, the exhaustive understanding of the problem presented in the project and what can be achieve through dynamics and techniques such as brainstorming; 2nd the transformation of the verbal understanding of the problem presented in the project into written language; 3rd searches for images that identify or translate the project's objectives, the transformation of written language into visual; 4th creation of the visual ambience, made through the composition of the map; 5th definition of the palette of colors, shapes and textures to be used in the final product; 6th creation of a descriptive text to help its understanding.

In the teaching of graphic design, a briefing usually initiates the project and later definition of the concept and / or ideas that define the projectis followed by the creation of a mood board. This visual research tool is often used in the initial stage of a project as it helps to translate verbal language into visual signs. According to Bruseberg, McDonagh and Wormald (2004, p. 124) "images are a powerful resource to transmit meanings, particularly values and emotional experiences". As Gusmão observes (2012), it is up to the designer to articulate abstract or metaphorical concepts, translating them and evoking their meaning interconnected with the concepts.

After executing the mood board, analyzing the colors and typography present in it can help to highlight the emotional stimulus characteristic of the project in question. For Noble and Bestley (2005), to carry out experiences EXPERIMENTS?? focused on certain groups, in order to generate feedback on a certain criterion: use of color, typography, image and legibility, allows the designer to gather more specific and detailed information. Using mood boards and exploring these visual aspects can also highlight the emotional sense of the project, when analyzing each of these elements separately, we seek to define in detail the conceptual and visual direction to apply to the work.

The understanding of the processes used by the student, leads to the understanding of critical thinking, the deepening of research and analysis techniques, the resolution of creative problems as well as the learning of graphic techniques. The documentation of the entire work process, will allow the student to show the development of the different stages of the project, providing the justification for their decisions and allowing a final presentation that is easy to understand.

6 Visual Identity Signs: Color, Typography and Symbol

For Slade-Brooking (2016), the creation of successful brands depends not only on good design, but also needs to have meaning. However, concepts and ideas can only be represented through the words that define them as well as through images and visual signs.

Semiotics is the science that studies signs, the relationships between written or spoken signs, as well as the physical references created from ideas (Noble and Bestley 2005). A designer can use semiotics to create meaningful forms as well as to study existing signs. Lupton (2011, p. 88) states that "(…) when creating a logo or a system of icons, designers can look at the basic categories of visual signs in order to generate ideas with various degrees of abstraction or familiarity". There are three different types of signs: icons, indexes and symbols (based on the categories of the relationship between the sign and Peirce's object).

An icon has a similar relationship with what it represents (for example, the drawing of a flower); an index refers to the elements that compose it and has a continuous relationship with what it represents (symbolizes a physical action or process: smoke symbolizes fire; dark clouds indicate rain); in a symbol it is abstract and arbitrary, its representation is not similar to its meaning and its relationship is purely conventional (for example, the symbols proper to mathematics or the graphic mark of a certain brand or company).

According to Raposo (2008, p. 10) "a brand can be an icon, an index, a symbol or all of them simultaneously" for the author, a visual identity that is an image, can also be a metaphor that represents a certain entity and its style, being able to allude to the style of the designer who created it. It is essential, for its creation, to appreciate and manipulate the level of meaning contained in its identity, as well as to understand the reactions of the target audience. It is based on its message and meaning that the way it should be communicated is determined. For this, the use of typography, color and symbol is extremely important.

The multiple possible combinations to be made through the design of a graphic brand depend on the strategy adopted and, on the characteristics, and functionalities of the different elements that compose it (typography, color and symbol) and that translate what each sign represents from a semiotic perspective to a symbolic one (Costa et al. 2013). These three elements are the basis of any visual identity and it is through these that a brand may or may not impact its target audience.

However, when defining the message, it is necessary to correctly define the markets in which the brand operates, as well as to investigate its acceptability and linguistic and cultural adequacy (Costa et al. 2013). Often, a seemingly harmless word, combination of words, image or symbol, suggests unexpected associations that may be offensive to some people or cultures and, therefore, must be evaluated. It is therefore important to take into account all possibilities (using imagination or common sense) depending on the complexity of the project/brand.

7 The Importance of Semantics and Mood Boards in Brand Mark Creation

The information collected through the mood board leads to the creation of conceptual routes at a semantic level that, and in turn, determines the message that a project or brand must express. The way the subject interprets the sign depends on their mental models, as well as the way the designer chooses the representation of the object (Isherwood 2009).

When viewing a graphic brand for the first time, the consumer immediately perceives its shape and color. These two aspects instantly create a visual pattern that is completed by being associated with a previous message or experience, according to Formiés and Vázquez (2006) and this visual pattern is completed through the semantic attributes that relate to its meaning and how it is recognized (Fig. 2).

As mentioned earlier, semantics is a linguistic branch that leads to the study of the relationships between signs, symbols and the meaning they represent. It is a field of knowledge that studies the systems of signs that allows people to communicate with each other and "refines why a letter, a set of words, an object, a photograph, a mathematical symbol, a hand gesture, a color or a series of pictograms, acquire concrete meanings in a given society" (Miranda and Quindós 2015, p. 23). Semiotics allows the valuation of a form, if it is relevant in relation to what one wants to understand (meaning), and if it proves that the messages of a system of pictograms are correctly understood and interpreted by the target audience.

According to the aforementioned authors, the basis of the concept of semiotics rests on the work of two philosophers: Ferdinand de Saussure and Charles Peirce, who founded their bases. Their theories centered on the belief that an individual is programmed for verbal language and that it is through words that their view of the world is explained.

Morris (1985) states that the semiotics process relates three factors: The first is the sign itself, the second is what the sign means, the third being the effect that the sign produces on a given target audience considering its interpretation. It also states that the target audience can be considered as a fourth factor. It is through these that the common claim that a graphic brand means something to someone can be justified. The author also states that the sign can be a vehicle or a bridge that transports the target audience to the real sense of the graphic brand.

Miranda and Quindós (2015) point out that Morris (1985) adopts the three categories of relationship between sign and object established by Peirce, stating that if the sign is seen as a symbol, it will be the spokesperson for abstract concepts, establishing an arbitrary relationship between emitter and receiver. The relationship it establishes with the object it represents is founded on a basis established by a previous convention. Thus, depending on the context, there are several conditions that affect the meaning of a symbol or graphic mark. These conditions are the environment in which it is understood; the degree of recognition of its meaning; the particular culture of the recipients; social circumstances and different combinations of symbols.

As previously mentioned, if through the use of mood boards, conceptual routes of semantic level are created, then the relationship between semantic attributes and previous experience allows the brand positioning in the brain to be generated. It is through memory that the link and information related to the brand are remembered.

According to Formiés and Vázquez (2006), the semantic differential technique allows the evaluation of opposite adjectives by observing whether there is any relationship between elements such as color, set, visual pattern and semantic attributes that the brand intends to transmit. When conducting a study to assess whether the brand values were fixed in the memory and whether it was striking enough to be recognized and distinguished among other similar brands, its symbols and colors are analyzed separately. The differentiation between the quality and the origin of a brand classifies it in categories such as physical characteristics, functional aspects and emotional characteristics.

The application of semantics can be a tool for analyzing a brand's proposals, referring to its values and representing them by adjectives. This would allow for visualizing dominant visual elements such as the figure, color, size, scale,

Fig. 2 Example of a mood board created for the rebranding of the olive oil brand mark "Galo". Photos of the author and work of students from graphic design classes

proportion or contrast and adjusting the final brand so that its graphic representation faithfully reflects the values it intends to transmit (Formiés and Vázquez 2006).

Different studies report that objects, concepts or functions, require a high level of abstraction in order to be represented, making this task almost impossible. The intrinsic relationship between the graphic brand and what it represents can be described as a semantic differential, this relationship can also be used to determine brand recognition.

Isherwood (2009) points out that all the studies already carried out on semantics suggest that it has an important role in the way the graphic brand is interpreted. This may be related to how the brand and the consumer are related. This proximity may be an index of the semantic and lexical visual connections. The same author notes that familiarity is also an important factor to take into account when creating a graphic brand, as well as response times, as familiar signs activate the consumer's memory more quickly. The author clarifies that the way in which information about a graphic brand is transmitted from person to person, is often not so direct, and cannot be based only on the association made through signs, but it needs to refer to the personality of the brand and the values that are inherent in it, these being understood in its image. "On its own, a logo is just a mark. For it to become more than a graphic device it must acquire meaning in the mind of the consumer" (Slade-Brooking 2016, p. 27), in order to build a relevant and meaningful graphic brand it is necessary to resort to a series of interconnected elements that can represent or transmit the brand's values.

8 Conclusions

In design education, the use of active methodologies helps in recreating the way in which design process works and there are several effective methods and techniques that teachers use in graphic design classes. These kinds of methodologies help this type of teaching since the student is responsible for their own learning process. In the area of graphic design, it is proven that the use of tools such as mood boards and concept boards, among others, help in visual thinking, especially when used in the early stages of a project because they help the students understand the meaning and concepts in an objective graphic design product.

Mood boards are an imagery tool that support students with the association of semantic elements with graphic elements, they are an aesthetic-symbolic reference tool that give adequate space to produce conceptual alignment and sensory inspiration.

This type of analysis is especially important in the creation of brand marks, since they contain a great symbolic load. Through the analysis of mood boards, students can analyze references in terms of color, typography and shape, which are essential elements in the creation of brand marks.

References

Ambrose G, Harris P (2010) Design thinking. AVA Publishing (UK) Ltd
Ausubel DP et al (1980) Psicologia educacional, 2nd edn. Interamericana, Rio de Janeiro
Baxter M (2011) Projeto de Produto: guia prático para o design de novos produtos. Tradução, Itiro Iida. 3. ed. São Paulo: Edgard Blücher
Blumenfeld C et al (1991) Educational psychologist. Motivating project-based learning: sustaining the doing, supporting the learning

Bruseberg A, Mcdonagh D, Wormald P (2003) The use of images to elicit user needs for the design of playground equipment. In: Mcdonagh D et al (eds) Design and emotion. CRC Press, London, pp 114–118

Bürdek B (2015) Design: history, theory and practice of product design, 2nd edn. Birkhäuser Basel, Basel

Cassidy T (2011) The mood board process modeled and understood as a qualitative design research tool. Fash Pract 3(2):225–251

Costa J, Bosovsky G, Fontvila I, Radabán A, Culleré A (2013) Los Pilares Del Branding: anatomy of the brand. Costa Punto

Dillenbourg P (1999) Collaborative learning: cognitive and computational approaches. advances in learning and instruction series. Elsevier Science Inc., New York, NY

De Wet A (2016) An educational tool to encourage higher level thinking skills in the selection of images for fashion design mood boards: an action research approach. Int J Fashion Des Technol Educ 10(1):16–25

Endrissat N, Islam G, Noppeney C (2016) Visual organizing: balancing coordination and creative freedom via mood boards. J Bus Res 69(7):2353–2362

Formiés I, Vázquez A (2006) Brand analyzes through the semantic differential. Automotive brand cases

Garner S, McDonagh D (2002) Problem interpretation and resolution via visual stimuli: the use of 'mood boards. Des Educ Int J Art Des Educ 20(1):57–64

Garner S et al (2015) Mood boards as a design catalyst and resource: researching an under researched area. Int J All Aspects Des 7(3):16–31

Gusmão C (2012) Semantic panel as a methodological technique in the teaching of design practice in design

Herrera E, Fernández L (2008) Diseñar es transformar las cosas en signos. Convergências— Revista de Investigação e Ensino das Artes, VOL I (1) Retrieved from journal URL: http://convergencias.ipcb.pt

Isherwood S (2009) Graphics and semantics: the relationship between what is seen and what is meant in icon design

Jacques J, Santos R (2009) The semantic panel as a tool in product development. Annals V CIPED

Jones C (1992) Design methods. John Wiley & Sons, New York

Lawson B (2011) Como arquitetos e designers pensam. São Paulo: Oficina de Textos

Löbach B (2001) Design industrial: bases para a configuração dos produtos industriais. Edgard Blücher, São Paulo

Lucero A (2012) Framing, aligning, paradoxing, abstracting, and directing: how design mood boards work. Designing Interactive Systems Conference, DIS '12. Anais. ACM Press, New York

Lupton E (2011) Graphic design thinking: beyond brainstorming. Princeton Architectural Press

Miranda E, Quindós T (2015) Diseño y Pictogrmas Campgrafic Editors 1st edn

Morris C (1985) Psychology: an introduction. prentice hall college div, 9th edn

Noble I, Bestley R (2005) Visual research. AVA Publishing, SA

Raposo D (2008) Identity design and corporate image. IPBC

Slade-Brooking C (2016) Creating a brand identity: a guide for designers. Laurence King Publishing

Categorising the Sonic Experience in the Soundscapes of Videogames

João P. Ribeiro, Miguel Carvalhais, and Pedro Cardoso

Abstract In this paper, we address the categorisation of sounds in the soundscapes of videogames. Analysis and classification of sounds in their relationship with humans are essential to help us assess how we interact with acoustic components. We also provide an outline of sound concerning player perception, game design, interaction, realism, and communication. To compile information, we combined an autoethnography methodology with the soundwalking practice applied to videogames. The findings indicate that rules and actions can make the soundscape of videogames anthropophonic. However, such happens with all audiovisual media, so this categorisation is only hypothetical. The categories of Krause's taxonomy may be insufficient to analyse soundscapes that are too varied. As such, the categorisation of sounds as technophonic is also examined. We also show how repetition, patterns, and rhythm are used in games to make sounds mechanical and improve game design. This understanding will allow designers to deliver distinct experiences to players.

Keywords Soundscapes · Videogames · Repetition · Ecological listening

J. P. Ribeiro (✉)
Faculty of Engineering, University of Porto, Porto, Portugal
e-mail: up201601392@edu.fba.up.pt

M. Carvalhais
i2ADS, and Faculty of Fine Arts, University of Porto, Porto, Portugal
e-mail: mcarvalhais@fba.up.pt

P. Cardoso
Universidade de Aveiro/DigiMedia, Aveiro, Portugal
e-mail: pedroccardoso@ua.pt

1 Introduction and Methodology

In this essay, we present our analysis of a particular aspect of the soundscape ecology of videogames, the classification of sound sources. Sound is a physical phenomenon which is usually studied in the natural sciences. Still, the study and the classification of sound in its relation to human culture are essential for allowing us to better understand how we deal with the acoustic elements in the world.

While classifying the sounds of the soundscapes of videogames within Bernie Krause's taxonomy (Krause 2015), we aim to clarify the logic behind our thesis that those sounds might be *anthropophonic*. To do so, we reviewed the concepts of soundscape and acoustic ecology. We also present current theories on the measurement of sound, aesthetic context, acoustic areas, and soundscape analysis.

Then, we introduce existing ideas on the form and function of videogame soundscapes. This outline includes sound concerning player perception, game design, interaction, realism, and communication. A summary of the most relevant frameworks for the study and design of videogame soundscapes is also presented. At the time of writing, we were not able to find any thesis sustaining our specific argument. As such, after the literature review, we will present our argument.

To do this, we needed to adopt a methodology for studying the soundscape, define it, and find out which frameworks exist to categorise sounds and their contextual significance. However, there are no proven techniques for evaluating the soundscape from the viewpoint of the cultural and social sciences (O'Keeffe 2011).

A mixed research methodology must be followed to determine what may be crucial regarding a soundscape. One approach is *soundwalking*, initially proposed by Hildegard Westerkamp as well as R. Murray Schafer (O'Keeffe 2011). However, *soundwalking* does not provide us with an explanation of the social or cultural significance, so we need to consider other qualitative methodologies. Standard sociological approaches can play a role in the study of sound significance and creation (O'Keeffe 2011).

Recognising the existence of various approaches to explore a game space is a crucial prerequisite for determining what a soundscape can be within an interactive environment (O'Keeffe 2011). Our physical reality and interactive technology are becoming interwoven, increasing significance and sense. Intrinsically, authors suggest the need for methods that promote the exploration of ways in which the player experiences a videogame. Chamberlain et al. suggest that autoethnography can help us find the design possibilities in combining digital content and physical locations (Chamberlain et al. 2017).

We believe that the methodology is appropriate for our study as we explored videogames that manifest through five different spaces, both digital and physical. We combined autoethnography and *soundwalking*, applying them to videogames. With this, we were able to reflect on the significance of many case studies and use our expertise and real-world knowledge to examine videogame soundscapes.

2 Literature Review

2.1 Soundscape and Soundscape Ecology

Sound has objective features such as *acoustic pressure*, *audible frequency*, and *phase velocity*. However, it also has subjective properties such as *pitch*,[1] *loudness*, and *tone quality*. Our perception of sounds is also *objective* and *subjective*. Due to its subjective nature and our perception of it, a particular soundscape can present elements which are liked by some, while being repulsive for others, they can be *noise* (Loupa 2020).

The entirety of the sounds perceived in a given context form the *soundscape*. Researchers focus on how the soundscape is interpreted and comprehended by a person. Sound value judgments can vary according to the specific area and visual look of the soundscape (Miller 2013). The study of the soundscape allows for aesthetic reflection on the sound environment of a specific context, allowing us, for example, to understand that the soundscape of cities is defined by urban sounds, which also express temporality, evanescence, and urban sprawl. Sound icons, characters, and symbols are recognisable and are in line with the physical elements of the urban structure, and qualify it. Listening as a process includes the immersion of the listener in the recording and assessment of the sound environment (Quintero and Recuero 2018).

The definition of soundscape is proposed by R. Murray Schafer (1969) to describe any acoustic area which can be explored as a text. The soundscape is comprised of all the sounds of a particular location, whether that location is a country, region, community, mall, office or a programme on radio. The soundscape constitutes a sonic representation in which the sounds make people feel their actions and activities through sounds, which are understood in their cultural context. The critical components of the soundscape are (1) *keynote sounds*; (2) *sound signals*; and (3) *soundmarks*.

As defined by Schafer, the sounds produced by the terrain and the environment of an ecosystem are the *keynote* sounds. Sometimes, such sounds may have prototypical meaning.[2] They can also shape a community's actions or mode of living (Schafer 1993). *Signals* are the forefront sounds that we consciously listen to.

---

[1]"(…) pitch is subjective, resulting from human perception. This means that under specific conditions two sounds produced at two different frequencies may be perceived as having the same pitch" (Davenport and Hannahs 2020).

[2]The keynotes are the foundational sounds that help in making all the other sounds possible. A keynote is the basis of the soundscape. These sounds often form an unrecognized, yet always-present, framework of sounds. As such, we deliberately hear the additional two categories of sound in opposition to the keynote sounds. They operate like a communal auditory component for the people hearing them. They bind people to an acoustic culture (Hansen 2017; Pigott 2017).

Sound signals are frequently arranged in very complicated patterns, as "is the case with the cor de chasse, or train and ship whistles" (Schafer 1993). *Soundmarks* originate from the idea of a landmark, and the concept relates to a cultural sound that is distinctive or holds characteristics that make it especially esteemed (Schafer 1993).

Schafer (1977) also defined the terms *figure* and *background* with the expression "signal-keynote sound" which means that the keynotes constitute the background, and the figure is constituted by the sound signals and the soundmark (Hedfors and Berg 2003). In intricate sonic environments, the *scale* is a relevant characteristic. Payne et al. (2009) showed that a two-scale paradigm, composed of sounds and soundscape, is by far the most prevalent across over 500 papers. Individuals *soundwalking*[3] in Manchester and London defined what they heard mostly from the sounds, but spoke too about the more expansive soundscape (Davies 2015).

Quintero and Recuero propose a soundscape-based methodology for street analysis that is phenomenologically and psychoacoustically focused. The problem is explored in two stages: seeing the picture and listening, observed using the soundwalk method, spectrogram analysis and surveys. A multidimensional perception of space emerges that makes it possible to describe the landscape distinctions from the soundscape. Thus, revealing simple or distinct associations with the levels of the readability of the urban picture (Quintero and Recuero 2018).

In addition to the description of the main elements of the soundscape, R. Murray Schafer tells us that there are two distinct modes of a soundscape created by the environment: *hi-fi* and *lo-fi*. This terminology was used by R. Murray Schafer to differentiate between soundscapes filled with relevant sounds and others which are too obscured by "noise" (Schafer 1993). A *hi-fi* soundscape suggests an acoustic setting in which an uncorrupted configuration of a sound is transmitted. It is replicated, distributed, and received with high fidelity to a quintessential form (Rasmussen 2017). Andrea Polli argues that every sound is characteristically distinct. They happen in one location at a moment, and cannot be repeated. The replication of any sound in precisely the same way is theoretically unfeasible in nature (Polli 2012).

Bernie Krause established a concept of soundscape ecology in *Voices of the Wild* that divides soundscape elements into three groups: (1) *geophony* for naturally occurring non-biological sounds; (2) *biophony* for sounds of biological systems; (3) *anthropophony* for sounds created by humans or for humans (Krause 2015). One of the concerns of many soundscape ecologists is whether human beings cause changes in the sound environment that reduce the existence of natural soundscapes across all life forms (Cowan 2016).

---

[3]"Soundwalking is a listening and composition method that focuses on the exploration of the environment" (Carvalhais and Lee 2019).

2.2 Soundscapes in Videogames

Aki Järvinen tells us that game environments are made of five audiovisual elements. They are (1) *dimension*; (2) *point of perception*; (3) *visual outlook*; (4) *soundscape*; and (5) *senso-motority*. He argues that soundscapes typically resemble the distinction seen between diegetic and extradiegetic sounds in film. The diegetic sound may be a city scuffle or the humming of animals. Environmental awareness is essential in play, so diegetic sound is quite crucial to set that awareness (Järvinen 2002). When we press on a mouse button in a play session of *Doom* (id Software 1993), we anticipate a gun to fire alongside the appropriate sound effects. In setting up atmosphere or anticipation, including intents like tension, the extradiegetic sounds are essential. If a player takes a particular direction or an exit door, the soundtrack will shift and imply that in that direction there must be something important. Soundscapes frequently run via the context of the visual disposition of the game. They are differently selected per game world (Järvinen 2002). Järvinen uses examples of videogames like *Parappa the Rapper* (NanaOn-Sha 1996), *Dance Dance Revolution* (Konami & Bemani 1998) and *Vib-Ribbon* (NanaOn-Sha 1999) to state that some game genres utilise music to push play. In those kinds of videogames, navigating the game world moves towards experiencing the soundscape. The soundscape of a videogame is often the collection of in-game (*diegetic*) and off-game (*non-diegetic*) sounds (Järvinen 2002).

Daniel Kromand analysed "the affordances of the soundscape in survival-horror games by examining the barrier between diegetic and non-diegetic sounds and how the validity of a sound cue is challenged", claiming that videogames categorised as horror use the "discrepancy between soundscape and perceived reality to create an ambience of fear"(Kromand 2008). Games are simulated worlds with hard-coded assets. Some sounds can be programmed to function in a specific manner as the player traverses different spaces. This kind of dynamic structure in audio design builds a precisely designed soundscape, "where sound can provide a dramatic increase of tension" (Kromand 2008).

Mark Grimshaw advocates for a soundscape framework in video games by using soundscape ecology concepts. He describes the soundscape ecology of competitive *first-person shooters* (FPS) as "a set of relationships between players founded upon sound" (Grimshaw 2007). FPS gaming can be seen as a cultural artefact. This view, as well as its ramifications, can also be extended to FPS single-player games. AI-enabled bots are seen as (simplified) social players (Grimshaw 2007). The software frameworks[4] in which videogames run are the performance stages of the acoustic ecology, its building foundations. They offer several scenographic sounds as well as other sound features. They also offer a game template inside which there is much space for creativity. The more advanced FPS software system will recast

---

[4]Such as 3D scenegraph APIs, game artificial intelligence, engines, and modification tools.

the sound of the player via a real-time DSP[5] that positions their character in various spaces, places and periods. The game engine might sometimes play a unique role as a scripter or may supply signals like game statuses.

Shortly after Grimshaw's model, another framework for game audio was published, the IEZA Framework (Huiberts and Tol 2008). It can be employed for the study and processing of sound in videogames. The framework includes two axes to explain the sound of videogames. Four domains are rooted in the two axes: *Interface, Effect, Zone,* and *Affect*.

Sound throughout the *Interface domain* communicates what is going on in the game world. In several games, it is a sound connected with HUD action, like sound connected directly to health or progress bars, pop-up windows and performance indicators. Sound in the *Effect domain* reflects the action of the game environment. Sound typically includes a combination of one-shot auditory stimuli and persistent sound sources. In several titles, it is the portion of the game sound that is dynamically encoded. Sound within the *Zone domain* reflects the world of the game. The Zone can be interpreted as a particular spatial environment containing a set amount of visual and acoustic items. Sound in the *Affect domain* reflects the psychological, cultural and symbolic significance of the game (Huiberts and Tol 2008).

Milena Droumeva discusses how the concepts of accuracy and realism present themselves traditionally as global cultural norms in digital technology, and as design criteria for the development of sound in videogames. She states that there still are insufficient tools and theoretical structures for analysing the importance of sound in videogames. She points to Grimshaw's conceptual model of acoustic ecology in first-person shooter games as one of the few instances of a model. Hence the demand for the creation of broader theoretical and methodological structures to explain the different principles of game sound. Droumeva suggests a structure for the analysis of game sound which elicits a multi-disciplinary viewpoint with a clear emphasis on hearing (Droumeva 2011). This system, based upon the work of Truax (2001), the IEZA framework (Huiberts and Tol 2008), and inspired by Schafer (1977), integrates media history with present technical and cultural real-life situations (Droumeva 2011).

The idea of acoustic communication is a model which seeks to bring interdisciplinary viewpoints to the research of acoustic receiving and sound production. Its origins can be traced back to R. Murray Schafer's context of acoustic ecology (Droumeva 2011). Its push into realism is something which Droumeva sees as an abstract trend that intersects multiple styles and innovations in art and culture. Examples range from interactive movie soundscapes on wide screens and digital audio technology to full VR technology (Droumeva 2011). Listening merely becomes a different way to focus. There is a chain of command in listening modes

---

[5]"Digital signal processing (DSP) is concerned with the representation of signals by a sequence of numbers or symbols and the processing of these signals. Digital signal processing and analog signal processing are subfields of signal processing" (Goyal and Gupta 2010).

throughout gameplay. Droumeva outlines the standard concepts of hearing to gameplay sounds and organises them as per the established categories of game functions, attentional positions, and states of diegesis. She claims that doing so fails to acknowledge sounds external to the game world, which can be representative of the play activity. Some examples are "the acoustic soundscape of group play, the arcade environment or online audio conferencing such as Teamspeak" (Droumeva 2011).

A group of listening types arose from Droumeva's explanation of "fidelity, verisimilitude and the ecology of game sound." Such types represent and seek to classify the broader patterns that have been borne out by ongoing changes in the characteristics, strategies, and features of game sound across history. They are (Droumeva 2011):

1. *Imaginative Listening*: "A listening that supplies the perceptual conditions for immersion—building up a mental image of an environment from the little that is provided acoustically by the game's soundtrack (…)"
2. *Nostalgic Listening*: "An analytical, culturally-critical type of listening that has emerged over time in experienced players who look for iconic game music themes through platforms and generations of a particular game (…)"
3. *Disjunctive Listening*: "A listening position that describes the ability that gamers develop to very quickly and fluidly interchange listening attentions (…)"
4. *Naive Listening*: "A non-analytical, electroacoustic listening that allows the player to feel immersed into the game reality with the minimum amount of auditory complexity."
5. *Conditioned Listening*: A type of listening which Truax (2001) defines as media listening, in which players hear the flow of soundscapes, tacitly acquainted with the acoustic features of the games, and with an implicit premise.
6. *Inter-textual Listening*: "A result of cross-pollination of different media genres, this listening position addresses situations where game soundscapes contain radio, telephone, or TV sounds (most famously featured in Grand Theft Auto)."

3 Sonic Experiences in Videogames

3.1 Are the Sounds in Videogame Soundscapes Anthropophonic?

In Sect. 2, we analysed a variety of authors that described the various elements of the soundscapes of videogames but we were unable to find a concise description of the concept in their works. We have thus opted to define it ourselves using concepts initially set down by the authors reviewed in Sect. 2.

The soundscape of videogames consists of each acoustic output created by a videogame system, the mediation devices, and players. We can separate the components of the soundscape in relation to their position in one of videogames' spaces, and we can analyse their features in isolation or relative to each other. We cannot, however, devise an exact notion of the soundscape in videogames, considering that the spaces and devices in which they manifest themselves are vastly diverse.

We focused on those that do not make use of current emergent or online technologies but of conventional mediation devices and that are single player.[6] Conventional mediation devices include consoles or PCs, TVs or computer monitors, controllers or keyboard and mouse, and speakers. The inclusion/exclusion criteria were: (1) occurs only in virtual environments; (2) require only non-wearable bidimensional displays for visual output; (3) do not make use of online communication networks; (4) are single-player games. We acknowledge that videogames' manifestations far exceed these restrictions, however, due to the scope of this text, we will limit ourselves to the implementations mentioned above.

If we try to take Krause's taxonomy in consideration when thinking of soundscapes in videogames, we find that most sounds depend on algorithms either for storage and reproduction or synthesis. Therefore, they might be classified as *anthropophonic* sounds. However, there are cases where they can be recordings of *geophonic* and *biophonic* sounds like we find in film.

Both film and videogame soundscapes rely on mediation. One may e.g. find nature documentaries that include recorded natural soundscapes, and despite mediation, those sounds are still non-anthropophonic. As such, although videogame soundscapes' mediation is usually algorithmic, one might also argue that sounds from non-anthropophonic sources remain non-anthropophonic.

The method of composition of the soundscape of videogames, which depends on rules and actions, can also make the soundscape anthropophonic to some. An analogue to this can be found in the compositions of Olivier Messiaen as well as in composers of *musique concrète*[7] and biomusic, who accurately transcribed and recorded geophonic and biophonic sounds for use in their music. Accordingly, there is human agency behind the way in which those sounds are presented, so the argument can be made for them to be classified as anthropophonic (Psimikakis-Chalkokondylis 2016). One could argue that a videogame may present soundscapes that reflect on recordings of biophonic or geophonic sources that are scientifically accurate. However, a film viewer or a player's perception of the origin of the sound will not come from a living ecosystem. Those sounds can then be considered anthropophonic or not, depending on one's view on whether the *mediation* element overlaps all others. As a result of their algorithmic nature, digital representations of living organisms in videogames are codified, regardless of

---

[6]We opted to exclude online technologies because their emphasis on socialization, much present in online games, can lead to sound output variables we are yet to consider.

[7]*Musique concrète* is a musical movement in which composers utilize recorded sounds as materials for their music. Most people agree that the incorporation of natural sounds alongside musical instruments, human voices, and synthesizers, originates musical artefacts—which are inherently synthetic.

accuracy. Even videogames that incorporate full-motion video only attempt to merge the two media or achieve "life-like" visuals in videogames. It is creating plausibility in a videogame scene, an imitation of life within a computer, almost like a facsimile.

Accordingly, we find that using Krause's taxonomy is limiting in the context of videogames. However, distinctions can be made between recorded and synthesised sounds. We can also identify the diegetic origin of a sound, which might lead to a different categorisation of the origin of sounds in videogame soundscapes and players' experience with them. To illustrate our point, we provide some examples that distinguish the use of recorded sounds both in film and in videogames.

3.2 Soundscapes of Film

In *King Kong* (Cooper and Schoedsack 1933), the soundscape is composed of both diegetic and non-diegetic sounds. Character dialogues and object-related sound effects can be considered diegetic since they pertain to the fictional world that the viewers are being shown. However, the soundtrack is considered non-diegetic, since it is only a stylistic element, used to elicit specific reactions in the viewer. When looking at this film and other classics in the Hollywood style, we can classify most diegetic and non-diegetic sounds as anthropophonic since they are either synthetic or human.

Still, let us look at Werner Herzog's *Grizzly Man* (Herzog 2005). Alongside anthropophonic sounds, we can also find sounds from geophonic and biophonic origin in the soundscape. They can be, e.g. the wind rustling through trees or the sound of a bear growling. One may reason for us to be able to classify those as not being anthropophonic is because they correspond to the diegetic presence of the trees and the bears. They are also straightforward recordings of those sounds, which were taken from real-world ecosystems, they are field recordings. However, one may also argue that they are mediated by the film medium. Someone chose to record them, with specific techniques and technology, and arranged them in a specific position in the film. In so doing, one can argue that they are in fact anthropophonic, as the recording, montage and distribution was made by humans. Looking at another example, the origin of a grasshopper's sound in 1994's *The Lion King* (Allers and Minkoff 1994) will not be a grasshopper that had been recorded to appear on the screen as it did in the real-world. However, it is the recording of an actual grasshopper. This duality leaves room for both interpretations on the categorisation of the sound.

Despite this, we argue that some of the non-diegetic sounds in *Bill Oddie's Wild Side* (Oddie 2008) are decidedly anthropophonic despite seeming biophonic. This confusion happens precisely in the soundtracks composed for the series. Some of those tracks contain samples from recordings of e.g. amphibians and vertebrates. However, those samples are cut, manipulated and, above all else, arranged within other—anthropophonic—sounds. This arrangement makes them part of the soundtrack; it makes them music, either as a whole or as part of a larger composition.

3.3   Soundscapes of Videogames

If we establish an analogy between film and videogames, firstly we can observe that videogames also have both diegetic and non-diegetic sounds. For instance, in *Donkey Kong Country* (Rare 1994), the sounds produced by sources like enemies and barrel explosions are diegetic. They are directly related to the characters and objects of the narrative game world. However, the soundtrack and the sound effects related to object collection are non-diegetic. They either break the fourth-wall or can pertain to information that is being transmitted just to the player.

Donkey Kong Country, as well as other videogames published up to 1994, utilises synthesis of sound and not recordings. Therefore, sounds from biophonic or geophonic sources could not be present at all. With the introduction of better media storage technologies in the mid-1990s, the use of recorded sound in videogames became considerably more widespread. One example of the use of such technologies can be found in *Never Alone* (Upper One Game 2014). The game's soundscape contains sounds that are anthropophonic, e.g. the orchestrated soundtrack and human voices. However, it also contains sounds that we would typically consider biophonic and geophonic. The game's designers recorded sounds from foxes running on the snow, bears in caves, and ice crystals tinkling, among others from real-world ecosystems. The sounds of foxes running in the game are recordings of actual foxes running, however those sounds only play when the player moves their avatar to run along with the foxes—they are algorithmic and depend on player action.

There are also instances of recorded sounds that only play due to algorithmic processes but do not depend on player action. Alexander Galloway tells us that these moments happen when a "game is in an ambient state, an ambience act" and defines it as a game that "is running, playing itself, perhaps" (Galloway 2006). For instance, *The Witcher 3* (CD Projekt Red 2015) has day/night and dynamic weather systems. When a player is idle, that is, they are not interacting with the game, it is still running: time passes, the weather changes, non-player characters move, along with other systems that contribute to the game's ambience act. In this "state of pure process" (Galloway 2006), recordings of wind rustling through trees and rain falling will start and stop playing over time, without the need of player action, but due to algorithmic processes.

The soundscape of *Resident Evil 7* (Capcom 2017) also includes elements that, despite having been recorded from biophonic sources, can become anthropophonic and part of an entirely anthropophonic soundscape. Various rationales arise in favour of this argument, among which: (1) They are presented in a non-diegetic way; (2) They are integrated into the soundtrack of the game, being arranged into a composition; (3) Like all the other sonic elements, these are algorithmic. For example, the audio team recorded the sounds of bees and the wind and included them in the soundtrack of the game. This does not mean that we might consider them anthropophonic because they are non-diegetic, but rather because they are part of a musical composition. In interviews (Morimoto et al. 2017), the game's audio team states that they were inspired by the composition methods of *musique concrète*. Their goal was to create a sense of horror by combining macabre imagery with a sonic experience that prioritized horror aesthetics. The composers conceptualized this idea into the term "horror you could hear", highlighting the importance of the soundscape in establishing the videogame's intended horror experience and aesthetic coherence (Morimoto et al. 2017).

Algorithmic composition is a method used to compose music through algorithms. It can encompass methods traditionally used in generative music, which often relies exclusively on algorithms for sound generation. Nevertheless, it can also include the use of recorded sounds and use soundscapes as sources for machine learning. We reason that it is recognizable that algorithmic composition generates purely anthropophonic artefacts. However, videogames also rely on rules, chance procedures, mathematical models, grammars, and artificial intelligence. Even if these rules are used to build simulations of reality, the code behind them would have been written by humans or human-created machine intelligence. Let us take the example of a hypothetical simulation of a deep-sea ecosystem. Might we regard the sounds produced by that ecosystem as anthropophonic or geophonic and biophonic? From an ontological standpoint, since the simulation was built by humans or human technology, it must be considered anthropophonic. However, from a phenomenological perspective, the sounds present in that soundscape mimetise the sounds produced by agents of a real-world ecosystem, and players experience them as such. So, they should be considered non-anthropophonic. Given the possibilities, a concrete answer as to whether they should be considered anthropophonic sounds or not depends on one's philosophical standpoint. Even so, we state these considerations so that they may be gauged in future studies.

Some videogames use interactive interfaces which allow for user action, which distinguishes them from some forms of purely algorithmic composition. However, the comparison can still be made if we consider performance methods like *live coding*. It is a method of algorithmic composition, which might use recorded sound as a base for composition. With the analogy between music composition and videogame soundscapes, if we consider the results of one purely anthropophonic due to its algorithmic nature, then so can be the resulting soundscape of the other. Both constitute aesthetic objects which, due to their artificial nature, make us consider whether they are anthropophonic or if computational artefacts need to be classified in a different category altogether, and if such category can be technophony or one that is more directly correlated with computational devices and artificial intelligence. This distinction would differentiate computers from preceding technologies that do not make use of algorithms for operation.

3.4 Repetition, Patterns, and Rhythm

To get hold of players' interest, videogame sound designers often use repetition, which contributes to players' perception of the possible anthropophony of the soundscapes. Overall, in game design, repetition is used as a tool for aiding players in learning the rules and mechanics of a game or game section. As players experience the event or mechanic many times, they become acquainted with it. Once players are acquainted with a game world, it becomes more comfortable and intuitive for them to navigate it and become attached to its locations and characters.

Let us establish an analogue with interaction design. Throughout the years, most messaging desktop apps' text fields have displayed a message that usually read something like "Press Enter to Send a Message". This message could be found in popular applications like LinkedIn and Facebook. Since this was ubiquitous not only in messaging apps but across multiple software in various operating systems, users memorised it. As it is memorised, most contemporary applications and operating systems kept the function but removed the instructions.

Similarly, in many videogames, users are confronted with messages that instruct them on how to perform some actions at the beginning of the game, only to have such instructions removed later. This removal happens because once users become accustomed to doing it, they repeat it. Hence, they no longer need such assistance. For example, in the starting section of *Warriors Orochi 4 Ultimate* (Omega Force 2020), there is a permanent UI box on the screen informing players of the buttons for performing primary actions. However, these instructions are no longer there in subsequent screens. This omission happens because players will have repeated those actions multiple times and will no longer need to be informed on how to perform them.

We used a visual example to illustrate how repetition can be used in videogames since it is easier to understand it in a written essay. However, the effect also applies to the soundscape. For example, in *The Legend of Zelda: Breath of the Wild* (Nintendo EPD, & Monolith 2017), when players collect an item like a *Hylian Shroom* for the first time, a sound effect meant to represent item collection plays, and a popup message appears alongside the sound effect describing the item. However, in subsequent collections of the same item, the same sound effect plays, but the message never appears again. Due to repetition, and because players have been previously informed, we associate that sound with the successful collection of a previously discovered item.

In loud city environments, there are birds that sing small tunes which they repeat quickly (Slabbekoorn and Boer-Visser 2006). To our knowledge, such repetitions consist of similar sounds, but not the same as they typically vary in frequency and amplitude (Katti and Warren 2004; Cardoso and Atwell 2011; Slabbekoorn and Peet 2003; Hu and Cardoso 2010; Halfwerk et al. 2011). While this repetition happens with small changes in nature, in videogames these recordings are played repeatedly unchanged. They are mechanical. Hence, while a game can be repeating the recording of a biophonic sound, we must consider whether that sound is still biophonic. As this change into a mechanical sound is caused by human scripting, it may be considered an anthropophonic sound.

We can view repetition as the successive recurrence of the same sonic artefact throughout play. Nevertheless, there are additional techniques of repetition which we can find in videogame soundscapes: *patterns* and *rhythm*.

A *pattern* is a repetition in which several sonic components in the soundscape join together as a whole. For example, in *The Legend of Zelda: Link's Awakening* (Grezzo 2019), players need to find items like keys and compasses to progress in dungeons. Often, those items are found in hidden chests which players need to unveil by solving puzzles inside the dungeons. When players are successful in solving them, the chests appear, and players can open them and release the items contained within them. What interests us here is that such sequence produces a pattern of sound effects, which typically are ordered in the following manner:

Star Dropping → Chest Materialization → Puzzle Solved → Link Walking → Chest Rumbling → Chest Opening → Get-Item Music.

This is a pattern because the combination occurs multiple times across play, almost always in the same order, and at different intervals. A pattern of sounds can repeat in play at set intervals, but with small changes, it can be *rhythmic*. We have identified 5 types of rhythmic repetition in videogame soundscapes, correspondent —but not equal—to the five types of rhythm found in interaction design (Soegaard 2020). The five types are *Haphazard*, *Uniform*, *Interchanging*, *Flowing*, and *Gradual*.

Haphazard rhythms are produced by repeating sonic components without a fixed uniform period. The gap might vary from milliseconds in one location to hours in another, whilst the components may be scattered across locations. *Uniform rhythms* occur in equal cycles over time. A player may quickly discern a uniform rhythm by spreading sonic trends on a score over time and always getting the same result. The player's ear can immediately identify a uniform rhythm, checking for any anomalies in so doing. An *interchanging rhythm* occurs when we have two or more sonic components being used interchangeably. Variation is represented in a very consistent way. In music, we can verify this happening when we have, e.g. a powerful and weak beat, or a short and long note. While being mindful of the rhythm, players need to be able to predict it. The *flowing rhythm* reveals repetitive features like twists, loops, and ripples. If the sounds were to be put in a score as notes, we would see a repetition of shapes and forms. It leads to a feeling of motion and stream. Game designers may produce a *gradual rhythm* by modifying one of the features of the pattern when it repeats. For example, there might be a combination of five notes in a sequence, and the designers slightly alter the frequency of one of them each time the sequence repeats.

4   Conclusions

In this article, we provided an analysis of the soundscapes of videogames. From that analysis, we concluded that due to their algorithmic nature, it is possible that they are composed entirely of anthropophonic sounds, depending on one's viewpoint. Before reaching this conclusion, we conducted a review of frameworks and theories for the analysis and design of videogame soundscapes present in current literature. Although we did not present an innovative approach for conducting this research, we produced a distinctive arrangement of the autoethnography methodology with the *soundwalking* practice, using what we defined as "conventional videogames" as case studies. Our findings demonstrate that a succinct explanation of the notion of videogame soundscapes had not previously been provided. As such, we identified the elements of the soundscape and illustrated how and when they can be inter-related or not. In this clarification, it was made evident that a general characterisation of videogame soundscape cannot be provided.

Using film as a starting point, we found that one can classify most diegetic and non-diegetic sounds as anthropophonic. However, we were also able to find cases in which geophonic and biophonic sounds were present. Those presences allow one to use Krause's taxonomy to the fullest in film and in videogames. Film soundtracks may have sounds of non-anthropophonic origin that become anthropophonic due to their inclusion in the composition.

The soundscape of some videogames also includes elements that have non-anthropophonic sources. However, since they are algorithmic, these elements can become anthropophonic as well, depending if one agrees or not that mediation transforms non-anthropophonic sounds into anthropophonic ones.

Across the analysis of our case studies, we showed how repetition, patterns, and rhythm are used in videogames. These make sounds in games become mechanical, further supporting our thesis that they might be classified as anthropophonic.

These conclusions help researchers envision a more stable foundation of the concept of videogame soundscapes. Game designers can take advantage of the explanations presented about the notions of repetition, patterns, and rhythm to describe how these can be implemented to assist players in creating routines, which can be understood and employed in real-world situations of game design. The implementation of the various types of repetition will ultimately assist players in understanding and navigating a videogame's world through the soundscape.

We have hypothesised the categorisation of the soundscapes of videogames as anthropophonic. However, our proposition is still hypothetical. Different perspectives are possible, as to whether they are entirely anthropophonic or not. Therefore, future studies need to be focused on further researching the subject so that a more conclusive answer can be obtained, possibly using different methods.

Our essay stands supported by several case studies and authors that were examined in this paper. Nonetheless, we believe that some fields still need to be studied with regards to the categorisation of videogame soundscapes. The hypothesis that the sounds that compose a videogame's soundscape are entirely anthropophonic needs to be analysed within the context of emergent technologies of videogame mediation. We have identified some instances of such mediation that have not been addressed in this article. Those instances include videogames that make use of *composited environments*, *brain-computer interfaces* and *augmented reality*.

As it can be seen, Krause's taxonomy needs evaluation as well. With regards to the clarity given with artificial intelligence systems, future studies must consider whether a different category should exist for sounds created by AI systems. For example, Google's Duplex[8] voice is generated by an AI. The implementation of such a technology in videogames leads us to question if the sounds produced by AI really would be anthropophonic. It is possible that anthropophony (sounds generated by or for humans, or human activities) and technophony (sounds created by or for humans but by means of technology) can be distinguishable by the listener, but that too introduces potential issues, such as the categorisation of music produced using computer systems according to Krause's taxonomy (Krause 2015). For one thing, it is still music produced by humans, but it is produced by means of technology. So should we consider such music anthropophonic or technophonic (Psimikakis-Chalkokondylis 2016)?

A few game genres use music to steer play, often as film does it to push narrative and emotional response. It is more noticeable in games of the rhythm genre. However, the practice can also be observed in other genres, like FPS. Both in videogames and film, every genre possesses a different number of musical properties and codes, a pattern they typically follow, and that distinguishes them. For this reason, we believe that it is also essential to develop this parallel in future studies.

References

Allers R, Minkoff R (1994) The lion king. Buena Vista Pictures, United States

Capcom (2017) Resident evil 7: biohazard. Capcom

Cardoso GC, Atwell JW (2011) On the relation between loudness and the increased song frequency of urban birds. Anim Behav 82(4):831–836. https://doi.org/10.1016/j.anbehav.2011.07.018

Carvalhais M, Lee R (2019) Soundwalking and algorithmic listening. In: RE:SOUND 2019—8th international conference on media art, science, and technology. BCS Learning & Development. https://doi.org/10.14236/ewic/resound19.8

CD Projekt Red (2015) The witcher 3: wild hunt. CD Projekt

Chamberlain A, Bødker M, Papangelis K (2017) Mapping media and meaning: autoethnography as an approach to designing personal heritage soundscapes. In: Audio Mostly, pp 1–4. https://doi.org/10.1145/3123514.3123536

---

[8]"(…) a new technology for conducting natural conversations to carry out "real world" tasks over the phone. The technology is directed towards completing specific tasks, such as scheduling certain types of appointments. For such tasks, the system makes the conversational experience as natural as possible, allowing people to speak normally (…)" (Leviathan and Matias 2018).

Cooper MC, Schoedsack EB (1933) King kong. United States: Radio Pictures

Cowan JP (2016) The effects of sound on people. Wiley & Sons, Chicester, United Kingdom

Davenport M, Hannahs SJ (2020) Introducing phonetics and phonology. Taylor & Francis Group

Davies W (2015) Cognition of soundscapes and other complex acoustic scenes. In Internoise 2015

Droumeva M (2011) An acoustic communication framework for game sound: fidelity, verisimilitude, ecology. In: Game sound technology and player interaction: concepts and developments, pp 131–152. IGI Global

Galloway AR (2006) Gaming: essays on algorithmic culture. University of Minnesota Press

Goyal P, Gupta SC (2010) Design of real time image recognition system using digital signal processing. National conference on emerging technological trends (NCETT-2010)

Grezzo (2019) The legend of zelda: link's awakening. Nintendo

Grimshaw M (2007) The acoustic ecology of the first-person shooter. University of Waikato, Hamilton, New Zealand. Retrieved from https://hdl.handle.net/10289/2653

Halfwerk W, Bot S, Buikx J, Van Der Velde M, Komdeur J, Ten Cate C, Slabbekoorn H (2011) Low-frequency songs lose their potency in noisy urban conditions. Proc Natl Acad Sci USA 108(35):14549–14554. https://doi.org/10.1073/pnas.1109091108

Hansen SMO (2017) Designing an interactive installation with sounds from rural areas— explorations of the interactivity with sounds. Malmö högskola, Faculty of Culture and Society

Hedfors P, Berg P (2003) The sounds of two landscape settings: auditory concepts for physical planning and design. Landsc Res 28:245–263. https://doi.org/10.1080/01426390306524

Herzog W (2005) Grizzly man. Lions Gate Films, United States

Hu Y, Cardoso GC (2010) Which birds adjust the frequency of vocalizations in urban noise? Anim Behav 79(4):863–867. https://doi.org/10.1016/j.anbehav.2009.12.036

Huiberts S, Van Tol R (2008) IEZA: a framework for game audio. Retrieved from https://www.gamasutra.com/view/feature/131915/ieza_a_framework_for_game_audio.php

id Software (1993) DOOM. GT Interactive

Järvinen A (2002) Gran stylissimo: the audiovisual elements and styles in computer and video games. In: Proceedings of computer games and digital cultures conference

Katti M, Warren PS (2004) Tits, noise and urban bioacoustics. Trends in ecology and evolution. Elsevier Ltd. https://doi.org/10.1016/j.tree.2003.12.006

Konami, & Bemani (1998) Dance dance revolution. Konami

Krause B (2015) Voices of the wild: animal songs, human din, and the call to save natural soundscapes. Yale University Press

Kromand D (2008) Sound and the diegesis in survival-horror games. Audio Mostly 2008:16–19

Leviathan Y, Matias Y (2018) Google duplex: an AI system for accomplishing real-world tasks over the phone. Retrieved 3 Dec 2020, from https://ai.googleblog.com/2018/05/duplex-ai-system-for-natural-conversation.html

Loupa G (2020) Influence of noise on patient recovery. Curr Pollut Rep 6(1):1–7. https://doi.org/10.1007/s40726-019-00134-3

Miller N (2013) Understanding soundscapes. Buildings 3(4):728–738. https://doi.org/10.3390/buildings3040728

Morimoto A, Velasco C, D'Oliveira B (2017) The sound and music of resident evil 7: biohazard. SoundWorks Collection. Retrieved from https://soundworkscollection.com/post/the-sound-and-music-of-resident-evil-7

NanaOn-Sha (1996) PaRappa the rapper. Sony Computer Entertainment

NanaOn-Sha (1999) Vib-ribbon. Sony Computer Entertainment

Nintendo EPD, & Monolith Soft (2017) The legend of zelda: breath of the wild. Nintendo

O'Keeffe L (2011) Sound is not a simulation: methodologies for examining the experience of soundscapes. Game Sound Technol Player Interact Concepts Dev 44–59

Oddie B (2008) Bill oddie's wild side. British broadcasting corporation, United Kingdom

Omega Force (2020) Warriors orochi 4 ultimate. Koei Tecmo

Payne SR, Davies WJ, Adams MD (2009) Research into the practical and policy applications of soundscape concepts and techniques in urban areas. HMSO

Pigott M (2017) The soundproof box—using phonography to investigate the workplace of the cinema projectionist. Invisible Places 2017.

Polli A (2012) Soundscape, sonification, and sound activism. AI & Soc 27(2):257–268. https://doi.org/10.1007/s00146-011-0345-3

Psimikakis-Chalkokondylis L (2016) Rewilding music: improvisation, wilderness, and the global musician. Konstuniversitetets Sibelius-Akademi

Quintero CA, Recuero M (2018) El espacio urbano 'calle' a través de la mirada del paisaje sonoro. Una propuesta metodológica. Territorios, (38):191–214. https://doi.org/10.12804/revistas.urosario.edu.co/territorios/a.5484

Rare (1994) Donkey kong country. Nintendo

Rasmussen AW (2017) Resistance resounds: hearing power in Mexico City. University of California. Retrieved from https://www.proquest.com/docview/1972030112?accountid=43623

Schafer RM (1969) The new soundscape: a handbook for the modern music teacher. Berandol Music Limited, Scarborough, Ontario

Schafer RM (1977) The soundscape: the tunning of the word. McClelland & Stewart, Toronto

Schafer RM (1993) The soundscape: our sonic environment and the tuning of the world. Simon and Schuster

Slabbekoorn H, den Boer-Visser A (2006) Cities change the songs of birds. Curr Biol 16 (23):2326–2331. https://doi.org/10.1016/j.cub.2006.10.008

Slabbekoorn H, Peet M (2003) Birds sing at a higher pitch in urban noise. Nature 424(6946):267. https://doi.org/10.1038/424267a

Soegaard M (2020) Repetition, pattern, and rhythm. Retrieved 22 Oct 2020, from https://www.interaction-design.org/literature/article/repetition-pattern-and-rhythm

Truax B (2001) Acoustic communication (2nd ed) Ablex Publishing, Westport, Connecticut. ISBN 1-56750-537-6

Upper One Game (2014) Never alone. E-Line Media

Social Representations of Communication Design: Symbolic Universes

Maria Luísa Costa, Fernanda Daniel, Inês Amaral, and Ilda Maria Morais Massano Cardoso

Abstract The development of Design as a discipline in Portugal was slow. Therefore, only in the '80s, visual culture was implemented through Communication Design. Its rises were just at the beginning of the twentieth century, which constrain the identification of Communication Design as a specific field of Design, isolated from other areas of knowledge such as Advertising. Communication Design is strategic to conveying messages in a world that converges on visual culture. Its role in society is to facilitate informational and cognitive processes that enhance the human being's physical, neurological, and psychological behavior and the connection established with objects, others, and the world. The messages' interpretations are anchored on symbolic representations that compose collective memories, i.e., shared social construction derived from social representations validated by media and social systems. This chapter aims to explore how social representations influence perceptions of Design. We conducted an exploratory study based on the Free Word Association Test with Design students was implemented to put the analysis forward. The main conclusions refer to a central design association for Advertising, and peripheral associations for Marketing, forms of expression, and Design and media products.

Keywords Communication design · Social representations · Collective memory · Portugal

M. L. Costa (✉)
Research Centre of Architecture, Urbanism and Design (CIAUD), University of Lisbon, Lisbon, Portugal

M. L. Costa · F. Daniel · I. M. M. M. Cardoso
Instituto Superior Miguel Torga, Coimbra, Portugal

F. Daniel · I. M. M. M. Cardoso
Center for Health Studies and Research, University of Coimbra, Coimbra, Portugal

I. Amaral
Faculty of Arts and Humanities, University of Coimbra, Coimbra, Portugal

I. Amaral
Communication and Society Research Centre, University of Minho, Braga, Portugal

© The Author(s), under exclusive license to Springer Nature Switzerland AG 2022
D. Raposo et al. (eds.), *Perspectives on Design II*, Springer Series in Design and Innovation 16, https://doi.org/10.1007/978-3-030-79879-6_21

1   Introduction

Design is a comprehensive concept that encompasses multiple fields of activity, one being the Design of Communication, which is of strategic importance in transmitting messages in a world that focuses on visual culture. It has roots in Graphic Design, whose name emerged in the mid-twentieth century to define a set of practices associated with the production and publication of books and other printed pieces. In Portugal, during the twentieth century, the Design's growth follows its development: it is a slow development, industrialization is scarce, and education is neglected. In this context, Design evolves slowly. The main works are related to the propaganda of the Estado Novo dictatorship. Only in the 80s, with the formation of Designers by the Schools of Fine Arts of Lisbon and Porto and the entry into the European Economic Community, Communication Design reaches maturity and relevant importance in Portuguese society and culture.

Design is directly associated with social representations that people make of others or objects, considering that these result from the socialization process and are directly associated with collective identity and memory (Daniel et al. 2015).

This chapter aims to understand the symbolic universe of Communication Design and identify the structure of the social representations associated with stimulus "Communication Design Reminds…" among Design students. A study was carried out based on the Central Nucleus Theory (Abric 1998). This theory supports the hypothesis that all social representations are organized based on a central nucleus and a peripheral system. The central nucleus is related to collective memory, which means that groups' history is consensual and gives consistency and permanence to the representations and, therefore, are stable, coherent and rigid (Sá 1996).

2   Communication Design: Concept, Practice and Designation

Design is a comprehensive concept that describes a set of activities. According to Margolin and Côrte-Real (2014), "Design, is the process that human beings have used over time to develop the contexts necessary for their survival and progress (…) Design is the activity that results from our capacity to give answers to problems, starting from the imagination towards the action". However, this perspective of Design is distorted. Bonsiepe (2013) argues that, in public opinion, Design is identified as a wrapper, moving further and further away from the idea of intelligent problem solving, moving closer to the commercial and marketing functions.

Concerning Communication Design, the reality is not different. The communication designer's role is to develop and facilitate informational and/or cognitive processes by studying the physical, neurological, and psychological behavior of the human being and the relationship he establishes with his surroundings (anthropometry and ergonomics). This reality is often unknown to most people, who consider Communication Design a beautification or styling process, as Bonsiepe (2013) argues, associating it with analog or digital media, which attract attention and promote trade.

This connotation is due to the permanent association of Communication Design with advertising and the creation of ephemeral and futile products, but of excellent visibility, which does not promote knowledge or improve people's lives. Whereas determinant products for the life and well-being of individuals, such as schematic indications to facilitate the use of a machine, the pagination and editing of a book, a signage system that allows us to walk safely and without mistakes in an airport or in any other space, are entirely devalued as an effective practice of Communication Design.

According to Icograda (2020), the specific areas of Communication Design activity are increasingly diversified because "Design is a constantly evolving and dynamic discipline. The professionally trained designer applies intent to create the visual, material, spatial and digital environment, cognizant of the experiential, employing interdisciplinary and hybrid approaches to the theory and practice of Design. They understand the cultural, ethical, social, economic and ecological impact of their endeavors and their ultimate responsibility towards people and the planet across both commercial and non-commercial spheres. A designer respects the ethics of the design profession".

Communication Design consists of a disciplinary area that responds to the needs of society. It is based on a theoretically grounded practice, promotes knowledge and information in a predominantly visual way, through the articulation between visual signs and verbal signs, suitable for the transmission and reception of messages, observing the most appropriate communication means and channels from analog to digital. Thus, Communication Design returns to social, cultural, and environmental needs.

Although the concept of Design is originated from the Industrial Revolution, the designation of Graphic applied to Design appeared only in 1922 when the book designer William Addison Dwiggins coined "Graphic Design" to the professional practice that created structural order and visual form in printed communication (Meggs and Purvis 2009). The term Communication Design appears later associated with the appearance of new means of communication. The terminology associated with the practice of this branch of Design is not consensual. In some cases, Design is called Communication, and in others, it is Graphic. However, we consider that Communication Design derives from the designation, still used today as Graphic Design, which according to those mentioned above and following Falcão (2018), defined the type of Design practiced as Graphic linked to the printing industry. This author also mentions that although "graphic" is not the same as "communication", both are commonly used to define the same design practice, and the second designation (Communication) places Design, to which is a more appropriate context. For this reason, Icograda, which was founded in 1963 as the International Council of Graphic Design Associations, was renamed as The

International Council of Communication Design to exhibit the development of Graphic Design within the new media environment.

3   The Twentieth Century of Communication Design

Design, regardless of the group it belongs to, originated from industrialization. In Portugal, we know that industrialization was a slow and late process, that at the end of the nineteenth century, the country continued to be predominantly rural. However, with industrialization, there was a need for the creation of specialized education. According to Santos (1997), "in 1916–1918 the Republic reformed the industrial technical education, (…) entrusting secondary education to three schools then created, industrial schools (designed to train specialized workers), schools of Applied Art (dedicated to specialized teaching of industrial arts) and schools of Arts and Trades (which provided an elementary cultural formation to empirically trained workers and craftsmen) (Santos 1997).

From the beginning of the twentieth century to the middle of the century, numerous visual communication practices, embryos of design and whose designation are decorative arts, develop. "Disciplinary awareness about design is late in Portugal," and the separation of design from architecture, fine arts, and so-called minor arts are difficult or impossible to determine (Baltazar and Português 1940). With the creation of the National Propaganda Secretariat (SPN) in the 1930s, and later named by the National Information Secretariat (SNI), a graphic expression was built based on historical evocations and moral values of political and ideological propaganda. It evolved towards a modernist aesthetic, which stimulated visual exploration and added countless artists who developed different high aesthetic quality works, such as exhibitions, pavilions, illustrations, posters, books, and scenography. These artists learned by doing (Fragoso 2012).

In 1948, the António Arroio School of Decorative Arts was re-founded, where new study plans were introduced, namely Lithographer Engraver Designer. In graphic arts, this program will allow the formation of professionals in the universe of Design. This reform was extended to the Soares dos Reis School of Decorative Arts, in Porto, where programs with the same characteristics were created (Almeida 1959).

Modernism asserts itself as a particular time of graphic expression in Portugal, where works of high aesthetic value and great names in communication design emerge. However, many are self-taught, other architects, illustrators, and painters without specific training in the area. For many decades, the profession has been closely linked to graphic arts, where professionals were referred to as graphic artists or graphic designers.

In the 1960s, with the increase in consumption, several advertising campaigns were carried out, some at the State's initiative, such as those for promoting tourism in Portugal and the promotion of Portuguese and foreign companies (Almeida and Português 1960). That is how we arrived in the '70s, with advertising and publicity instigating the development of Communication Design, but still without higher education in the area.

In 1973, IADE created the program of studies in Design and Graphic Arts, and in 1975 the Higher Schools of Fine Arts in Lisbon and Porto created degrees in Communication Design and Graphic Arts and Design, respectively (Almeida 1959). The curricula will only be recognized in the 1980s. The recognition of the profession of the designer by the Portuguese State, with the attribution of its code by the General Tax Directorate, only happens in 2007 (Almeida 1959). The '80s are decisive in the history of Portuguese Design. The first designers are trained by higher education. As a reflection of the importance that Design assumes in the national context, the Portuguese Design Center is created. With Portugal in the EEC, there was an opening to the foreign market, free movement of people and goods, and also community funds that brought a set of problems and challenges, but also opportunities for industry, the country and Design, to which support and incentives also come (Silva 1980).

In the 90s, information and digital communication expanded and changed our visual culture. Significant national milestones promoted the recognition of Design and designers in Portugal, highlighting editorial projects such as the launch of newspaper Público or the magazines K, the launch of the Experimenta Design biennial, and the installation of the Design Museum at CCB and finally Expo98 (Silva 1980). After a long journey of development and affirmation, Communication Design reaches the twentieth century, on the rise, with the affirmation and recognition of its importance entirely assumed in the society. Much of this long journey was carried out by great professionals with no specific training in Design, stimulated and sustained both by advertising the Estado Novo regime and by commercial advertising.

Only at the end of the century with the formation of designers, the country's social and cultural opening to the world, Design, despite its connection with the promotion of consumption, peaked and recognized its value. In the twenty-first century, Communication Design incorporates new activities and behaviors that question the practices linked to advertising and promotion of consumer goods, directing its activity towards social interventions, cultural and environmental aspects, fulfilling their social responsibility to promote a better life for citizens.

4 Collective Memories and Social Representations

The process of building social representations is considered social because it occurs in a determined social context that is decisive, being composed of ideologies, values, and systems of social categorization shared through communication and its systems (Vala and Monteiro 2000; Daniel et al. 2016). It follows that the representations are social and not just shared by a group of people. Moscovici (1984) argues that modern societies' social representations are equivalent to myths and belief systems of traditional societies. Therefore, social representations are constituted as forms of practical knowledge oriented to understanding the world and communication. Thus, representations appear as constructions of social subjects regarding socially valued objects (Jodelet 1994), contributing to collective memory construction.

Social representations are something that exists and that remains beyond the individual. Thus, Design refers to the "construction of symbolic representations shared by members of social systems inhabiting a universe of specific socialization" (Daniel et al. 2015). Social representations are a modality of knowledge that is socially elaborated and shared, contributing to the construction of a reality that is common to a social group (Daniel et al. 2016).

Collective memories arose from social representations and generational and intergenerational contexts (Amaral and Brites 2019). Corsten (1999) coined the term "We Sense" to decode the sense of presence to a group from "historical and social experiences, whether individual or collective, within the public or private sphere, allow identification with groups" (Amaral and Brites 2019). Therefore, collective memory and collective identity refer to sharing historical and social experiences (Corsten 1999), anchored to the importance of image and communication in perceptions, beliefs and attitudes (Koltay 2011). Indeed, collective memory refers to social representations about a shared past that allows the construction and maintenance of collective identity. Furthermore, social representations of History refer to collective memory, often reconstructed by media and visual environments. By considering the importance of design in its multiple aspects in the communication and creation of conceptions of the past, the visual images have a strong capacity to create social representations validated and credited by media products through persuasion, an evocation of emotions, and the creation of a sense of identification with the subject or object or value represented.

5 Empirical Study

5.1 Methodology

Based on the Free Word Association Test (FWAT), a dictionary was created, taking into account the different evocations and the respective frequencies (Table 2). The initial homogenization took into account the transformation of the feminine into male or female or vice versa, the plural in singular or vice versa, and the synonymous words written in English in Portuguese or vice versa, using as a criterion of converting the maintenance of evocations with the most significant frequency. The words were also grouped based on the etymological root. There was no concern with carrying out any content analysis. In this sense, only the words used whose reproduction had a frequency equal to or greater than three were considered.

5.2 Data Collection Instruments

The FWAT was the instrument used in this study to collect data. The Free Association allows a type of open research structured to evoke responses given from an inducing stimulus (in this study, the words "Communication Design"), which allows highlighting prominences. This study has two distinct parts. In the first part, we collected data for the sociodemographic characterization of the interviewees. In the second stage, we asked interviewees to write short answers to the inducing stimulus, which was the expression "Communication design remembers …". It was intended a direct and spontaneous production of associations or free evocations, assuming that the terms or simple words are always covered with meanings. Despite emerging from a vocabulary coming from common sense, they have an internal coherence to the emitter, revealing elements of its symbolic universe. Likewise, was taken into account the order of the words. According to Sá (1996), the order of answer is essential since, in addition to the representation's content, it allows us to know the same internal structure and organization. The Free Word Association Test, as well as the hierarchy of the evoked items, is one of the main methods of identification of the central nucleus, as that it combines the frequency of the emission of words and/or expressions with the order in which they are evoked, allowing to delimit the elements of the central nucleus, as well as those of the peripheral nucleus (Sá 1996).

In the Central Nucleus Theory (Abric 1998), the nucleus is composed of the stable or more permanent social representation elements, which are of a normative and functional nature. The functional aspects are linked to the nature of the represented object. The normative ones refer to the social values and norms belonging to the group's social environment. The peripheral system is responsible for updating and contextualizing the representation. For Flament (1994), the periphery of a social representation is considered a "bumper" between reality and a central nucleus that does not change quickly. According to the Central Core Theory (Abric 1998), a social representation is constituted as an organized and structured set of information, beliefs, opinions, and attitudes. A social representation is composed of two subsystems—the central and the peripheral-, which function precisely as an entity, where each part has a specific and complementary role. According to Vergès (1992, 2002), the four quadrants can be interpreted as follows: the first contains the most relevant elements and, therefore, possible to constitute the central nucleus. These elements are the most readily evoked and cited with high frequency by the subjects. The second and third squares correspond to the least salient elements in the representation structure; however, they are significant in their organization. In the second quadrant are the elements that obtained a high frequency but that were mentioned in the last positions; in the third quadrant are the elements mentioned at a low frequency but were evoked first. In the fourth quadrant are the elements that correspond to the distant periphery of the second periphery. In it are the elements less mentioned and less evoked firsthand by the subjects.

5.3 Participants

Participants are aged between 17 and 48 years old ($M = 21.38$; $SD = 4.15$), are mostly female (71 = 73.2%), single (92 = 96.8%) and Design students (61 = 62.9%) (Table 1).

6 Results and Discussion

Table 2 shows the indicators related to the vocabulary originally obtained (total of different words) and the vocabulary retained in two different phases. Phase 1 includes the vocabulary resulting from groupings according to the criteria described in the methodology (total of different words after grouping); phase 2 includes the vocabulary eliminating words whose frequency was less than 3.

Table 3 shows 34 different words resulting from the evocations obtained through the word association test administration. Among the most evoked words comes Advertising (41 frequencies), which presents twice the second most evoked word (posters).

Table 4 presents the Central nucleus's possible elements of the social representations of the inducing stimulus "Communication Design reminds…". The evocations in the upper left quadrant are the evocations that are probably part of the central nucleus. In contrast, the evocations in the lower right quadrant belong to the peripheral system. The rest are considered to be intermediaries.

The advertising category was the one that stood out the most in the word association test with 41 evocations. Posters' evocations, Communication, Creativity, Illustration, and Brands are also represented in the central nucleus. The peripheral system components found in the 2nd and 3rd quadrants are Peripheral Nucleus 1 and 2. In these quadrants—the upper right and lower left quadrant—we

Table 1 Sociodemographic characterization of the sample ($N = 97$)

	N	%
Sex		
Female	71	73.2%
Male	26	26.8%
Marital status		
Married or cohabiting	3	3.2%
Single	92	96.8%
Program attending		
Design	61	62.9%
Communication Design	17	17.5%
Global design	19	19.6%

Table 2 Associations obtained and retained

Obtained	Retained (Phase 1)	Retained (Phase 2)
185	125	34

Table 3 Categories resulting from evocations obtained from the free word association test

Categories	Frequency	n × order of evocation	Order average of evocation
Advertising	41	81	1.98
Posters	20	41	2.05
Communication	19	46	2.42
Creativity	18	45	2.50
Illustration	11	28	2.55
Marketing	11	32	2.91
Art	9	29	3.22
Brand	9	25	2.78
Typography	9	30	3.33
Ads	8	19	2.38
Logos	8	21	2.63
Aesthetics	7	24	3.43
Information	7	25	3.57
Innovation	7	24	3.43
Message	7	23	3.29
Social networks	7	19	2.71
Interaction	6	17	2.83
Internet	6	8	1.33
Magazines	6	10	1.67
Color	5	12	2.40
Graphic design	5	19	3.80
Ideas	5	13	2.60
Image	5	12	2.40
Television	5	20	4.00
Adobe	4	9	2.25
Marketplace	4	13	3.25
Wayfinding/Signage	4	8	2.00
Draws	3	9	3.00
Expression	3	8	2.67
Graphics	3	9	3.00
Product	3	9	3.00
Promotion	3	10	3.33
Videos	3	8	2.67
Visual	3	10	3.33
	274	716	94.70
	8.06		2.79

Table 4 Identification of possible elements of the central nucleus of social representations of the inductive stimulus "communication design reminds…"

Central core OMF > 8.06 OME < 2.79	Peripheral core 1 OMF > 8.06 OME > 2.79
Advertising (41) 1.98	Marketing
Posters (20) 2.05	Arts
Communication (19) 2.42	Typography
Creativity (18) 2.50	
Illustration (11) 2.55	
Brands (9) 2.78	
Peripheral Core 2 OMF < 8.06 OME < 2.79	**Peripheral Core 3 OMF < 8.06 OME < 2.79**
Ads (8) 2.38	Aesthetics (7) 3.43
Logos (8) 2.63	Information (7) 3.57
Social networks (7) 2.71	Innovation (7) 3.43
Internet (6) 1.33	Message (7) 3.29
Magazines (6) 1.67	Interaction (6) 2.83
Color (5) 2.40	Graphic design (5) 3.80
Ideas (5) 2.60	Television (5) 4.00
Image (5) 2.40	Market (4) 3.25
Adobe (4) 2.25	Draws (3) 3.00
Wayfinding/Signage (4) 2.00	Graphics (3) 3.00
Expression (3) 2.67	Product (3) 3.00
Videos (3) 2.67	Promotion (3) 3.33
	Visual (3) 3.33

AOE average order of evidence; *AOF* average frequency order

can observe the intermediate elements that can approach the central nucleus or the peripheral elements. In the peripheral core 1, we find 3 different words—Marketing is the word with the highest average order of frequency—while in the peripheral core 2, there are 12 different words, Ads and Logos are the words with the highest average order of frequency. The words located in the lower right quadrant constitute the peripheral elements most distant from the representation—Aesthetics, Information, Innovation, and Message are the words that have the highest average order of frequency.

7 Conclusion

This study intended to explore how Design students understand the symbolic universe of Communication Design and identify the structure of the social representations associated with the stimulus "Communication Design remember…". Data showed that the immediate and ephemeral visual communication character and its close connection to social, economic, and political life. It reflects, like no other expression, the spirit of the time, that is, the trends and cultural preferences of a given time (Meggs and Purvis 2009).

Considering that the central core is related to collective memory (the history of the group), we find that advertising comes first, which is a predictable fact since much of Designers' work is aimed at promoting consumption. It is not always to trade but is generally interpreted as such. The reality is that advertising has been a source of work and value for Designers, probably due to the lack of awareness on the part of different organizations of the importance that Design can assume in solving environmental, social, and cultural problems.

From the need to counter the idea of Design associated with advertising, as well as the frequent trivial advertising practices, in 1964, the Manifesto "First Things First" is published, by Ken Garland along with 20 other designers, photographers, and students, to appeal the need for designers to concentrate efforts to direct Design towards works such as signs for streets and buildings, books, periodical, catalogs, education, and public service tasks that promote the improvement of society (Ken Garland et al. 1964). In 2000, this message was considered increasingly relevant and urgent, giving rise to a 2nd manifesto (First Things First Manifesto 2000), signed by Jonathan Barnbrook and an extensive list of Designers, Art Directors, and Visual Communicators (Barnbrook et al. 2000).

Thus, according to this manifesto (Barnbrook et al. 2000) "Designers who devote their efforts primarily to advertising, marketing and brand development are supporting, and implicitly endorsing, a mental environment so saturated with commercial messages that it is changing the very way citizen-consumers speak, think, feel, respond and interact. To some extent, we are all helping draft a reductive and immeasurably harmful code of public discourse."

This reality makes many designers feel uncomfortable with the world's view of Design and "propose a reversal of priorities in favor of more useful, lasting and democratic forms of communication—a mind shift away from product marketing and toward the exploration and production of a new kind of meaning. The scope of debate is shrinking; it must expand. Consumerism is running uncontested; it must be challenged by other perspectives expressed, in part, through the visual languages and resources of Design" (Barnbrook et al. 2000).

References

Abric J-C (1998) A abordagem estrutural das representações sociais. Estudos Interdisciplinares De Representação Social 2:27–38

Almeida V (1959) Design em Portugal, um Tempo e um Modo—a institucionalização do design Português entre 1959 e 1974. Doutoramento em Belas-Artes. https://repositorio.ul.pt/bitstream/10451/2485/2/ulsd059655_td_Tese_Victor_Almeida.pdf. Accessed on 6 Dec 2020

Almeida V (2015) Design Português - 1960/1979. Vol IV (Coord. Bártolo, J.). Vila do Conde e Matosinhos: Ed. Verso da História, ESAD

Amaral I, Brites MJ (2019) Trends on the digital uses and generations. In: Proceedings of INTED2019 Conference, Valencia

Baltazar MJ (2015) Design português—1940/1959. Vol.III,) p, 45 (Coord. Bártolo, J.) Vila do Conde e Matosinhos: Ed. Verso da História, ESAD

Barnbrook et al (2020) Emigre essays first things first manifesto 2000. https://www.emigre.com/ Magazine/51. Accessed 16 Dec 2020

Bonsiepe G (2013) Design, cultura e sociedade. Editora Blucher, S. Paulo

Corsten M (1999) The time of generations. Time Soc 8(2–3):249–272

Daniel F, Antunes A, Amaral I (2015) Representações sociais da velhice. Análise Psicológica 33 (3):291–301

Daniel F, Caetano E, Monteiro R, Amaral I (2016) Representações sociais do envelhecimen-to ativo num olhar genderizado. Análise Psicológica 34(4):353–364

Falcão G (2018) O que é que o Designer de Comunicação Faz—Mais uma tentativa de clarificação do campo de actuação do designer de comunicação. Convergências—Revista de Investigação e Ensino das Artes 22(21)

Flament C (1994) Structure et dynamique des représention sociales In: Jodelet D (dir) Les représentations sociales, pp 204–219. Presses Universitaires de France (Sociologie d'Aujourd'hui), Paris

Fragoso M (2012) Design Gráfico em Portugal. Formas e expressões da cultura visual do século XX. Livros Horizonte, Lisboa

Icograda: defining the profession ratified by the 25 icograda general assembly, Montreal, Canada. https://www.ico-d.org/about/index/sb_expander_articles/9.php. Accessed on 6 Dec 2020

Jodelet D (1994) Représentations sociales: un domaine en expansion. In: Jodelet D (dir) Les représentations sociales, pp 36–57. Presses Universitaires de France (Sociologie d'Aujourd'hui), Paris

Ken Garland et al (1964) First things first manifesto. http://www.designishistory.com/1960/first-things-first/. Accessed 16 Dec 2020

Koltay T (2011) The media and the literacies: media literacy, information literacy, digital literacy. Media Cult Soc 33(2):211–221

Margolin V, Côrte-Real E (2014) Design e risco de Mudança. Verso da História

Meggs P, Purvis A (2009) História do Design Gráfico. Cosac Naify, S. Paulo

Moscovici S (1984) The phenomenon of social representations: social representations. Cambridge University Press, Cambridge

Sá CPD (1996) Representações sociais: teoria e pesquisa do núcleo central. Temas Em Psicologia 4(3):19–33

Santos RA (1997) O design e a Decoração em Portugal, 1900–1994, p 443. In: AAVV (Coord. Pereira, P.) Do Barroco à Contemporaneidade, Vol. III, História da Arte Portuguesa. Lisboa: Ed. Círculo de Leitores

Silva HS (2015) Design Português—1980/1999. Vol V (Coord. Bártolo, J.). Vila do Conde e Matosinhos: Ed. Verso da História, ESAD

Vala J, Monteiro MB (2000) Psicologia social. 4rd edn.. Serviço de Educação Fundação Calouste Gulbenkian, Lisboa

Verges P (1992) L'evocation de l'argent: Une méthode pour la définition du noyau central d'une représentation. Bulletin De Psychologie 45(405):203–209

Vergès P (2002) Conjunto de programas que permitem a análise de evocações: EVOC: manual. Versão 5, Aix en Provence

Interior, Fashion and Product Design

"Playful Spaces": A Design Approach in Contemporary Jewellery

Mónica Romãozinho

Abstract In 1932, Gabriele Chanel (1883–1971) presented an unprecedented jewellery collection at the *Bijoux de Diamants* exhibition (London), inspired by stars, planets, and comets, working in partnership with Paul Iribe (1883–1935) and producing transformable pieces in precious materials. This idea of changeability was explored by other jewelers or companies such as *Van Cleef*, but after the middle of the 20th century, we assist to changes greatly stimulated by artistic fields and by the desire to transform the society that will be reflected not only in language but also in materials and techniques. This theme is still pertinent to us. With one single object, we can answer to different occasions and aspirations. Jewellery can be an extension of ourselves, communicating our personality, our moods and breaking at the same time with the tendency to a standardization very present in the fashion field. The present collection entitled "Playful spaces" is part of a post-doctorate in Design called "Possible but improbable spaces" developed within the CIAUD (Lisbon School of Architecture, Universidade de Lisboa). Architecture and nature are our concepts, side by side with the manipulation of volumes and masses and its possible games of transformation. The present objects resulted from the construction of a system of fitting so-called mobile elements that were replicated in all components of the same collection to make their appropriation more intuitive and playful for the user. The same solution was applied to more mimetic scales.

Keywords Product design · History of design · Jewellery · Changeability · Sustainability

M. Romãozinho (✉)
CIAUD, Lisbon School of Architecture, Universidade de Lisboa, Rua Sá Nogueira, 1349-063 Lisboa, Portugal

M. Romãozinho
University of Beira Interior, Labcom-UBI, R. Marquês de Ávila e Bolama, 6201-001 Covilhã, Portugal

1   Context: Subject and Background

The History of Design reveals to us remarkable experiences in the context of the creation of transformable jewellery pieces, a theme addressed in this project, but fundamentally produced in precious metals and gems of exotic colors. Alba Cappelieri, professor of Jewellery Design at the Faculty of Design of the Polytechnic of Milan and curator of important jewellery exhibitions, refers the importance of the growing connection between art and jewellery giving the example of the 1946 exhibition that took place at MOMA in New York, which exhibited the works of Calder, Bertoia, José de Rivera, Jacques Lipchitz, Richard Pousette-Dart, Margaret De Patty, Adds Husted-Anderson, Paul Lobel and others (Cappellieri 2010, p. 36). Elsa Schiaparelli (1890–1973), for instance, involved in this field of accessories artists such as Alexandre Calder (1898–1976), Christian Bérard (1902–1949), Salvador Dali (1904–1989), Jean Cocteau (1889–1963) although some of their results were closed to miniaturization of details or compositions taken from their artworks. After the development of partnerships of the jeweler sector with plastic artists such as Calder or Picasso (1881–1973), a new tendance that marked the Milan Triennale in 1951, catalyzed by Mario Pinton, founder of the *Padua School*, came to contradict this attitude, exalting the forge work that brings up the essential quality of the forms, the molded and dominated material, the light (Cappellieri 2016). The *Massana School* is also an unavoidable reference from the 1960s pursuing an international trend that converted personal ornament into a field of plastic and conceptual research. This institution played a key role with Manuel Capdevila (1910–2006) and his contacts with the School of Art of Pforzheim, a path later consolidated by several artists linked to the school, such as Ramón Puig Cuyàs (1953). These changes were felt the same way at costume jewellery field, more aligned to fashion trends. Paco Rabanne (1934), a Spanish stylist and cocreator of the 1960s *Space Age movement* (along with André Courrèges and Pierre Cardin) turned clothes into jewels. Rabanne had trained as an architect and he made plastic buttons and jewellery for Paris couture houses. This background was certainly important and explains the way he used techniques borrowed from jewellery, creating sculptural dresses in unconventional materials which broke all the rules (Cappellieri 2010, p. 45) and jewellery also made in squares, circles, and spirals: "I wanted to produce jewellery that would recall the paintings of that period, oversized, mad and uninhibited. Women too wanted to change, rejecting the traditions of the past. Their jewellery had to belong to the new aesthetic. I made jewellery for the alternative side of a woman's personality, for her madness".[1] In 1966, he presented at the Hotel George V in Paris his first collection, presented as a performance: "Twelve Unwearable Dresses in contemporary materials", composed of dresses made of paper, plastic, and metal, which were pieced together with wire chains and glue (Borelli-Persson 2017).

---

[1] *V&A Search the collections.* https://collections.vam.ac.uk/item/O121985/evening-mini-dress/.

How do these changes translate into Portugal? Like Italy and Spain, Portugal experienced a period of dictatorship, marked by a mostly conservative society, which never nullifies the avant-garde attitude inherent in personalities linked to Literature, Fine Arts and Design in its pioneering times. Throughout the 1960s, during the Marcellist period (1968–1974), we can point to an initial desire for change, of the search for innovation that translates into the support given to multiple initiatives, namely competitions and exhibitions in the area of Design. The INII (Institute of Industrial Research), proposed by António Magalhães Ramalho (1907–1972) and created in 1958, would have contributed, in particular, to the establishment of strategic partnerships with foreign research and vocational training centers in order to fill gaps in the areas of engineering, technology and management (Almeida 2015). The same institute made it possible for some national companies to allow technological and product tests, such as the *Fábrica-Escola Irmãos Stephens* (FEIS), in Marinha Grande, where Júlio Pomar, Alice Jorge, Maria Helena Matos collaborated (Almeida 2015, p. 17). It was also the *Industrial Design Center* of INII that, in 1971, organized the 1st Portuguese Design Exhibition (FIL, Lisbon), curated by João Constantino and José Cruz de Carvalho from the Furniture Store *Interforma-Equipamento de Interiores* with a catalog designed by Alda Rosa and Cristina Reis (Bártolo 2015). The jewellery would be an absence in this exhibition event as in the 2nd edition, realized in 1973, under the organization of the same nucleus and also the PRAXIS Cooperative (Fig. 1).

On the other hand, the involvement with the industry did not happen in the field of jewellery, with the former exception of the collaboration of the jeweler and sculptor Alberto Gordillo (1943) who, in 1967, worked with *Fábrica Cartene* directed by Carlos Carvalho, in Oporto, designing pieces to be produced in series and distributed in stores such as *Porfírios*, *Papelaria Progresso*, *Loja das*

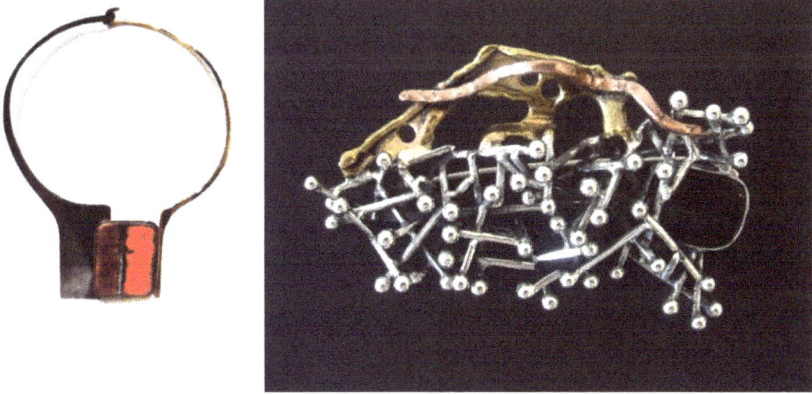

Fig. 1 Representative examples of the Massana School. Anna Font necklace (1945) in silver, refractory ceramic, and enamel. Collection of the *Museo del Disseny of Barcelona*. Photo: Mónica Romãozinho. | Brooch designed by Alberto Gordillo. Silver and onyx. 2011. *Source* movimentoartecontemporanea.com

Meias or *Ayer* (Filipe 2019, p. 129). The artists trained in the field of jewellery were scarce and their work gained recognition mostly thanks to the interaction between this area and the Fine Arts that would have stimulated a break with a revivalist tradition that was still felt in this area. Some changes are evident in the late 1950s, more specifically in 1958, when Gordillo designed a set of contestatory jewels he presented in 1963, integrated in the Vasco da Gama exhibition, at the *Galeria Nacional de Arte* (National Art Gallery in Lisbon) (Filipe 2019, p. 21). Gordillo developed his formative process in the workshop of his uncle, José António Nobre Fernandes and started to be known after his exhibition at *Dinastia Gallery* in 1968, winning one year later the *Prémio Nacional de Joalharia e de Esmalte* (National Jewellery and Enamel Award), attributed by the *Secretary of State for Information and Tourism* (Alves et al. 1972). Some Portuguese artists applied for scholarships which allowed them to contact other artistic currents. In the field of jewellery, we highlight the artist Kukas (Maria da Conceição Sousa Borges 1928) who studied at *École Supérieure des Arts Modernes* and socialized with some members of the non-conformable group formed in 1958 (Filipe 2019, p. 29) that was at the origin of the journal *KWY* whose designation arises from the three letters that do not belong to the alphabet Portuguese. Kukas would have known well René Bertholo (1935–2005), Lourdes Castro (1930), Christo (1935–2020), Gonçalo Duarte (1935–1986), António Costa Pinheiro (1932–2015), João Vieira (1934–2009), Jan Voss (1936) and José Escada (1934–1980), one of his best friends according to Cristina Filipe. It would be verified that Portugal, still resistant to abstract art, was not prepared for the return of these artists in 1960 on the occasion of the KWY Exhibition that would open at the SNBA that same year (Acciaiuoli 2001). Kukas, after his return from Paris, established some affinities with the designers Daciano da Costa (1930–2005) and Sena da Silva (1926–2001), but would not be part of the projects of this group (Filipe 2019, p. 36). Paradoxically, her methodology and concern about concept were very close to a design perspective: "Kukas, as a designer, always designed her pieces, made models and commanded the realization to traditional goldsmiths. Sometimes she approached Bruno Munari's creative process presented in his book "Das coisas nascem coisas", because, as Kukas points out, his jewels represent multiple forms, for example, "a cloud that collapses in rain" phrase that symbolically gave name to his retrospective exhibition.[2] In 1966, the first public presentation of Kukas's work took place in a solo exhibition, presented at *Diário de Notícias* gallery in Lisbon, and her pieces were all sold during the exhibition period, which means that there would be a target audience waiting for them, thirsty for conceptually innovative pieces (Filipe 2019, p. 21). Kukas' jewels in the 1960s reflected a language influenced by Nordic models, especially the jewels of Vivianna

---

[2]"A Kukas, como designer, desenhou sempre as suas peças, fazia maquetas e encomendava a realização a ourives tradicionais. Aproximava-se por vezes do processo criativo de Bruno Munari apresentado no seu livro "Das Coisas Nascem Coisas", pois, como Kukas refere, as suas jóias representam múltiplas formas, por exemplo "uma nuvem que desaba em chuva" frase que simbolicamente deu nome à sua exposição retrospectiva". Free translation. Interview to Cristina Filipe in 2020, June 16.

Torun Bülow-Hübe (1927–2004) that she saw in Paris (Filipe 2019, p. 26), also further away from the idea of manifest jewellery present in Gordillo, a trend felt at that time. The plastic and conceptual approach continues to be a reference for more recent generations in the present and the same author, responsible for the curatorship of Kuka's anthological exhibition at MUDE (Museum of Design and Fashion, Francisco Capelo Collection), found that the same artist was unknown to them.

In 1970, Alexandra de Serpa Pimentel (1954) and Tereza Seabra (1944) founded the jewellery course at Ar.Co (Centro e Arte e Comunicação Visual) in 1978 and later, in 1984, *Galeria Artefacto 3*, together with their disciple Pedro Cruz (1960), borning this way in Lisbon a jewellery gallery that would begin the process of dissemination of the so-called New Jewellery (Santos 1995). Until then, most of the jeweler designers exhibited in art galleries that contributed to the internationalization of various artists, such as *Galeria 111*, where Kukas exhibited between 1968 and 1971 (Filipe 2019, p. 35). The *Calouste Gulbenkian Foundation* has received some jewellery exhibitions, namely the *Belgian Contemporary Jewellery exhibition*, inaugurated in 1988 in the headquarters building and the result of a co-production with the WCC-Flanders and commissioned by Johan Valcke (n.1952), as well as *News from the Netherlands: Study on Jewellery*, a proposal of the Dutch Form Foundation, produced by Eleonoor van Beusekom (1951), exhibited on CAM at the 1990s (Filipe 2019, p. 47).

The evolution of fashion in Portugal would also stimulate significant changes in mentalities. Mary Quant became a reference in that period, symbolizing the idea of a fashion accessible to all: "By bending the rules and testing different gender roles and identities with affordable clothes to enjoy, empower and liberate, she predicts the opportunities and freedoms of future generations".[3] We highlight the success of the role of *Porfírios* store, inaugurated in 1925 in Oporto and 1941 in Lisbon, with emphasis on the expansion of the Lisbon store in 1965 that sold ready-to-wear fashion made in Portugal, based on models purchased on King's Road and Oxford Street (Almeida 2015, p. 26). It is important to mention other stores such as *Rampa*, designed in 1955 by Conceição Silva (1922–1982) and Daniel Santa-Rita (1929–2001) with the collaboration of the painter Rolando Sá Nogueira (1921–2002), located in Lisbon, which provided women's clothing and artistic objects (Almeida 2015, p. 25). The *Loja das Meias* store would also be a lever for a more cosmopolitan taste, propagating the English fashion of those days and because it was the first one to sell jeans (Filipe 2019, p. 42). Ana Salazar's store called *A Maçã* (1941), which opened in 1972, was a total success and also sold pieces imported from London. Manuela Gonçalves (1946), after returning from London, opens, in 1976, the *Carmim* store on Castilho Street and, three years later, the unavoidable *Loja Branca*, in Praça das Flores, where she sold "unique pieces, of apparent simplicity and various ways of using." Almost as if they needed an instruction

---

[3]Text integrated in the *Mary Quant exhibition*, V&A, 2020, April 6–16 February 16.

book.[4] We are talking about a time marked by the opening, in 1982, of the *Frágil Bar* of Manuel Reis (1946–2018), a meeting point for various artists and entrepreneurs, referred to by Manuela Gonçalves as her second house and also by Filomeno Pereira de Sousa (1949), artist-jeweler who created the school *Contacto Directo* in 1989 (Filipe 2019, p. 58). According to Pinharanda, the 1980s and the public debate of postmodernism began publicly through the initiatives of *Depois do Modernismo* (SNBA-National Society of Fine Arts 1983) which encompassed exhibitions of fine arts and architecture, fashion, dance, and music manifestations (Pinharanda 1995). In this decade, marked by the diversity of languages and projective attitudes, the work of Ana Silva e Sousa stands out, which presented simultaneously in the SNBA her exhibition *De Passagem*, invited by Julião Sarmento, member of the advisory committee that would challenge the artist to present a performance within the scope of this event, in which a set of models paraded simply dressed in gauze and plaster, becoming a work built by the hands of the artist and also a model (Filipe 2019, p. 50).

A new generation of jeweler artists broke out in the 1990s, such as Ana Cristina Melo (1963), Cristina Filipe (1965), the duo Pedro Cruz (who worked in the previous decade with the duo Abbondanza/Matos Ribeiro) and Luís Moreira (1964), and Teresa Milheiro (1969) who, in 1991, were invited to participate in the Exhibition *Tendências: Dias Intensos* that took place at the Picoas Forum, Lisbon (Filipe 2019, p. 52). Likewise, Madalena Braz Teixeira organized at the MNT (Costume Museum) a persistent program of consecrated and emerging authors that culminated, in 1990, in the 1st International *Symposium on Jewellery*, a biennial that continued until 1996 (Filipe 2019, p. 61). We highlight the birth of the *CPD* (Portuguese Design Center) that would enter into operation in 1990, providing articulation between companies, schools, public institutions, and the media. It was also responsible for design awareness campaigns, by its publications such as *Cadernos do Design* magazine (from 1992), seminars, exhibitions, training actions, and community funds were fundamental at this level, namely the specific *Program for the Development of Portuguese Industry*—PEDIP I and II (Silva 2015, p.35).

The contemporary jewellery would again be featured in the Exhibition *Manufacturas—Creation Portugaise Contemporaine*, part of the Europália program, which took place in Belgium in 1991, under the curatorship of Delfim Sardo (1962) and exhibition design by Pedro Silva Dias. According to Cristina Filipe, the artists were nominated by the production director, António Júlio Vilarinho, who elected Ana Silva e Sousa and delegated to Filomeno Pereira de Sousa the other choices that focused on the first disciples, namely Guta (José Augusto Silva 1961) and Manuel Vilhena (1967) (Filipe 2019, p. 62). In 1991, the first edition of ModaLisboa takes place, at Teatro Municipal S. Luiz, with scenography by Manuel

---

[4]"(…) peças singulares, de uma simplicidade aparente e várias formas de usar. «Quase como se precisassem de um livro de instruções»". Free translation. Vilela, J., Fernandes, P. (2016). Lisboa entra numa nova era: Lisboa: Lx 80 (p.57). Dom quixote.

Reis and the participation of Ana Salazar, Manuela Gonçalves, Luís Barbeiro, Júlio Torcato, Luís Buchinho, José António Tenente, Nuno Eusébio, Nuno Gama and the duo Abbondanza/Matos Ribeiro and Manuel Alves/José Manuel Gonçalves (Silva 2015, p.44). We also highlight the exhibition entitled *Isto é uma Jóia*—20 Years of Jewellery, promoted by Ar.Co and patent at the *Ricardo Espírito Santo Foundation*. Cristina Filipe's iconic piece, a multiple engraved in iron entitled "Thing (to wear attached to clothing)" would lend its name to the title of the exhibition (Fig. 3). The piece, dated 1991, represented a kind of "death" of the jewellery according to the artist's words: «The phrase "This is a jewel" appears because between 1988 and 1990, everything that was done outside the norm people asked if it was a jewel. When I do this piece entitled "Coisa, para se usar presa à roupa" I quote the intention/function, but it is the inscribed sentence that states that thing is in fact a jewel, without complying with the norm. It's a manifesto, an affirmation of the contemporary jewellery we were making».[5]

The *Experimenta Design* Biennial takes place for the first time in 1999, having contributed to the dialogue of various aspects of creation within Design. In the exhibition, *My World, New Crafts* of the 2015 edition, the objects exhibited were evidenced by their conceptual perspective, subjective dimension, and their unique character in denial of mass manufacturing (ExperimentaDesign 2005). We highlight the collection of contemporary jewellery entitled "Praline", by Leonor Hipólito (1975) which was evidenced by the unconventional of one of his materials, the silver paper of the candies *Mon chéri* and *Ferrero Rocher*. Fernando Brízio (1968) participated in the same exhibition with "Pata Negra", "Viagem-memória" and "Mesas Alcatifa". In 2004, Cristina Filipe, Marília Maria Mira, and Paula Paour founded PIN—Portuguese Association of Contemporary Jewellery, aimed at promoting events, exhibitions, and workshops for the dissemination of this artistic area.

In 2005, the *X International Symposium on Contemporary Jewellery* takes place, resulting from the will and initiative of Cristina Filipe that had already been in two editions in Cologne and Zurich. The theme of the symposium was "Everywhere nowhere", and a part of the program would be held at CCB (Belém Cultural Center), whose educational service was directed by Barbara Coutinho, future director of MUDE (Design and Fashion Museum) and, thus, an important connection is established that will stimulate the creation of the current collection of contemporary jewellery of the same museum.[6]

This first look allowed us to expand our knowledge within what is produced in the present, creations guided by the application of new materials and languages/methodologies that continue to affirm a strong connection to the field of Fine Arts.

---

[5]«A frase "Isto é uma jóia" surge porque entre 1988 e 1990, tudo o que se fazia fora da norma as pessoas perguntavam se era uma jóia. Quando faço esta peça intitulada "Coisa, para se usar presa à roupa" cito a intenção/função, mas é a frase inscrita que afirma que aquela coisa é de facto uma jóia, sem cumprir com a norma. É um manifesto, uma afirmação da joalharia contemporânea que estávamos a fazer.» Free translation. Interview to Cristina Filipe in 2020, May 16.

[6]Interview to Cristina Filipe in 16/6/2020.

We set out for the realization of a jewellery project assuming architecture and interior design as references to its narrative, its concept, through a project methodology common to the field of design, a container of specific phases, but open to setbacks and reformulations resulting from tests on usability and users feedback at a functional and emotional level.

2 Architecture as Concept and Objectives

The jewellery project presented was based on experiments parallel to a process of graphic speculation from the search for new models and answers that we can explore in architecture. We refer to sketches that translate housing typologies, strongly anchored in the relationship with nature, not only reflected in the organic morphology of the outer volumes but in the interior solutions, marked by the modularity of the compartments (volumes that unfold within the outer volumes) and fixed equipment, by the lightness of the furniture modules themselves often suspended in the similarity of architecture with its pilotis, as well as by the texture and clarity of the dominant material that is wood or its derivatives (Fig. 2). Finally, color and identity are fundamentally conferred by textiles that divide spaces, replace glass in cabinets, or function as versatile coating following a role played

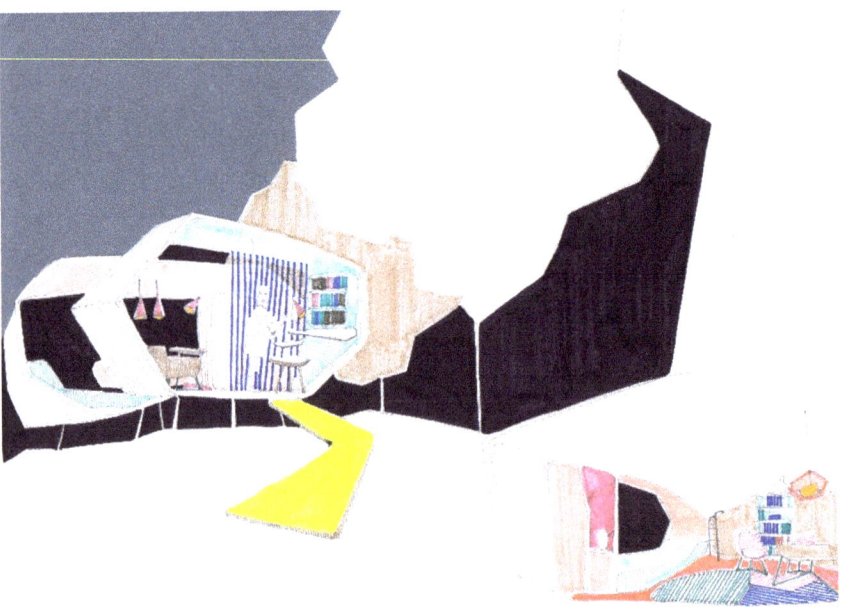

Fig. 2 Example of experimental architectures that are in the genesis of the jewellery project. Pencil, *Tombow* and collage 2020. Drawing: Mónica Romãozinho

Fig. 3 Collection "Playful spaces": studies that focus on the positioning of the piece and the fitting system of the respective blades, 2019. Sketches: Mónica Romãozinho

throughout the history of interior design. For centuries, the arming fabric have coated the walls, changing from season to season, together with other movable elements such as cushions or tapestries. This scenic function make us reflect on the active role that the user can play by transforming the spaces and even objects around him. The spatial principles resulting from this experimentation would be reinterpreted at the scale of the jewel, integrating the research project that equates this possibility of mutation, almost game. The present collection entitled "Playful spaces" is part of a post-doctorate in Design called "Possible but improbable spaces" and developed within the CIAUD (Lisbon School of Architecture, Universidade de Lisboa) under the supervision of Professor Fernando Moreira da Silva.

One of the fundamental premises in this series is versatility, thinking of jewellery as an object opened to a more playful appropriation by the user. The History of Design reveals to us these remarkable experiences in the context of the creation of transformable jewellery pieces, a theme addressed in this project, but most of them were fundamentally produced in precious metals and gems of exotic colors. In 1932, Gabriele Chanel (1883–1971) presented an unprecedented jewellery collection at the Bijoux de Diamonds exhibition (London), inspired by stars, planets, and comets, working in partnership with Paul Iribe (1883–1935), producing transformable pieces.

Chanel would declare: "My (jewels) are flexible and detachable [...] You can take apart the jewellery and use it to match a hat or fur. In this way, the set of jewellery is no longer an immutable object. Life transforms it and bends it to its needs" (Doulton 2019). In 1938, an original necklace by the house *Van Cleef &*

Arpels (founded in 1896) was patented, the "Pass-partout" necklace, under the influence of the Art Deco style, which consisted of a "snake chain", executed in yellow gold, whose clips could be autonomous (Cappellieri 2010, p.19). Still, in the 1930s, Wallis Simpson, Duchess of Windsor, proposed to Renée Puissant, the brand's artistic director and the daughter of the founding couple, to create a necklace inspired by the zipper closure that was introduced in fashion earlier this decade by designer Elsa Schiaparelli (Garrahan 2016). This piece took about ten years to be deepened under the point of its flexibility and multifunctionality: "Featuring interlocking gold teeth peppered with precious gems, the Zip could be worn as a necklace or, when zipped up, as a bracelet—perfectly timed with the dawn of international travel and the need for a versatile wardrobe" (Garrahan 2020). It should be added that, in the 1930s and 1940s, it was clear how much the discipline of jewellery benefited from an approximation to the field of fine arts. We intend with this series to continue this experimentation at a multifunctional level, however, away from a high-jewellery concept and available to a wider public just like Gordillo aimed. The program included precisely one multifunctional piece, a necklace formed by brooches that can conquer its autonomy as artistic objects.

The second question concerns the concept, with this desire to create a narrative that connects the user to the jewel: the history of an architecture that reconciles with nature and that contributes to the (re)invention of society and the individual. This idea of exploring spatiality is intended not only to communicate a specific message, an idea of architecture and city but to awaken emotions, to make us dream, fundamental functions also performed by jewellery. A piece of jewellery is not necessarily utilitarian and its dimension requires a broader look, an anthropological perspective. Its primary function may be to constitute itself as a platform of our individuality, such as a house, intimate space and intimacy. Thus, there is no intention to think only of the ergonomics of the productions inherent to the project. We reinforce the idea of jewellery as the object of emotions, something that happens with objects in the field of design. Donald Norman (1935) defends precisely the concept of emotional design using the example of his three teapots that he likes to expose in the alcove formed by the window, which he does not resort to in everyday life and which illustrate various aspects of product design: usability (or lack thereof), aesthetics and functionality. The first one is a copy of a coffeepot that was not supposed to be used and it was invented by Jacque Carelman while the second one called "Nanna teapot" was designed by Michael Graves and: "looks clumsy but actually works rather well" (Norman 2004, pp. 3–4). The last one answers all stages: placing the leaves in the pot's interior, lay the pot on its back while the leaves steep, set the pot upright when the tea is ready, and in this way the leaves will not float in the tea. The same author notes that designers, when designing, consider various factors such as the choice of material, the production method, its communication, cost and functionality, and whether the product will be easy to handle and understand (Norman 2004, p. 5). But the emotional side of the object can be more critical to its success, so it should be thought of by the designer or producer: "A favorite object is a symbol, setting up a positive frame of mind, a reminder of pleasant memories, or sometimes an expression of one's self. And this object always has a story, a remembrance, and something that ties us personally to this particular object, this particular thing" (Norman 2004, p. 6).

The third problem lies in the fundamental question of understanding the extent to which it would be viable to impose on this artistic area a project methodology specific to the field of Design, as well as the explanation around principles such as rationality, modularity, functionality, and the use of technology in prototyping/final product. It is intended since the beginning of the research to explore standardization as a solution of formal coherence and not as a form of serial production since we intend to create unique pieces. The experiment in 3D printing, begun in 2014 from *Beethefirst* (a Portuguese brand) allowed us to expedite the application of some of these principles.

3   From Process to Production

In this series, we use a geometric lexicon previously manipulated in other collections, which translate interior volumes, roofs, or furniture present in our imaginary architectures. At the same time, the sense of intimacy that opposes the concept of an anonymous living cell is evoked, because each piece can be customized. We can give the user some chromatic and texture combinations within the available range of polypropylene for upcycling purposes. We tried to explore a system consisting of so-called movable elements that were replicated in all parts of the same line to make its appropriation more intuitive and predictable by the user. It works like a game in which we can insert or replace blades of various chromatism or even add volumes. The angular contour pieces feature a double layer formed by white PLA and reused polypropylene (glued to each other), flowing along openings operated on the modular parts that make up the base of the collar (Fig. 3).

In addition to the question of the possibility of transformation, we have addressed a dual function. The collar was unfolded into three components. The central one, made of copper, ensures the ergonomics of the assembly and it is possible to sustain at its extremes the pins that integrate the side arms corresponding to brooches. These pieces are developed from the sequence of three modules of irregular contours that demarcate the left piece and the sequence of two of the previous modules on the right side that affirm the asymmetric design of the set, emphasized by color (Fig. 4). The intermediate module of the most extensive component is complemented by a volume that is supported by the colored blade itself as if it were a new interior space. Gluing became a problem, derived from the heat along with the Summer, and it was necessary to resort to an epoxy glue capable of ensuring the durability of the solution. Colors such as black, indigo blue, and transparent base as well were adopted in the previous series. Its configuration corresponds to an open structure that surrounds the body without losing its freedom. The clamping system of movable blades proved to be more functional. The sense of depth is worked on the various pieces through a simple succession of vertical surfaces, far from any attempt of *trompe l'oeil* or perspective illusion.

Fig. 4 Collection "Playful spaces": multifunctional piece: necklace on the right and brooches on the left. PLA, copper and polypropylene (reuse), 2019. *Photo* Mónica Romãozinho

In the case of earrings (Fig. 5), the sense of depth is again contextualized in the various pieces through a simple succession of planes that provides possible transformation games. In this case, the polypropylene surfaces would transcend the perimeter of the central body where they fit, speeding up the gripping process hampered by the mimetic scale of these reused polypropylene surfaces. The hollow and identical organic modules are arranged vertically and horizontally, causing an

Fig. 5 Collection "Playful spaces": transformable earrings and ring. PLA, polypropylene (reuse) and copper. *Photos* Mónica Romãozinho

asymmetry in the pair of earrings, reinforced by the reading of the two upper modules, entirely symmetrical, in which the silver pins fit. In this second exercise, it would be unthinkable to operate identical openings in order to fit parts, and because the PLA only achieves print quality from 1.5 mm thickness. We played only with polypropylene blades that would eventually transcend the perimeter of the central body where they fit. In this way, we have overcome the problem of grip hampered by the mimetic scale of these reused polypropylene modules.

Contrary to what happens in the multifunctional collar, the opacity gives way to transparency, continuing the texture of the material to assume relevance, more dramatized by the parallel lines of the turquoise blue polypropylene. Given the greater fluidity of the fitting of the parts, it is more operative to adapt this typology of the fitting solution of the movable blades to more mimetic scales, emerging in this perspective the second proposal for a transformable ring (Fig. 5). We resorted to the lexicon of modular shapes previously applied as well as the decentralization of the ring, allowing two distinct positions. White appears as a background option at the base level. Contrary to what happens in previous collections, more neutral from the point of view of the season, the reading of these solutions does not cease to evoke the seasonality of summer by the lightness of the overlapping transparencies, by the introduction of transparent and textured polypropylene and two new colors that have expanded the chromatic palette (pale yellow and turquoise blue). The blades recollect into the volumes. We can alternate opaque, transparent surfaces, including textures that recall textiles previously explored at the level of architectural design, marked by a pattern of parallel lines.

4 Conclusion

This last series has enabled us to apply the principles underlying serial production, namely planning, modularity, repetition, even if production in series is not a goal to achieve. The concept allows almost unlimited variations in the composition, color, and even introduction of new modules. It reaffirms a concern with the monetization of residual materials, an attitude that has had repercussions in the work that we continue to develop in the present. We are interested in sharing a set of experiences and meanings with someone even if sometimes anonymous. We explored principles such as versatility and mutability that provide a manual transformation experience, but above all the idea of conveying a critical narrative of how our cities, architecture, and interiors evolve. This dimension of communication is fundamental, and we have found that these pieces have linked several professionally connected users to areas such as Architecture, Design, Design Teaching, Fine Arts, Curatorship or Gallery Management/Culture, with some exceptions to this rule, which means that society is still changing and sometimes still stuck to some conservatism in aspects such as the materials or the language itself. We addressed fundamental issues such as the concept, linked to the idea of a connection between jewellery and space, as well as the project methodology, supported either in universal instruments such as the sketch or the cardboard model or in technological options such as the use of 3D software and rapid prototyping, creating pieces that are intended to be changeable and innovative.

References

Acciaiuoli M (2001) KWY: a revista, as edições e o grupo. In KWY: Paris 1958–1968. Catálogo da exposição, p 28. Centro Cultural de Belém/Assírio & Alvim

Almeida VM (2015) Design em Portugal 1960–1979. In: Bártolo J (Coord) Design Português, vol 4, pp 16–17. Colecção exclusiva do Jornal O Público. Verso da História-Edição e Conteúdos, SA

Alves C, Lourenço J, Pinheiro S, Andrade N, Simões M (1972) Um dia com... Alberto Gordillo. https://arquivos.rtp.pt/conteudos/um-dia-com-alberto-gordillo/

Bártolo J (2015) Cronologia 1960/2015. In: Bártolo J (Coord) Design Português, vol 4. Colecção exclusiva do Jornal O Público. Verso da História-Edição e Conteúdos, SA

Borelli-Persson L (2017) The space age designer making a big comeback all over the fall runways. Vogue. https://www.vogue.com/article/trends-paco-rabanne-fall-2017-ready-to-wear

Cappellieri A (2010) Twentieth-century jewellery: from art nouveau to contemporary design in Europe and the United States, p 36. Skira Editore S.p.A

Cappellieri A (2016) Brilliant! I futuri del gioiello italiano. XXI Esposizione Internazionale della Triennale di Milano. Corraini Edizioni

Doulton M (2019) Chanel 1.5: one camellia five ways to wear it. The Jewellery editor. http://www.thejewelleryeditor.com/jewellery/article/chanel-15-one-camellia-many-ways-wear-it-diamond-jewels-2019/.

Existir SH [Madredeus, 1990] (2015) In: Bártolo J (Coord) Design Português 1980/1999, vol 5. Colecção exclusiva do Jornal O Público. Verso da História-Edição e Conteúdos, SA

ExperimentaDesign (2005) Bienal de Lisboa, 15 Set-30 Out (2005). Agenda ExD'05. Guide— Artes Gráficas, Lda

Filipe C (2019) Joalharia contemporânea em Portugal: Das vanguardas de 1960 ao início do século XXI. MUDE, p 129

Norman D (2004) Emotional Design: why we love (or) hate everyday things, pp 4–5. Basic books

Pinharanda J (1995) O declínio das vanguardas: dos anos 50 ao fim do milénio. In: Pereira P (Dir) História da Arte Portuguesa, Do Barroco à Contemporaneidade. Círculo de Leitores, Vol III

Rachel G (2016) Experimenting with 3-D Jewelry. The New York Times. https://www.nytimes.com/2016/12/05/fashion/jewelry-3-d-printing.html

Rachel G (2020) How Wallis Simpson inspired a jewellery icon. Vogue UK. https://www.vogue.co.uk/fashion/article/wallis-simpson-duchess-of-windsor-van-cleef-and-arpels#:~:text=A%20perfect%20union%20of%20jewellery,by%20the%20Duchess%20of%20Windsor.&text=Wallis%20Simpson%20was%20photographed%20for,necklace%20by%20Van%20Cleef%20%26%20Arpels

Santos R (1995) O Design e a Decoração em Portugal, 1900–1994. In: Pereira P (Dir) História da Arte Portuguesa, Do Barroco à Contemporaneidade. Direcção de Paulo Círculo de Leitores, vol III

Design Applying Creativity and Its Process, with Different Types of Embroidery

Ana Margarida Fernandes and Isabele Lavado

Abstract The design process has various elements that require understanding the implications for creativity and product development to create different and innovative products. While it is critical to design for a customer or for a purpose the creativity is often stagnated by a lack of understanding of the different components that can make up a creative approach to an area that seems traditional and often outdated. By directing students to observe the embroidery as a starting point to a creative process it is possible to deconstruct the embroidery into its different parts and interpret it as whole creation and entity as well as a sum of parts that have their creative elements that can be structured or restructured to create new, innovative and invocative design pieces.

Keywords Embroidery · Deconstruction · Restructured embroidery · Design process · Interpret

1 Design Processes

What is design? It is important to understand that Design is essentially the answer to needs and essential questions, it represents an idea, allied to a product that is appealing, for example by the beauty of its form. A design product performs functions, transmits values and creates an undeniable emotional connection with the user.

In addition, design has an undeniable connection with psychological aspects. In other words, a design product, whatever it is, will have to differentiate itself and call consumer's attention—become an object of desire—much because the product itself appeals to emotions, is visually attractive, and so the consumer will want to buy it. Therefore, more than the product fulfilling a particular function, it will also have to create an emotional connection with the consumer—appeal to sensations, to the senses. So, apart from the key components which are form and function, the

A. M. Fernandes · I. Lavado (✉)
Polytechnic Institute of Castelo Branco, Castelo Branco, Portugal

D. Raposo et al. (eds.), *Perspectives on Design II*, Springer Series in Design and Innovation 16, https://doi.org/10.1007/978-3-030-79879-6_23

315

product must go beyond this if it is to become an object of desire—something which is extremely important nowadays if a particular brand or product wants to differentiate itself from the rest, in a very competitive market. Its beauty can differentiate the product in terms of form, or the manipulation it exerts on the consumer, inducing them to purchase the product in a certain way.

Many designers argue that a product can create an emotional connection with the user, facilitates aspects such as differentiation between brands that compete in the same market, and also causes a stronger connection between product and user. Furthermore, design is not only fundamental in answering essential questions, but also in formulating them: that is to say, design can lead to new concepts, through studies, sketches, idea sharing, experimentation and in this way lead to new questions, which in turn will provide new challenges and consequently new creations and new products. It responds to needs and creates new questions.

Identify design processes, and how they can be relevant to creating a product and to answer essential needs and questions by reflecting on creativity and using a project methodology. Having reflected and to putting into practice all this methodology starts with the execution of the project reflecting that for the construction of any design product, it is necessary to reach a set of logical ideas and be well dazzled. For this there must first be a series of disorganization of ideas, in which the designer should feel an explosion of ideas. To start the process a set of ideas are created, starting sketches from the proposed theme that over the studies will be more refined, eliminating ideas that are not compatible with the initial purpose of the research. Following the reflection from which sets of proposals must be selected to create a chain of products, with tests and analysis to subsequently develop new products in order to observe if they are coherent with the initial starting question. With the existence of creativity that ideas and sets are created up to the limit of our creative skills. These ideas have to be selected and refined in order to answer the questions in a logical manner.

1.1 How Creativity Can Be Arrived At

Creativity is the first part from within us, related to sensitivity, has enough expertise to score a point. That is created by a set of experiences, memories, research. They relate to our inner self and so we end up putting a part of us into the object, fruit of our sensibilities. These are transposed, but they already have to come as an interpretation for the type of object we want to make, and from there a set of hypotheses is given, some of which are excluded, and those that remain are conjugated, refined and structured until they respect the design object in terms of functionality.

1.2 Design Processes to Apply in Embroidery Projects

It is crucial to identify design processes, and how they can be relevant to creating a product and answering the essential needs and questions starting from the reflection on creativity and starting from the use of a project methodology. For the development of the collection stages with embroidery, the following methodology is proposed:

1. Starting point—Development of a collection starting from the embroidery inspiration.
2. Identification of the problem starting from a need.
3. We will create what and for Whom?
4. Research of what exists, brands, concepts, values, cultures.
5. What theme will we explore within the previous data.
6. "Creativity" process, where the previously analyzed components are synthesized.
7. Connection between the previous ideas.
8. Coordinate the connection between the previous elements in order to develop proposals for the solution of the problem.
9. Design proposals.
10. Collection development.
11. Illustrations.
12. Technical sheets—technical drawings, materials.
13. Collection plan.
14. Prototyping.
15. Analysis of results to the initial problem.
16. Redesign in case it does not answer the initial question.

The question that starts the process, fomented fundamental research and analysis: research about the different embroideries and their symbology. To prove the hypothesis, it was pertinent to define the best way to reach the final product, developing several work stages, methodologies used to disseminate research, evaluate and compare, which were made from different types of research approaches.

2 Deconstruction of Embroidery

Creativity is a fundamental and intrinsic part of the design process, without which there would be no potential for innovation. Having a strategy of design-driven innovation Dziadkiewicz (2017) can be made to achieve the final product. In this sense with an understanding of the processes that lead to creative designs interests both individuals and organisations. It can be challenging for students to create and develop from a brief it can be difficult to create a bridge between their creative minds and a design brief that may align with their own options and tastes. Fundamentally, students are taught how to abstract themselves from specific individual ideas to become creative in the design process. In this sense students can establish a creative design process to produce an innovative process model to lead to a clear and consistent design path leading to a creative product that they are being asked to develop.

The last few years have seen more interest and popularity in embroidery be it patches on denim and floral-inspired designs to intricate patterns flowing on dresses. The great advantage is how versatile embroidery is and how it can be used to create or enhance different fashion styles. A piece of embroidery can be machine embroidered or created by hand. There are many fashion designers and big brands who have been incorporating embroidery into their clothing lines.

Part of the students' learning path needs to incorporate techniques that can be used in the conception and design of pieces that are fundamental to their knowledge base. As such the deconstruction of embroidery demonstrates to students how they can transform an existing piece into a new creative piece.

When confronted with various different types of embroidery during a creative process one way of proceeding is with the deconstruction of the embroidery. This will divide the embroidery into different parts that will create different elements that can be used independently or collectively in a future design element. What is meant by deconstruction is taking the different elements that make up the embroidery from its conception to the final piece. This final piece of embroidery can be part of a garment or other textile like bedding or even decorative wall hangings.

2.1   Visual Image

On examining the embroidery, the fundamental element is the visual image of the piece. Very often the purpose of the embroidery will decide what the visual of the piece will be. Some endless images and patterns that are used, and it is these that we retrieve from the embroidery. When deconstructing the embroidery, the objective is to find the different patterns and make an attempt at an interpretation of how the patterns are used. These are both abstract images as well as the more detailed images. From there it is possible to interpret what can be subjective in terms of the image itself, or objective as to the interpretation that each one can have of the image.

Geometric patterns: Numerous geometric patterns that are used in embroidery all around the world. These may come in the form of strips as well as large patterns that resemble mosaics.

In Figs. 1 and 2 the geometric patterns are used as strips as well as a large pattern that was often used in larger pieces. Some of the most common shapes are those which are found in the North of Europe as well as South America as are in Figs. 4 and 5 (Fig. 3).

Fig. 1 Organisation chart of the working methodology

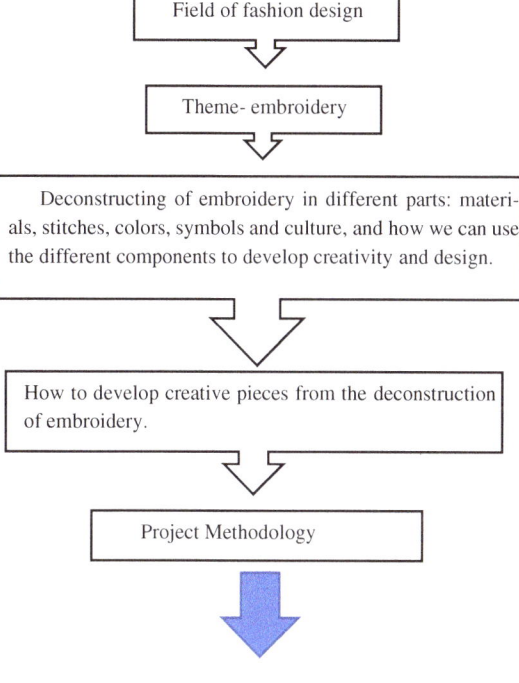

Field of fashion design

Theme- embroidery

Deconstructing of embroidery in different parts: materials, stitches, colors, symbols and culture, and how we can use the different components to develop creativity and design.

How to develop creative pieces from the deconstruction of embroidery.

Project Methodology

Fig. 2 Native American embroidery pattern

Shapes: Shapes such as triangles and circles are often used in embroidery as too are symbols such as arrows and diamond shapes. This is especially true of tribal and ethnic embroidery that is found in Africa and South America. A look at Mexican traditional textile work, the motifs mainly consist of geometric shapes and zigzags and spiral shapes.

Flowers and animals: Some of the most common embroidery images that can be found, particularly in more intricate embroidery are that of flowers and animals. The

Fig. 3 Hungarian embroidery pattern

Fig. 4 Scandinavian embroidery strips

Fig. 5 Peruvian embroidery strips

variety of these is limitless as they depict not only natural and original flowers and animals from nature and imaginary animals such as dragons and unicorns. The images of nature are found in all parts of the world and in different forms. Some patterns are very detailed and use many different colours and stitches. Some of these embroideries are as detailed as a painting and very life like while are others are decorative pieces that can be pretty abstract. It is possible to find entire costumes decorated with embroidery in different forms. These can be with strips of geometric shapes as well as flowers. The Embroideryes in many Ukrainian folk costumes are done using a cross stitch which does not always allow for great detail or a life like image. It is possible to have more detailed flowers, animals and shapes with the stitching providing a texture to the flowers that make these more detailed in the petals and the shapes of these appear more natural and lifelike. Using materials and stitching a different texture is possible which is very emblematic of embroidered textiles in particular from south America. A particular the Mexican Chiapas Embroidery and Tenango Embroidery with flowers and birds and a very distinct textile that is obtained from the stitches used as well as the thread.

Oriental embroidery is very detailed in images as these may depict village scenes and intricate images of flowers and animals. Whether it is Chinese or Japanese embroidery they are highly recognisable for these specific figures. Figure 6 is a classic embroidery of birds and flowers as well as the typical colours used in the embroidery.

When referring to the Orient in terms of embroidery it is done as an umbrella term to refer to areas of Asia. In this sense it also refers to embroidery from countries like Thailand, Indonesia and India. These countries have a very rich culture in embroidery with details of flowers and animals as well as images of everyday life that is extremely detailed. Figure 7 is typical of an embroidery that is detailed and very intricate.

It is in the Orient that it is possible to find many detailed embroidered costumes and clothing that is used for specific occasions. In Fig. 8 the thread and stitching create a texture on the silk. Very often these garments that are used for special occasions also used metallic thread and beading. The use of therich threads is seen in wedding outfits as in Fig. 9 and other ceremonial occasions. One of the most important of these occasions are related to royal appearances and military occasions.

Fig. 6 Textile, embroidered silk satin square embroidery; red ground with large floral spray and two birds

Fig. 7 Chinese embroidery of boat men and river with flowers, butterflies and a cabin

Fig. 8 Chinese embroidery
piece from a robe Guangxu
(1875–1908)—Qing dynasty
(1644–1912) —Chinese
Dynasty and Reign Periods;
Unknown

Fig. 9 Chinese bridal
wedding gown

There are endless images that can be used to illustrate the variety that is available in the embroidery area. However the small selection has some examples that are appropriate for the objective of deconstructing embroidery in terms of images.

At this stage the deconstruction of the embroidery must consider the importance of the meaning of the images as to the symbolism that these represent. The typical example that is obvious is that of the symbolism that exists in the images of flowers and animals that are found in Chinese embroidery. The example of the Dragon and Phoenix which were traditionally reserved for royalty and symbols related to the military and civil service ranking system. Taking examples of flowers, a peony represents wealth and spring, riches and honour, respectability and being the symbol of masculine beauty, while the chrysanthemum represents mid-autumn and pleasure and is the symbol of feminine beauty.

In all of the embroideries that are found in the world they will all have some kind of meaning and will represent the crafts people, tradition and the culture of the people who make and wear the embroidery. There are numerous garments, clothing, textiles and decorative pieces with embroidery that have significant uses and meaning which need to be understood if the embroidery is to be correctly interpreted and, in this process, to be deconstructed to be part of the creative process.

2.2 *Colour*

Each embroidered item and its colour are essential in their own way. The colours have different meanings in different countries and different cultures. Some embroideries that typically use more colours than others. The example of Russian and Ukrainian embroidery use a lot of red and blue. Typically red symbolizes love life, the sun energy and joy, while blue is the symbol of the sky and water and is regarded as healing and having a spiritual calmness.

Chinese use of colours in threads as well as the fabrics are used to create different items for celebrations such as weddings, birthdays and New Year which are rich, vibrant and in high contrast. Just as in other cultures, specific colours and/ or shades were reserved for specific uses. Particularly in the orient this was also for military and civilian ranks.

2.3 *Materials*

The materials that are used for embroidery can be both luxury silks and threads and plain cotton and linen. Throughout the world the use of embroidery is both for decorative purposes and to show prestige and status. The materials will also determine to a certain extent how the embroidery is used. In terms of clothing the garments will have a specific use whether is for everyday use or for a specific purpose as is the case of ceremonial or formal wear. In the deconstruction process the materials are important since in the creative process the objective of the garment or fashion piece is fundamental to the final product.

The fabrics most commonly used in hand embroidery are hand embroidery are linen, satin, cotton, silk, georgette, chiffon and velvet. Most traditional embroidery has very specific uses for the fabrics and these were also dependent on availability and cost.

Embroidery thread is also very typical to the region and the type of embroidery being done. The threads which are traditionally prepared are hand spun specifically for the embroidery. These can vary in the number of strands as well as the thickness of the stands to make the thread. With regards to the thread, it is crucial to consider the dying of the strands and the depth of colours that are used. There are also the metallic threads in different weights, structures and colours which offer another spectrum of opportunity. These can be found in royal and military embroidery and well as very luxurious garments in traditional oriental clothing.

The stitching is also a fundamental part of the embroidery process. The stitches chosen for a pattern or to create the images are specific to both the materials, such as the fabric and the thread, as well as the technique. It must always be taken into consideration that much of the embroidery process is a cultural element and the embroidery itself is a sum of the parts.

3   Conclusion

It is through an understanding of the design process and the creative process that it is possible to develop new innovative products. The process of deconstruction of the embroidery is done to illustrate to students that it is possible to take a traditional craft and use it not just like a replica of an image or the use of materials but that the various parts of the embroidery can be exploited to create other embroidery patterns that are original, and which can be inspired from the different traditional embroideries that are available. The ability to combine the different materials and the images from different origins allows students to become more creative in their design process. If there is an important lesson to be learnt here it is that there is still a lot that can be learnt and reproduced from traditional embroidery that is more than just its replication. By encouraging design students to view the traditional crafts from a different perspective they can be creative by interpreting new elements that they can create and develop through deconstruction of the whole piece.

Bibliography

Dziadkiewicz A (2017) Managing design process. Exploring the differences in and the relationship between the analitycal, multiplying and visionary design process. Handel Wewnętrzny 2 (367):69–81

Figures

https://clevelandart.org/art/1928.231.a 1870 Plain weave with supplementary weft wrap; wool (homespun and Germantown) Cleveland Museum of Art (This work is in the public domain in its country of origin and other countries and areas where the copyright term is the author's life plus 70 years or fewer.)

2005–11–12 18:01 PKM 1024×581× (1024627 bytes) *Detail of [[cross-stitch]] [[embroidery]]. Tea cloth border, black and red cotton floss, Hungarian, mid-twentieth century. Black and red cross-stitch patterns are characteristic of the folk embroidery of eastern and central [[Europe]]. Photo by Paula K*

https://pixy.org/2502525/ SCANDINAVIAN STYLE KNITTED EMBROIDERY CC0 Public Domain

Author: Perrine Aguiar 3 June 2018. This file is licensed under the Creative Commons Attribution-Share Alike 4.0 International license. https://commons.wikimedia.org/wiki/File:Girls_traditional_Peruvian_clothing.jpg

Auckland Museum Page 556.56 Object #55655 15688 Image 6/12 http://api.aucklandmuseum.com/id/media/v/82776

By Wikipedia Loves Art participant "va_va_val"—Uploaded from the Wikipedia Loves Art photo pool on Flickr, CC BY-SA 2.5, https://commons.wikimedia.org/w/index.php?curid=8444836

By Auckland Museum, CC BY 4.0, https://commons.wikimedia.org/w/index.php?curid=65310404

Design Methodology: From the Interpretation of Portuguese Interior Design Projects Through Virtual Reality

Liliana Nevesⓘ **and Fátima Pombo**ⓘ

Abstract This article discusses a design methodology's model to interpret Portuguese historic interior design spaces from the project's definition to its recreation in Virtual Reality. This methodology is based upon 5 phases: Project Definition; Data Collection; Data Processing and Analysis; 3D Space and Virtual Space. As this investigation intends to interpret interior design and architecture projects, hermeneutics appears as the elected framework for the design methodology presented in this study. The hermeneutical design interpretation enhances to understand the project's collected data and its context till the application in the three-dimensional modelling of the space and consequently how its recreation occurs in the virtual space. This methodology is intended to be replicated in other historical interior spaces, even those that are no longer physically available. In this sense, the study is aligned with the Digital Era challenges and the opportunities within contemporary paradigms. This research interacts with Digital contents as a channel to learn and to preserve knowledge and cultural heritage.

Keywords Design methodology · Interior design projects · Hermeneutics · Virtual reality

1 Introduction

This article, part of a doctoral research in Design, aims to translate domestic interior projects into Virtual Reality, as a way to preserve its memory and contribute to ensure its cultural heritage. It discusses the design methodology developed as a proposal to achieve the main goal referred. Therefore, the spaces transformed into Virtual Reality become a digital content that offer information in a more accessible and captivating format. Current times have turned the moment of the digital era and as consequence our day-to-day life has started to consume and produce digital content massively. Thus, this investigation is in line with the spirit of time pro-

L. Neves (✉) · F. Pombo
Aveiro University, Aveiro, Portugal

© The Author(s), under exclusive license to Springer Nature Switzerland AG 2022
D. Raposo et al. (eds.), *Perspectives on Design II*, Springer Series in Design and Innovation 16, https://doi.org/10.1007/978-3-030-79879-6_24

327

moting and facilitating access to information of Portuguese historical interior design projects.

Starting from the Post World War II, it is to say that the social and economic framework of the world required a new approach to respond to the production of goods, services and information. In the 1960s, at the HfG Ulm, design methodology became an essential discipline, as it allowed the designer to respond to problems that consisted not only of form, aesthetics or production, but also of a context and target audience. The names of Tomás Maldonado and Gui Bonsiepe stand out and are known to turn the project activity into something more 'scientific', through a methodology more based on mathematics and functionalism. During the 1970s the paradigm and the methodological orientation has changed, it is clear that the production of knowledge is not a uniform and linear process, highlighting the work of Feyerabend who was opposed to the thought of the existence of a single method and in turn believed that knowledge should favour variety and be compatible with the humanist conception. In the 1980s, human sciences gained strength and the design methodology started to be dictated by two components: the experience and hermeneutic. Designed objects came to their own language not only ordered by their function, but they have also started to be seen as a form of communication, being susceptible to interpretations. In this way, semiotics, hermeneutics and phenomenology became a research instrument allowing the interpretation and meaning attribution as a contribution to the methodological process in Design.

As this investigation intends to interpret Interior Design and Architecture projects, hermeneutics appears as the elected basis for the Design methodology applied in this study. Thus, this hermeneutical design interpretation allows not only to understand the project and its context, but also to interpret the collected data, making connections and creating designed phases that integrated and complemented each other, allowing their application in the three-dimensional modelling of the space and consequently in the creation of the Virtual Space.

Once this methodology is based on documents' analysis as technical drawings, photographs and texts, it can also be applied to historical domestic interior design projects that are no longer physically available or are not possible to be accessed.

2 Design Methodology: State of the Art

With the Post World War II Era, the social context, economic power, the increase in wages and population, products and services provided offer was much more than of essential goods like products and services for private consumption and tourism. In these circumstances, Design starts to play a fundamental role in society, to create functional and aesthetically appealing products and services. According to Maldonado (2012) in 1961 the role of the designer "consisted of designing the shape of the product" (p. 13) as "supposed aesthetic appearance, without taking into account the nature of the technical-productive process" (p. 13).

In 1962, the first *Conference on Design Methods* takes place in London, where Design Research Society was born, contributing strongly to the development and creation of new design methodologies.

According to Bürdek (2006, p. 251), the design methodology originated in the 1960s at HfG Ulm followed the increase in the types of task developed by Design for the industry of the time. In 1964, Christopher Alexander was considered one of the fathers of Design methodology and professor at Ulm. He developed a methodological process focused on the problem between the form and the context, addressing the problems of the project in a deductive way. The First-Generation Systems were characterized by dividing the design process into several well-defined steps: (1) the problem; (2) collecting information; (3) information analysis; (4) development of alternative solutions; (5) evaluation of solution; and (6) test and implementation (Bürdek 2006, p. 252).

Tomás Maldonado and Gui Bonsiepe were, in 1964, responsible for the first retrospective on "the scientification of project activities" (Bürdek 2006, p. 254). Both professors at HfG Ulm were able to translate their interest in science and methods into design teaching, basing their methodologies on mathematics and on functionalism. By the end of the 1970s, there was a change in paradigms with a new methodological orientation. "With the term paradigm shift it should become clear that science does not advance or collect more knowledge in a uniform way, but that from time to time it lives on revolutionary failures or radical modifications that change current thinking" (Seiffert cit in Bürdek 2006, p. 256). In this sense, Feyerabend's (1993 [1975]) work was very imperative, as it was opposed to the thought of the existence of a determined method that should be accepted unanimously. Thus, objective knowledge lacked several ideas, favouring variety as the only method compatible with a humanistic conception.

Until the 1970s, the methods used were mostly deductive (from the outside to the inside; from the general problem to the specific solution), but with those new paradigms the work started to be more intuitive (from the inside to the outside; specific project for a specific market). In the 1980s, the humanities gained prominence and Christopher Alexander took a fundamental role in the development of a new methodological approach that had the unity of form and context as its main concern. This argument was developed in *Pattern Language* (Alexander et al. 1977), being the *context* generally referred to practical requirements that the designer must take into account when designing a new project. These requirements are no longer just a matter of form but are as well a matter of the meaning of things. In this decade, two authors stood out, and they are still a reference in the teaching of design methodology nowadays: Bruno Munari, with his work in *Das Coisas nascem Coisas* (2014) [*Da Cosa nasce Cosa,*f 1981] and Gui Bonsiepe in *Metodologia Experimental: Desenho Industrial* (1984).

According to Munari "the design method is nothing more than a series of necessary operations, arranged in a logical order, dictated by experience. Its objective is to achieve the best result with the least effort" (2014, p. 20). For Munari "the design method for the designer is neither absolute nor definitive; it is something that can be modified if other objective values are found that improve the process" (2014, p. 21). Munari draws his methodology between the problem and the solution, creating several steps, where experimentation is the main contribute to get the solution. Also, Bonsiepe (1992) argues that the design methodology should offer two things "a series of guidelines and clarify the structure of the design process" (p. 204–205), thus containing "a praxiological component and a hermeneutic component" (p. 205). For this author, the mindset is not just to present a step-by-step structural way of solving problems, but to interpret several hypotheses or alternatives to achieve the solution. The 1990s brought a new reality —digitalization. In this sense, Alexander's methodology gains a new context in the development of hardware and software where the user starts to have a fundamental role. In short, it is considered that mainly from the 1970s on, Design presents itself as an everyday language life associated with the product's language. Selle also argues that "Language is a mean of interpreting reality and the language of the product allows the consumer the possibility of identification with the product and its verbal proposal of reality level often seems irrational and dreamlike" (Selle cit in Bürdek 2006, p. 286). Following this argument, Donald Norman (2013) writes: "What people need, and what designers must provide are signifiers. Good design requires, among other things, good communication of the purpose, structure, and operation of the device to the people who use it. That is the role of the signifier" (p. 14).

Since this investigation is focused on understanding and interpreting the language associated with Architecture, Design of Interior Spaces and its interconnection, we could consider semiotics, hermeneutics and phenomenology as possible methodological approaches. However, for this investigation, hermeneutics was the selected one, once it allows the researcher to relate content of various contexts theoretical frameworks. Regarding this methodological approach, Snodgrass and Coyne wrote:

> The operation of the hermeneutical circle is not the employment of a method. It is not something we can choose to use or not, in the manner of a tool. It is, rather, embedded in all thought and in all action. (Snodgrass and Coyne cit in Soares and Pombo 2010, p. 1353)

In effect, for Snodgrass and Coyne (1997) the interpretation is always based on pre-existing references, which will question and formulate hypotheses for a better understanding of the project. Interpretation based on hermeneutics recognizes and understands signs in order to interpret their meaning. The hermeneutic circle relates the meaning of the parts to the whole in each interpretation: "The whole and the part give meaning to each other; understanding is circular" (Snodgrass and Coyne 1997, p. 72). For both authors, interpretation is a continuous circle of small interpretations that contribute to interpret the whole. Indeed, studying an interior design/ architecture project is not just about the building as a structure. There is a need to analyse its historical, cultural context, the physical environment where the building will take place, the materials to be used and the architect/designer intentions expressed or emphasized in the interior space in dialogue with the exterior environment.

3 From the Interpretation of Projects to Virtual Reality

3.1 Project Context

As mentioned above, this article is part of the investigation related with the PhD thesis in Design entitled *Da interpretação do projeto à realidade virtual para a preservação do design de interiores doméstico Português* [From the interpretation of the project to Virtual Reality for the preservation of Portuguese domestic interior design]. This PhD research has been developed around the documentary base *Arquitectura* Magazine which allowed us to select the domestic projects involving architectural design and interior design that were most prominent in Portugal, paying special attention to Portuguese modernism (Neves and Pombo 2018, 2020). Naturally the *Ofir* House (1957–1958) by Fernando Távora was a project to try out for several reasons (Neves and Pombo 2021): (1) marks a turning point at the *Arquitectura* Magazine Editorial's perspective on Portuguese modernism style; (2) it is recognized as a landmark in the history of Architecture and Interior Design in Portugal; (3) it almost disappeared after a violent fire that left it in ruins and abandoned for some years. As one of the PhD project goals is to contribute to learn about Portuguese Interior Design history, recently it was developed a preliminary study that has allowed to understand if Virtual Reality could be a complementary learning tool (Neves et al. 2020). The results showed that students are more willing to learn through Virtual Reality because they consider it to be an innovative teaching methodology, a more engaging technology and more captivating way to study.

Therefore, in the path of previous research, this article is consequently focusing on the establishment of a design methodology that not only will recreate the *Ofir* House in Virtual Reality as an experimental project (Neves and Pombo 2020), but will also offer a methodological tool to recreate other historic domestic spaces in Virtual Reality as a contribution to the History of Portuguese Interior Design.

With this methodology it is intended to: (1) accomplish the three-dimensional digitalization of historic spaces and make it available to the public, especially as a tool to learn about history; (2) recreate digitally historical domestic space, whether it still physically exists or not, with the great potential to enable the designer/ researcher to create virtual spaces that have already been destroyed or that went through processes of transformation and change.

3.2 Proposal Methodology

Regarding this project, it is important to emphasize that its core is not just about creating a methodology per se but about developing a methodology that can be applied to different historical interior design projects to create virtual spaces.

The methodology then consists of 5 phases namely: Project Definition, Data Collect, Data Processing and Analysis, 3D Space and Virtual Space. As can be seen in Fig. 1 these phases are intertwined with hermeneutical phases, as: Definition, Understanding, Interpretation, 3D Application and Virtual Reality Application.

The image above also shows in detail several topics for each phase that will be discussed below.

Phase 1—"Project Definition" defines and selects the project that will be studied. At this point is necessary, first and foremost, to make a literature review about the project that will be interpreted and translated into Virtual Reality. As it is possible to observe in Fig. 2, two types of criteria have been taken into account with the intention of finding and delimiting the project that fits the current research aims and goals: inclusion and alignment.

The inclusion criterion defines that this is a Portuguese domestic space project, with the Interior Design component designed by a well-known author, goes through a project of historical relevance, ensures that the project was executed/built and that it is possible to access several types of documentation/information about it. The chosen project must check all these pointed criteria.

The alignment criterion complements information about the project by keeping the focus on the research objectives, offering multiple choices.

Phase 2—"Data Collect" describes three types of data: (1) technical documentation (plans, sections and construction details), especially from a documentary archive of the architect/designer, (2) photographs of the constructed building (interior and exterior), and (3) complementary textual information (descriptive memory, author's notes, scientific and non-scientific texts). Figure 3 shows the collected data interconnection that promotes the understanding of the project.

It was decided to make a distinction between the two types of images because the photograph reports the building as a constructed piece and the technical drawing only reports the intention of the architect/interior designer. On the other hand, because photography is not an orthogonal image, it enables to differentiate volumetry, spatial and object relationships, light-shadow, materials and textures.

Phase 3—"Data Processing and Analysis" regards the step of interpretation. It is developed through the empirical triangulation of the three data entry mentioned in phase 2. As depicted in Fig. 4 this "Data processing and analysis" expands through six complementary sections, creating a representation of and hermeneutical circle.

In this Phase 3 the know-how of the researcher is important because it facilitates the design of data interconnection and the interpretation of the collected data. It was used a vectorial software that enables to place the collected data side by side and therefore to make connections between the information and take notes for further developments. For that reason, the six established sections are translated into six parameters of interpretation:

1. Digital plan: convert the documentary plan into digital, CAD. The scale of technical drawing must be respected.
2. Structure: analysis and interpretation of the plan with section, technical details and its interconnection with the collected photographs.

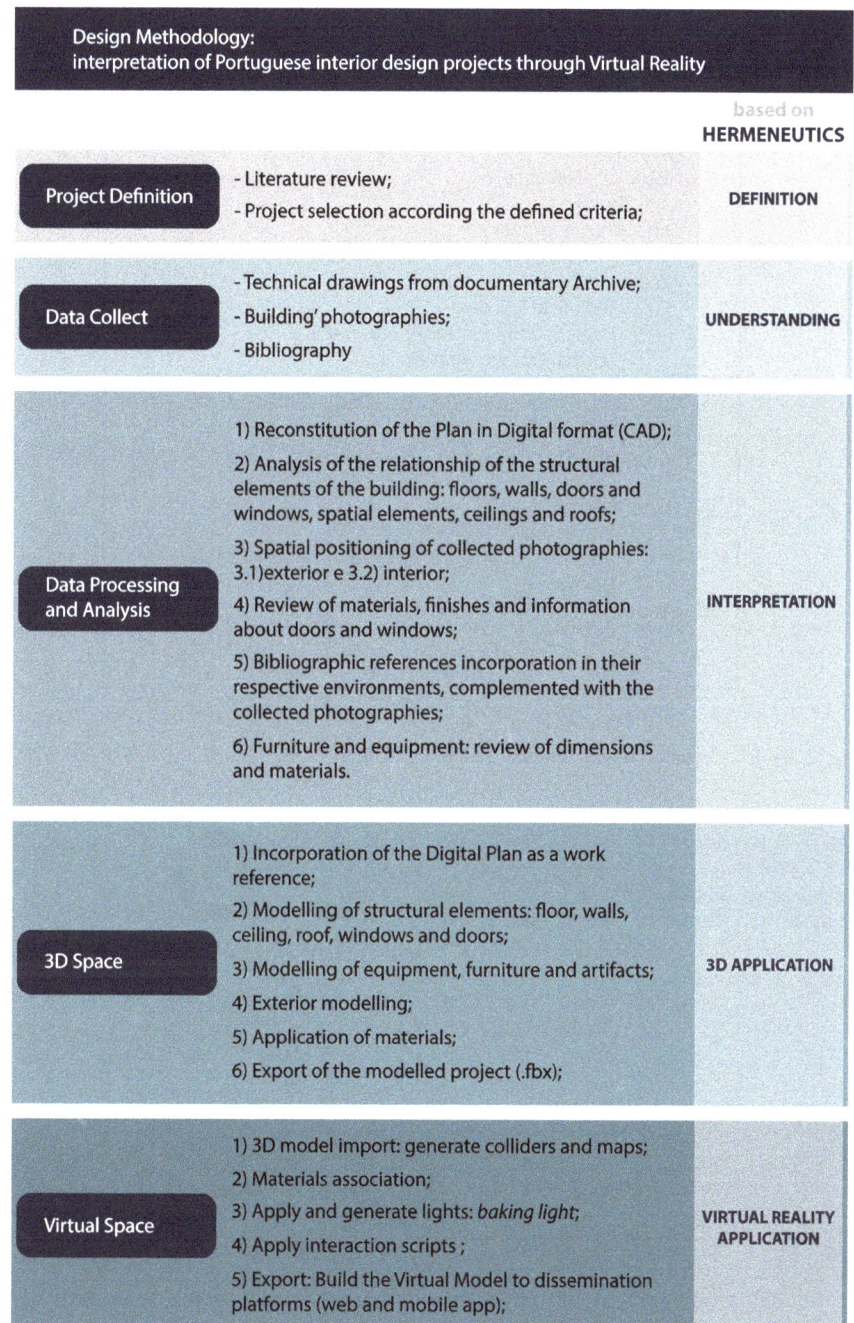

Fig. 1 Design Methodology based on Hermeneutics. *Source* authors

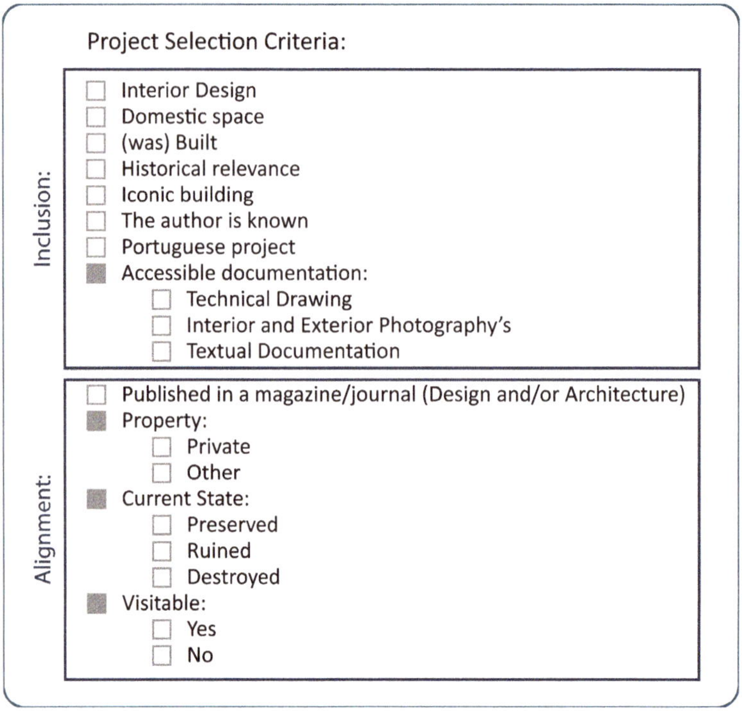

Project Selection Criteria:

Inclusion:

☐ Interior Design
☐ Domestic space
☐ (was) Built
☐ Historical relevance
☐ Iconic building
☐ The author is known
☐ Portuguese project
▨ Accessible documentation:
    ☐ Technical Drawing
    ☐ Interior and Exterior Photography's
    ☐ Textual Documentation

Alignment:

☐ Published in a magazine/journal (Design and/or Architecture)
▨ Property:
    ☐ Private
    ☐ Other
▨ Current State:
    ☐ Preserved
    ☐ Ruined
    ☐ Destroyed
▨ Visitable:
    ☐ Yes
    ☐ No

Fig. 2 Project Selection criteria definition. *Source* Authors

Fig. 3 Representation of Data Collection Triangulation. *Source* Authors

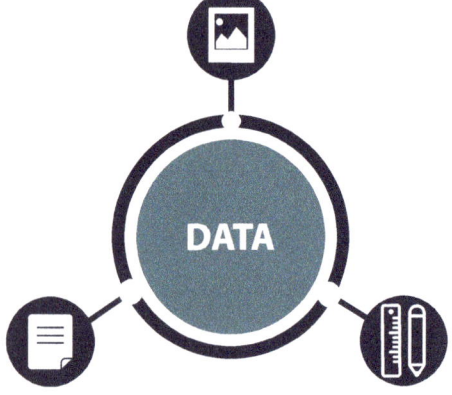

3. Spatial positioning of the collected photographs: understand and relate photography with the space and its point of view. It allows to interpret the volumetry of space and objects, light and shadows, materials and textures. At this point is possible to observe the global project.

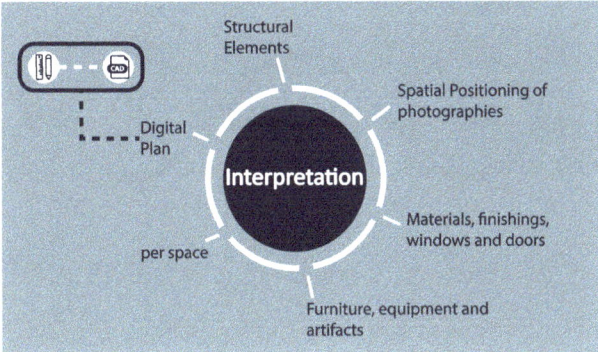

Fig. 4 Representation of the hermeneutical circle design for the interpretation of Portuguese historical domestic spaces. *Source* Authors

4. Materials, finishings, windows and doors: intertwine the plan with meta data annotation. These meta data are collected through the analysis of the bibliography. Here it is possible to become aware of some details that are not showed in photographs.
5. Furniture, equipment and artifacts: interconnection with photographs and technical drawing to find the right dimensions, materials and finishings.
6. Per space: if possible, aggregate on the same page all the information collected about a given space.

Phase 4 and Phase 5 are related to the interpretation applicability.

Phase 4—"3D Space" is central. Here the three-dimensional space is modelled, which means all structural elements: windows, doors, equipment, furniture, other artifact, exterior environment and materials applied to all of them—this step is done in 3D max (or other compatible software). It is very important to pay attention to details because the collected and analysed data (interpretation) are ensuring and crediting all components modelled. So there is a constant feedback that complete each other. After its conclusion, the 3D model is exported using.fbx extension and becomes a digital object by its own.

Phase 5—"Virtual Space" expresses the Virtual Reality applicability. Here the 3D model is imported from a program that allows to create a Virtual Reality Space (it can be used Unity). While importing the model it must be generated the maps for the correct application of the textures and the automatic colliders. It was chosen the URP (Universal Render Pipeline) in Unity because it is a Scriptable Render Pipeline compatible with the largest types of dissemination platforms as it is an interest of this research to convert this project into web and android platform. Materials were here reapplied, upgrading the imported materials to the URP, created and baked lights, and scripted interactions for future users with *first person view* and other scripts that allow users to know more about the Portuguese historical domestic space chosen to be interpreted.

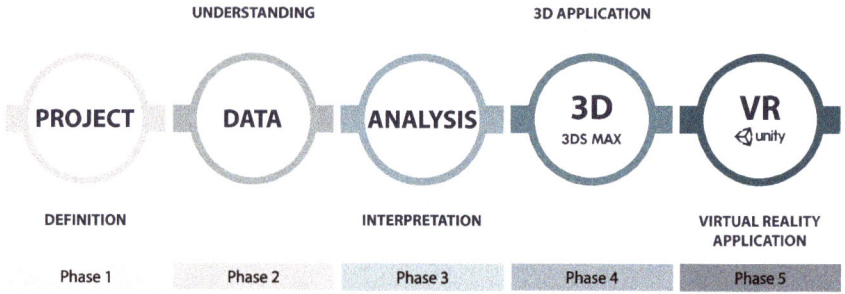

Fig. 5 Infographic of the proposal methodology. *Source* Authors

In summary, the model of the methodology proposal is visually synthetised as depicted in Fig. 5, and it begins with the definition of the project (phase 1) through the designed criteria, then is necessary to understand the project by collecting all the reliable data available (phase 2). The interpretation (phase 3) is then initiated, where the hermeneutical circle has a major importance to interconnect the collected data and create reasoned hypotheses. After that, all information and interpretation is applied for the 3D Space creation (phase 4) and becoming a 3D model that can be applied to the creation of a space in Virtual Reality (phase 5).

As already mentioned above, the dissemination process involves creating two ways of Virtual Reality access: through the web or using the mobile phone. However, on both platforms, the project is accompanied by an integrated side page where future users can find information about: (1) this particular investigation; (2) a brief description of the historical project; (3) a brief note about the author of the project (architect/designer); (4) complementary bibliography and technical information, namely instruction about how to navigate across the virtual space.

4   Final Considerations

This article demonstrates a design methodology that comes from a research that has been developed in a PhD thesis in Design, where is intended to create historical projects in Virtual Reality. This research has the *Arquitectura* Magazine as documentary base and focuses on Portuguese domestic interior design spaces, with special attention to Portuguese Modernism. *Ofir* House appears as the case study for this experimental project.

A Design methodology proposal is discussed in 5 phases, each one intertwined with a hermeneutics framework.

The knowledge gathered enabled the creation of a reliable virtual space based on the interpretation of historical domestic project. With this innovating research it was conceived a design methodology that has been tested in all phases in order to be ahead successfully implemented. In effect, this methodology is intended to be replicated in other Portuguese historical domestic interior spaces, even those that are no longer physically available. Thus, this methodological approach enhances the preservation of the memory of specific projects and the study of Portuguese Interior Design. In this sense, this research is aligned with the Digital Era challenges and opportunities within contemporary paradigms. This research interacts with digital contents as a channel to learn and preserve knowledge and cultural heritage.

Acknowledgements This research was funded with a PhD scholarship by Fundação para a Ciência e Tecnologia (SFRH/BD/146842/2019).

References

Alexander C, Ishikawa S, Silverstein M et al (1977) A pattern language: town, buildings. Oxford University Press, New York, Construction

Bonsiepe G (coord.) (1984) Metodologia experimental: desenho industrial. CNPQ, Brasília

Bonsiepe G (1992) Teoria e Prática do Design Industrial: elementos para um manual crítico [Teoria e Pratica del Disegno Industrial: Elementi per una manualistica critica, 1975]. Centro Português de Design, Lisboa

Bürdek B (2006) História, Teoria e Prática do Design de Produtos. Blucher, São Paulo

Feyerabend P (1993) Against method, 3rd edn (1st edn, 1975). Verso, London

Maldonado T (2012) Design Industrial [Disegno Industriale: un riesame, 1991]. Edições 70, Lisboa

Munari B (2014) Das Coisas Nascem Coisas [Da Cosa nasce Cosa, 1981]. Edições 70, Lisboa

Neves L, Pombo F (2018) Interiores domésticos dos anos 50 em Portugal: a construção do fluxo espacial segundo a Revista Arquitectura. Convergências—Rev Investig e Ensino das Artes XI: 21

Neves L, Pombo F (2020) Portuguese modernism from arquitectura magazine (1927–1988). Three cases of interior design in the 1950s. In: Raposo D, Neves J, Silva J (eds) Perspective on design: research, education and practice. Springer Series in Design and Innovation 1, Cham, pp 369–384

Neves L, Pombo F (2021) Virtual Reality for Interior Design History. The Ofir House as Experimental Project. In: Raposo D, Neves J, Silva J, et al. (eds) Advances in Design, Music and Arts. Springer Series in Design and Innovation 9, Cham, pp 461–471

Neves L, Beça P, Pombo F (2020) Virtual reality and interior design history: learning about three interior spaces by Frank Lloyd Wright. In: Senses & Sensibility '19: Lost in (G)localization. Proceedings of the UNIDCOM 10th International Conference. EDIÇÕES IADE, Universidade Europeia, Lisbon, pp 56–67

Norman D (2013) The design of everyday things. The MIT Press, Massachusetts

Soares L, Pombo F (2010) Interpretation as a design method. In: Conference proceedings of design & complexity: design research society international conference. Université de Montreal, Montreal, pp 1350–1357

Snodgrass A, Coyne R (1997) Is designing Hermeneutical? Archit Theory Rev J Dep Archit Univ Sydney 1:65–97

The Offland Exploratory Project as a Starting Point to a Literature Review on Types of Immersion in VR

Rafael Silva, Daniel Brandão⬤, and Nuno Martins⬤

Abstract The immersion in virtual reality is separated into multiple concepts as proposed by different researchers, essentially, we create a comparison between sensorial immersion, challenge-based immersion, mental or imaginary immersion and emotional immersion. We analyze Offland, an exploratory project which consisted in the creation of a fictional world and virtual reality experience, to explore this medium's immersion and storytelling. The lessons taken from brief user testing helped understanding which narrative and interactive elements may help toward each type of immersion. From this study we concluded that sensorial immersion is natural to virtual reality and advancements in technology will certainly help it become stronger. As in videogames, it is through challenge-based immersion that the user enters a flow-state, achieving satisfaction through a balance of challenge and skills. Mental or imaginary immersion happens when the user connects with the fictional world which inspired the narrative. We also concluded that the use of details to indicate a larger fictional universe can engage the user in this kind of immersion. A deeper state of immersion allows for the narrative to reach protected values related to the identity, affection, morality, decision-making and social cognition. We use this deconstructed view of immersion to help understand it, but this approach does not cover the complexity of total immersion. Finally, we believe that future advancements in virtual reality open a door for much valuable research and testing of the causes and effects of each type of immersion.

Keywords Virtual Reality · Interactive storytelling · Immersion · Flow · Interactivity

R. Silva · N. Martins
Research Institute for Design, Media and Culture, School of Design,
Polytechnic Institute of Cavado and Ave, Barcelos, Portugal
e-mail: rafsilva@outlook.pt

D. Brandão (✉)
Communication and Society Research Centre, Institute of Social Sciences,
University of Minho, Braga, Portugal

1 Offland: A Virtual Reality Experience

Offland is a project which consisted of creating and testing a fictional universe and the corresponding virtual reality (VR) experience. With this project we have studied the process of creation of digital media, world-building, virtual reality, interaction and user experience, with the goal of understanding how immersion, narratives and interactivity work in VR. This was achieved through literature review and regular and informal user testing throughout the project.

An original fiction world was used: Offland, which is a fantasy approach to the western genre, centered around an inhospitable wasteland. The project is based on McDowell's methodology (McDowell 2019), in which the design of a world precedes the telling of a story. Therefore, we have adopted an iterative and exploratory methodology, where different steps in the conceptual, creative and technical development process were taken following the feedback informally gathered from typical VR and videogames users (from an audience of 94 participants of an initial enquiry, 17 were chosen due to their interest in VR experiences) (Fig. 1).

The VR experience in Offland is about ten minutes long. It portrays one specific scenario of an illusion inducing oasis, centering the experience in exploration, survival and altered states of mind such as hallucinations (Fig. 2). The virtual environment serves us as a sandbox for experimentation and testing different techniques, multiple iterations and prototype, in order to look for answers for what ways fiction storytelling can be enhanced by VR's interactivity. We interpreted Brett Leonard's concept of Storyworlding (Bailenson 2016) through short narratives distributed through space, in which the user participates naturally through interaction with the environment. The Offland virtual system also explores user participation, allowing for users to leave voice recordings for the next users, and creating a more collective narrative.

Fig. 1 Design for the title screen of the experience. *Self-source* 2020

Fig. 2 Screenshot of The Oasis of Illusions, in which the narrative is based. *Self-source* 2020

After building the prototype, testing sessions were taken with real users. From the group of 17 users included in the development phase of the VR system, we have selected five participants. Four of them represented the four player types proposed by Bartle (Bartle 1996): Killers, Achievers, Explorers, Socializers, and the fifth participant was someone who had no interest or knowledge of video games. These testing sessions allowed us to understand what techniques and methods work better towards the comprehension and engagement of narratives in virtual reality. We found that the experience should start with a goal to guide exploration, balancing linearity and nonlinearity allows for a narrative that's both comprehensive and engaging, the lack of characters or their representation causes little emotion and empathy, details make the fictional world more discernible, and participation should feel simple to the user and not be forced.

The experience was developed for Oculus Quest, using Unity 3D 2018. A big part of the production was focused on translating aspects of a fictional universe to a narrative told through virtual space as the sensorial immersion in space is natural in VR. For the user to feel truly immersed in the narrative and experience Aristotle's catharsis or Csikszentmihalyi's flow (2004), more effort is needed.

The theoretical research of relevant authors, different projects and latest improvements in these fields were continuously developed throughout the project, providing guidance for each development phase. Based on literature review, next we will break down immersion into multiple concepts as proposed by different authors, essentially creating a parallel between sensorial immersion, mental or imaginary immersion, challenge-based immersion and emotional immersion, aiming at identifying which type we have achieved with our project.

2   Immersion in Virtual Reality

Talking about stories and how they are told through the virtual environment, it is relevant to understand how the user perceives the environment and its narratives. Qin et al. (2009) question about how users experiences immersion of said narratives, creating a general model that encompasses terms like flow, cognitive absorption, immersion and presence.

Flow can be considered a state of total absorption or engagement in an activity (Pace 2004) and its characteristics are similar to Play, a broader state of mind that is related to freedom of movement within a rigid structure (Fullerton 2014). Immersion is a metaphor for being totally surrounded by a different reality (Murray 2017), but it also implies substituting the perception of our daily reality by a virtual reality (Brooks 2003).

For Qin et al. (2009) immersion happens not only physically but also mentally and emotionally. Ermi and Mäyrä (2005) explain how several dimensions of immersion can be considered, focusing on sensorial immersion, challenge-based immersion and imaginary immersion. The model we draw in Fig. 3 represents how a fictional world exists across media and its relation with the person interacting with it. The psychological connection is what gives value to fiction, allowing for cognitive and emotional immersion to happen, as the user is influenced by its values and influences.

2.1   Play and Flow

Besides the numerous applications (Sackman 2015), VR is seen as related to the game industry because of the close connection between games, interactivity, play and storytelling. Fullerton's definition of games (2014) can closely relate to VR experiences, and while they do not necessarily have the same formal and dramatic structure, they are at least similar in boundaries and play.

Boundaries are what separate the virtual from the physical reality, the headset provides this transition, but in some experiences the physical setting is a complement of the virtual setting, assisting in the transition, either by replicating virtual space on the physical (Pouke et al. 2018) or by starting the fiction immersion on the physical (Nafarrete 2018). Conceptual boundaries are something more natural to storytelling: the suspension of disbelief to imagine stories and enter play-state (Tolkien 1947).

To Fullerton (2014), play is essentially a state of mind, that can be applied to even serious subjects. It is in its essence, cheerful, spontaneous, fun, relaxing, with effortless behavior, leading to a good time. But play has utility: it helps developing skills, acquiring knowledge, feeling the world, socializing, problem-solving and allows us to see in different perspectives.

Mediatic Relations

DIFFERENT TYPES OF IMMERSION

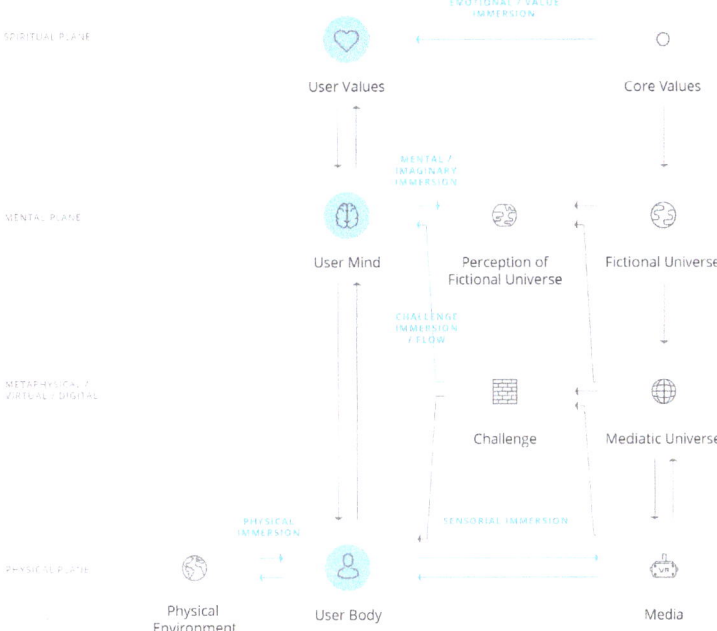

Fig. 3 Media relations and different types of immersion. *Self-source* 2020

Serious games make transformation the key goal of the player's experience (Games for Change 2019). Play can also be serious in the process of experimentation, pushing boundaries for artists, scientists and children. Most children's gathering of information and learning comes from play (Bergen 1988), they engage in it naturally, and for Tolkien (1947), one must enter fiction with the "heart of a child" (humility and innocence).

For Beasley (2017a) play is triggered in adults when they are facing novel sensations, and the brain rewards them for exploring new ways to move or interact in different scenarios, causing the brain to enter the play-state.

Sutton-Smith (2006) considers daydreaming as a form of play, and it interestingly relates to Tolkien's comparison of an immersive drama with dreaming. Milk (2016) describes VR as a shared dream, because the users know it is not reality, but their senses are telling them that it is. Imagining fiction presents a similarity with the functions of dreaming, which is considered as an evolutionary trait to prepare us for uncertain futures (Revonsuo 2000), and so were the first games, which were created to prepare men for hunting and warfare, instead of idle amusement (Miller 2004).

Play allows for the flow experience (Csikszentmihalyi 2004), which is a balance between challenge and ability, avoiding frustration and boredom, and resulting in a deep state of concentration, effortless involvement, control over actions, automatic activity, no concern for the self or everyday life frustrations and altered time perception. The combination of these elements causes a deep enjoyment, that is considered worth the expense of energy used to feel it. Flow's measurement can be subjective based on one's perception and past experiences. Flow is experienced when both challenge and skill are above average levels of that person's usual levels (Nakamura et al. 2002).

2.2 Physical and Sensorial Immersion

Physical immersion is about a new environment and doing things that become possible in that environment (Qin et al. 2009), like being submerged in water and learning how to swim. What happens in VR is not entirely physical but more a sensorial immersion that brains perceive as physical, to the point that users feel discomfort and sickness as their bodies react adversely to sensorial inputs presented by the virtual (Fagan 2018).

Sensorial immersion is natural for the vision in VR, however, the intensity and variety of senses add more interest to the experience. Imagining the perfect scenario for VR pornography (Wood et al. 2017), many of the research participants idealized an experience that used multiple senses. Lee (2013) presents an experience scoring system for each sense, showing how experiences that cover more senses are perceived as better.

In Offland, the test users reported to feel as if they were in another space, and upon asking, would answer clearly about what they were seeing and hearing in the virtual environment. Some participants also showed a lack of attention to their physical surroundings, getting too close to physical objects because of their focus in the virtual. Settings for using VR should account for a space that allow for unconditioned interaction and user safety, as advised by VR hardware manufacturers.

Total sensorial immersion assumes that the user is surrounded by active sensorial inputs, this would be possible to be mediated digitally in a setting such as the one proposed in Matrix (Wachowski and Wachowski 1999), through electromagnetic inputs to the brain. But even so, total sensorial immersion would only happen if all the senses were being stimulated at the same time.

With this notion of sensorial immersion in sight, Slater (2018) makes a relation between the higher levels of immersion coming through technology advancement (wide-field of view, high resolution, stereo, full real-time motion capture and multisensorial feedback). However, it is possible for a user to feel a large amount of presence in a virtual environment and not be fully invested mentally or emotionally.

2.3   Challenged Based Immersion

Challenges in an interactive medium are presented physically and mentally. In a medium that requires active participation, this kind of immersion has an essential role. Ermi and Mäyrä (2005) consider this feeling very similar to the flow experience, being that the user enters this state when he achieves a satisfying balance of challenge and skills.

For Fullerton (2014) conflict emerges from creating rules, procedures and situations that will not allow players to accomplish their goals directly. The procedures will imply that the user is forced to use a specific set of skills for the given task (many times less efficient). Obstacles might be physical or mental and make use of opponents and dilemma-based questions. The physical is present when the user is required to act, while the mental is present when he is required strategic thinking or logic problem solving.

Challenges should provide the right amount of effort and satisfaction, avoiding boredom or frustration and should adapt to the user's growth. For a person without skills the challenge is meaningless. The user must have minimal skills and be uncertain of the outcome. This uncertainty and the ability to influence the outcome will give the user a sense of control. The user needs clear goals and feedback of his actions in order to feel immersed in challenge (Csikszentmihalyi 2004; Fullerton 2014).

Because the nature of immersion is of substituting our perception of reality, when immersed in virtual challenge, our attention will fade away from other life problems, providing "escapism", as we become extremely focused on the task at hand (Nakamura et al. 2002).

In Offland, our tests presented no major action or puzzle challenges, but even so, participants reported both finding it too hard or too easy. These perceptions of difficulty are most likely due to the novelty of VR. Most of the participants felt a mild sense of gratification by reaching the final Oasis. This feeling could possibly be intensified if the story structure was better: employing techniques from traditional storytelling, such as increasing difficulty and tension to reach a rewarding climax.

To be physically immersed in challenge would mean a whole environment where everything is challenging, while to be immersed in the action would be to act with full focus upon the challenge. This is where flow would happen, under optimal conditions. Mental immersion in challenge would be related to our perception of challenge: perceiving that we are surrounded by it. Acting upon a challenge would also mean assimilating a goal, planning the action, perceiving what happened after the action and interpreting it (Norman 2013). In these phases of action, the user might become mentally immersed in the action and challenge, in a way that these become his focus.

2.4   Mental and Imaginary Immersion

Mental immersion is broader but also more related to narratives and schemas, which are constructs by which we view the world (Lotto 2016; Douglas and Hargadon 2000). Both are perceived and interpreted in a mental domain. While sensorial immersion is natural to the VR medium, mental immersion also happens in a more passive medium experience such as reading books (Douglas and Hargadon 2000), when the reader's cognitive process is aimed towards the fictional world instead of the physical reality.

Cognitive immersion is more likely to happen when the user feels familiar and understands narratives (Douglas and Hargadon 2000), this is something achievable by story schemas, which will provide a common point through which the user can understand the new narrative.

The early prototypes of our project Offland, presented a non-conventional story, with only objects spread across the space, each with narrative value. Upon testing it, we concluded that generally it lacked consistency, context and purpose. The addition of a starting event with tension and goals to the experience helped guide the rest of the narrative, helping the user to make sense of every event until the ending (Fig. 4).

For Ermi and Mäyrä (2005), imaginary immersion is related to the fictional world, characters and narratives. Their research indicates that children are attracted to this kind of immersion because it allows them to do things that were not possible otherwise. Bailenson (2018) defends that this the purpose of VR as a medium: experiencing what would not be possible otherwise, or what is too costly and risky.

In Ermi and Mäyrä's research (2005), the games in which players felt more imaginary immersed are the ones with a more complex background story and

Fig. 4 Screenshot from Offland. Tension and goals help the user understand the narrative. *Self-source* 2020

broader fictional worlds (i.e., Knights of the Old Republic 2, which represents the whole Star Wars fictional universe), and the less imaginary immersive are the ones related to pure simulation and representation (i.e., Pro Evolution Soccer 4).

According to Pacat (2017), details are what makes a fictional world interesting and compelling. In Offland we went through a process of world building focused on the project and many of the aspects of the fictional world weren't included in the experience, but small details made the users question the existence of huts in the desert and the corresponding civilizations who built and dwell in them. Using equipment with a fictional brand indicates the existence of commerce, craftsmanship and societies. Using references to a fictional mythology indicates the existence of history, religions, cultures and communities (Fig. 5). In our test participants had difficulty understanding all the aspects of the fictional world, but even so they reported to feel like they were in another place, and manifested interest in gaining deeper knowledge about that fictional world. In an experience with more length and freedom to explore, this kind of imaginary immersion is more likely to happen.

In short, the sense of imaginary immersion can be increased through:

- Presenting relatable narratives (Douglas and Hargadon 2000);
- Focusing on world, characters and narratives (Ermi and Mäyrä 2005);
- Creating empathy, enjoyment and emotions with the imaginary elements (Ermi and Mäyrä 2005; Douglas and Hargadon 2000);
- Accounting for the players expectations and interpretations (Douglas and Hargadon 2000);
- Presenting scenarios that otherwise would be impossible or unlikely (Ermi and Mäyrä 2005; Bailenson 2018);
- Indicating a fictional world that seems real and deep (Sanderson 2016);

Fig. 5 Screenshots from Offland. Objects representing mythology make fiction more believable. *Self-source* 2020

- Causing immersion through reasoning and realistic consistency within the fictional world rules (Fagerholt and Lorentzon 2009);
- Using fictional worlds that the user already has affinity or familiarity with (Qin et al. 2009; Ermi and Mäyrä 2005);
- Creating familiarity with the presented world (Qin et al. 2009);
- Reducing conditions in the physical environment that will take the attention away from the virtual environment (Brown and Cairns 2004; Mestre 2005).

The effects of imaginary immersion will be related to those of play and fiction. As the user have a stronger, more memorable experience with fiction, so will the values of fiction be more effective to the user and make it easier for emotional immersion to happen.

2.5 Emotional and Value of Immersion

For Brown and Cairns (2004) total immersion is when it impacts a person's thoughts and feelings, this is what we are considering as emotional and value immersion. According to Beasley (2017b) it would be constraining to consider this purely inside the mental domain, as emotions happen through and in the body and are perceived mentally. The barriers to this kind of immersion are the relevance of the virtual environment and empathy, but it will result in narrative that can reach protected values which are related to identity, affection, morality, decision-making, and social cognition (Kaplan et al. 2016).

A relevant virtual environment is essential for this deep state of immersion, as it will require the user to use multiple senses, invest more attention and effort, and experience a seamless interaction, being that high levels of emotion will result in the user feeling emotionally drained (Fagerholt and Lorentzon 2009).

VR is being called the empathy machine (Milk 2015), because of the perspective change happening through the close contact with other represented beings, and body transfer (Bailenson 2018). VR presents a highly influential alternative to less emotional traditional medium, like Tricart (VR director) points out: "viewers have become numb, in a way to what's unfortunately become all too familiar" (Carlton 2019).

Through empathy and emotional experiences, users of VR are presenting more results of behavioral change, in awareness campaigns experiments, when compared to users of other medium (Bailenson 2014). VR can make people more helping to each other, when they are active participants of the narrative (Rosenberg et al. 2013), and it has proven effective in changing behaviors related to trauma (Sackman 2015) and treatment of real cases of phobia (Maples-Keller et al. 2017).

Behavioral change is related to the core of humans: their values and identity. Through deep emotional and mental immersion users subconsciously access these dimensions, being immersed in abstract values and ideologies which were the root of the fictional world they are experiencing.

Bielskyte (2016) sees a resemblance of accessing these inner values and more traditional, medicine-induced, immersive experiences. In her view what people experience is what was already in their subconscious, and there is a relation between this kind of experiences and virtual reality, which can easily trigger inner values through immersion. Ayahuasca VR (Haridy 2019) is an example where the traditional experience is recreated through virtual, and while the review is of superficiality and dullness, this might be due to the viewer not feeling emotionally immersed (which is variable from person to person).

In Offland, the experience might not be very deep from an emotional point of view, but the mood, art and consistency of the experience being intimate, surreal, desert-like and eerie takes the user into a more emotional state. The feelings of being lost, discovering and exploring are a common thematic in the Offland fictional world and were successfully implanted in the user.

2.6   Overall Sense of Immersion

We considered the sense of full immersion as an ideal state, but in a literal interpretation, immersion does not imply a satisfactory experience, but instead to be surrounded or involved in something. This would mean that despite challenge-based immersion is someone being challenged in a way that surpasses that person's perception, we considered the ideal state of a challenging immersive experience, the flow-state. Total immersion would mean that the physical, mental, and emotional dimensions of the user are simultaneously being stimulated in all their subdomains. An optimal immersion experience would mean that each dimension of immersion is being stimulated to an optimal state (which is subjective according to the user).

Mental immersion can happen on many levels. Ermi and Mäyrä (2005), suggest additional studies relating immersion to emotions, social contexts, player expectations and interpretations, and it is possible to study how immersion happens on each of these dimensions and what are its effects on the user. However, the different types of immersion will most likely overlap and influence each other, changing over time, being that the common user will only remember an overall immersive experience.

Drawing relationships between the states of immersion, Qin et al. (2009) propose a model for measuring player immersion in game narrative, which can easily be applied to VR, consisting in the player self-evaluating different dimensions based on the researcher's questions. The dimensions are: Curiosity, Concentration, Challenge and Skills, Control, Comprehension, Empathy and Familiarity. Offland user evaluation was based on these parameters, and it allowed us to understand when immersion was present and which improvements could be made in each dimension of immersion.

3   Conclusions

Narratives in virtual reality are different than other medium, digital or traditional, but the same principles are still relevant, as the different types of immersion by the user are independent of the medium. Narrative value can be deepened by virtual reality's natural immersion, changing the user's perception of reality to convey experiences which are meaningful and rich.

Virtual reality's guidelines for creating narratives are still being discovered and defined, but it is probable that the best storytelling practices reside in what is natural to the medium: space, immersion and interactivity.

Milk (2016) and Bailenson (Bailenson 2016) explain that the techniques and language of storytelling in virtual reality is not yet defined. There might be a dullness in the interest of general audience for most media and perhaps, if the play-state found in entertainment lost its function of preparing and teaching humans (Milk 2016; Revonsuo 2000), VR as a medium will provide a more efficient way to do this through play and immersion.

Immersion happens in many levels but is essentially about substitution: the substitution of sensorial information of the physical world by a virtual world; the substitution of what we know to be truth by a fiction story (a willing suspension of disbelief); the substitution of the harshness of life by a gamified balance between challenge, skill and reward; the substitution of our notion of presence in the physical space by presence in the virtual environment; the substitution of our sense of body ownership by the control of a virtual body; the substitution of our perspective, identity and values to learn something new and achieve personal growth.

Practical experimentation is relevant to determine good practices in the overall process of world building, storytelling, immersion, interaction and production. Future iterations in Offland should account for more possibilities and differentiation to test each kind of immersion. A more perceptible narrative and richer fiction details will help in mental immersion, and more action and puzzle challenges will allow to testing challenge-based immersion.

References

Bailenson J (2014) Infinite reality: the Dawn of the virtual revolution with Jeremy Bailenson [YouTube Video]. https://www.youtube.com/watch?v=1jbwxR8bCb4
Bailenson J (2016) The trials and tribulations of narrative in VR: The stanford ocean acidification experience. Sensing and tracking for 3D narratives [Conference Video]. https://www.youtube.com/watch?v=mF78lwAKrRw&feature=emb_logo (2016)
Bailenson J (2018) Experience on demand: what virtual reality is, how it [...] [Conference Video]. https://www.youtube.com/watch?v=HZKGde91Xfs
Bartle R (1996) Hearts, clubs, diamonds, spades: players who suit MUDs. http://mud.co.uk/richard/hcds.htm. Accessed 8 Dec 2019
Beasley C (2017) Activate the brain to play in VR. Hack Reality with Cris Beasley [YouTube Video]. https://www.youtube.com/watch?v=ykeQuTN_mxg

Beasley C (2017) Using the full body as the controller in VR. Hack Reality with Cris Beasley [YouTube Video]. https://www.youtube.com/watch?v=sE6GJNSkBUY

Bergen D (1988) Play as a medium for learning and development: a handbook of theory and practice. Heinemann, Portsmouth, N.H

Bielskyte M (2016) The new storytellers II: world-building: best practices for creating story worlds. Centre Phi [YouTube Video]. https://www.youtube.com/watch?v=jtr0AZK64Do

Brooks K (2003) There is nothing virtual about immersion: narrative immersion for VR and other interfaces. Alumni Media MIT

Brown E, Cairns P (2004) A grounded investigation of game immersion. In: Extended abstracts of the 2004 conference on Human factors and computing systems—CHI '04. ACM Press, Vienna, pp 1297–1300

Carlton B (2019) TRIBECA: 'The Key' Wins Tribeca's Storyscape Award For Best Immersive Media. VRScout. https://vrscout.com/news/the-key-wins-tribeca-storyscape-award/. Accessed 28 May 2019

Csikszentmihalyi M (2004) Flow, the secret to happiness. TED Talks [Conference Video]. https://www.ted.com/talks/mihaly_csikszentmihalyi_flow_the_secret_to_happiness

Douglas Y, Hargadon A (2000) The pleasure principle: immersion, engagement, flow. In: Proceedings of the eleventh ACM on Hypertext and hypermedia, San Antonio, Texas, USA, 30 May-3 June 2000. Association for Computing Machinery, pp 153–160

Ermi L, Mäyrä F (2005) Fundamental components of the gameplay experience: analysing immersion. Worlds Play Int Perspect Digital Games Res 37(2):37–53

Fagan K (2018) Here's what happens to your body when you've been in virtual reality for too long. Business Insider. https://www.businessinsider.com/virtual-reality-vr-side-effects-2018-3. Accessed 18 May 2019

Fagerholt E, Lorentzon M (2009) Beyond the HUD: user interfaces for increased player immersion in FPS games (Master of Science Thesis). Chalmers University of Technology

Fullerton T (2014) Game design workshop: a playcentric approach to creating innovative games. CRC Press, Boca Raton

Games for change. http://www.gamesforchange.org/. Accessed 7 Oct 2019

Haridy R (2019) Tripping on virtual reality: The artists trying to replicate psychedelic experiences in VR. New Atlas. https://newatlas.com/vr/tripping-virtual-reality-ayahuasca-vr-psychedelic-experiences/. Accessed 07 Oct 2019

Kaplan JT, Gimbel SI, Dehghani M, Immordino-Yang MH, Sagae K, Wong JD, Tipper CM, Damasio H, Gordon AS, Damasio A (2016) Processing narratives concerning protected values: a cross-cultural investigation of neural correlates. Cereb Cortex 27(2):1428–1438. https://doi.org/10.1093/cercor/bhv325

Lee, J.: Design for all 5 senses. TED Talks [Conference Video]. https://www.ted.com/talks/jinsop_lee_design_for_all_5_senses

Lotto B (2016) The new storytellers II: world-building: best practices for creating story worlds. Centre Phi [YouTube Video]. https://www.youtube.com/watch?v=jtr0AZK64Do

Maples-Keller JL, Yasinski C, Manjin N, Rothbaum BO (2017) Virtual reality-enhanced extinction of phobias and post-traumatic stress. Neurotherapeutics 14(3):554–563. https://doi.org/10.1007/s13311-017-0534-y

McDowell A (2019) Storytelling shapes the future. J Futures Stud 23(3):105–112. https://doi.org/10.6531/JFS.201903_23(3).0009

Mestre DR (2005) Immersion and Presence. http://www.ism.univmed.fr/mestre/projects/virtual%20reality/Pres_2005.pdf

Milk C (2015) How virtual reality can create the ultimate empathy machine. TED Talks [Conference Video]. https://www.ted.com/talks/chris_milk_how_virtual_reality_can_create_the_ultimate_empathy_machine

Milk C (2016) The era of VR storytelling. TechCrunch [YouTube Video]. https://www.youtube.com/watch?v=5CqPyT3G_SE

Miller CH (2004) Digital storytelling: a creator's guide to interactive entertainment. Taylor & Francis

Murray JH (2017) Hamlet on the holodeck: the future of narrative in cyberspace. MIT Press, Cambridge, Massachusetts

Nafarrete J (2018) SPACES debuts multi-sensory terminator VR experience. VR Scout. https://vrscout.com/news/spaces-multi-sensory-terminator-vr-experience/. Accessed 23 May 2019

Nakamura J, Csikszentmihalyi M (2002) The concept of flow. In: Snyder CR, Lopez SJ (eds) Handbook of positive psychology. Oxford University Press, New York, pp 89–105

Norman D (2013) The design of everyday things (revised and expanded edition). Basic Books, New York

Pacat C (2017) Fantasy worldbuilding: the power of detail. Writing Queensland 258:14–15

Pace S (2004) A grounded theory of the flow experiences of Web users. Int J Hum Comput Stud 60(3):327–363. https://doi.org/10.1016/j.ijhcs.2003.08.005

Pouke M, Ylipulli J, Minyaev I, Pakanen M, Alavesa P, Alatalo T, Ojala T (2018) Virtual library: blending mirror and fantasy layers into a VR interface for a public library proceedings of the 17th international conference on mobile and ubiquitous multimedia, Cairo, Egypt, November 2018. Association for Computing Machinery, pp 227–231

Qin H, Patrick Rau P-L, Salvendy G (2009) Measuring player immersion in the computer game narrative. Int J Hum Comput Interact 25(2):107–133. https://doi.org/10.1080/1044731080 2546732

Revonsuo A (2000) The reinterpretation of dreams: an evolutionary hypothesis of the function of dreaming. Behav Brain Sci 23(6):877–901

Rosenberg RS, Baughman SL, Bailenson JN (2013) Virtual superheroes: using superpowers in virtual reality to encourage prosocial behavior. PLoS ONE 8(1):e55003. https://doi.org/10.1371/journal.pone.0055003

Sackman D (2015) Real change through virtual reality. TEDx Talks [Conference Video]. https://www.youtube.com/watch?v=gpOZIdqYMlU

Sanderson B (2016) 318R—#4 (World Building). Camera Panda [YouTube Video]. https://www.youtube.com/watch?v=v98Zy_hP5TI

Slater M (2018) Immersion and the illusion of presence in virtual reality. Br J Psychol 109(3): 431–433

Sutton-Smith B (2006) Play and ambiguity. In: Salen K, Zimmerman E (eds) The game design reader: a rules of play anthology. The MIT Press, Cambridge, Massachusetts, pp 296–313

Tolkien JRR (1947) On fairy-stories. Oxford University Press, Oxford

Wachowski L, Wachowski L (1999) The matrix. Warner Bros, Village Roadshow Entertainment

Wood M, Wood G, Balaam M (2017) "They're Just Tixel Pits, Man": disputing the 'Reality' of virtual reality pornography through the story completion method. In: Proceedings of the 2017 CHI conference on human factors in computing systems, Denver, Colorado, USA, 6–11 May 2017. Association for Computing Machinery, pp 5439–5451

Design Principles in the Development of Dashboards for Business Management

Nuno Martins⊙, Susana Martins, and Daniel Brandão⊙

Abstract This paper presents a set of Design principles for the development of dashboards for the area of business management. The objective of this study is to guide and help the designer in his dashboard design process in order to obtain efficient results. The adopted methodologies were focused on literature review of design principles in dashboard creation, namely in the areas of interface design; data visualization; usability; UX and UI design; interaction design; and visual identity. The study demonstrates the importance of design, namely in establishing a convergent relationship between the graphic and functional components, in order to guarantee adequate and efficient interface solutions for the user.

Keywords Dashboard · Infographic · UI & UX design · Interface design · Interaction design · Digital design · Communication design

1 Introduction

This paper aims to demonstrate the importance of design in the creation of dashboards and to present, through literature review, guiding methodologies that help designers create user-friendly solutions. It is also intended to contradict the reductive idea of design as a means with the exclusive function of beautifying the visual aspect of an interface. The visual design of the information, which includes the use of infographics, aims to contribute to the clarification of data in order to be efficiently read and understood by the user.

N. Martins (✉) · S. Martins
Research Institute for Design, Media and Culture, School of Design,
PolytechnicInstitute of Cavado and Ave, Barcelos, Portugal
e-mail: nmartins@ipca.pt

D. Brandão
CECS/Institute of Social Sciences, University of Minho, Braga, Portugal
e-mail: danielbrandao@uminho.pt

The information presented on the dashboards is essentially visual and the designer plays a key role in the process of creating and unifying graphics, readability, colour definition, interaction and in the global translation of dense and complex information into visual and interactive systems that are easy and fast to understand.

This paper begins by addressing the concept of dashboards; the importance of design in building these visual tools; and presents a set of theories, authors, and design methodologies considered to be crucial to a dashboard design process.

2 Dashboard and the Importance of Design

2.1 The Dashboard Concept

In the area of management, the dashboard can be defined as a tool for the graphical visualization of data from companies' Key Performance Indicators (KPI's). In a more comprehensive definition, by Gröger et al. (2013), the dashboard is considered to be a panel that gathers information presented throughout different visual resources (such as graphs or maps) capable of being combined with each other, with the main objective of monitoring, analyzing and facilitating decision making at all hierarchical levels of a company.

According to Stephen Few (2012), the dashboard is a visual representation of the most important information, organised on a single screen so that it can be read and monitored quickly. Caldeira (2010) goes further by saying that the dashboard can be considered as a management tool, which allows decision making to be sustained.

Tokola et al. (2016) defines the dashboard as a management communication medium for monitoring the company, with the objective of being a response for decision-makers in terms of interpretation, visualization and data analysis.

From these authors' perspectives, it can be concluded that the dashboard is an information presentation panel, functioning as a means of communication. Thus, design assumes an important role in the process of transforming complex and dense information into concise graphic solutions that allow easy reading and understanding of that data.

2.2 The Role of Design When Building Dashboards

The development of dashboards should use design procedures in order to apply an interactive solution that involves users in viewing data and making decisions. In this way, it also contributes to reduce the probability of errors in their design (Matheus et al. 2020).

According to Matheus et al. (2020), dashboards are not only intended to provide data. They also highlight problems and play a key role in understanding them in order to solve them.

Caldeira (2010) argues that the construction of dashboards should be based on design techniques by identifying six advantages resulting from their introduction:

1. The dashboard can have more data;
2. Relate more information at the same time;
3. The user perceives the information more quickly;
4. Guide the user in reading;
5. Highlights what really matters;
6. The dashboard image will be consistent with the company image.

Caldeira (2010) considers that designers being "experts in the rules of visualization", their skills allow them to highlight, reveal, differentiate and aggregate aspects of the data that compose the dashboard. Problems such as the meaning of colour, visual coherence, information hierarchy or noise suppression are central concerns in the designer's activity. The involvement of this type of specialists ensures the construction of dashboards with good readability for the user and a layout consistent with the graphic standards of the respective company.

In the specific case of dashboards for the management area, in the business sector, it is recommended to prioritize functionality over aesthetics (Tableau 2017). For complex data, the dashboard should consist of minimalist graphical elements, with soft colours that allow easy and straightforward reading of the company's financial data. It is also recommended to provide personalised views using tables, graphs, pictograms and numbers, so that it is possible to read the information from different perspectives, thus allowing a more detailed analysis and, consequently, better decision making (Matheus et al. 2020).

2.3   The Representation of Data Through Infographic

Infographic is considered to be included in the field of information design and is used in areas such as education, journalism or economics, namely for visual representations of data.

Alberto Cairo (2011) defines the concept of infographic as a diagrammatic representation of data that conveys an explanation of a given subject. The same author states that the main component of an infographic is the diagram, defining it as an abstract representation of reality. For Cairo (2011) abstraction is essential for the development of diagrams, as it is through it that unnecessary information can be removed in order to highlight the necessary information.

According to Cairo (2011), the word "design" implies structure. The main task of information design is to shape what appears to be disorganized and difficult to understand. Through this process, data is grouped and organized into relevant information that serves as a guide for a given action, eventually turning itself into knowledge.

In order to create good graphics, the right information must first be chosen. If the analyses or data are deficient, it is not possible to develop a graphical solution of quality data (Cairo 2019). According to Krum (2014), the recipients of infographics are not interested in seeing only data, their main interest is understanding the relationships between the data—and a good infographic product can fulfil that mission.

2.4 The Data Visualization

Finally, it is important to understand why graphic and infographic representations are an effective means of reading and understanding information.

According to Krum (2014), 50–80% of the human brain is dedicated to forms of visual processing, such as vision, memory, colours, shape, movement, patterns, spatial awareness and image recall. For Krum (2014), data visualization uses the ability of the brain to recognize patterns to accelerate data understanding. The author reinforces that it is possible to look at a data graph and understand it quickly by seeing patterns. This ability is the main reason why graphical representations of data can be highly effective in reading and quickly understanding information.

For Edward Tufte (2001), visual coding of data represents one of the most important steps in the visualisation of information. This visual transformation must be structured according to the type of data presented, and must be structured with different visual attributes, namely position, saturation and size, in order to culminate in a representation in different types of graphs to allow a good understanding of the data (Brath and Banissi 2016).

3   Design Principles in the Creation of Dashboards

In the creation of dashboards, it is important to achieve a convergence between usability and aesthetics. In the following chapters, a set of methodologies, theories and authors in the field of design are presented, which are a fundamental resource in the process of building dashboards.

3.1 The Interface Design: Page Organisation, Colour and Typography

There are three main guidelines for interface design: page organisation, colour and typography. Regarding organisation, organisational details can make a big difference in the interpretation of dashboards (Juice 2015).

It is important to define the most appropriate location for the graphics and the amount of information that can be placed on the dashboard. Trying to put as much information as possible on a dashboard increases the risk of making the maximum information compression error, penalizing reading.

According to the Gutenberg Diagram (Fig. 1), which demonstrates the reading behaviour of the western user (from left to right and from top to bottom), the main information should be inserted in the top left area of the layout, as it is in this area that the user will focus first (Andrade 2013). And, according to Jacob Nielsen (2017), the lower right area is the one that the user will pay least attention to.

When building a dashboard, the use of a grid system is an important support in the organization and coherence of the various graphic elements. As well as the concern for the existence of blank spaces in the layout in order to allow visual breaks and contribute to the focus on relevant information.

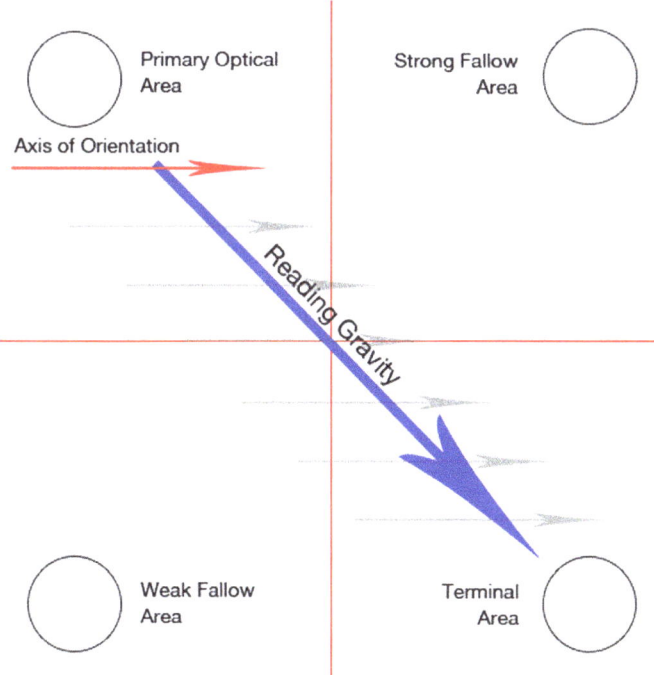

Fig. 1 Gutenberg diagram. *Source* Bradley (2011)

The creation of blank spaces is central to a comfortable interaction with the platform. The whitespace allows you to define hierarchies in order to distinguish information. A high density of information, without white spaces at the outer edges of the layout or between the elements, can make the reading of the information and the user's concentration harder (Schlatter and Levinson 2013a).

According to Stephen Few (2004), the content cannot be placed anywhere, nor should the sections of the dashboard be sized to contain as much information as possible in the space available.

Regarding the colour concept, the report "A Guide to Creating Dashboards People Love to Use", developed by Juice Analytic (2015), states that "more often than not, dashboards get lit up with colour like an over-dressed Christmas tree", i.e. most dashboards make inexplicable and impulsive use of colour that doesn't add significance. The colour should be used with moderation. Dashboards should initially be designed in shades of grey and only then should colour be added gradually so that they can convey useful information. Concerns such as defining colour shades to connect related data or increasing colour saturation to create highlights, are precautions that should be taken into account when designing a dashboard.

It should also be noted that colour influences usability issues by its influence in capturing the attention of the user. Colour is a means that contributes to the prioritisation and harmonisation of information and the expression of emotions, helping to improve user interaction with the dashboard (Schlatter and Levinson 2013b).

According to Juice Analytics (2015), colours are categorised into three types, namely: Sequential, referring to high and low level values; Divergent, when there is a critical point, such as the value zero; and Categorical, when we portray different groups of data, which requires colour contrast.

In relation to typography, the following aspects should also be taken into account when designing dashboards: readability of the text should be the top priority; the headings that name the main sections of the dashboard should be highlighted in the typography (through different scales or weights); the notes should be positioned in the background; the main highlight of the typography should always refer to the data that is to be highlighted; and the option for the adoption of a serif or sans serif typeface should be taken at the beginning of the construction of the dashboard, always preserving the coherence and readability of the layout (Juice 2015).

In summary, the basic rule that should guide the layout design process is to create and organize the different graphic elements that prioritize the reading and visual comfort of the user and never overvalue aesthetic issues over functional ones.

3.2 The Main Data Visualisation Tools

Data analysis and visualization tools are essential pieces to help in the management of companies, allowing to read a high amount of data in a simple way and contributing to a better analysis and a more informed decision making.

Graphics are the most common data visualisation tools, because they are a visual solution that allows to read, compare and evaluate trends in a more immediate way.

However, graphics are not always the best solution for translating information. For example, according to Knaflic (2015), when there is only one or two numeric data to show, the most effective will be to put the number in evidence, and not to use graphs. The use of simple text supported by a brief captioning makes it possible to read the data more directly and quickly. However, when the volume of data is larger, the use of a table or graph is recommended (Knaflic 2015).

Tables usually work when comparing values. Colour maps, on the other hand, help reduce the mental process, as they use colour saturation to highlight points of interest (Knaflic 2015).

There are different software solutions on the market for data management and analysis. Microsoft Excel software has become the most used tool in companies due not only to its ease of use, but also because it is a software integrated in the Windows operating system, the most used worldwide. After the mass use of Excel, companies invested in the Business Intelligence (BI) platforms that were committed to offering data integration and analysis, starting with reports and later developing dashboards, which with the technological advance became increasingly interactive (Accenture 2014).

3.3 Usability

The concept of usability refers to the ability to meet the user's needs in their interaction with a given product.

For the development of a dashboard solution that is intended to be a tool to support professional activity and decision making, it is essential to understand the concept of usability and meet its objectives in order to obtain an effective result.

The design process must be user centered and usability is the key principle to maximize your user experience.

If an interface is difficult to use, users will most likely give up and eventually seek another platform that meets their expectations (Nielsen 2012).

Nielsen (2012) states that usability is defined by five quality attributes: learning, efficiency, memory, error and satisfaction.

According to the author, learning refers to the ease with which the user interacts with the application at first contact. The efficiency interprets how quickly the user performs a task. As for memory, Nielsen highlights that the user must be able to remember his actions after a period of non-use. The memory evaluates the ease with which the user reconnects to the platform. Regarding errors, the author states that the errors made by users should be studied, how serious they are and how easily users recover from them. Finally, the level of user satisfaction regarding the use of the platform should be assessed, seeking to detect and correct errors and improve the necessary components in order to improve that level of satisfaction.

3.4 UX Design

According to Edward Stull (2018), the human being is a collection of experiences and these experiences are increasingly digital, whether they are in websites, e-mails, video games.

According to Don Norman (2013), the term User Experience (UX) refers to the quality of the user experience with a product. For the experience to be successful, the first requirement is to meet the user's needs, avoiding problems or complications in their activity. Therefore, the essence of the User Experience is to understand the user in detail, not only in terms of his needs, but also to understand his limitations. User Experience aims to ensure that users find value in the platforms presented to them (Martins et al. 2020a).

Peter Morville (2004) has developed a diagram illustrating the seven factors that qualify the user experience. These factors are critical to the success (or failure) of a product (Morville 2004) and serve as a guide for creating a good user experience:

1. **Useful**: the purpose of implementation should be to make the decision-making process more rapid and effective.
2. **Usable**: the application should be easy to use.
3. **Findable**: the user should be able to view all the necessary data and find what they need.
4. **Desirable**: the application should make daily professional management simpler and pleasant.
5. **Accessible**: the application should provide a good user experience to all type of users including the ones with disabilities.
6. **Credible**: the application should present on the first page a set of basic information about the reliability of the company
7. **Valuable**: the application should seek the satisfaction of the user and the information should be valuable to him.

In order to optimize the user experience, the UX Design process should start with a user-centered search by collecting the user's needs; analysis of data processing platforms; analysis of management process optimization platforms; and understanding of the dashboard concept and the principles for its creation.

The user profile should then be defined, using interviews with company employees and the focus group method.

Subsequently, meetings should be developed with the target audience (the company's managers and employees) in order to understand the motivations, objectives and limitations that users may encounter when interacting with the application. Consequently, it will be possible to understand the environment of the future users of the application, which allows to evaluate its effectiveness. Information sharing between the designer and the end users is a fundamental strategy to provide scenarios that will allow a better response to real situations.

For structuring the interface of a dashboard application, it is recommended to use the development of wireframes to speed up the structuring and navigation process. This initial draft version of low fidelity helps in defining the sections of the interface, positioning of elements, evaluation of the functionalities with higher priority and in understanding potential problems of the application at an early stage.

Once the wireframe development phase is complete, the next step should be to seek to identify the actions users will take, developing a consistent navigation flow that allows easy use of the dashboard application.

3.5   UI Design

The interface design is an iterative and interactive process, in which research on user profiles, the construction of prototypes and testing with users are fundamental to ensure a good interactive experience with the designed product (Wood 2014).

The UI Design process aims to improve the interactions described in UX design by combining visual design, interaction design and information architecture. The UI Design is responsible for the visual part of the application, i.e. the graphic interface. The objective of UI Design is to promote a pleasant interaction experience minimizing the difficulties of using the interface.

As a consequence of constant research, it is predictable that wireframes and navigation flows have changed during the dashboard development process. The wireframes are not the end of the UI Design process, instead they are a method to find out and help decide what needs to be included in the final solution (Wood 2014). It is in this process that the elements of UI Design are defined, such as colour, typography and visual identity.

The study is a continuous iterative work process that results in constant changes and back and forth. In the same way, a prototype does not necessarily represent the final solution. A prototype usually results in several versions until a completely effective solution is achieved (Saffer 2010).

3.6   Interaction Design

The Interaction Design is based on users' understanding and their cognitive principles (Cooper et al. 2007). According to Bill Verplank (2009), Interaction Design facilitates interactions between humans and interactive systems, allowing to balance the relationship between interaction and functionality, thus promoting good usability.

Verplank (2009) states that Interaction Design's main goal is to focus on the user and how he/she interacts with the product. According to this author, Interaction Design can be summarized in three questions:

1. **How do you DO?** The aim is to understand what the user needs to interact, understand how the application will behave and how it affects the user.
2. **How do you FEEL?** It consists of the analysis of the user's feedback concerning his interaction with the system.
3. **How do you KNOW?** It is related to the verification that the user recognizes actions and knows how the product works. The aim is to help the user understand what happens during interaction.

The Interaction Design balances a variety of concerns, using various methods or representations. These methods are the framework for checking whether needs have been addressed (Verplank 2009).

Verplank (2009) illustrated the stages of the Interaction Design process, from the beginning of the idea to its presentation. According to the author, a project can start from two situations: the discovery of an error or an idea that will be the motivation for the designer.

The project must have a meaning. Several scenarios are created in order to understand the meaning of the application: what is it for?; where can it be used?; and what are the user's expectations?

The set of all user expectations suggests the creation of a model that meets those expectations. The model should be represented through mapping representations and controls. The essence of an Interaction Design is to achieve the product objectives without disrespecting the user objectives (Cooper et al. 2007).

3.7 Visual Identity

As Raposo (2008) argues, to understand and manage a brand, it is not enough to develop and paste a logo. Success is more dependent on the general conduct of the institution and on the way in which the graphic identity is implemented, in order to make it unique and impossible to be copied (Raposo 2008). In the same sense, Smith (2010) warns that branding exercises should not focus only on the tip of the iceberg, changing only what is visible.

Visual identity has the function of aggregating and making coherent a whole communication system, in order to build a single voice, with a properly measured and calibrated tone. The various forms and means of expression (visual, sound, interactive, etc.) must be convergent with the company's philosophy, thus contributing to the robustness of its identity (Martins et al. 2020b).

Building an identity also implies a technical component. Namely, the selection of a typeface for a brand should take into account not only its visual expressiveness, but also its suitability for the different situations in which it will be applied, namely in terms of legibility.

3.8 Usability Tests

Usability tests act as an evaluation that is made to a product, using users that represent its target audience. Its main objective is the identification of usability problems and the evaluation of user satisfaction. A good usability test should take into account not only the time of the test but also the post-test phase, i.e. the subsequent analysis of the tests carried out on the basis of feedback from users (Usability.gov 2013).

After the usability tests, a final prototype should be carried out, including any failures detected in interaction with the application, as well as improvements suggested by users.

4 Conclusions

Through literature review, an attempt was made to define a guide to support designers' work in developing dashboards. Although the study focuses on dashboards directed to the area of Business Management, it is believed that their relevance is not limited to this area, as they address methods that are transversal in the area of Design.

It is argued that the focus of the study on a solution for the Management area is of additional importance because it requires a design solution where functionality is the most important element. For this reason, the technical component, related to the achievement of the objective of maximum efficiency in the reading and understanding of information, is a priority compared to the aesthetic component. This is not to say that functionality and aesthetics are unrelated. Quite the contrary. As the present study has shown, issues such as colour, graphics or typography are decisive visual elements to ensure an efficient solution, namely to contribute to a good reading and understanding of information.

For this set of reasons, the importance of design in the dashboard design process has been defended, and it has been shown that the visual component is not a matter of *personal taste*, but a complex problem that requires the application of logical methods in order to ensure the design of an efficient solution.

References

Accenture (2014) Entendendo a visualização de dados. https://www.accenture.com/_acnmedia/PDF-45/Accenture-Entendedo-De-Dados.pdf

Andrade M (2013) Gutenberg diagram—why you should know it and use it. Medium. https://medium.com/userexperience-3/the-gutenberg-diagram-in-web-design-e5347c172627

Bradley S (2011) 3 design layouts: gutenberg diagram, Z-pattern, and F-pattern. Vanseo Design. https://vanseodesign.com/web-design/3-design-layouts

Brath R, Banissi E (2016) Using typography to expand the design space of data visualization. She Ji 2(1):59–87. https://doi.org/10.1016/j.sheji.2016.05.003

Cairo A (2011) El Arte Funcional. Alamut, Madrid

Cairo A (2019) How charts lie: getting smarter about visual information. W. W. Norton & Company, New York

Caldeira J (2010) Dashboards—Comunicar Eficazmente a Informação de Gestão. Edições Almedina, Coimbra

Cooper A, Reimann R, Croni D (2007) About face 3: the essentials of interaction design. Wiley Publishing, Indianapolis, Indiana

Few S (2012) Show me the numbers: designing tables and graphs to enlighten. Analytics Press, El Dorado Hills

Gröger C, Hillmann M, Hahn F, Mitschang B, Westkämper E (2013) The operational process dashboard for manufacturing. Procedia CIRP 7:205–210. https://doi.org/10.1016/j.procir.2013.05.035

Juice Analytics (2015) Whitepaper: a guide to creating dashboards people love to use. http://bit.ly/DashboardsPeopleLoveToUse

Knaflic C (2015) Storytelling with data. John Wiley & Sons, Hoboken, New Jersey

Krum R (2014) Cool infographics: effective communication with data visualisation and design. John Wiley & Sons, Indianapolis

Martins N, Campos J, Simoes R (2020a) Activerest: design of a graphical interface for the remote use of continuous and holistic care providers. Adv Sci Technol Eng Syst 5(2):635–645. https://doi.org/10.25046/aj050279

Martins N, Martin-Sanroman J, Suárez-Carballo F (2020b) The design process in the improvement of the experience between a brand and its target audience through a digital product: the Lexus Portugal's used car website case study. Adv Sci Technol Eng Syst J 5(5):620–629. https://doi.org/10.25046/aj050576

Matheus R, Janssen M, Maheshwari D (2020) Data science empowering the public: data-driven dashboards for transparent and accountable decision-making in smart cities. Gov Inf Q 37(3):101284. https://doi.org/10.1016/j.giq.2018.01.006

Morville P (2004) User experience design. http://semanticstudios.com/user_experience_design/

Nielsen J (2012) Usability 101: introduction to usability. Nielsen Norman Group. https://www.nngroup.com/articles/usability-101-introduction-to-usability/

Nielsen J (2017) F-shaped pattern of reading on the web: misunderstood. But still relevant (Even on Mobile). Nielsen Norman Group. https://www.nngroup.com/articles/f-shaped-pattern-reading-web-content/

Norman D (2013) The design of everyday things. Basic Books, New York

Raposo D (2008) Design de Identidade e Imagem Corporativa: Branding, história da marca, identidade visual corporativa. Edições IPCB, Castelo Branco

Saffer D (2010) Designing for interaction. creating innovative applications and devices. New Riders, Berkeley

Smith S (2010) A experiência da Marca. In: Clifton R, Simons J (eds) O Mundo da Marcas. Actual Editora, Lisboa

Stull E (2018) UX fundamentals for non-UX professionals: user experience principles for managers, writers, designers, and developers, vol 63, issue 2. Apress, Berkeley, CA. https://doi.org/10.1007/978-1-4842-3811-0

Tableau (2017) 10 best practices for building effective dashboards. Tableau. https://www.tableau.com/learn/whitepapers/10-best-practices-building-effective-dashboards

Tokola H, Gröger C, Järvenpää E, Niemi E (2016) Designing manufacturing dashboards on the basis of a key performance indicator survey. Procedia CIRP 57:619–624. https://doi.org/10.1016/j.procir.2016.11.107

Tufte E (2001) The visual display of quantitative information, 2nd edn. Graphics Press, Cheshire

Usability.gov (2013) Usability testing. https://www.usability.gov/how-to-and-tools/methods/usability-testing.html

Verplank B (2009) Interaction design sketchbook. http://www.billverplank.com/IxDSketchBook.pdf

Wood D (2014) Interface design: an introduction to visual communication in UI design. Bloomsbury Publishing, London

Inclusive Product Design: Applicating the Montessori Methodology into the Design Conception of Children's Products

Leonardo Moreira and Tomás Queiroz Ferreira Barata

Abstract This article presents the results of an ongoing scientific initiation research, as well as the contributions attained from a Research Internships Abroad Program (BEPE/FAPESP) which sought to expand the theoretical framework on design processes regarding sensory products in the European Market. The study focuses on toys for children with blindness or low vision, including its design process, all the way though its physical prototyping. Here follows the adopted structure of analysis: (a) Theoretical review on the design of sensory products and the contribution of the Montessori method; (b) Application of synchronous analysis amid similar children's toys from the European market, specifically those commercialized in Portugal; (c) Project development with generation and selection of alternatives; (d) Experimental execution of the physical prototype at the Prototype Laboratory. Thus, this research aims to contribute to the development of sensory products through the Montessori method, as well as stimulating further research in the areas of Product Design and Inclusive Design.

Keywords Inclusive design · Product design · Montessori method · Sensory products

L. Moreira (✉)
Universidade Estadual Paulista, UNESP, São Paulo, Brasil

T. Q. F. Barata
Faculdade de Arquitetura e Urbanismo da Universidade de São Paulo, FAU-USP, São Paulo, Brazil

1 Introduction and Background

This paper presents the results of an ongoing scientific initiation research project in Brazil (grant provided by FAPESP[1]) namely "Development of prototype furniture for children in pre-school phase: Articulation between Sustainable Design and Inclusive Design" (FAPESP). The scope of that project regards the design of sensory products aimed at five- to six-year-old children, with the objective of providing a theoretical and projective deepening on inclusive and sustainable design.

The results presented here also points out to contributions obtained through a Research Internship Abroad Program (BEPE) that explored the theoretical foundation on the design processes of sensory products, with an emphasis on toys for children with visual impairments in the European market.

The study was carried out in conjunction with the School of Architecture, Arts and Communication (Brazil) and the Faculty of Architecture at the University of Lisbon (Portugal). Its focus is researching and gathering knowledge in relation with product design and human senses, with an inclusive approach for the population of children, without neglecting the application of sustainable design guidelines, in regard to the impacts generated by the studied products (Fig. 1).

Furthermore, among the broad results obtained, this article presents a fraction of the specific and significant contribution of the Montessori methodology in the process of developing inclusive products for children. Thus, the following aspects will be highlighted in this study: (a) Theoretical review on the design of sensory products and the contribution of the Montessori method; (b) Application of synchronous analysis amid similar children's toys from the European market, specifically those commercialized in Portugal; (c) Project development with generation and selection of alternatives; (d) Experimental execution of the physical prototype at the Prototype Laboratory.

2 Theoretical Foundation

Inclusive Design uses a transversal approach to the different areas of projective discipline, as a strategy to meet a more comprehensive planning that includes human diversity.

> It is possible to design and produce products, services or environments suitable for such human diversity, including children, older adults, people with disabilities, sick or injured people, or, simply, people placed in disadvantage by circumstances. This approach is called "Inclusive Design". (SIMÕES and BISPO 2006, p. 8)

---

[1]São Paulo Research Foundation, Brazil.

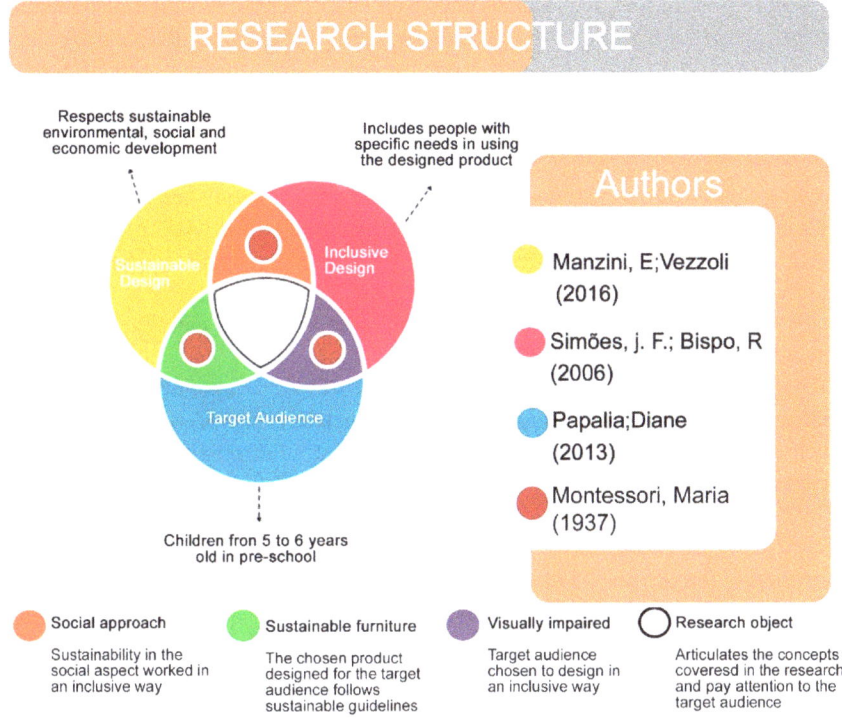

Fig. 1 Infographic Research Structure. *Source* prepared by the author (2021)

When thinking about Inclusive Design, the targeted audience for the application of the concepts, in addition to the elderly, are often people with disabilities. The Brazilian Law for Inclusion defines:

> A person with a disability is considered to be one who has a long-term physical, mental, intellectual or sensory impairment, which, in interaction with one or more barriers, can obstruct their full and effective participation in society on equal terms with the other people (Law 13.146/20015), art. 2nd.

Within the realm of the design of inclusive products, it is worth mentioning as an example those intended for people with visual impairment, approached more deeply in the scientific initiation research which based this paper. The childhood of a person can be considered a strategic period for interventions and sensory enrichment, which can be achieved with the aid of objects, and consequently product design, as a tool.

The cited consideration is supported by several theorists, including Hatwell (1986) and Rosa and Ochaíta (1993), pointing out that children with visual impairment may be delayed by two to three years in acquiring the symbolic function; and up to four years in the tests of manipulation of figurative and spatial elements. According to Enderle (1987), this is because the first five years of life are the most important for psychomotor improvement of a child, thus, it is also the most efficient phase for learning. According to the same author, from five to six years of age, the child goes through a phase that includes the acquisition of gait, speech, autonomy for self-hygiene and food habits.

As an important tool to product development for children, there is the Sensory Integration Theory, which describes how the individual develops the ability to perceive, learn and organize sensations, received from his body and the surrounding environment to perform voluntary and significant activities. According to Ayres (1970, 1979), during their search for broadening the perception of their bodies in the world, the children perform multiple interactive experiences. A newborn starts to experiment with sensations, without being able to signify them, acquiring only later the ability to organize their sensory inputs.

That being said, it is worth highlighting the work of another theoretical and medical-educator Maria Montessori, who identifies five important areas for human development as part of a method initiated by her through observations which then became tools that can be used in favor of processing and their application. In a simplified way, according to the author, the learning contents can be classified in: Cosmic Education, Language, Practical Life, Mathematical Education, and Education of the Senses (Montessori 1965 and Lagôa 1981). Within these areas, the materials produced by her were arranged as follows:

Cosmic Education: comprises the knowledge of Socio-historical Sciences and Natural Sciences.

- Language: especially in Early Childhood Education comprises of materials for preparing the child's hands for writing; literacy has an emphasis on phonetics; reading; and textual production.
- Practical Life: a context in which children can develop motor skills through the execution of daily activities, such as washing and drying dishes, handling liquids, clamping, drawing, painting, cutting, pasting; caring for the environment and for themselves (watering plants, washing hands, washing clothes, etc.).
- Mathematical Education: referring to materials that develop the notions of numbers, as well as addition, subtraction, division, multiplication, among others.
- Education of the Senses: consists in the development of the senses through materials such as color boxes, smells, flavors, porosities, in addition to developing concepts such as high and low, heavy and light, strong and weak, smooth and rough, etc.

The materials chosen and produced by Montessori are of a concrete nature, so that the children can handle them, which emphasizes the education of the senses, as the author "defended that the path for the intellect passes through the hands, because it is through movement and touch that children explore and decode the world around them" (Ferrari 2008, p. 32). Such consideration regarding the use of the senses is supported by several other authors (Vygotsky 1983; Martin and Bueno 1997; Mendonça et al. 2008; Papalia 2013). It is appropriate to establish a parallel with the concepts presented by Vygotsky, in which the assimilation of concrete sensory knowledge helps to form necessary conceptions, without separating the sensitive from the rational, and it is fundamental for a more effective development (Vygotsky 1983).

Among her achievements during her clinic period, Montessori taught some children with disabilities how to read and write, who were then subjected to exams in public schools and obtained surprisingly positive results. After her teachings, the children from that clinic achieved similar results compared to those obtained by children without any disability (Montessori 1965 and Lagôa 1981). For Montessori, that level of success was probably attained because those children were treated pedagogically in a different, unconventional way (Montessori 1957b).

[…] according to the same author, starting from the work developed children with disability, Montessori assumed that there is, between children considered normal and those with disabilities, a correspondence of behaviors and responses. The difference focuses only on different moments and rhythms, both of which, according to the premises of this scholar, have the possibility of learning and developing. (Tezzari 2009, p. 129).

Thus, for the author, people with disabilities should be understood beyond their clinical condition: "[…], I, unlike my colleagues, had the intuition that the issue of disabled people was probably pedagogical before clinic" (Montessori 1957b, p. 23). This alternative method is summarized in the application of an appropriate educational program, which according to Ferrari (2008) stands out for the fact that: "her method did not contradict human nature and, therefore, it was more efficient than the traditional ones" (Ferrari 2008, p. 32).

3   Application of Synchronic Analysis

For the application of the demonstrated concepts, the typology of furniture named "sensory table" was widely used within the Montessori methodology, as it consists of an object that supports several sensory activities, which delimits an area of sensory exploration, consisting of a table with built-in containers and objects for activities. Applied in this context, Montessori points out that the choices of materials, especially the components, must be well-founded, they must be attractive and aesthetically pleasing, allow for gradual difficulties, and present one stimulus at a time. Another suggestion is making the materials modifiable, that is, possible to be assembled, disassembled, and used in various stages of the learning process, in addition to being proportional to the size of the child (Montessori 1965 and Lagôa 1981).

Still in her notes, the projected sensory product must be self-correcting, that is, the child must be able to perceive their mistakes, either because the pieces do not fit together or because of characteristics that induce him to try to relate the object to a purpose, such as congruent colors, sounds or textures. The sum of all observations regarding the use of the material, according to the author, favors the child's concentration on the activity, which in turn, induces the child to work in silence spontaneously (Montessori 1965 and Lagôa 1981). Thus, it is noticeable that her method self-complete and self-regulate, giving it its conceptual sustainability.

For the projective start, a synchronous analysis was performed by collecting data of the registered sensory products available in the city of Lisbon, with emphasis on projects aimed at stimulators that benefit children with visual impairments, considering the analysis of the product characteristics and the conditioning parameters. Therefore, it was visited traditional toy stores, shops specialized in more sustainable and educational products, as well as websites with availability of similar toys and toy types. It is worth emphasizing the importance of visiting physical stores at this stage, because when designing for children with visual impairments, the multi-sensory is fundamental, so, in person, one can analyze the textures, materials, shapes and sounds of each object.

Among the products studied, two examples of sensory tables and two examples of components to be used in those pieces of furniture were listed for this article (Table 1).

4 Project Development with Generation and Selection of Alternatives

This stage comprises the generation of alternatives, selection of promising ideas, improvement and feasibility investigation with definition of shape, color, texture and finishes, through the use of manual sketches, virtual modeling and renderings.

4.1 Generation of Alternatives

The planning of generating ideas was carried out by understanding the bibliographic data and synchronic analysis, previously presented with the use of handmade sketches, drafts, and notes of possible products and operations. A few Sensory Table alternatives were initially created, followed by the elaboration of its components.

Two table alternatives were selected for study and improvement, according to the image below (Fig. 2).

Several component options were generated to be used in the sensory table (Fig. 3).

Table 1 Analysis of similar products. Photos extracted from shopping sites; text written by the author

PRODUCT	ANALYSI
•Flisat Sensorial Table 	Built in wood, it has a very simple and elegant design made with inserts and glue, which make maintenance and exchange of parts difficult, but guarantee an advantage at the end of the life cycle with its easy decomposition. Only the table is sold without the activities, vats, and benches that are purchased separately. It has little contrast in its original colors and a uniform texture.
•Mamielo Sensorial Table 	Made of wood, it is a more robust version with a more traditional design, accompanying two mobile plastic vats and a paper roll holder. It has the function of a common table, a sensory table and also the free activity of the drawing with the roller attached to its top. Its construction has a high use of raw material, does not provide a great contrast in the colors of the product and maintains a uniform texture throughout the surface.

PRODUCT	ANALYSI
•Plastic Tools 	Made of petroleum-derived plastic, it has a smooth and homogeneous texture.Found in several stores and manufacturers, this set provides great improvement of the engine and has vibrant colors, however, the choice of colors does not favor the contrast for various visual needs, such as color blindness.
•Tactile Memory Game 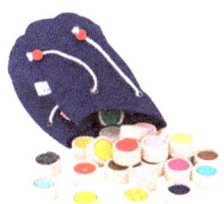	Made of wood combined with several textures and materials on its top surface. Product from the shop "Happy Grove ". It shows great motor and sensory improvement, mainly because of the wide range of textures and bold colors working independently, which enables the cognitive development of memory, a crucial skill for the target audience.

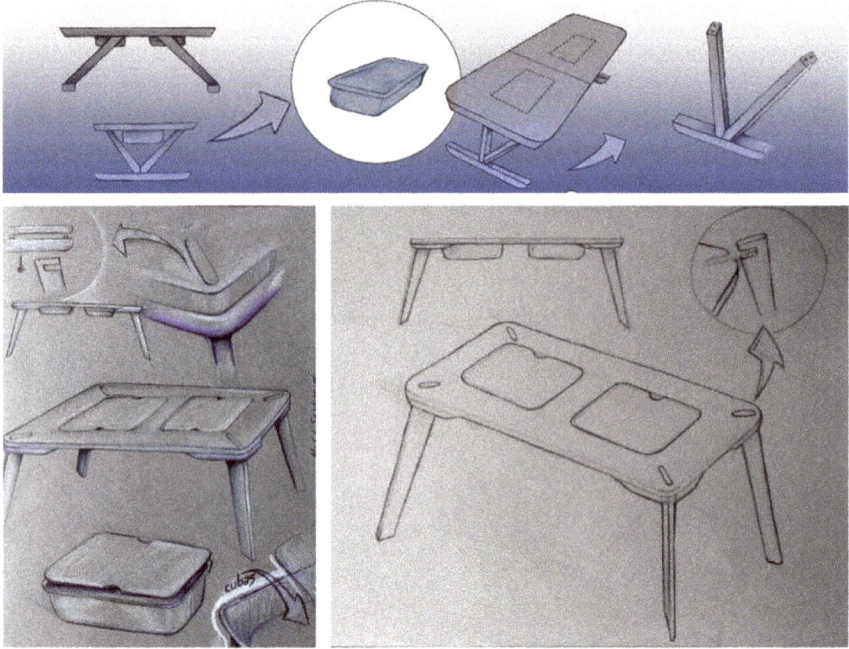

Fig. 2 Sketches made by hand, by the author (2021)

Fig. 3 Sketches made by hand, by the author (2021)

4.2 Selection of Alternatives

Initially, a productive feasibility study was carried out among the sensory table options that have been raised. A simulation was also conducted to study its manufacturing complexities, with 1: 4 scale model of the initial idea (Fig. 4).

Fig. 4 1:4 Scale Model, by the author (2021)

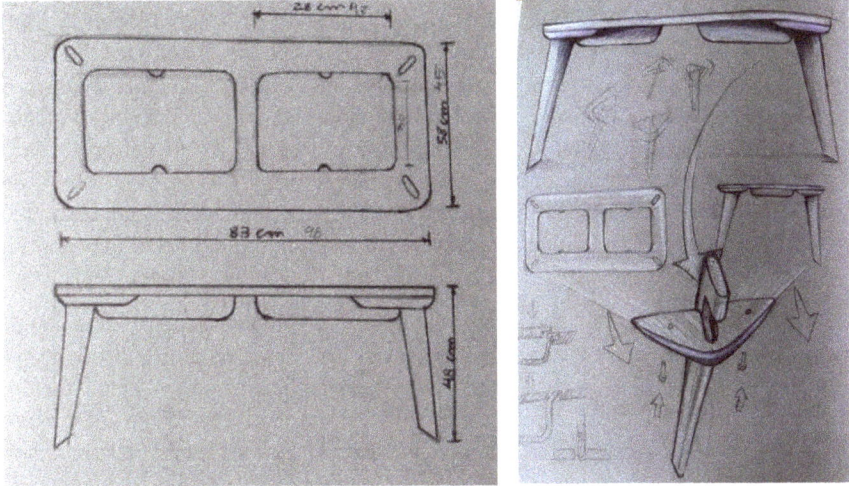

Fig. 5 Sketches made by hand, by the author (2021)

Through this model, it was possible to identify points of structural weakness, possible crushing points, and a great demand for the use of raw materials. This led to the improvement of a second creation, by demonstrating a promising reduced use of raw materials, ease of manufacture and distinguishable design. To optimize the time use, the second idea was perfected using sketches, solving as many conceptual problems as possible, before starting the new physical prototype. Like the main concept, the table was conceived in sober forms and provided a great contrast for the future components, without dispersing the user's attention, also functioning as a frame for guidance during the activities (Fig. 5).

Fig. 6 Sketches made by hand, by the author (2021)

After the selection and improvement of the sensory table, the choice of sensory components was initiated, with two promising ideas being chosen for improvement:

(1) The first idea consists of a multisensory game, which benefits touch, hearing and vision simultaneously (Fig. 6). The created product emphasizes the action of playing and uses sensory exploration to guide the experience in a self-corrective way. That is, through attempts and fails, the child stimulates their own "action systems" (a process of combining skills in motor development) and establishes a parallel between the logic of this operation with the logic of the effects caused by playing. In this sense, the children can learn how to create a motor repertoire and to continuously merge the skills they already have with those they are acquiring, while building more complex capacities.

In total, the interior of the box has 18 pieces, varying in shape, texture, color, material, and sound. When removing the pieces, the process of investigating their content begins, and then sorting the pieces by similar characteristics. Shape, texture, and sound are the levels of increasing difficulty, respectively. After the assimilation of the characteristics, the use of the pieces is expected for the arrangement of simple games, such as, the memory game.

Like the previous process of attempting to sort the pieces, the memory game can be performed following shapes, textures, and sound, allowing for an expansion of difficulty, and learning in the process. Thus, the gestures of "picking up", "interpreting" and "signifying" the objects can be done in a multisensory way, including a great diversity of specific needs, among them, the visual ones.

The second idea consists of a set of tools, in which it aims at motor improvement, with varied gestures and delicate fine movements. This toy introduces mathematical proportions—one half and one third, for example—and geometric elemental shapes such as rectangles, circles, triangles, and simple polygons in the design of the pieces. In addition, it encourages fanciful thinking in the simulation of activities of possible professions, while encouraging creative development. Its pieces have an initial configuration that can be rearranged in several ways and the tools have the

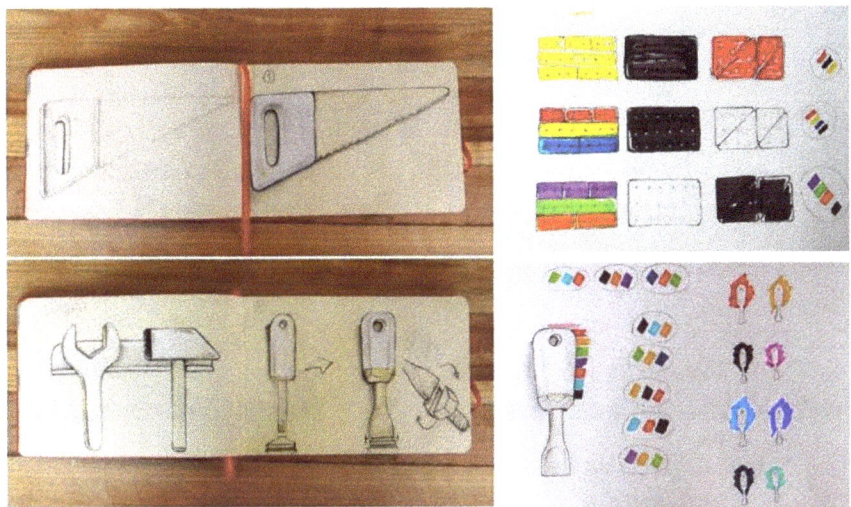

Fig. 7 Sketches made by hand, by the author (2021)

same functional character. In this sense, the tools can be used to build various objects that, in turn, can be reframed while playing with the ones already created by the child (Fig. 7).

4.3 Virtual Modeling and Renderings

After the previous definitions, it was carried out a tridimensional virtual modeling of the proposals, which are important for the verification of the constructive viability and for obtaining a preview of the aesthetic functionality (Fig. 8). After modeling, both proposals were digitally rendered (Fig. 9).

4.4 Experimental Execution of a Physical Model in Prototype Laboratory:

In this phase, a physical prototyping was started to study the proportions and materials. The sensory table was produced in the prototype laboratory of the School of Architecture, Arts and Communication (UNESP, Brazil), while the components were manufactured in the prototype laboratory of Faculty of Architecture (UL, Portugal) (Fig. 10).

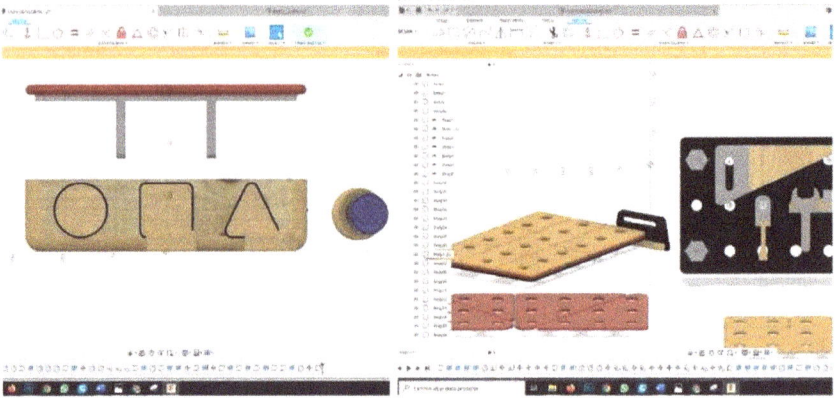

Fig. 8 Virtual Model, Autodesk Fusion software, developed by the author (2021)

Fig. 9 Digital renderings, prepared by the author (2021)

4.5 Prototyping Results

Next are presented the photos of the result from the production of the proposed functional prototypes (Fig. 11).

The colors black and red were chosen to compose the sensory box (Fig. 12), the black details help to contrast with the light wood, thus helping those children with residual vision in the process of identification and positioning of the pieces when storing them in the box. The hollow side-handles become visible after removing the

Fig. 10 Photos of the prototype production, prepared by the author (2021)

Fig. 11 Photo of the finished prototype, prepared by the author (2021)

box from the bowl of the sensory table. The handles are much smaller than the pieces of the game to prevent its entry by mistake, but large enough to present a safe handle for the child to lift the box.

The pieces that make up the box are hollow inside, and can be filled with different materials, to provide three different types of sounds (Fig. 12). Three pieces were produced, out of a total of eighteen constituents, the three representing the three types of elementary shapes, textures, colors and sounds possible in the game.

Fig. 12 Photo of the finished prototype, prepared by the author (2021)

The set of tools, on the other hand, has several reinforcements of association, in which the tool and its correspondent piece have both congruent colors, shape and texture, to facilitate the assembling, disassembling, and playing for the visually impaired children (Fig. 13).

Finally, the components were combined in use on the sensory table (Fig. 14).

5   Conclusion

Finally, when analyzing the results, it can be concluded that the objective of developing inclusive sensory products using concepts from the Montessori methodology were met. It is worth remembering that the present study presents the results of a much denser research in progress (Fig. 1), thus representing a small theoretical and practical outline developed so far. In general, the results were promising, and it is expected that such a study will contribute to the bibliographic discussion on the subject because it can be further reproduced and tested, for greater popularization and improvement of the design of sensory products, that is still not widespread in the Brazilian market.

Fig. 13 Photo of the finished prototype, prepared by the author (2021)

Fig. 14 Photo of the finished prototype, prepared by the author (2021)

References

Ayres AJ (1970) Integração Sensorial e a Criança. Serviços Psicológicos Ocidentais

Ayres AJ (1979) Sensory Integration and The Child, Los Angeles, WPS

Enderle C (1987) Psicologia do desenvolvimento. O processo evolutivo da criança. Porto Alegre: Artes Médicas, 2ª

Ferrari, Marcio (2008) Maria Montessori, a médica que valorizou o aluno. https://novaescola.org.br/conteudo/459/medica-valorizou-aluno. Accessed on 29/01/2021

Hatwell Y (1986) Toucher l'espace, la main et la perception tactile de l'espace. Presses Universitaires de Lille, Paris

Lagôa V (1981) Estudo do Sistema Montessori. São Paulo. Loyola

Martin MB, Bueno ST (1997) In: Bautista R (ed) Special educational needs. Lisbon: Dinalivro. 1997 MEC. Benjamin Constant Institute. Magazine Benjamin Constant, vol 3, paragraph 6. Rio de Janeiro

Mendonça A, Miguel C et al (2008) Alunos Cegos e com Baixa Visão. Orientações Curriculares. Lisboa: Ministério da Educação/DGIDC

Montessori M (1957b) La scopeta del bambino. Milão: Garzanti

Montessori M (1965) Pedagogia científica. São Paulo: Flamboyant

Papalia D (2013) And human development

Rosa A, Ochaíta E (1993) (Org) Psicologia de la Cegueira. Madrid: Alianza Editorial

Simoes JF, Bispo R (2006) Inclusive design: accessibility and usability in products, services and environments. Manual to support training activities of the project Design Inc

Tezzari ML (2009) Educação Especial e Ação Docente: da medicina à educação. 2009. 46 f. Tese (Doutorado)—UFRGS, Porto Alegre, Cap. 5 e 6

Vygotsky LS (1983) Problems essenciales de la therapeutic pedagogy. Ed. Russian, Trad. Cuban, p 144

Local Refuge for Pollinating Insects, BEEbedor and a BEElhário Project

Fernando Miguel Marques⊙

Abstract The goal is to help the proliferation of pollinating insects, that throughout the years, according to scientists, have suffered—thanks to various causes—a drastic reduction of the populations, which has been reported in many scientific studies, and becomes concerning given that these animals are important for the reproduction of vegetable crops and consequently for humanity. Within the concepts of animal design, a nesting place and a waterer for pollinating insects were developed: the "aBEElhário" and the "BEEbedor". This study, still in the initial phase, had promising results given that the bee waterer is the most highlighted object regarding the utility demonstrated during this time sample. The nesting place was occupied by pollinating insect species but needs to be monitored for longer.

Keywords Ecodesign · Animal design · Pollinating insects

1 Introduction

The animal focused design is essentially based in two branches: the pet design one which is, by default, an emotional design in which the products reflect in many aspects the ideals thought out for humans, not reflecting sometimes the animals' true needs, while the animals themselves adapt to the objects, that suit any home decoration, but far from being close to the animal design. Another branch, with a more technical and scientific approach, is the design thought out to operate closely

F. M. Marques (✉)
ISEC Lisboa—Instituto Superior de Educação e Ciências, Alameda das Linhas de Torres, 179, 1750-142 Lisbon, Portugal

F. M. Marques
Tgraf—Centro internacional de estudos e investigação em tecnologias gráficas e comunicação cientifica, Lisbon, Portugal

F. M. Marques
CIAUD—Centro de investigação em arquitectura, urbanismo e design, Rua Sá Nogueira, 1349-063 Lisbon, Portugal

© The Author(s), under exclusive license to Springer Nature Switzerland AG 2022
D. Raposo et al. (eds.), *Perspectives on Design II*, Springer Series in Design and Innovation 16, https://doi.org/10.1007/978-3-030-79879-6_28

to veterinarians, intimately connected to the investigation or the practice of veterinarian exercises. This branch essentially reflects the technical characteristics associated to the products that are intended to fulfill a certain job.

How can the design contribute to a better enjoyment of nature's paradigms.

When we talk about animal design, we want products that are designed not for humans but to help the lives of animals. This is not about nice and "cute" objects to have at home where animals can accommodate. Animal design does not think solely about objects for humans to have in the house. It thinks about objects that fulfill purposes or that help to fulfill animals' functions. It is a wide field of work, that can work for the advantage of our four-legged friends but it does not end with them. However, the aesthetic function must be always present because it is meant to be used by animals but enjoyed by people.

At the moment, the planet needs the healthy design to come out and look at animals with a responsible attitude and to help the preservation of species. To do so, the designers must leave their comfort zone and seek information in other areas that are usually not explored in their professional practice.

There is some dispersed information that circulates in more important media such as traditional media and, specially, social media. Who has not yet come across the information that the oceans are full of plastic in the depths and of the existence of monumental islands with the size of several countries? There are organizations and other ONG that alert to these issues, like sea animals that are suffering thanks to human negligence. Regarding this matter, there are already some engineering products and designs that were developed to help in the capture of trash and in the cleansing of water and beaches.

These are problems that need to be solved, and as they are very visible and media covered, there are already a number of entities concerned with minimizing and making efforts to resolve them.

However, there are other problems that are appearing in the media and go unnoticed by most citizens. For now, only the most attentive are concerned and the rest think there is nothing they can do to alleviate it. It is the case of the abrupt decrease of insects, namely bees and other insects of the same species, which are pollinators and therefore of vital importance to mankind's agricultural crops.

2   Contextualization

Regarding a study conducted in the University of Sydney, the researcher Francisco Sanchez-Bayo (2019) talked to "The Guardian", where he commented the concerns of his study "The Decline of Insect Populations"[1], in which he claims insects are with a loss of population of about 2.5% per year, in last the 25–30 years. The author estimates that in 10 years, there will be one quarter less of the current insect

---

[1]Sánchez-Bayo (2019).

population. If nothing is done about it, in 50 years there will only exist half of the current population. And until 2120, a great number of insect species will be extinguished.

The predominant factors pointed out are the massive intensification of agriculture, as well as the consequence of the massive use of agro-toxic agents, such as insecticides to control certain species of insects that are considered agricultural predators, or herbicidal species considered as invasive of crops. In some countries of the European Union, such as France, certain agro-toxic agents like fluorophosphate[2] were forbidden.

According to the website "wilder.pt",[3] pesticides like chlorothalonil,[4] which has been used against potato mildew since the 1960's, were banned from the UE. This happened over studies showing that this pesticide is responsible for possible damages to the human ADN, having already been responsible for damages in amphibians, fish and insects, according to studies conducted by the EFSA— European Food Safety Authority. This decision will only have repercussions when the EU directives are released, foreseen to be approved in May of 2019, having already been postponed to 2020.

3 Problem

3.1 Decline of Insects

According to Carla Rego[5] (2019), entomologist (insect researcher), there are currently 680 species of bees identified in Portugal. And of all these species, very few are the "good" ones for producing honey, although they're all pollinating insects.

In the cities, says the researcher, when the spring comes, the grass we call "weeds" starts to flower (the entomologist prefers the term "spontaneous grass"), which then sprouts throughout urban areas which makes the people in charge hurry to cut or destroy them with herbicides because they are considered invasive.

Cristina Faria Moreira[6] (2019), a journalist, writes in her article in the "Público" newspaper, (25 of March of 2019) mentioning a study published in January of 2019, in the *Nature Ecology and Evolution* journal, in England, led by the researcher Katherine Baldock, who spoke to the British newspaper "The Guardian" about the study. In her interview, she talked about her study object: the presence of

---

[2]Fluorophosphate—Main agro-toxic agent of some pesticide brands.

[3]wilder.pt. (2020).

[4]Chlorothalonil—fungicide used by farmers against mildew in crops of potatoes, tomatoes, wheat and others.

[5]Author's note: Carla Rego is a researcher from the Centre for Ecology, Evolution and Environmental Changes of the Faculty of Sciences of the University of Lisbon.

[6]Moreira (2019) [*weeds also grow flowers in spring*].

bees and other pollinating insects in four cities in the United Kingdom—Bristol, Reading, Leeds and Edinburgh—between 2012 and 2013, in urban farms, domestic gardens, cemeteries, green surfaces built in buildings (like parking lots and other urban facilities), green parks and public gardens, natural reserves, and other green spaces, including spontaneous grass that appears in curbs and sidewalks all over the urban areas of these cities.

In this study, one of the plants referred as an example of spontaneous grass for being an important supplier of nectar and pollen to insects is the Dandelion (*Taraxacum sp.*), common in some countries in Europe, including Portugal.

The study author says in her interview that "*people tend to think of these plants as weeds, but they are really important for pollinators*". The cited study concludes that urban farms, despite the reduced area that they may have, are good places for pollinating insects within cities as they have a wide variety of flowers, fruits and vegetables, in addition to native plants.

On the other hand, hydrangeas, forget-me-nots and daisies proved to be the plants less sought-after by pollinating insects, as they offer low or very low pollen and nectar resources.

According to Carla Rego, a University of Lisbon researcher, referred by C.F. Moreira (2019) in her article in the "Público" newspaper, these pollinating insects are responsible for "*about 80% of the foods of vegetable origin*" that are consumed in the human diet and by the other animals that depend on the pollinating process.

The loss of pollinator biodiversity is not occurring on a local scale, nor is an exclusive problem of the European Union. This is data that is showing on a worldwide level, regardless of the type of habitat. "*It is a very worrying aspect because we live within an ecosystem and we are all very interdependent. We depend on plants and insects. This loss that we are observing can have very big consequences in our future*", says Carla Rego. "*When we start to apply a chemical product, the manufacturers write the effects that they consider to be beneficial against the agricultural plagues, but there have been more and more indications that there are secondary effects that will affect other insects and organisms*", explains the researcher. "*There are less insects because they end up being sensitive to the applied pesticides*". This decline also has direct consequences on pollinating insects and on other species such as frogs, birds, and other animals that feed on them.

What actions can be taken to minimize these facts.

According to Rego, 2019, there are already some municipalities in Portugal aware of this reality, building spaces to promote the pollination of plant species, either by not cutting them or by spraying spontaneous plant species as soon as they start to sprout. But sometimes the understanding of the local population is a complicated issue. "*Even when towns want to make some effort to keep some vegetation available, people complain because that is an indicator of sloppiness. Things don't look as nice and people don't like it. It is important to always let it stay for a few more weeks* (the spontaneous species[7]) *while there is the flowering*

---

[7]Author's note.

'boom' so that our insects in the cities can enjoy those plants", which can be cut when they start to dry, says the researcher. Urban farms are considered the best refuges for pollinating insects. They are better than gardens because ornamental flowers are unappealing to these insects, as they have little nectar and pollen, and often the flowers are closed as is the case with roses. For gardens, the plants best suited for pollination are the said aromatic plants, such as rosemary, lavender and basil.

The importance of pollinating insects is proven by several scientific studies, as well as their decline due to aggressions to the environment. Therefore, it is urgent that some measures are taken to mitigate their decline, since the insects with the greatest capacity to adapt to insecticides are flies and cockroaches.

In 2008, the Royal Geographical Society of London, at the "Earthwatch" event, nominated bees the most important living beings on the planet, as they are responsible for pollination and for 90% of the plant species that need to be pollinated.[8]

The various species of bees and pollinating insects are therefore the starting point for this study.

4 Starting Question

Would an object that allows the mitigation of insects at a domestic level be able to be used by the recipients, pollinating insects and, or, preferably, bees?

4.1 Incentive to Pollination

Pollination of plant species is essential to life, both human and animal. The main pollinating agents are winds, birds and insects, and within the latter those that are the most important regarding pollination are the various species of bees. According to the Belgian author, Maurice Maeterlinck,[9] in his book The Life of the Bee (1944), *"It is estimated that more than a hundred thousand varieties of plants would disappear, if bees could not visit them."* (p. 225).

This project is directed to people who have some kind of plant background knowledge, whether with gardens, urban community farms or other green spaces. In order to carry out pollination, the various species of bees need a place to nest and also a place to drink water in order for the process of transforming pollen and nectar into food to be possible.

---

[8]Gamble (2008).
[9]Maeterlinck (1944) [*The life of the Bee*].

It is not the intention of this project to create an object for a specific species of bee, much less develop a hive to extract honey. It is an incentive for bees to regularly visit the space where the nest and the drinker are placed. That is why a nesting place ("aBEElhário") and a waterer ("BEEbedor") were developed, in order to try to understand if these places will be occupied by solitary or social bee species.

4.1.1 Bees as an Example to Incentivize Pollination

The various species of bees that exist in the country and in the world are important and their needs are studied. In particular, the ones that nest in urban and rural spaces in closed places and sheltered from light, are important agents of pollination of crops and flowers.

According to her dissertation, presented at the Animal Biology Department of the Faculty of Sciences (in Lisbon, Portugal), Mafalda Carvajal Rocha[10] (2017), states that:

> In Portugal there is a lack of studies concerning wild bees, and regarding the scope of the present study - abundance and diversity of bees (Hymenoptera: Apoidea) in urban centers - there are no published Portuguese works. The last publication on the diversity of bees present throughout the entire Portuguese territory dates back to 1960 and had only 143 species. (Diniz 1960)
>
> There is currently a temporary list (Baldock et al. to be published) of all species identified in the Portuguese continent to date, which has already registered 663 species of bees. In the last 15 years there has been a considerable increase in the collection of bees for registration in Portugal, with a special focus on Algarve, which has already added about 350 species to the current list, whereas on the north is still underestimated. On the other hand, Nieto et al. (2014) had estimated for Portugal between 315 and 434 species of bees, of which 11–25 species would be endemic, 1–3 threatened and for 92–137 their conservation status is unknown (Data Deficient). (p. 4)

According to this study conducted by Rocha (2017) 66 species of bees were captured. In it, states that most of the captured bees were of the solitary species that are flower generalists that nest in cavities and on the ground. The author also mentions that the floral diversity is beneficial to these pollinating insects. According to studies consulted by the author (p. 7) namely the one by Matteson there are species nesting in several places. Cavities, walls and others account for 46% of the species. Hives account for 19%. Fences and wood logs 1.6%. Rotten wood 1.2%. Dense bushes 7%. Worth noting that 50% of these are the type of solitary bee that does not produce honey and approximately 39% are social bees.

Within these species, in the various studies consulted by the author, she states that larger bees seek food over longer distances than smaller ones.

---

[10]Rocha (2017) [Diversity and abundance of bees in a green urbanized space in Lisbon: The Tapada de Ajuda].

The size of the bees can also have a significant role, given that social species of considerable size, such as bumblebees, are able to fly longer distances to find food compared to the smaller species (Klein et al. 2008; Holzschuh et al. 2008). Smaller bees of the Lasioglossum genus, for example, do not fly further than 600 m for food. Consequently, the flower and nesting resources of the smaller bees will have to be in closer proximity than for other larger species.

Within the various species of bees, whether they produce honey or not, there are 2 generic types of bees: the ones that have a regular pollen diet, called polylactic, and the ones that have a specialized pollen diet, called oligolectic bees.

In her dissertation, Rocha (2017) describes her study (p. 32) "*Of the 57 identified species, 41 (72% of the species) had a general polylectic pollen diet, whereas 16 (24% of the species) had presented a specialized oligolectic pollen diet. Regarding the individuals, 89% of the individuals presented a generalized diet and 11% presented a specialized one. However, when the Apis genus was not taken into account, 79% of the individuals presented a generalized diet and 21% presented a specialized one*".

Bees are predominantly a seasonal insect given that they are a pollinating one that feeds on pollen. They are almost inexistent in the winter period and they start to appear in March, with their busiest time coinciding with spring, from April to July, and returning to the nest from October to November, according to said study.

For the present study, the bees that we are more interested in are the ones that nest in cavities that, according to Rocha (2017) (p. 46) "(…) *On the other hand, the most diverse family in this study, Megachilidae, lodges species that usually nest in cavities. In fact, Cane et al. and Matteson et al. found that bees that nest in cavities tend to thrive in urbanized habitats. The Apidae family, on the other hand, was the most abundant, which can be explained by the presence of the social species A. mellifera, B. terrestris and B. ruderatus which were very common. These results diverge somewhat from the study by Fortel et al. where different green spaces were sampled in Lyon, France, and in which the most diverse and abundant families were the Halictidae and the Apidae, while the least diverse and abundant was the Megachilidae*."

In Portugal there are only 5 types of bees that produce honey, and for feeding on nectar and pollen they are important pollinators. But they do not seek food crops like tomatoes and blueberries, that continue to depend on wild bees and bumblebees. These honey bees of the *Apidae* family are the *Apis mellifera mellifera*, the *Apis mellifera iberiensis*, the *Apis mellifera ligustica*, the *Apis mellifera carnica* and the *Apis mellifera caucasica*. These bees have what can be considered a greater flight ability compared to the other types of wild bees. Within these, they can be polylectic or specialized in a single species of flower, oligolectic.

All other species of bees, bumblebees and pollinating wasps only produce food for their own consumption, but all are responsible for the pollination of approximately 76% of the flora produced in the EU.

The European Union launched in July 2020 the publication "*Know your pollinators*"[11] directed towards the youngest, about the main pollinating insects. Of these, the most important ones for this study will be the various species of bees. The main information was taken from the references below as well as from the website of the organization "Bumblebee Conservation Trust".[12]

Solitary bees (*Osmia* spp) are the types of wild bee species that build small nests at the care of a single female, on the ground or in a wall cavity. This family has species that reproduce once a year, remaining in a cluster during winter and borning during spring. It is an important bee for pollination of food and flowers.

Eastern carpenter bee (*Xylocopa virginica*)—19–22 mm; large size bee; digs tunnels in dead wood to lay eggs; males have no sting. In its physiognomy it barely looks like a common bee, due to its lack of yellow and black fur. It is a black bee with purple-blue reflections on its wings. They can live for more than a year and are solitary and essentially pollinate fruit trees and some flowers. They have a long range flight. In danger of extinction in some places.

European orchard bee (*Osmia corrnuta*)—10.6 mm; begins flying in early March; nests in wooden holes or walls. Can also use dry stems in gardens or orchards and is a common resident of insect hotels. They are important pollinators of fruit trees and flowers. It has a medium flight range within the pollinating bee species.

Spined mason bee (*Osmia spinulosa*)—6 mm; small bee that nests in empty snail shells. Offers no contribution to food pollination and prefers the flowers of the daisy family, from which it collects nectar and pollen. It has a short flight range. In danger of extinction in some places.

Alfalfa leafcutting bee (*Megachile rotundata*)—10.3 mm; started to be used as a pollinator by some farmers; is important when it comes to pollinating carrots, alfalfa and other vegetables and flowers. It nests in old tree trunks or other holes and builds the cells of the nests with cut leaves. It can nest in insect hotels and has a short flight range.

Leafcutter bee (*Megachile*) is a solitary bee that builds nests with flowers or vegetation leaves. They easily nest in bee hotels as long as the hotels are in isolated places. They make nests in holes and existing cavities, especially in sunny places facing south. They fly with leaf parts to make nests for their larvae. The females chew the leaves and create a cozy cell to lay an egg. In each cell, they will place a pollen mixture and nectar for the larvae to be fed. At last, they seal the cavity with the leaf paste and the bees hatch in the next spring.

---

[11]Europeia, DG Environnement União, and Direção-Geral do Ambiente (Comissão Europeia) (2020).
[12]Bumblebee (2020).

Painted nomad bee (*Nomada fucata*)—8.5 mm; very similar to a wasp in terms of physiognomy. Infiltrates into the nests of the yellow-legged Mining bee and there it lays its eggs in the pollen that these had collected. These bees do not collect pollen but they visit the flowers to collect the nectar, therefore acting as pollinating. They have a very short flight time and they only visit flowers, having no contribution to food. It can present two flight seasons per year. In danger of extinction in some places.

Gray Wrinkled Bee[13] (*Lasioglossum sexnotatum*)—8.5 mm; uncommon species of mining bees. Lives in hedges and shrubs. Nests in the ground, in urban farms and gardens or vacant lots. Flies during spring and summer. Its flight is very important for food and flowers. It has a short flight range. It is in danger of extinction.

Yellow-legged Mining Bee (*Andrena flavipes*)—9 mm; is an important bee for fruit trees. It nests in the ground and can present two generations per year, in the spring and in the summer. It is important for the pollination of food crops, while it also visits flowers. It has a relatively short flight range.

Ivy mining bee (*Colletes hederae*)—10 mm; is one of the fastest spreading bees in the world, at this time. It flies in the autumn and collects pollen from ivies, being of vital importance for this plant. It has no contribution to food pollination. They nest in large bee cities. They can have their nests close to each other. It has a good flight range.

Rare-horned bee[14] (*Eucera nigrescens*)—10.5 mm; this bee owes its name to the very long antennas of the males, that collect pollen from flowers of the pea family, which is also important for flowers. They fly mainly during the month of May. It has a good flight range. In danger of extinction in some places.

Common mourning bee (*Melecta albifrons*)—11.5 mm; it is considered a big sized bee. It has a large coat that allows it to pollinate. It essentially visits flowers in search of nectar. This bee is a kleptoparasite. "It infiltrates in pre-made nests built by the hosts, the Hairy-footed flower bees, and lays its eggs there. The larvae hatch before the host's and consume the competition as well as the stored pollen, ready to emerge as adults the following spring."[15] They prefer flowers but also seek fruit trees such as apple and cherry trees. There are different species of mourning bees, some in danger of extinction.

Hairy-footed flower bee (*Anthophora plumipes*)—approximately 10 mm. It is a solitary bee that can build nests in large groups. In this species, the male and female are quite distinct. The males are brown with colored coat in their faces. The females are basically black with orange/reddish colored hair in their back legs. Once having mated, they collect pollen in their back legs and carry it to the cells of the nest,

---

[13]Author's note: Literal translation from the portuguese common name [Abelha de sulco cinzento].

[14]Author's note: Literal translation from the portuguese common name [Abelha cornuda rara].

[15]https://www.bumblebeeconservation.org/mourningbee/.

where the larvae are. When these have enough food, the cells are sealed and, in the next spring, the new bees will hatch. The nests can be on the ground or in soft mortar walls.

Buff-tailed bumblebee (*Bombus terrestris*) is the generic name of the species. It builds nests with 50 individuals. Nests in the ground or in trees and is important for the pollination of flowers and food.

Tree bumblebee (*Bombus hypnorum*)—11 mm. Commonly found in gardens. It nests in tree holes and bird houses. The community is composed by a queen and 150 individuals. It flies in the spring and has a preference for fruit trees and raspberries.

Red-tailed bumblebee (*Bombus lapidárius*)—12 mm; it is a bumblebee with a distinctive bright orange tail; lives in urban or rural areas; nests on the ground and in rat burrows; important for wildflowers and very important for food crops. It flies during spring and summer. With a good flying ability it can travel long distances.

Gypsy cuckoo bumblebee (*Bombus bohemicus*)—16 mm; is a kleptoparasite; nests in the nests of white-tailed bumblebees; does not collect pollen but visits flowers in search of nectar. More important for flowers and wildflowers than for food. With a good flight ability.

Like bees, wasps are also pollinating insects. Some species of plants are pollinated exclusively by wasps, as with some types of fig trees.

German wasp (*Vespula germanica*)—11–13 mm; the nests are above ground, which can be on the walls of buildings or in holes and can contain up to thousands of individuals. Queen wasps hibernate during winter and in the spring they start building their nests. The nests, which seem to be made of paper, can lodge up to 7500 workers, before the cold kills all the workers, except for the queens. They offer a good contribution to the pollination of flowers and food. It has a diverse diet that can range from human-processed foods such as sweets to other insects. They have a great flight range.

Paper wasp (*Polistes biglumis*)—16 mm; a social wasp species; builds water resistant paper nests above ground, using wood fibers or plant stems. They use a system of recognition based on smell that is the basis of all wasp interactions. The wasp colony queen produces a homogeneous and specific odor that it impregnates in the paper nests and identifies all the colony. This system also acts as protection of the colony, identifying strange agents. They have an average flight range and fly during the spring and the queens hibernate during the winter.

Common wasp (*Vespula vulgaris*) or **European wasp** (*vespa crabro*)—11–17 mm; builds nests in cavities or trees and shrubs; the community ranges from a few dozens up to 2500 individuals. The characteristics are similar to the german wasp.

European hornet (*Vespa crabro*)—can reach 25 mm; it is a native insect from Portugal; it builds its nest with paper fibers on tree trunks, in crevices at home, wooden bird nests and places with poor lighting; they rarely do it on the soil as it is usual with some wasp species; they can attack bees but only the dying ones. These nests are normally protected from the weather and can be inside an abandoned space.

Median wasp (*Dolichovespula median*)—16–22 mm; is a social wasp; the nests are made of some kind of paper that can come from wood or plant fibers; they are built above ground and can contain up to 800 individuals. During the winter, the queen hibernates. The nests are in the shape of a pine cone, hanging from trees or shrubs and the entrance is through a hole under the nest. It is attracted to sweet food, so it can disturb people, although it is not considered an aggressive wasp.

European beewolf (*Philantus triangulum*)—12 mm; it supplies its nests on the ground with honey bees, which made it earn the nickname "wolf of the bees"; is a common species in Europe that nests in sandy places and likes to visit flowers; offers little contribution to food; has an excellent flight mobility being able to fly long distances.

4.1.2 Propper Conditions for a Bee's Nest

The nest should be placed facing the sun most of the day; it should be facing south or west if we are in southern Europe.

It must be placed at least one meter from the ground and close to vegetation but without it covering or shading it; it should not shake when subjected to wind.

According to the website "Bumblebee Conservation Trust", a bee and pollinating insect hotel must have long enough tubes, preferably close to 15 cm. It is beneficial that there are tubes with different diameters ranging from 2 to 10 mm, thus attracting various bee species. These tubes must have one of the ends closed, otherwise the bee will not nest. The alignment tubes must be protected from rain and humidity so they will not get wet. These tubes must not be made of plastic so that there is no condensation nor fungus and other plagues that can lead to the destruction of the larvae. The entrance of the tubes must be smooth and clean. Tunnels must be accessible and removable so that they can be removed and replaced.

This type of nest can attract several species of bees, but also solitary wasps that will act as the garden's pest control, collecting flies, caterpillars and aphids to supply their nests.

These are the construction principles for an insect hotel. As the ones that can be found for sale, their design is based on overlapped tubes in order to encourage the nest building of various species of bees and other pollinating insects.

5   Case Study

5.1   *Construction of a Nesting Space*

Development of a pollinating insect nest receptacle | aBEElhário

Development of a drinking water container | BEEbedor

For this study, a nesting space and a drinking pool/waterer for bees were developed. It is this project's intention to help in the proliferation of pollinating insects that usually inhabit gardens, urban farms and other green spaces, where the land owners intend to carry out the pollination of its crops and surrounding spaces.

These objects were thought out to be produced with ceramic, a weather-resistant material, easy to clean, with a significant industry and handicraft culture in Portugal, being a cost-effective material, traditionally used in some cultures in the construction of beehives for honey production.

This project is not intended to be targeted towards insects that produce honey in particular, but rather for any insect that wants to nest there.

The project took into account its geometry, important for this type of insect. It was developed having in mind the golden ratio, given that bees are insects with a great ratio and mathematical instinct in the construction of their nests, that normally are based in hexagons with a pyramid base.

The cells of the bee nests are made up of three planes that are laid in a point— claims Maeterlinck (1944) in his book (p. 114)—which allows a large saving of matter (wax) and labor. According to studies consulted in this same book. hexagons consist of angles of 109, 28° for the largest ones and 70.31° for the smallest ones. The author makes a comparison between the combs of bees and wasps, in which both animals build them in hexagonal form (p. 115).

> For example, wasps, that build combs with hexagonal cells like bees, had the same problem, and they solved it in a much less ingenious way. (...) Therefore, the wasp combs are less solid, more irregular and represent a waste of time, matter and space, that can be assessed in one fourth of effort and one third of the necessary space. (Maeterlinck 1944)

This project is focused towards bees or wasps, as they both are pollinating insects. Wasps that are considered pests (such as the Asian hornet) do not seek this type of refuge to nest (Fig. 1).

However, this species' bigger proportions were considered so that their entrance into the aBEElhário (receptacle) is hindered.

The aBEElhário project was based on a geometric base that rests on a hexagon section, a common shape for bees and wasps. The basic shape of this project is a rhombus seen from above, and the combination of various elements can form a hexagon.

In the image, it is illustrated the geometric principle applied to this aBEElhário, exemplified with some figures of the drinker, which is one of the elements that comprises this nest building project: the aBEElhário and the BEEbedor, shown in the image, that are essential for the pollination to be carried out.

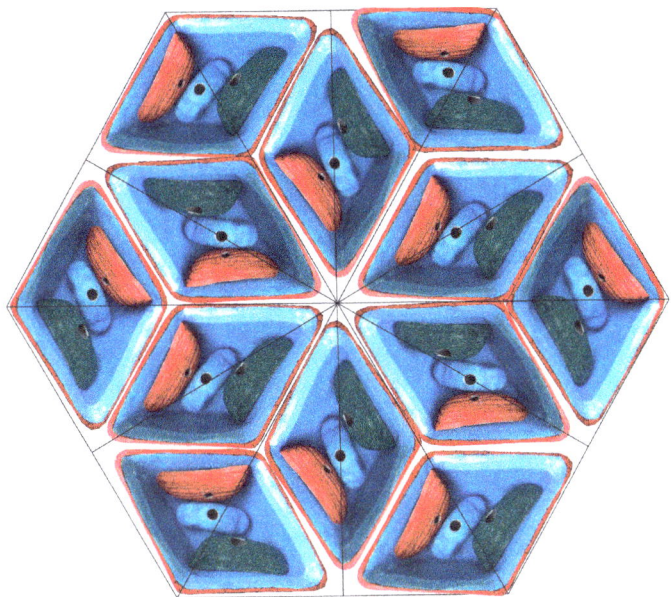

Fig. 1 Combination of several pieces of "BEEbedor" that form the hexagon. Author's photo

This principle is demonstrated in a photomontage in which it can be seen that each base element (in this case the BEEbedor) can be divided into four triangles, two with an equilateral base, that if divided in a longitudinal direction will make two isosceles triangular figures.

The sum of the angles of a triangle is 180° and this shape is the sum of two triangles, which makes up 360° in the total sum. The equivalent of saying that the shape has the same angle of a circumference, 360°. That is why some authors say that the rhombus has a circumcircle, being the latter considered the perfect plane geometric shape.

The shape of the drinking pool is the simplest one of the aBEElhário design. The BEEbedor consists in taking advantage of the base of the receptacle's production mold for the bees, without the remaining components that would turn it into the nests' receptacle (Fig. 2).

In addition to the rhombus-shaped water container (from a top view), the BEEbedor is comprises three fake stones, also made with ceramic, making the best use of the technology and the requirements of the material. To be baked, ceramic has to be hollow. The used technique was filling. The opening of the stones was pointed upwards thus allowing water to enter the stones and evaporate more slowly, conserving drinking water for insects for a longer period of time. The stones normally have an irregular surface and are glazed on the top, leaving the ceramic to be seen in the lower part, so that the porosity of the material does its job and leaves the water to be absorbed and be expelled, while is evaporating, allowing the water to

Fig. 2 Wasp drinking water from the drinker BEEbedor. Author's photo

last longer in the drinker. If the fake stones were not glazed on one of the sides, the water evaporation would occur faster (Fig. 3).

The color of the stones preferably contrasts with the color of the bottom of the bowl, to let the bees know the water limit, thus avoiding drowning. In this drinker, that is visited by countless insects that satisfy their thirst, no drowning was ever observed during the study period.

During the pollen and nectar collection and transportation process, these insects have the need to consume water, either for the construction of their nests (as is the case, for example, of the paper wasps), either to supply the food to the small larvae where the pollen and the nectar are mixed with water. In some cases, the water may be able to help lower the ambient temperaturz\e of the nest, according to Paulino[16] (2007).

5.2   The aBEElhário Receptacle

Most beehives are settled directly on their horizontal base. They could be (or not) settled directly on the ground, which for some materials it is not very advisable, thanks to the direct contact with the humidity and thanks to being more prone to plagues and other invaders, which in many cases leads to stands being needed to lift them off the ground (Fig. 4).

---

[16]Paulino (2007).

Fig. 3 View of the drinker set BEEbedor. Author's photo

As it was already mentioned in this text, some bee species prefer to make their nests on the ground but most pollinating insects prefer to find places further away from the ground, in a way to ensure more protection. With these bee species in mind is why the aBEElhário was developed. It must be hung a meter from the ground and is a receptacle that works vertically and can be placed on a wall or a tree.

Of the existing species in Portugal, the most likely to nest in this receptacle are the following; Lone/Mason bee (*Osmia* spp); European orchard bee (*Osmia cornuta*) 10.6 mm; Alfalfa leafcutting bee (*Megachile rotundata*) 10.3 mm; Ivy Bee (*Colletes hederae*) 10 mm; Rare-horned bee[17] (*Eucera nigrescens*); Hairy-footed flower bee (*Anthophora plumipes*) 10 mm; Tree bumblebee (*Bombus Hypnorum*) 11 mm; German Wasp (*Vespula germanica*) 11–13 mm; Paper wasp (*Polistes biglumis*) 16 mm; European hornet (*Vespa crabro*). As a general rule, they will be the species that inhabit darker and above ground places that will not need wood or a softer land. The size of the bee species is important so that it allows the entrance and exit of the resident insects but prevents the entrance of some predators. In this case, the size of the entrance was 10 mm of diameter.

The aBEElhário comprises two parts. The body of the receptacle and a rhombus-shaped lid. This lid has a rubber jamb in the back to help with the light isolation and water entrance, and a type of cover over the entrance with the goal of preventing the water entering the insect's entrance hole.

During the making process, initially, the lid did not have the back flap. But during the oven cooking process the pieces started to curve, not fitting properly on the base part.

---

[17]Author's note: Literal translation from the portuguese common name.

Fig. 4 aBEElHário placed on a wall. Author's photo

The base part is, like the cover, only glazed facing the outside part to allow more friction on the inside. Different glazes were applied to tell which ones would better attract bees, as they can distinguish colors. According to the electronic digest "The Magazine",[18] bees are sensitive to a variety of colors and ultraviolet waves (Fig. 5).

Depending on the species, and within them the types of individuals and their functions, bees can have up to five eyes, 2 complex and 3 simple ones. The

[18]The Magazine (2020).
[Like a bee sees: a spectrum of color vision, what colors they distinguish and which ones they do not.].

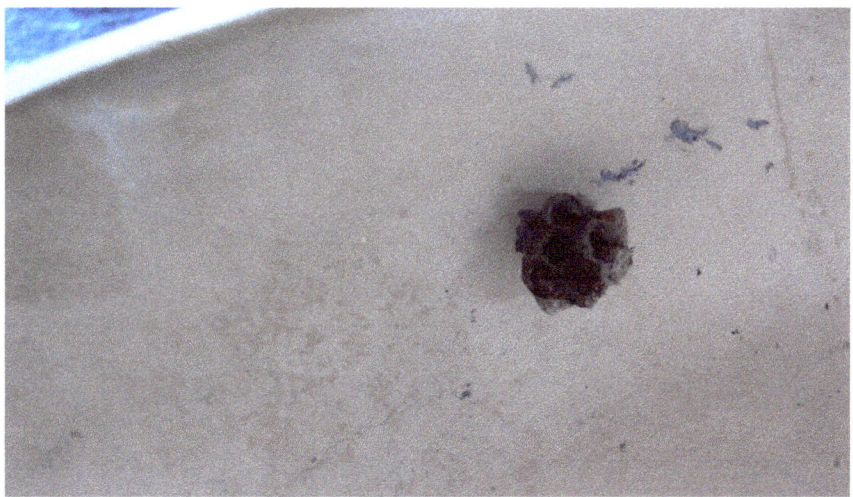

Fig. 5 Start of the construction of a paper wasp nest

complex ones help in the perception of nearby elements and the simple ones are more optimized towards flight orientation by perceiving the sun's position. The colors that bees distinguish best are white, yellow, orange and green, also managing to perceive red, which they can transform into ultraviolet, using it for orientation.

To date, no significant preference in terms of color has been registered. However, the largest wasp colony settled in an aBBElhário with a gray front and a blue cover.

In this aBeelhário, a colony of paper wasps was introduced, which developed during the spring, reaching a significant number of individuals. In another aBBElhário, where the bluish green is the dominant color, with the same solar orientation, the social proliferation was smaller, which leads us to assume that it is another species or that the nesting was not successful.

6   Final Considerations

This study is yet to be concluded given that only a spring season and a summer season have passed since the pollinating assistants were installed. However, it can be confirmed that the BEEbedor is of vital importance and that it is visited by countless species of insects, not only bees and wasps, but also other kinds of insects, including dragonflies (Fig. 6).

The duration time of the water in the BEEbedor depends directly on the solar incidence as expected. But even with the drinker placed in the sun with a western incidence (sunset), the water lasts fifteen days during the summer months.

Fig. 6 Paper wasp that colonized within the nesting site aBEElhário

Three drinkers were placed in a space of approximately ten square meters, all with the same solar orientation, the only thing differing being the place exposed to the sun. One was placed under direct sunlight, on top of the stones (red glaze on the outside and blue on the inside). Another was placed on top of the ground and the grass, only 5 m away from the first (green on the outside and the same blue glaze inside), in the shade of a shrub very sought-after by insects. A third one was made using a black glass bowl where real stones were placed on the inside, under direct sunlight but for less hours per day.

The drinker most sought-after was the first one (red glaze on the outside and blue on the inside) with the other two having a residual demand, almost null. Regarding the duration time of the water inside the containers, the difference in liquid conservation is clear. The BEEbedor, for having hollow rocks with water on the inside, lasts more than a week, on average, than the container with regular rocks. In terms of water and stone dirt it is similar. These must be cleaned once a month.

It leads us to believe that bees and other pollinating insects have preference for water with a higher temperature or with a longer solar incidence.

Of the three aBEElhários placed they all created insect colonies, the paper wasp having been the colonizing insect.

The proximity of crops may be important in the proliferation of several bee species. The test took place in a place without close proximity to abundant human crops, being close to a garden and a spontaneous plant area.

Text translation: João Teixeira Pinto.

Bibliographical References

Beylerian GM, Dent A (2005) Material connexion; the global resource of new and innovative materials for architects, artists and designers, 1st edn. Thames & Hudson, London

Bumblebee (2020) Mourning bee (Melecta albifrons). https://www.bumblebeeconservation.org/mourningbee/. Accessed outubro 2020

Europeia, DG Environnement União, and Direção-Geral do Ambiente (Comissão Europeia) (2020) Conhece os Polinizadores Publications Office of the EU

Gamble Z (2008) Bees declared the winners in Earthwatch's 'irreplaceable species' battle. Ecology, The Environment and Conservation. https://www.innovations-report.com/ecology-the-environment-and-conservation/bees-declared-winners-earthwatch-s-irreplaceable-122930/. Accessed abril 2019

Johnson PD, Besselsen DG (2002) Practical aspects of experimental design in animal research. ILAR J 43:4

Kohl PL, Thulasi N, Rutschmann B, George EA, Steffan-Dewenter I, Brockmann A (2020) Adaptive evolution of honeybee dance dialects. In: Proceedings da royal society B. Biological Sciences. The Royal Society Publishing, The Royal Society

Maeterlinck M (1944) A vida das abelhas [The life of the bee] (C. d. Figueiredo, Trans. 9ª ed.). Lisboa: Livraria Clássica Editora

The Magazine (2020) Como uma abelha vê: um espectro de visão de cores, que cores distinguem e quais não. https://ao.tomahnousfarm.org/6505-as-a-bee-sees-a-spectrum-of-color-vision-which-color.html. Accessed 0utubro 2020

Mahendra SH (2005) Mechanical life cycle handbook: good environmental design and manufacturing. Taylor & Francis

Martins V (2018) As abelhas são declaradas o ser mais importante do planeta, mas estão a morrer. https://kids.pplware.sapo.pt/curiosidades/as-abelhas-sao-declaradas-o-ser-mais-importante-do-planeta-mas-estao-a-morrer/. Accessed April 2020

Moreira CF (25 de Março de 2019) Não corte já as ervas daninhas. As abelhas agradecem Publico. https://www.publico.pt/2019/03/25/local/noticia/ervas-daninhas-tambem-dao-flores-nao-cortadas-mal-comeca-primavera-1866480?fbclid= IwAR1RRQfxq0gToVLhTapRX8djfNxABsMvxtshN9UhY12kfTiA7Ps–tzHHJk. Accessed September 2020

Paulino FDG (2007) Alimentação em Apis Mellifera L.: Exigências nutricionais e alimentos. Paper presented at the 1 Simpósio de Nutrição e Alimentação Animal realizada na XIII Semana Universitária da Universidade Estadual do Ceará—UECE., Ceará, Brasil, Data Deficient

Pinto DNR (2015) Estudo de hábitos de nidificação de abelhas solitárias em ecossistemas agrários: O caso dos pomares de pêra Rocha no Oeste., Universidade de Lisboa Faculdade de Ciências, Lisboa

Rocha MC (2017) Diversidade e Abundância de Abelhas (Hymenoptera: Apoidea) Num Espaço Verde Urbanizado Em Lisboa: A Tapada da Ajuda. Universidade de Lisboa Lisboa

Sánchez-Bayo F (2019) Insect population faces 'catastrophic' collapse: Sydney research. https://www.sydney.edu.au/news-opinion/news/2019/02/12/insect-population-faces–catastrophic–collapse–sydney-research.html. Accessed October 2020

University of Würzburg (2020) Dialetos de dança das abelhas. www.maisconhecer.com/tecnologia/1675/Dialetos-de-danca-das-abelhas. Accessed outubro 2020

wikiwand (2020) Espécies potencialmente perigosas. https://www.wikiwand.com/pt/Lista_de_esp%C3%A9cies_perigosas_em_Portugal. Accessed outubro 2020

wilder.pt (2020) Pesticida banido da UE por danos ao ambiente e à saúde humana [Pesticide banned from the EU for damage to the environment and human health]. https://www.wilder.pt/historias/pesticida-banido-da-ue-por-danos-ao-ambiente-e-a-saude-humana/?fbclid=IwAR2_UPIRS0AIO_NOjyWTGMrPsgnfyGLglK8Srma2P-lhfwWIQWTqObfQ. Accessed october 2020

CPSIA information can be obtained
at www.ICGtesting.com
Printed in the USA
LVHW080001061022
730050LV00006B/231